Barbara La Marr

BARBARA LA MARR

The Girl Who Was Too Beautiful for Hollywood

SHERRI SNYDER

UNIVERSITY PRESS OF KENTUCKY

Copyright © 2017 by Sherri Snyder

Published by the University Press of Kentucky, scholarly publisher for the Commonwealth, serving Bellarmine University, Berea College, Centre College of Kentucky, Eastern Kentucky University, The Filson Historical Society, Georgetown College, Kentucky Historical Society, Kentucky State University, Morehead State University, Murray State University, Northern Kentucky University, Transylvania University, University of Kentucky, University of Louisville, and Western Kentucky University.

All rights reserved.

Editorial and Sales Offices: The University Press of Kentucky
663 South Limestone Street, Lexington, Kentucky 40508–4008
www.kentuckypress.com

Frontispiece: Barbara as she appeared in an advertisement for Richelieu pearls, 1924. Unless otherwise noted, all photographs are from the author's collection.

Cataloging-in-Publication data is available from the Library of Congress.

ISBN 978-0-8131-7425-9 (hardcover : alk. paper)
ISBN 978-0-8131-7427-3 (epub)
ISBN 978-0-8131-7426-6 (pdf)

This book is printed on acid-free paper meeting the requirements of the American National Standard for Permanence in Paper for Printed Library Materials.

Manufactured in the United States of America.

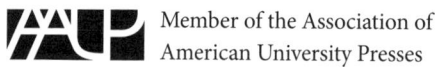 Member of the Association of
American University Presses

For Barbara and Don, with all my heart.

Sherri has brought my mother back to life for me. She has generously given of her time and energy to fulfill my lifelong need to tell the true life story of Barbara La Marr, a woman who was decades ahead of her time. I can never thank her enough.

—Donald M. Gallery, 2014

Contents

Preface xi
Prologue 1

I. Dreamer
One 7
Two 14
Three 18
Four 29

II. Notorious
Five 39
Six 55
Seven 62
Eight 72

III. Terpsichore
Nine 85
Ten 97
Eleven 108
Twelve 120
Thirteen 127

IV. Screenwriter
Fourteen 139
Fifteen 148

V. Film Star
Sixteen 161
Seventeen 171

Eighteen 181
Nineteen 193
Twenty 205
Twenty-One 213
Twenty-Two 226
Twenty-Three 235
Twenty-Four 244
Twenty-Five 254
Twenty-Six 262

VI. Outcast

Twenty-Seven 279
Twenty-Eight 286
Twenty-Nine 297

VII. Butterfly

Thirty 315
Thirty-One 326
Thirty-Two 335
Thirty-Three 344
Epilogue 352

Appendix: Musings of a Muse 367
Acknowledgments 371
Filmography 375
Notes 385
Selected Bibliography 423
Index 425

Preface

I first heard the name Barbara La Marr from Karie Bible, a film historian and author with whom I became friends when we both modeled for a vintage-fashions designer. Karie contacted me one morning in July 2007 about an opportunity I couldn't refuse. The Pasadena Playhouse and Pasadena Museum of History were casting *Channeling Hollywood,* a play involving the life stories of five Hollywood notables. One of the producers had asked her if she knew anyone who could portray silent screen star Barbara La Marr—"a fascinating woman," she told me, "who led a short, stormy, unbelievable life." The producers wanted an actress who could both play Barbara and write an account of her life in monologue form (each actor's part would then be interwoven to create the play). Karie said she had given them my name and they would be contacting me to schedule an audition.

I immediately began researching Barbara and discovered how right Karie was. Barbara La Marr was indeed an incredible, multitalented woman, often tortured by great adversity. What touched me most, beyond Barbara's frailties and her life's tragic elements, was her underlying strength and determination. I quickly wrote my audition piece. A mere day and a half later, I stood anxiously before the director and producers and performed it.

What followed was a journey beyond anything I could have imagined. First, I won the part. My research took on greater urgency as I sought deeper insight into Barbara than readily obtainable, sparse resources afforded me. From the beginning, I was convinced that her true story lay beneath her achievements and the astonishing events that marked her life. It was to be found, I believed, in her heart and soul. "To be understood," she reportedly stated at the pinnacle of her fame, "—that is the greatest thing you can give to any person, and it is . . . the greatest thing any person can give you."[1] I sought to *understand* Barbara La Marr, turn her inside out, think as she thought, feel as she felt. Probing her core became an adventure.

Preface

I was put in touch with Barbara's only child, her son, Donald Gallery. Merely three years old when Barbara died, Don welcomed my regular e-mails and phone calls, gladly sharing all he knew. The joy he expressed when my research uncovered new information about Barbara and photographs of his mother and himself that he hadn't seen before was heartwarming.

I was delighted when Don flew to California from his home in Puerto Vallarta to see the play, and I looked forward to meeting him. Our first face-to-face encounter occurred while I was onstage during the play's final performance. I hadn't meant to look at him in that moment; I was nervous about his being there and was trying *not* to look at him. I raised my face toward the audience and there he was—dead center in the front row—a handsome, white-haired gentleman in a blue suit. He was wiping tears from his eyes.

Don complimented me a short while later when he commented, "I was amazed and thrilled to see this very beautiful and talented young woman step back in time to recapture the tempestuous life of my mother during the silent days of Hollywood." Shortly thereafter his wife, Patricia, added, "Don said he really feels the essence of his mother in your words, movements, and smile."

In the ensuing years, Don became one of my dearest friends (he jokingly called me his surrogate mother), and my intensive research on Barbara continued. Don gave his blessing when people who saw the play suggested I write an entire script about Barbara's life. I also wrote a one-woman performance piece about her that I present beside her crypt at the Hollywood Forever cemetery each October as part of an annual tour hosted by the Art Deco Society of Los Angeles. The most unexpected honor, however, came when Don asked me, just days after our face-to-face meeting, to author Barbara's biography. His passing in 2014 at age ninety-two (ironically, at the same time that I was portraying Barbara in my annual performance) prevented him from reading this book in its entirety, but to the end he remained passionate that his mother's remarkable story be told. When I completed the manuscript for this book, Don's wife was the first person I called. "I know if Don were still with us he would be crying right now," Patricia told me. "You made his dream come true."

Working on Barbara's story as both an actress and a biographer has been, for me, a dream come true. I received one of the greatest compliments of my life after sending Don and Patricia a stack of completed chapters. "Don said he feels a peace inside him that he has never had before about his mother and how she felt about him," Patricia said. "Thank you for giving this to him." The gratitude is all mine.

It is with great joy that I share the story of the amazing woman known as Barbara La Marr.

Prologue

Barbara La Marr first made headlines in January 1913. She was an unknown sixteen-year-old named Reatha Watson then, inexplicably missing from the Los Angeles apartment she occupied with her parents. On the third day after her disappearance, Reatha's agonized parents received their first news of her: a cryptic letter signed with her name arrived in their mailbox. The next morning, newspapers screamed, "Beautiful Girl Disappears; 'Kidnapped,' Says Her Father."[1]

The headlines continued unabated. Reatha eventually reappeared as mysteriously as she had vanished. She stood before rapt reporters and recounted being heinously deceived by a monstrous man. The court proceedings that followed exposed an astonishing series of events, revealing that someone's story wasn't all it seemed.

Reatha again made headlines a year later. She had left her parents and their new home in El Centro, a diminutive town deep in southeastern California's barren desert; hurtled headlong into the gaieties of Los Angeles nightlife; and garnered a substantial reputation. When tales of her activities reached El Centro, her father beseeched authorities to rescue her from impending ruin. Statuesque, chestnut-haired, and with a face which, according to journalist Adela Rogers St. Johns, "could no more go peacefully through a world of men than a cobblestone could pass through a plate glass window without busting things up," Reatha was tracked down.[2] Newspapers throughout the country proclaimed, "Beauty Too Dangerous, Girl Ordered From City."[3]

The "too beautiful" Reatha soon returned to Los Angeles and the headlines. Becoming further mired in scandal, she was subsequently barred by film studios from working as an actress. Reborn as Barbara La Marr, she emerged as a celebrated cabaret sensation at the height of the pre–World War I dance craze. She next partnered with veteran comedian and vaudeville headliner Ben Deely, touring the vaudeville circuits and earning acclaim as the female constituent of his three-person act. Capitalizing upon her innate writing abilities and piercing intellect, she then became a highly paid storywriter for the Fox Film Corporation in the same town that had cast her out. Finally, she succeeded in burying her turbulent past long enough to reign as a preeminent silent screen goddess.

The quintessence of a rising breed of 1920s screen idol—a seductress who ensnares men with her femininity—Barbara La Marr was a film producer's dream, the titillating antithesis of the standard saccharine heroine. A product of the inflammatory film roles she played, shrewd marketing, and fantasy, she bewitched the world with her volatile sex appeal. "No woman has ever been able to walk across the screen with such golden allure," asserted writer Jim Tully. "Voluptuous, caressing, undulating, and fascinating as a beautiful tigress, she was vibrant with life."[4] Homosexual film star William Haines, romanced by Barbara in 1923, maintained, "Of all the screen sirens I think she was the greatest—she was always so much the real woman."[5] Celebrated American cartoonist Al Capp looked to Barbara's sinuous proportions when creating Daisy Mae, the beautiful, busty feminine lead in *Li'l Abner*, a comic strip that achieved unparalleled worldwide fame during its 1934–1977 run.[6]

Barbara's meteoric film career, encompassing just over five years and twenty-six films, left an indelible impression upon the film industry. Ramon Novarro, leading Latin lover and Barbara's costar, reputedly considered her one of the screen's greatest artists. In 1932, RKO Radio polled over one hundred fifty film critics, asking them to name the most glamorous woman in American cinema history. Of the thirteen actresses heading the nominations, Barbara was listed along with Greta Garbo, Marlene Dietrich, Theda Bara, and Clara Bow. Edgar S. "Ed" Wheelan, another American cartoonist, drew inspiration from Barbara when crafting *Minute Movies*, a beloved comic strip parody of silent films, throughout the 1920s and early 1930s. Endowing one of the strip's star players with Barbara's sleek, dark tresses, graceful profile, heavily lined eyes, "piquant expression," and alluring elegance, Wheelan christened her "Lotta Talent."[7]

One of the few actresses to transcend sex-symbol typecasting with inherent sensitivity, emotional depth, and multidimensional characterizations, Barbara inspired a succeeding generation of Hollywood's most brilliant stars. Garbo and Fay Wray professed to admire her. Joan Crawford was influenced by her. (Until her death, Crawford cherished a black feathered fan entangled with rosary beads that adorned Barbara's bedroom during her final weeks. Crawford acquired the fan from producer Paul

Prologue

Bern, their mutual friend, during a period of intense discouragement; Paul told her he believed Barbara would want her to have it.)

In the late 1930s, film producer and Metro-Goldwyn-Mayer mogul Louis B. Mayer discovered a stunning, intelligent Austrian actress who he believed to be star material, but thought her name, Hedwig Eva Maria Kiesler, unsuitable. When signing her with Metro-Goldwyn-Mayer, he renamed her after his favorite actress, a woman whose presence he saw reflected in his new find. Mayer's young discovery dominated the screen throughout the 1940s and is today remembered as a star perpetually cast as an exotic temptress, the glamorous Hedy Lamarr.

While Barbara's artistic achievements hung as a bar before her contemporaries, her predilection to live against the grain of the stifling conventions of her day provided an example to a culture hungry for alternatives. In looking to none but herself to determine her place in the world, by spurning societal rules in favor of unbridled self-expression, she was among the rare women to scale the heights of the professional world, commanding a salary commensurate with her male colleagues in an age where laws ensuring uniform treatment and equal pay for the sexes were virtually nonexistent. No matter the form and even to the end, she clung to her calling to express—as an actress, as a dancer, behind a typewriter—and implored others to do likewise.

Through it all, her explosive private life incited gossip columns, and the headlines kept coming. After her death at age twenty-nine caused a furor in downtown Los Angeles in 1926, her publicist Bert Ennis confessed, "There was no reason to lie about Barbara La Marr . . . Everything she said, everything she did was colored with news-value. A personality dangerous, vivid, attractive; a desire to live life at its maddest and fullest; a mixture of sentiment and hardness, a creature of weakness and strength—that was Barbara La Marr."[8]

Her extraordinary life story is one of tempestuous passions and unbending perseverance in the face of inconceivable odds. It is the story of a woman's fierce determination to forge her own destiny amid the constant threat of losing it all to scandal, and ultimately, death.

I

Dreamer

I can look back and see scene after scene . . . each one very much the same . . . the family sitting around a table, cards, talk, games, and I, sitting on the floor, elbows on the windowsill, star-gazing.

—*Barbara La Marr, "The True Story of My Life"*

One

At the crest of her prominence as a world-renowned actress, when her image emblazoned the covers of fan magazines and films in which she appeared filled theaters to capacity, Barbara La Marr reputedly penned "The True Story of My Life," a nine-article series for *Movie Weekly* magazine. With captivating flair, it is written in the first article: "I had no parents—properly speaking. That is a bad or sad beginning for anybody's life story. It is the beginning of mine."[1]

Barbara's mother, the article continues, was a French actress from a distinguished family while her father, an Italian of exceptional birth, bore a title. In the article, Barbara laments that her mother died when she was a baby, and she was thus "shipped to America at the brilliant age of five." It is then related that "the people who brought me over, friends of my mother's, knew Mr. and Mrs. Watson on the West Coast" and "at the time the Watsons took me, as they did, they were very well-to-do."

Next it is claimed that the facts of her parentage were at first kept from her by the Watsons, who raised her as their own daughter. Barbara attests to receiving her first inkling of her true identity around age ten: while exploring an old trunk in the Watsons' attic, she uncovered a delicate figurine nesting among finely fashioned baby clothes and Venetian lace. "You don't see Venetian lace on American baby clothes," she supposedly wrote. The discovery of the concealed treasures and their implication "stirred my heart in a way that it had never been stirred before . . . I looked like that miniature. And I was *glad!*"

While stars of the 1920s regularly collaborated with publicists and journalists to produce writings attributed to them, it's impossible to know just who wrote Barbara's *Movie Weekly* series and similar articles. Given Barbara's talent for writing and that sections of articles credited to her are characteristic of her phraseology and mind-set, it's likely that such articles were at least partially authored by her. In addition, since portions of these articles are verifiable through cross-checking, they contain truthful elements. (Unless otherwise noted, only verifiable information has been culled from these and other fan magazine articles.)

The truth of Barbara's origins was far less intriguing than she would ever acknowledge: "Born, Tuesday to the wife of W. W. Watson, a daughter." This single sentence, tucked quietly away among the town's shop advertisements, was the *Yakima Herald*'s pronouncement two days after Reatha Dale Watson entered the world on July 28, 1896, in North Yakima, Washington. The girl who would become Barbara La Marr was the biological child of William Watson and Rosa Contner Watson.

Deeply embellished and outright fictionalized background accounts often accompanied film stars in early Hollywood. Audiences were largely unaware, for example, that reigning movie vamp Theda Bara, purportedly imported from the swirling sands of the Sahara, was actually Theodosia Goodman from Cincinnati, Ohio. Studios, managers, and press agents were highly adept at igniting the fantasies of a public that didn't yet distinguish between the luminous image on a movie screen and its human counterpart.

Yet Barbara withheld the details of her ancestry from even her closest friends, obscuring them with a web of distortion. What she ostensibly confessed concerning her parents is that, beneath the "clashes of temperament" and feelings of being misunderstood, "I loved the Watsons very dearly."[2] Her exceedingly protective mother and father likewise deeply loved her. Certainly, her reason for cloaking herself in a fictitious history doesn't appear to be a sense of contempt toward her parents.

Predominantly of Welsh descent with traces of Scottish and English, the Watsons reached America—specifically, Massachusetts—shortly after the Pilgrims arrived at Plymouth Rock. They were "not of the so-called nobility," according to Barbara's cousin Warren Orr, but rather "uncompromising dissenters" who fled the oppression of their mother country in search of religious freedom, bountiful land, and adventure.[3]

By the 1850s, Barbara's grandfather William T. Watson and grandmother Jane Mitchell Watson had left their native state of Ohio, settled into their own farm in Pike County, Illinois, and were rapidly enlarging their family. Barbara's father, William Wright Watson, was born on this farm March 15, 1857.

Despite the hardships imposed by a rural existence, tremendous value was placed upon education in the Watson farmstead. Seated beside a corncob fire in the evenings as his father and older brother, Chandler, read aloud from the *New York Tribune,* young William, dark-haired and gentle-eyed, listened attentively and dreamed of being a writer.

His cherished aspiration was nearly extinguished in the aftermath of the Civil War. His father had abandoned the plow for a musket, marched off to battle for the Union, and returned so badly compromised he was unable to work in his corn fields. The responsibility of the farm and the entire family—soon to include nine children—now rested squarely upon thirteen-year-old Chandler and six-year-old William. William immersed himself in farm life for thirteen years, working unrelenting hours with his four brothers and continuing his schooling whenever he could. In 1876, his writer's heart and pioneer's spirit got the better of him. Borne on the surge of fortune-seeking migrants headed for the Western frontier, William followed Chandler to Oregon.[4]

The tall, good-natured young man first channeled his sharp mind and commendable writing skills into composing editorials for the *Portland Oregonian.* He then traversed the state to Lakeview, where, in December 1878, he and Chandler published south-central Oregon's first newspaper, the *State Line Herald.* The brothers' siblings Mary and Benjamin joined them by 1880, hiking up their sleeves and working as printers alongside William. Chandler, who began practicing law three years previously and had established the region's first law office, served as the paper's editor. (Chandler would become one of Oregon's leading citizens as a lawyer, presidential elector for James A. Garfield in 1880, deputy district attorney in multiple counties, spokesperson for the Republican State Central Committee, and a lobbyist who worked to preserve a considerable portion of Oregon's natural resources.)[5]

If William's brief time with the *Oregonian* hadn't given him a proper introduction to the potential hazards of the newspaper business, his experience with the *State Line Herald* did. He and Chandler made enemies by using the paper as a platform for their fiercely Republican convictions. "The Watson brothers were very vigorous in their denunciation of Democrats," remembered *Oregon Journal* reporter, Fred Lockley, "and so continued in spite of frequently being licked or shot at."[6]

William's profession would give him more than bullets and fistfights to worry about. "The newspaper business is not a dream," he later admitted. "Too frequently it is a haunting nightmare, from a business standpoint. Its pursuit is not a pleasure excursion into realms of delight, luxury, and leisure. Too often it is a mad and disheartening chase after the means with which to insure the morning doughnut and the evening flapjack."[7]

He stayed the course. When the Watsons sold the *State Line Herald* in early spring 1881, he wandered west into Ashland, where he served as a newspaper editor, picked up a clerical job in a land office, and taught English to college students at the Ashland Academy. Then he set off again, bent on success and determined to find the next big thing—something better, he said.

Back to Lakeview and the *State Line Herald* he went. (His brother Benjamin had repurchased the paper in August 1881.) This time William assumed the editor's seat. Braving bodily injury—and death—the brothers recommenced their attacks on local Democrats. By the following year, the *State Line Herald* had either attained a sizable portion of the town's patronage, ruffled enough feathers, or both. The *Lake County Examiner,* the paper's Democratic rival, bought the publication. The brothers got out of town.

They made their way to Portland. When newsboys scampered onto the icy streets the morning of January 1, 1883, with the premiere issue of the *Northwest News* tucked beneath their arms, William and Benjamin were setting the type in the paper's composing room. The publication rapidly became the *Oregonian*'s toughest contender. But again, William chose to move on.

Possibly prompting his decision to leave Portland was a strikingly lovely young woman he met in the nearby town of Hillsboro—a woman who would become his wife.

Barbara's mother, Rosa May (Rose) Contner, was born in Corvallis, Oregon, on November 26, 1858, the daughter of James Contner, a Pennsylvania-born tailor, and Charlotte Brown Contner of Ohio. (The family name appears as Countner in later records.) Barbara's maternal ancestry originated in the British Isles and Germany, later branching into families that reportedly included notable Southern citizens. After an interview with William and Rose following Barbara's death, writer Adela Rogers St. Johns claimed that Barbara's maternal grandmother was the granddaughter of a Miss Davis, the niece of Samuel Davis, who was the father of Jefferson Davis, president of the Confederate States of America. St. Johns's statements, however, often forged by her colorful imagination, aren't always factual.

Barbara's maternal grandparents ventured from Ohio to the Oregon

One

Territory in 1855, when the region was rife with turbulence. Incoming settlers were under constant threat of Indian attacks, which the U.S. Army had grown powerless to prevent. The migrants took up arms, joined the soldiers, and eventually drove the Indians onto reservations. As stillness reclaimed the wooded countryside, Rose, the youngest of six children, enjoyed a safe, sheltered youth.

Her life changed abruptly after she set out on her own. She apparently wed a William Liles in Clark County, Washington, in July 1874. The identities of the bride and groom, however, cannot be confirmed; the original marriage record was destroyed in a fire, and surviving Clark County documentation provides only names and an imprecise age range. Were Barbara's mother indeed the bride, two things are certain: she represented herself as being over eighteen when she was in fact fifteen; and the marriage was short-lived.

On April 5, 1876, seventeen-year-old Rose married Caleb Austin Barber, a blacksmith, at Goose Lake, California. They lived in Redding, California, where on January 16 of that same year Rose had already birthed a son, Henry Clay. (The boy would use the surname Barber throughout his life and list Caleb as his father on his wedding certificate.) Rose bore a daughter, Violet June Barber, on February 22, 1880. The existence of another son—not readily identifiable through available records and potentially fathered by Liles—is implied both by later census reports in which Rose lists the number of her living children and testimony given by Henry when on trial in 1928 for a crime that ultimately landed him in jail. The children hadn't known their father long when tragedy struck. Rose was widowed August 15, 1882. In his final hours, Barber requested that the church bells be rung thirty-two times at his funeral, once for each year he lived. After burying her husband, Rose returned with her children to her family in Hillsboro, Oregon.[8]

She soon met the man she came to regard as the love of her life. That man, William Watson (married and divorced as of 1880), wed her June 11, 1883.[9]

That William undertook to raise another man's children on his newspaperman's salary surely attests to his love for his new bride. It also added urgency to his quest for that "something better" he was forever seeking—particularly after the birth of his son, William Jr., in Tacoma, Washington, June 6, 1886.[10]

William veered into other professions and cities over the next two years, including a brief stint in Astoria, Oregon, where, indubitably owing to Chandler's standing as the city's deputy district attorney, he judged misdemeanor cases as Astoria's deputy U.S. commissioner. But the pull of the printing press was strong. By April 1889, he had resettled his family in Tacoma, acquired the editorship of the *Orting Oracle*, and returned to cranking out newspapers full-time. He also kept searching.

Sometime in 1890, after his brother Benjamin took over as proprietor of Portland's *Sunday Mercury*, William moved his family back to Oregon and began editing that publication. What's more, he walked back into the line of fire. The *Mercury*, as reported by the *Oregonian*, was garnering a reputation as "a publication insidiously demoralizing as well as unspeakably offensive."[11] The *Mercury*'s allegedly "indecent" articles of "lust and crime" had many citizens shelling out their coins to get their weekly dose from one of Portland's avowed "smut-mills."[12] Others were outraged. In November 1891, the *Mercury* was indicted by the U.S. grand jury for sending "obscene papers" through the mail.[13] Benjamin pleaded guilty, paid a $500 fine, and returned to his press. Charges kept coming; within the next two years, the *Mercury* was indicted for criminal libel against at least eight city officials. Benjamin was found guilty in an indictment involving the defamation of high-ranking attorney C. E. S. Wood, though he temporarily evaded sentencing while his petition for a retrial was considered.

Meanwhile, in November 1893, district attorney W. T. Hume took action. Benjamin received an urgent telegram from the *Mercury* office at his home, imploring him to "come at once."[14] He arrived to find that his operation had been shut down; his entire staff, including fifty-six newsboys, had been shoved into police wagons and carted to the station. Charged with violation of a statute prohibiting the publication of morally offensive literature, Benjamin was likewise arrested. He blamed his arrest and the seizure of his paper upon a vendetta Hume had against him. It made no difference. His request for a retrial in the case brought against him by Wood was denied, and he was sentenced to a year in jail.

William had vacated the *Mercury* office by the time the detectives raided it. Possibly seeking to dodge the brewing storm, he had taken his family to Yakima, Washington, that August. With a clean slate, he established a reputation as, according to one of his peers, a "gentlemanly and courteous" writer "of more than usual ability and force," working first as editor for the *Yakima Herald*, then moving to the *Yakima Daily Times*.[15] He

One

was still not opposed, however, to boldly printing his opinions whenever he deemed it necessary.

Nor was he opposed to making an extra buck. Surveying the verdant, freshly irrigated lands nestled among Yakima Valley's sweeping hillsides, William smelled opportunity. Here was a chance to profit from both his literary talent and his farming background. He became the Yakima Commercial Club's publicity agent in 1894, promoting local enterprises and enticing settlers to the city through advertising campaigns. Returning to his roots, he used his agricultural expertise to help maximize the area's farmland and extend its irrigation systems. In many of the cities in which he would live in the next twenty-five years, William would act as promoter and irrigationist, supplementing his newspaperman's salary with additional income.

He assuredly needed it.

Rose was pregnant again.

Nearing age forty and believing this pregnancy to be her last, she longed for a little girl. As midnight approached on July 28, 1896, her wish was fulfilled in a Yakima maternity home when she cradled tiny, dark-haired Reatha Dale in her arms for the first time.

Two

The world into which Reatha Watson emerged in 1896 wasn't far removed from the world that had welcomed her parents. Aside from firmly rooted clusters of populations along the Atlantic, the United States was a vast canvas of rural, undisturbed frontier unfolding all the way to the Pacific. Many Americans were unacquainted with such novelties as indoor plumbing and electricity. Newly developing "horseless carriages," better known as automobiles, were jeered as "devil wagons," and their drivers "engineers."[1] American society remained in the grip of Victorian mores, imposing rigid moral values and a distinct separation of the sexes: men earned the wages while women kept house and reared children.

But tremendous change was afoot. The same summer Reatha was born, brothers Wilbur and Orville Wright, consumed by the notion that "the problem of flight might be solved by man," contemplated building a flying machine.[2] Their machine would take flight in 1903, but several years would pass before mankind acknowledged their accomplishment and reconsidered the limitations placed upon human potential and individual achievement.

Three months before Reatha's birth, Thomas Edison debuted his "Greatest Marvel," a film projector called the Vitascope. The *New York Herald* raved, "Wonderful is the Vitascope. Pictures life size and full of color. Makes a thrilling show."[3] Although Hollywood was little more than bucolic farmland, the world hovered on the threshold of what Peter Kobel later described as "a kind of communal waking dream shared in the darkness," an uncharted universe that "would reveal our own secrets to ourselves."[4]

The years surrounding Reatha's birth witnessed a rising rebellion against Victorian restraints upon the American way of life. Suffocated by a mundane existence, men and women of the rapidly expanding middle class sought liberation and control of their destinies. There existed "everywhere . . . a demand for vivid, masterful experience." Amid this upheaval, which would intensify throughout the years leading to World War I, the "New Woman" was spawned—daring, adventurous, and determined.[5]

Reatha Watson would be her epitome.

Two

From the beginning, Reatha's world was one of make-believe beauty. At age four, one story goes, she was no sooner tucked into bed before summoning her mother back into the room to behold the fairies she swore she could see alighting on the moonlit windowsill and twirling across the floor.

Reatha was easily swayed to laughter and tears. Her profoundly sensitive nature was an asset and a curse, yielding both a gentle heart and delicate nerves she couldn't allow to "be set on edge."[6] In *Movie Weekly*'s version of her life story, she dismissed dolls as "lifeless things," instead "wanting *real* things—or nothing."[7] Yet her parents, when confronted with the small children and various animals she was forever bringing home, often had to console their sobbing daughter after explaining that her newfound playmates needed to be returned. At age five, she was inconsolable when the family dog died. On another occasion, her beloved pet kitten vanished, finding a new home with a neighbor girl down the street. Reatha, unable to bear the girl's sadness when she tried to return the kitten, allowed her to keep it. Rose became increasingly concerned by Reatha's hypersensitivity and began keeping watch over her to safeguard against her runaway emotions.

Perhaps Rose wasn't the only one watching Reatha. A budding vision at six years old, with golden brown hair, fair skin, and large, intense eyes that somehow defied description—variously blue-gray, green, hazel, and the deepest sapphire—she was already noticed by boys. According to the (admittedly often embellished) writings of Adela Rogers St. Johns, Rose witnessed Reatha's first brush with romance while peering through the back window one day. Supposedly, the neighbors' boy, nine years old, slipped into the yard, declared his love for Reatha, and pleaded for a kiss. Reatha reputedly acquiesced with a fleeting peck.

When Reatha began her education in Portland in 1903, William and Rose opted for an all-girls school.

William, aside from a spell in Prairie City, Oregon, editing the *Prairie City Miner* in early 1902, had been working in Portland since at least 1898. He initially edited the *Sunday Welcome,* was next reinstated as editor at the *Sunday Mercury* (under new management and, minus the sensational articles, half its former size), then rejoined the *Oregonian*. All the while, the Watsons' address kept changing. The household now included Reatha, William Jr., Rose, and William. Reatha's half-sister, Violet, who had lived with the family in 1900 after marrying Orval Ross, a Portland shirt cutter,

Reatha Dale Watson, four years old. © 2017 The Liberty Library Corporation. All rights reserved.

had since moved out and given birth to a daughter, also named Violet. The whereabouts of Reatha's half-brother, Henry, a farmer, cannot be verified with accessible records.

St. Mary's Academy, founded by the Sisters of the Holy Names of Jesus

Two

and Mary, was regarded as Portland's leading girls' school when Reatha was enrolled as a day pupil in January 1903. Despite the bishop's initial intention to confine the curriculum to basic skills for girls—sewing, manners, language, and housekeeping—the innovative nuns had a higher vision for the young ladies in their charge. Each weekday morning, outfitted in her navy blue serge dress uniform and accompanying black hair ribbon, Reatha bounded up the stone staircase leading into the ornate four-story convent building. Seated among tidy rows of wooden desks, she was instructed by compassionate, highly educated nuns in reading, writing, grammar, and arithmetic (a subject the bishop deemed irrelevant for girls). Supplementary coursework involved art, music, and lessons in Christian doctrine. All girls attended daily Mass.[8]

Reatha's education continued into the evenings. As an adult, she fondly recollected her father's extensive library of "remarkable" books and how, like his father before him, he read to the family in the evenings. Like her father before her, Reatha eagerly listened. "My meals weren't meals," she would say of her girlhood. "They were lessons in English." Thus began her love affair with books, which, she later confessed, "I always preferred to any other kind of company."[9]

Even more than reading or listening to stories, Reatha adored telling them. She composed lines of verse and spun tales while lying in her darkened bedroom at night. She then recited them to the neighborhood children who happily gathered at her feet. Surely William also took pleasure in listening to his daughter and likely encouraged her fledgling talent.

For the time being, however, Reatha had another ambition in mind. Something about St. Mary's Academy resonated with her being, awakening her inherent spirituality. Perhaps it was the nurturing environment or the upstanding example set by the Holy Names Sisters. It may have been the exposure of her hungry intellect to stimulating new subject matter, or the mystical peace she felt there. Whichever it was, Reatha's six-year-old mind was resolved, and she adamantly announced her decision to her family: she would become a nun. Her declaration was dismissed as a passing whim.

Sadly for Reatha, St. Mary's records indicate she was removed from the school after just three months. That her tuition, $5.00 per semester (approximately $145.00 today), was paid in multiple installments offers one clue as to why she left; Rose's decision to work as a dressmaker in preceding years offers another. Money was tight for the Watsons.

Three

The Watsons' move to Tacoma, Washington, in 1905 was merely another in the long succession of migrations that dominated Reatha's childhood. By her own estimation, it wasn't until her teenage years that she remained in a single rented home or boarding room over a year. "Drab, unlovely places," she recalled as an adult, "ugly gray houses with hideously designed red wallpaper, chipped pitchers and dirty wash basins."[1]

She attributed her family's lifestyle to her father's latest moneymaking strategy: "He would go to some city or small town, start a paper, boom it, and then sell out."[2] As the Watsons wandered the Pacific Northwest, William put his children to work, teaching them a trade upon which they could rely in the future. Reatha and William Jr. (who quit school at fourteen, perhaps to help support the family) were given the arduous task of "sticking type"—manually arranging the tiny metal tiles that composed the headlines and columns of William's newspapers—into a printing press.[3] Although Reatha received thirty cents per column (roughly $7.50 today), she "loathed" the work; and, according to her, the job had its perils.[4] The tiles were stored in compartments within drawers according to size, upper-or lowercase, letters most frequently used, numbers, and special characters. Each drawer contained as many as eighty-nine compartments and slid into a large cabinet. If a drawer was accidentally pulled out too far, its contents emptied into the drawer below, resulting in "pied" type. "Many a spanking I got when I pied it," Reatha later conceded.[5]

In Tacoma, William established himself as editor and manager of the *Tacoma New Age* and then, moving the family to another part of town, as a reporter for the *Tacoma Daily News*. The Watsons appear to have been on more stable financial footing during this period in Tacoma; Reatha resumed her convent education and enjoyed occasional amusements in town.

The repeated moving, or "jumping about," as Reatha came to remember it, affected her tremendously. She acquired "the mental habit, as I was forced to have the physical one, of jumping from one point of interest to another."[6] Her self-confessed variability—which would, in her young adulthood, express itself in assorted hair colors, ranging from light champagne-pink to dark purple—surfaced. She also began a pattern of escaping more and more into realities of her own; "I read omnivorously," she recollected.[7]

An entirely new world soon consumed Reatha. One weekend at age eight, she was taken to a matinee performance given by the Allen Stock Company at Tacoma's Orpheum Theater. Seated beside Rose in the theater balcony, enfolded in hushed darkness and with her eyes fastened upon the stage, she felt destiny beckon. "I suddenly made up my mind," she was later quoted as saying in her *Movie Weekly* serial, "that what I wanted to be was a second Bernhardt."[8]

Sarah Bernhardt began life in Paris in 1844 as the illegitimate daughter of a courtesan and attained worldwide reverence as a theatrical sensation. Her debut in the United States in 1880 was preceded as much by accounts of her masterful acting as by tales of her astonishing lifestyle. The press was afire over her myriad lovers, extravagant jewels, and coffin in which she often slept (to prepare, it was professed, "for that final sleep"). Purportedly unrivaled in her ability to enact tragedy and completely immerse herself in characters she portrayed, "the Divine Sarah" drew hordes to her stages. She performed extensively throughout the United States for over three decades, seducing audiences with her serpentine grace, catlike agility, and what one newspaper called "the spell of her genius." According to another paper, theatergoers "reached delirium point" when she performed a male lead "as if she had never worn a skirt in her life." In her sixties, she played nineteen-year-old Joan of Arc so convincingly, audiences bestowed ovations when the judge in the play asked Joan to state her age.[9]

"I had read about Bernhardt," Reatha would later proclaim. "I had even seen her once, when I was very tiny. I didn't forget any of these glimpses."[10]

Reatha scurried home from plays she attended and enacted them herself. Her self-professed childhood longing "to be a great tragedienne and wield a dagger" trounced her inherent shyness.[11] She staged performances in the Watsons' parlor for her family and neighbors, amazing them with her resolve and emotional breadth. William Jr. and Violet may also have motivated these performances; William Jr. had been appearing in theater productions for the past four years, and Violet, now residing in Seattle, had performed with the Wiedemann theater company during their Seattle engagement in 1904.

When family friends hinted to William and Rose that they consider allowing Reatha to go on the stage, Reatha, according to her *Movie Weekly* narrative, announced to her parents that she was going to work. "They thought it was merely funny," she would declare in the narrative. "Another childish whim of mine. They thought it would last for a week or so."[12]

Reatha allegedly took matters into her own hands the Saturday after the Allen Stock Company performance. Her *Movie Weekly* story would recount her stealing away from home, marching back to the theater, and entering the main office—"fired" by her "great ambition." Supposedly Pearl Allen, head of the Allen Stock Company, and his stepdaughter, Verna Felton, the company's fourteen-year-old star, regarded her inquisitively. Reatha remembered that Allen, imposingly large at six feet one and over 350 pounds, spoke first. "What does this child want to do?" he asked. *Movie Weekly's* chronicle continues with Reatha's reply: "I want to go on the stage." Allen inquired if she had ever been on the stage. Reatha admitted she hadn't. He asked if she thought she could act. "Oh, YES, Sir," she assured him.

Allen likely saw something of himself in Reatha. He had left the idea of a career in his father's blacksmith shop behind long before, drawn by his own love for the stage. A job as a musician with Sam T. Shaw's stock company in the late 1890s led to a promotion to stage manager, a position managing the Jessie Shirley Company in 1900, and, in 1902, the formation of his own company.

The keen-minded, thirty-one-year-old Allen chose his players well, securing the services of Verna Felton, known as one of the most gifted child actresses on the stage (and, in later years, as an acclaimed Disney voice-over artist and radio, television, and film actress). For the next three years, the Allen Stock Company trouped around California, Washington State, and Canada, earning laurels. In mid-February 1905, after marrying Felton's widowed mother, Allen signed his players on for a four-week engagement at Tacoma's Odeon Theater. In under two weeks, the *Tacoma Daily News* reported they had "struck the public taste."[13] The company had also outgrown its overcrowded theater. They acquired a larger space at the nearby Orpheum, beginning an eight-week run March 13. Exceeding the management's expectations with continuously packed houses, they stayed an additional six weeks.

As summer neared, the company achieved a milestone in the itinerant world of stock theater: an invitation for an indefinite booking at Tacoma's Star Theater. Allen, ever determined to increase his fan base by aligning his company with his high standard of perfection, prepared for the engagement by scouting new faces for his cast of players.

According to William's recollection, Reatha was given a chance to appear in an amateurs' showcase at the theater, an event Allen periodically staged during his intermissions. To prepare for her role, she costumed herself in smudged, raggedy clothes and stockings with holes at the knees. She emerged onto the stage, a forlorn wisp of a girl, and delivered the words of a well-known poem, "Nobody's Child":

> Alone in the dreary, pitiless street
> with my torn old dress, and bare, cold feet
> all day I have wandered to and fro,
> hungry and shivering, and nowhere to go . . .
> Oh! Why does the wind blow upon me so wild?
> Is it because I am nobody's child?[14]

On she went through her depiction of a heartbroken waif, yearning for affection and eventually comforted by angels.

When her recitation concluded, William recalled, she was "received with such wild enthusiasm" that Allen immediately offered her a small part in a play.[15] Reatha's performance in that play was evidently engrossing. When the Allen Company began their run at the Star Theater July 3, she was a proud member of the lineup. Allen had given her a position for the summer.

Most stock theater companies, in addition to including a leading male and female, a juvenile male, an ingenue, a heavy (villain), a comedian, around six supporting actors, and an orchestra, featured a child or two. As Allen transitioned Felton from child phenomenon to mature roles, he looked to Reatha to fill the gap. The company welcomed Reatha as family, and soft-hearted "Daddy Allen," although predominantly focused upon Felton's career, took special interest in her. "They never put on a play without a child part in it," Reatha would recount, "or, if they did, they wrote one in for me."[16]

While Reatha's salary was likely modest, the hours she worked were extreme. The Allen Company, like all stock companies, drew from its extensive, ever-increasing repertoire of plays, staging a different bill each week. Reatha spent seven days a week at the theater, absorbing every aspect of her craft. Performances began nightly at 8:00 p.m. starting Mondays;

matinees were given Wednesdays, Saturdays, and Sundays; rehearsals for the following week's production commenced Tuesday mornings and continued throughout the week. Actors were expected to know their lines by the first rehearsal. The frenzied pace left Allen—also serving as the company's director—little time to develop his actors. Reatha relied upon trial and error, her observations of the other actors, and her instincts. Since the roles Allen assigned her were minor, she was called upon to perform "specialties." Between acts and during intermissions, as costumes were changed and stagehands shuffled scenery behind the curtain, she was often among the company members who gave dramatic recitals, sang songs, told jokes, or danced.

A full house of 1,200 patrons greeted the Allen players for their opening performance at the Star, and the crowds scarcely abated all summer, regularly packing the auditorium to the doors. The *Tacoma Daily News* approved the additions to Allen's assemblage of players, stating, "Good as was the original company, the present is vastly superior."[17] The *Tacoma Daily Ledger* was equally enthusiastic about the company's weekly showings, noting the "unusual ability" of the players, the repeated curtain calls, and that "a better pleased audience never filed out of the [Star] Theater."[18] The Allen Company, proclaimed the *Tacoma Daily News* midway through the summer, has earned the "right to the front rank in the dramatic world."[19]

The plays enacted by the Allen Company that summer undoubtedly impacted Reatha's receptive imagination. The players addressed such themes as honor, murder, and justice in *True to His Flag*; retribution and mercy in *The Count of Monte Cristo*; bravery and compassion in *The Two Orphans*; and promiscuity and ill-fated romance in Alexandre Dumas's *Camille*. The players tackled various genres, presenting dramas such as *Hazel Kirke*, adventures such as *Michael Strogoff*, comedies such as *A Texas Ranger*, and westerns such as *My Pardner*.

As Reatha grew as an artist, she appears to have assumed responsibility as a breadwinner. When discussing her theater experience nearly twenty years later, she emphasized that, to avoid disrupting her schooling, she performed only in the summer. Her statement, however, may have been an attempt to subvert rumors that she was uneducated (a falsehood likely resulting from her sex symbol image). Despite her claim, Reatha performed with the Allen Company at least twice during the school year. The extent to which her schooling was compromised cannot be verified, as newspapers' theater notices focus mostly on leading actors. While it's conceivable that Reatha worked only a few weeks during the school session, it's equally plausible that she worked additional weeks and that her wages were needed to augment the family income.

Impressed by Reatha's expressive voice, emotional range, and performances in the bit parts he gave her, Allen offered her a challenge that November. The selection for the week of November 20, 1905, was *East Lynne,* a worldwide sensation based upon Ellen Wood's scandalous 1861 novel of the same name. As the denouement nears, Isabel, the play's tragic heroine, has paid for her infidelity with ruination: her lover has mistreated her, her husband has wed her rival, and her son lies dying. Desperate to be with her boy, she disguises herself as a Madame Vine and obtains a position as her son's nurse in her ex-husband's home.

Reatha, cast as the dying child, Little Willie, was entrusted not only with a male role, but also with the play's most climactic scene. Her big moment came as Willie lay on his deathbed in the household nursery. Willie's pathetic longing for his mother prompts Isabel to expose her identity. Gripped in Isabel's arms, Willie utters a final word before dying—"Mother."[20]

Any reservations that Reatha, then nine years old, may have had concerning her readiness for the part were surely dispelled by the week's reviews. "The various members of the company are making new records for popularity" with the "excellence of their work," announced the *Tacoma Daily News.*[21] By midweek, crowds were being turned away from the brimming theater at the doors.

Reatha again triumphed when Allen cast her in another small, pivotal role the week of March 12, 1906. *Zaza,* a story of sacrifice, involves a Parisian singer, Zaza, who discovers that her lover is married. Zaza goes to the man's home to break up his marriage and encounters his young daughter, Totò, portrayed by Reatha. Totò's innocence and love for her father wrench Zaza's heart, preventing her from carrying out her plan. The week's newspaper write-ups confirmed another hit for Allen's players. Allen retained Reatha for a second summer. Her performance in *Zaza,* Reatha later related, decided it.

The Allen Company's second summer at the Star was as successful as its first. Newspapers reported standing-room-only showings, continuous encores, and the breaking of house records.

Reatha's performances now earned special mention in the papers. On July 14, the *Tacoma Daily Ledger* deemed the recitations she delivered between acts of the previous evening's play to have been "excellent." The following week, Allen gave her a supporting role in *Cad, the Tomboy*, a comedy-drama involving an impoverished tomboy (played by Felton) whose relatives deprive her of wealth belonging to her. "Miss Verna Felton and little Miss Watson," wrote the *Tacoma Daily News* after the opening performance, "received round after round of applause."[22]

By August, Allen sought further profit from his company's success. He accepted an offer from Sullivan and Considine, operators of the Star Theater chain, to relocate his troupe to the Star Theater in Portland, Oregon, a larger, more lucrative market. Rather than disappoint his Tacoma audiences, Allen formed the Allen Company No. 2 to occupy the Tacoma Star. After concluding their final performance in Tacoma August 19, Allen and his original players caught the midnight train to Portland.

Reatha had already said her good-byes. Remaining in Tacoma, she began rehearsals with the Allen Company No. 2. She and the talented new line-up closed the summer season playing to the same enthusiastic audiences that had attended Allen's first company.

Reatha's versatility and evolving acting skills, under the company's new director, John McCabe, continued to inspire. She received requests for curtain calls and a nod from the newspapers for her characterization in the Western tearjerker *The Man from Texas* the week of August 20. She earned critical acclaim for her "clever acting" and the "brilliant way in which [she] rendered [her] part" in the thriller *Zora* the following week.[23] She was commended for her enactment of another male role in the British drama *Queen's Evidence* the week after.

Reatha was ready for a bigger audience. She took her final bow with Allen's company at the conclusion of the summer season. "I don't believe I ever saw so many flowers in my life," she recalled. "We had to take a cab to get [them] home. In a little town of that size it was something unusual."[24]

Spokane, Washington, bustling and known throughout the country as "the best show town west of the Mississippi," was home to the famed Auditorium Theater, which then housed the world's largest stage.[25] The nation's most celebrated artists routinely staged lavish productions before the theater's triple tiers of 1,400 crimson seats. Even Reatha's heroine, Sarah Bernhardt, had graced the stage—and caused her usual frisson.

When Reatha arrived in Spokane at the dawn of 1907, the Auditorium was hosting the Jessie Shirley Company. Jessie Shirley, declared "the idol of

Three

the theatergoing public of Spokane" by the *Spokane Daily Chronicle,* had created her company with her orchestra-leader husband in 1897.[26] The company featured Shirley as leading lady and began an extended engagement at the Auditorium in April 1905, never failing to generate capacity business. The engagement would set a national record for continuous appearances—214 weeks' worth—in a single venue outside New York City before the company disbanded four years later.

Exactly what brought Reatha to Spokane is unclear. Since she was reportedly never apart from her mother until her early teenage years, Rose was presumably with her. Period newspapers indicate that William continued working for the *Tacoma Daily News* throughout most of 1907. It seems improbable that the family would shoulder the expense of Reatha and Rose living nearly three hundred miles across Washington for the benefit of Reatha's theatrical career. Perhaps Reatha and Rose stayed with Reatha's half-sister, Violet.

No longer with Orval Ross, her shirt-cutter ex-husband, Violet would marry Portland tiling contractor George Ake in Coeur d'Alene, Idaho, in April 1907.[27] Given that the city directory would soon record the newlyweds' presence in Spokane and their place of marriage is a resort town a short distance away, it's possible the two were already in Spokane by early 1907. Attractive, twenty-seven-year-old Violet had landed a catch. Ake, according to his great-granddaughter Ruthie Primiano, was every bit "the ladies' man" and loaded with money.[28] Violet would attest that she and Ake helped support Reatha during their marriage. Conceivably, they were already doing so before their wedding.

That February, on the strength of her success with the Allen Company, Reatha was hired by Jessie Shirley. It was a decisive achievement. She was engaged to appear in the company's production of *Uncle Tom's Cabin*—in her first leading part.[29]

Adapted from Harriet Beecher Stowe's widely read antislavery novel and set in the pre–Civil War South, *Uncle Tom's Cabin* centers on the character of Uncle Tom, a kindly middle-aged slave who is separated from his family and sold to a plantation owner. Reatha was cast as Little Eva, the plantation owner's angelic daughter. Envisioning a peaceful world where slaves are free and everyone is loved equally, she befriends Uncle Tom, and they are inseparable until a tragic illness claims her.

The production concluded with a tableau proclaimed by local newspapers to be a spectacle unlike anything witnessed in Spokane. Uncle Tom has ascended to heaven after being murdered; he kneels on the stage, gazing upward. High above, among shimmering clouds, Eva floats atop a dove, her arms outstretched in benediction. Stirring music rises from the orchestra.

Along with Shirley and the company's other stars, Reatha succeeded in her role. Newspapers pronounced the production a triumph. The Shirley Company, wrote the *Spokane Daily Chronicle* as performances ran the week of February 17, is "handling the play in an excellent manner" and "getting the best out of it."[30] Theatergoers, crowding each performance, agreed. The experience Reatha gained with the Shirley Company was significant. The elaborately staged production, coupled with the technical demands of performing in a theater that size, were uncharted territory for her.

So was the opulence surrounding her at the theater. Towering above her on the marble and onyx walls of the ninety-foot mosaic-tiled foyer were magnificent portraits of the world's legendary thespians. The theater was adorned with Turkish rugs, immense statues, and vivid frescoes by a renowned artist, upon which, it was reported, "one could gaze for hours, yet never tire."[31] The theater's seventeen dressing rooms were furnished with marble vanity tables. The stage was sumptuously accented by a curtain bearing a recreation of a famous painting: a castle on the edge of a forest.

It must have been thrilling for Reatha to tread upon the same stage as had Madame Bernhardt, performing for the theater's discerning audiences—the gentlemen in their silk top hats and opera capes and, according to one historian, "the ladies as glorious as jewels, ostrich plumes, and opulent gowns could make them."[32] Keenly aware of the "coarse cotton things" she herself had to wear, Reatha would admit of her childhood, "I longed to feel silk touching me" and "I was starved for beauty."[33]

As far as this gilded world was from her, it seemed to dangle within her grasp. William and Rose later recollected that Reatha's impressionability and predilection for pleasure and excitement were further fueled by the gleam of the stage lights upon her and the encouraging roar of the applause in her ears.

In "The True Story of My Life" *Movie Weekly* article series claimed to have been authored by her, it would be stated in 1924 that Reatha's migratory childhood prevented her from delivering a "coherent" account of her youth. She remembered the ever-shifting scenery and cast of characters comprising the tapestry of her early years "in patches," the article explains.[34]

Three

Presumably, after Spokane and Jessie Shirley's theater company, Reatha moved to Seattle. As with her move to Spokane, the details surrounding her appearance in Seattle cannot be determined with certainty. The extent of her employment by the Shirley Company is likewise unclear; her name doesn't appear in surviving newspaper write-ups and programs after *Uncle Tom's Cabin*. William was still on the *Tacoma Daily News* staff as of mid-July 1907 and would be working for the *Yakima Republic* by December; thus it appears he didn't accompany her to Seattle. Reatha and Rose likely went with Violet and her husband, George Ake, to that city, as records place the couple there after Spokane.

According to the *Movie Weekly* series, Reatha again felt the warmth of stage lights with an unnamed Seattle-based stock company, a group that included Myrtle Vane and Charles A. Taylor. But Vane and Taylor were evidently never in the same company in Seattle (or anywhere else). Vane made a fleeting appearance in Seattle (with the Casino Company) in May 1904 and played an extended run (with both the Sandusky-Stockdale Company and the Myrtle Vane Company) from August to December 1911. Taylor and his Charles A. Taylor Company appeared briefly in Seattle at the conclusion of a countrywide tour, remaining from around mid-September through December 1901. The company returned for a twelve-week engagement from June to August 1905, reappeared for several weeks in early 1906, then enjoyed a largely unbroken stay from August 1906 until February 1908.

Possibly Reatha was engaged by Taylor's company sometime between the spring of 1907 and the beginning of 1908. Although Taylor, arresting and suave, is described in *Movie Weekly* as the company's leading man, he was in fact a well-known producer and author of melodramas, not an actor. By 1907, the Charles A. Taylor Company was installed in Seattle's Third Avenue Theater. Taylor had just the drawing card to satisfy his patrons: appearing in his spectacle-studded productions and on her way to becoming a legend was his soon-to-be ex-wife, Laurette Taylor. Since the Taylor Company's daily newspaper reviews focus on the troupe's principals, Reatha (if indeed she was employed by Taylor) occupied a lesser position within the company.

It's also possible that Reatha instead performed with popular leading lady Myrtle Vane during Vane's August to December 1911 Seattle engagement at the Lois and Alhambra theaters. While this scenario places Reatha in Seattle within a different time frame than the one implied in *Movie*

Weekly, Violet and George resided there into 1912, and Reatha made at least one trip to the city around this time. In all probability, Reatha similarly played minor parts in the plays put on by Vane's companies, as she is once again apparently absent from production write-ups.

Whichever company Reatha performed with in Seattle, the experience she acquired was purportedly broad: she played in "everything from *The Squaw Man* up."[35] (It should be noted that Taylor and Vane's companies did not stage *The Squaw Man* in Seattle, and neither did the Allen nor Shirley companies in their respective cities; Reatha may have appeared in that play after the Watsons left Washington, although available sources do not confirm it.)

As exhilarating as it was for Reatha to be fulfilling her dream of acting on the stage, it was a chapter in her life that would soon come to a close.

As 1908 settled over Yakima, William had been employed by the *Yakima Republic* for under a year, Reatha and Rose appear to have joined him in Yakima, and he was itching to make a change. Forty miles east, bordered on the north and east by Washington's Columbia River, was a sagebrush wasteland known as Hanford. To William and the land's owners, the Hanford Irrigation & Power Company, this shriveled patch of earth with a population of a few hundred was a gold mine waiting to be tapped. Work on a massive power plant progressed along the river. That May, its mighty pumps would drench the Hanford region with twenty million gallons of water daily, creating, as declared by newspaper ads already circulating, an empire of the most fruitful agricultural lands in the world.

The Watsons moved to Hanford. William, assisted by twenty-one-year-old William Jr. as printer and publisher, established the settlement's first newspaper, the *Hanford Columbian,* disseminating the opening edition to surrounding towns in mid-April. As manager and editor of the publication, William provided more than local news; he advocated for the Hanford Irrigation & Power Company, promoting Hanford to potential settlers and major farming supply manufacturers. He also instituted another first for the town: its own electoral precinct.

As winter neared, William had gone as far as he cared to with his Hanford enterprise. He sold the *Hanford Columbian* in favor of what he anticipated would be a far more advantageous prospect.

The inconstant landscape of Reatha's life was changing again.

Four

As the editor of a fledgling agricultural trade paper in Turlock, California, in early 1909, William must have believed he had a sure thing on his hands. At least two hundred thousand acres of newly irrigated land, over six times Hanford's acreage, stretched in all directions. Bountiful harvests were being reaped, and more land stood ready to be leased and sold. William busied himself with providing the local farming industries and chief landowners with publicity.

While William lodged in Turlock, Reatha, Rose, and William Jr. lived eighty miles south in Fresno. Reatha acclimated to her new surroundings.

She enjoyed some success performing in Fresno's stock theater productions. When speaking of her experiences there in later years, however, she, William, and Rose didn't provide specifics, and Reatha is not mentioned in the theater sections of obtainable issues of the foremost Fresno newspapers of the day. The particulars of her theatrical career in Fresno are therefore difficult to ascertain.

Around this time, show business dealt Reatha a bitter blow. Now in her pre-teenage years, she had outgrown children's roles but was too young for adult parts. Her cherished ambitions reached a stalemate. A stock company manager explained to Rose that it would be a few years before Reatha should expect to appear on a stage again.

Reatha consoled herself by turning to her unbridled imagination. "Reading," she would be quoted as saying in the *Movie Weekly* version of her life story, was, "for me, the thing that was so eminently worthwhile all through my girlhood."[1] To satisfy a professed "avid and consuming mental curiosity," she ostensibly assimilated the philosophies of Darwin, Ibsen, Seneca, Plato, Aristotle, Socrates, Marcus Aurelius, and Alexander the Great.[2] Inspired once again to take up the pen, she also spent a great deal of time writing and uncovered a true talent for poetry.

Since Reatha's performance schedule had heretofore encroached upon her studies, William and Rose welcomed the resumption of her convent education. St. Augustine's Academy, a boarding and day school for young

Promotional photo of ten-year-old Reatha during her stock company days, before she outgrew child parts. © 2017 The Liberty Library Corporation. All rights reserved.

ladies directed by St. John's Church and the Sisters of the Holy Cross, offered courses in business (bookkeeping and penmanship), music, vocal instruction, sewing, and lace making. Beyond this, the Holy Cross Sisters, with their serenity and selflessness, continuously guided the students toward, in the words of the school's valedictorian, "higher aims and loftier ideals." Deeply affected by this influence, several of the young girls considered renouncing the world and joining the Sisters.[3]

Four

Reatha was among them. "I well remember how intensely religious I became during my stay at the convent," she later revealed. "I was absorbed by the desire to become a nun. It became an obsession with me."[4] Reatha was required to reach her fifteenth birthday before entering the monastery as a novice. With her childhood aspiration rekindled, she read her Bible and prepared herself.

As Reatha anticipated the future and reveled in the careless freedom of her waning girlhood, illness struck. Suddenly, she was no longer able to join friends who came knocking at the Watsons' door asking for "Beth" (a nickname she acquired at school; she preferred it to her given name). She instead spent her days convalescing in her house, physically drained, with Rose nursing her. Her unspecified malady is believed to have been related to a respiratory infirmity that would plague her at varying times throughout her life.

As Reatha's health worsened, the Watsons sought help through Christian Science, a religion founded by Mary Baker Eddy to honor the work of Jesus Christ. Healed from a crippling fall after reading of one of Christ's healings, Eddy experienced an epiphany in which she attained what she claimed to be an understanding of the science behind her healing. Her First Church of Christ Scientist was born of her desire to share her knowledge of these "mighty works," which she deemed "supremely natural" and available to everyone.[5] Operating on the principle of man's inherent perfection as God's creation, Eddy defined disease and disharmony as delusions of a mortal mind out of alignment with the divine Mind. The remedy, according to her tenets, is a complete surrender to God's loving, all-pervading presence.

Reatha's faith in the church and its methodology affected her physically and spiritually. As she immersed herself in the church's teachings and continued reading her Bible, her health returned. Bolstered by her newfound beliefs, her writing took the form of sermons, and she envisioned herself following in Eddy's footsteps as a proponent of Christ's principles. The church's devotees looked forward to Reatha joining their ranks.

Yet Reatha's inherent hunger for life experience, driven by her uncontrollable inquisitiveness and an emerging defiance, led her to forsake both the church and nuns. As her illness faded, her attention was incited by other pursuits. Some of them were unwelcome to Rose and William.

A favored pastime of Reatha's was one to which many young girls can wholeheartedly attest: "racing around with boys chiefly."[6] This diversion proved risky business for a girl with vigilant, protective parents. The *Movie Weekly* depiction of her life story would include a romantic escapade that resulted in disaster: twelve-year-old Reatha scales a garden wall to catch a glimpse of a butcher's boy, her heart aflutter over his "red cheeks" and "cheery whistle"; failing to notice she's being watched, she's peeled from the wall by her dress and given a paddling.[7] Though the story was perhaps enhanced to entertain 1920s film fans, Reatha undoubtedly resorted to secrecy in her romantic dealings.

At the convent, Reatha became ungovernable. Her "girlish pranks," she would one day relate, declining to elaborate, eventually went too far.[8] The mother superior expelled her.

William and Rose clamped down. To protect Reatha from what Rose termed "undesirable associates," public schooling was out of the question.[9] Private tutors were engaged to instruct her at home.

William and Rose felt justified in their concern. Thirteen-year-old Reatha, with her rapidly blossoming, shapely figure and refusal to leave the house unless she was well dressed—"always just a little better than girls who could afford it better than I could," she would reportedly assert—generally passed for older.[10] The drawn-out looks she received on the streets were noted by her parents.

But Reatha possibly broke more than a few of the hearts she captured. As far as being in love was concerned, she would supposedly insist, "I *know* that I never was back in those days of my teens. I was too excited about work, a career."[11] Indeed, Reatha's heart was set firmly upon motion pictures.

Flickers, as early films were called, debuted in America in nickelodeons in 1905. For five cents a show, these cramped, rudimentary, storefront theaters offered a ten-to fifteen-minute form of entertainment for those unable to afford plays or vaudeville. By 1908, nickelodeons had sparked such a craze—"nickel madness"—that nearly ten thousand of them existed throughout the country.[12] As the craze gained momentum, film producers accelerated their production of longer films. These films appealed to a larger audience, the middle class, fueling the necessity for greater numbers of upscale, spacious theaters than were already in existence.

In 1910, Reatha was among the 30 percent of Americans to pay a ten-cent admission fee, crunch through the occasional spattering of discarded peanut shells, and take a seat for a thrilling voyage into alternate worlds.

Four

The journey was heightened by live musicians, whose music and sound effects played upon the emotions and muted the puttering projector. The films themselves were soundless, but they communicated volumes and held fathomless promise. Producer Samuel Goldwyn foresaw that, through them, "every great novel, every great drama, might be uttered in the one language that needs no translation."[13]

Early filmmakers were hardly alone in their eagerness to fulfill an escalating demand. Film production companies emerged with the advent of motion picture cameras and enthusiastically experimented with this new medium. Their efforts were heeded by Thomas Edison, who possessed the majority of the American patents for filming devices. To monopolize the market, Edison joined with the major film producers and established the Edison Trust (Motion Picture Patent Company). Filmmakers excluded from the Trust were tormented by mandatory license fees, costly lawsuits, relentless spies, and raids upon their studios. Between 1907 and 1909, many filmmakers abandoned the established film centers in New York, New Jersey, and Illinois and moved their operations west. Among those evading the Trust were those seeking improved weather conditions in which to shoot their films. Los Angeles, with its pleasant temperatures, inexpensive land, extensive natural backdrops, and close proximity to Mexico (additional refuge from Trust officials), provided an ideal environment. Since the Trust had ousted the majority of foreign films from American theaters, American filmmakers dominated their industry. Los Angeles became their hub.

In 1910, the film industry gave birth to a cultural phenomenon. Previously, motion picture actors, although under contract with producers, did not receive screen credit for their films. Producers rationalized that they could avoid paying hefty salaries by keeping actors in relative obscurity. This changed when producer Carl Laemmle, in an endeavor to garner publicity for his company, staged a hoax. He announced in February that he had employed "the greatest moving picture actress in the world today," Florence Lawrence.[14] Next, he propagated a rumor that she had been killed in a trolley car accident. In March, after seizing the attention of a concerned public, Laemmle revealed that Miss Lawrence was alive, well, and making pictures with him. His tactic was successful. Now a recognized name, Lawrence gave interviews, made personal appearances, and was hailed as "America's foremost moving picture star."[15] Other companies soon promoted their stars, actors received screen credit, and the minds of young hopefuls were set awhirl with dreams of film stardom.

Reatha was doing her share of dreaming. Perhaps, by 1910, those dreams were all she had.

She lived alone with her parents. William Jr., married to Eleanor Ernst since January 1909, had left the newspaper business for a vaudeville career under the stage name Billy DeVore. He would spend the coming years performing a roller-skate dancing act and appearing in skits and musicals as a well-liked comedian and blackface performer. Violet, her daughter, and her husband remained in Seattle. Reatha's half-brother, Henry, now working as a rancher, resided with his growing family in Yakima, Washington.

William had left Turlock to strike out on his own again. The result was the *Inter-Californian,* a Fresno-based agricultural journal he started, managed, and edited. The going had been rough. Reatha would remember that William had hard luck from then on. Conceivably out of necessity, Reatha's schooling had ceased for good. Rose had fallen back upon her skills as a seamstress to make extra money. Reatha labored in a candy store.

Her life a distant cry from what she imagined it would be, Reatha begged William and Rose to allow her to travel to Los Angeles for a chance to break into movies. Her pleas were met with misgiving. William opposed her career choice. Perhaps he considered film acting an infeasible livelihood. He may have regarded films as second-rate entertainment (a commonly held belief in 1910), an undignified vocation for a young lady. Possibly, he didn't want her associating with film folk, particularly at her age. Undaunted and strong-willed, Reatha persisted in her campaign and eventually prevailed upon her parents.

At age fourteen, accompanied by Rose, she boarded a train for Los Angeles.

Reatha wasted no time in applying to Los Angeles producers for work. But with each unsuccessful interview, her spirits dampened. She had no experience before a camera, and her stage credits meant little in a town inundated with professional actors. Unwilling to abandon hope, she continued making the rounds of the studios. Finally, it happened. She was given a part in a film—a small part, but nevertheless, a chance.

Any joy Reatha felt over her hard-won victory was short-lived. Before the picture was completed, she was dismissed from the company. Her

Four

Fourteen-year-old Reatha with Rose. © 2017 The Liberty Library Corporation. All rights reserved.

hopes of success destroyed, she collapsed into Rose's awaiting arms and sobbed.[16] Her grand venture had ended in failure.

One reason, offered years later, for Reatha's inability to succeed in motion pictures at this time was the unrefined nature of early film. The technology of the day, it was said, was incapable of discerning her lovely features.[17]

While movie cameras may not have captured Reatha's burgeoning beauty, Los Angeles–based portrait and figure painter Antonia Miether Melvill did. Reatha met Melvill when she befriended Melvill's daughter, Viola, after Reatha and Rose moved into the same apartment building on Figueroa Street. In Melvill's painting *The Five Senses,* Reatha posed with four other beautiful young girls, her right hand cupping her ear. (A few viewers have suggested that Reatha appears to be exposing her breast, but this isn't the case; the shadowing that creates this illusion in photographic copies of the painting isn't present on the original.)

To her friends at the height of her fame, Reatha provided a different

Antonia Melvill, *The Five Senses*. Reatha is on the far left. (Melvill's daughter, Viola, is holding the pencil.) Courtesy of Joan Barry Liebmann.

explanation for her initial lack of success in films. Her discharge from the company, she said, occurred because she slapped the director when he attempted to kiss her. Alice Terry, Reatha's future costar and friend, said the director was "none other than Cecil B. DeMille."[18] (This seems unlikely, since DeMille didn't arrive in California or begin directing films until 1913, at least two years after the incident was claimed to have occurred.)

Reatha's dreams would have to wait. Her notoriety, however, would not.

II

Notorious

Snares Beset Beauty's Path; Beware! Warns Reatha Watson.
—Los Angeles Examiner *headline, June 15, 1914*

Five

December 30, 1912, dawned like any Monday morning in the Watsons' apartment at 1229½ South Figueroa Street. Shortly before 10:00 a.m., as the surrounding streets and business district awakened, sixteen-year-old Reatha was stirring in her bedroom. William, having abandoned Fresno and his *Inter-Californian* concern about a year earlier and now working for a Los Angeles paper, had already left for the day.

Rose heard a knock at the front door. Answering it, she found herself looking uneasily into the blue-gray eyes of the fair-haired caller. It was her daughter Violet, from whom she was estranged.

Much had changed in Violet's life between that morning and the Watsons' departure from Washington in 1908. She had separated from George Ake by 1911 and, charging nonsupport, divorced him shortly after. What William described as Violet's "spectacular" acting career on the Seattle stage had ended; the 1910 Seattle census records her occupation as "none," and the 1912 Seattle directory listed her as a clerk.[1] By mid-May, with her sights on film acting, she had left Seattle and her job as a milliner for Los Angeles, telling friends that Reatha would help her procure a studio engagement. She originally brought her daughter (whose name had changed from Violet to Mona), then sent her away to a Seattle convent school.

Violet had initially moved in with the Watsons. The sisters' sixteen-year age difference mattered little to Reatha, who, from age seven, had developed a self-professed knack for imitating adults. Reatha and Violet were inseparable, strolling the city and enjoying private talks. Rose, however, feared Violet's influence upon what she termed Reatha's "unusually romantic" nature.[2] After arriving in Los Angeles, Violet had taken up with Clark Boxley, a married man and father in his early thirties. Unbeknownst to his wife, Boxley had been plying Violet for months with tokens of his affection—including an expensive automobile. When William and Rose learned of Violet's amour, they evicted her from their home, and William forbade her to associate with Reatha. "Her chats with Reatha were not doing the girl any good," Rose averred.[3] William believed Violet influenced Reatha "to act on her own initiative and without regard to the desires of her parents."[4]

Standing at the Watsons' doorstep the morning of December 30, Violet asked to retrieve a photograph of hers from Reatha. Knowing that Reatha had just gotten out of bed, Rose permitted Violet to enter Reatha's room and speak briefly with her. Minutes later Violet reemerged with the photograph, exchanged a few words with Rose, and left.

Rose went into Reatha's room and found it startlingly empty. She noticed that several articles were missing, including Reatha's auto coat and the new black velvet suit Reatha planned to wear the following evening. Reatha and a friend had purchased tickets for a New Year's Eve opening at a local theater. Reatha had said nothing to Rose about going anywhere that Monday. Yet she was gone.

Three days later, on January 2, William and Rose received their first communication concerning Reatha. An envelope addressed to Rose, stamped "JAN 1 1913" and mailed from a train en route to Los Angeles from San Francisco, arrived. Inside, a letter read:

> Dear Mother and Dad,
> I am very sorry to have left you as I did and beg to be forgiven for any anxiety my hurried departure must have caused you, but when I tell you that I expect (and am) very happy in the step I have taken, I am sure you will not think harshly of me.
> We are on our way East and I shall write you fully on reaching our destination.
> We hope to repay you in many ways for the trouble I have given you. We have also made arrangements to have this letter mailed at a distant point given the place our train takes us.
> Hoping you will make no useless effort to find me. I remain,
> Yours with love,
> Reatha.[5]

As William read the letter, mounting panic seized him. It wasn't written in Reatha's handwriting. Forgery in hand, he charged to the police station. "I positively identify the handwriting of that letter as that of Mrs. [Violet] Ake," he proclaimed in a written statement. "It convinces me that she has

Five

Reatha as she appeared in the *Los Angeles Examiner,* January 4, 1913, beneath the headline "Efforts to Find Reatha Watson Unavailing."

denied my child the privilege of writing to her parents about her situation."[6] Begging the authorities to do something, he swore out warrants for Violet and Boxley's arrest.

A barrage of headlines striped California's newspapers the next morning. Touting Reatha as "the most beautiful girl in Los Angeles," reporters broadcast her description: sixteen years old, five feet seven, 130 pounds, blue-gray eyes, dark hair, fair skin.[7] The *Los Angeles Examiner* ran pictures of Reatha, Violet, and Boxley in a desperate attempt to obtain information on her whereabouts.

William revealed to reporters that Boxley was "madly jealous" of

Violet. He presumed the threesome might be on their way north to Violet's daughter in Washington. "[Boxley's] object in taking Reatha," he speculated, could be "as a sort of check on Violet at times when he is not with her."[8]

William told a *Los Angeles Evening Herald* reporter that Reatha and Violet had taken automobile trips to San Francisco in the past, and that the sisters had journeyed to Seattle together about a year earlier. Rose amended William's statement when speaking to a *Los Angeles Examiner* reporter the next day: "It is not true that Reatha has been going on long automobile trips with Boxley and [Violet]." She also asserted, "She has not been automobiling except when I was along."[9] The *San Francisco Call* quoted her as saying, "The child had never been away from me in her life."[10]

"She is a thoroughly good girl," Rose declared to the *Examiner*, "and I am sure it is not an elopement or escapade in which a man is concerned."[11]

According to William and Rose, Reatha had seen little of Violet recently, and they were unable to explain "how [Violet] could have gained enough influence over her to induce her to go away willingly with her and Boxley."[12]

When coaxed for personal details about Reatha, William and Rose spoke of her success as a child actress in the cities they had lived in. Rose told reporters Reatha had continued visiting Los Angeles film studios and appealing to directors for work. One such director was Al Christie, head of Nestor Studios in Hollywood. Many years later, Christie looked back upon the day Reatha, then fifteen, walked into his establishment. She "said she wanted to be a dramatic actress," the amiable Christie recalled. "So I hired her for comedies."[13] Christie's sidesplitting western one-reelers evidently weren't what Reatha had in mind. At the time of her disappearance, she had left Nestor and wasn't employed by any studio. "She was not offered salary enough to make it an inducement," Rose explained to reporters, "she did not want an engagement unless it was a good one."[14]

In addition, there had been fresh tension between Reatha and William over her acting ambitions. But, according to a statement William gave the *Los Angeles Times*, "the trouble was smoothed out" and "nothing further had been said about it."[15]

To a *Los Angeles Evening Herald* reporter, William asserted, "I will spend every cent I have to find her and rescue her."[16]

"I fear for Reatha as the result of her association with [Violet and

Boxley]," he admitted to the *Examiner,* "and I intend to prosecute them to the limit on a charge of kidnapping."[17]

After probing William and Rose, reporters descended upon the home at which, only a few days prior, Boxley resided with his wife and eleven-year-old son. Her face wet with tears, Mrs. Boxley confirmed, "My husband has not been home since Monday noon. I do not know where he is." She contended, "I never heard of [Violet] Ake before the officers told me."[18]

Police had visited Mrs. Boxley a few hours earlier, apprising her of the warrant out for her husband's arrest. When detectives disclosed that Boxley withdrew $600 (almost $15,000 today) from the bank the afternoon Reatha vanished, she was baffled. "I do not know where he got it," she insisted.[19] She then confessed that her husband frequently left home for days at a time and afterward assured her "that business had detained him."[20]

Boxley, investigators discovered, was leading a double life. A month before his disappearance, he was secretary-treasurer of a Los Angeles building and investment company. The company's members informed police he was let go when the firm reorganized. He then sold real estate. His former colleagues attributed his increased finances to success with his real-estate dealings. They knew nothing of his relationship with Violet, nor could they explain why he suddenly left the city.

An investigation of Violet's Ninth Street apartment uncovered additional complexities. The apartment manager told police Boxley and Violet had been living there under the aliases Mr. and Mrs. Clark. Violet was last seen leaving her room shortly before Reatha disappeared. She hadn't returned.

Telegraphs fired off by Los Angeles police beseeched San Francisco authorities to apprehend Boxley and Violet and take Reatha into protective custody. Deputies searched San Francisco's docks and railroad stations. Officers in every town from the Mexican border to Seattle were likewise on high alert. The story erupted in more newspapers, prompting an outcry of public concern encompassing several states. Soon, eyewitness accounts unfurled beneath headlines.

Around noon on New Year's Eve, the day after Reatha went missing, Boxley, Violet, and a girl matching Reatha's description reportedly entered the garage where Boxley stored the new car he had purchased for Violet. The garage owner, P. V. St. Clair, told police that the threesome drove off in the car without saying where they were headed.

Around 10:00 p.m. that night, Boxley pulled into a filling station in Santa Paula, a town about sixty-five miles northeast of Los Angeles. The station attendant later identified him, Violet, and Reatha from photographs. "The man said his name was Clark," the attendant informed police. The attendant also stated that he "gained the impression that they had no intention of returning" to Los Angeles, and "the girl seemed entirely willing to be with Boxley and Mrs. Ake."[21]

Another sighting was reported January 3 by Charles Avery, an acquaintance of Reatha's. Avery saw Reatha riding a trolley car into downtown Los Angeles that same day. At the time, he was unaware she had been reported missing. She was riding alone, Avery said, and he didn't speak with her.

The police soon were able to call off their search for Reatha. Shortly after midnight on January 4, four days after her disappearance, she walked through the front door of her parents' home and into their outstretched arms.

The morning of January 4 deputy district attorney Arthur Veitch met with Reatha and William, listening intently as Reatha rendered a graphic account of her experience with Violet and Boxley. Following this interview, Veitch told reporters, "I am convinced we have a strong case."[22] He pledged to do everything within his power to prosecute Violet and Boxley for child stealing, a charge carrying a maximum sentence of twenty years' imprisonment. William vowed that he and Rose would assist with the action.

That same day, in compliance with reporters' fervent requests, Reatha spoke publicly of "the most terrible experience of my life." Sympathy for Violet, she began, prompted her decision to leave home. "She said Mr. Boxley had been threatening her, and she showed me her arm where he had pinched it black and blue trying to get her into the automobile," Reatha explained. "She begged me to stay with her."[23]

Reatha stated she was under the impression they would drive to Riverside and return before evening. She trusted Violet would clarify the situation to Rose when they returned, she said.

According to Reatha, things took an unexpected turn: "I had not been with them long until I was bewildered by the discovery that I had been grievously deceived and that Boxley is indeed a monster."[24] Rather than return to Los Angeles, Boxley—whom Reatha described as drinking heavily, arguing with Violet, and "bullying us horribly"—drove north to

Burbank and Palmdale. Reatha spoke of being forced to sit in Violet's lap in the front seat, held "so I could hardly move," on a night ride laden with danger.[25] "The miracle," she continued, "is that we were not dashed over the precipices of Casitas Pass and crushed to death as a tragic denouement . . . It was a lucky star that guided our way with a desperate driver at the wheel."[26] The terror caused by her so-called "ride of horror" seemingly remained with her. "See," she exclaimed to her listeners, "I'm still trembling!"[27]

Reatha said that during a brief stop in Burbank, she slipped away from Boxley long enough to telephone her parents for help. Her call didn't go through, she claimed, "on account of a disconnected instrument."[28]

She contended that, upon learning of Boxley's plan to drive her north to Santa Barbara and then to San Francisco, she plotted an escape. "I was closely watched and did not dare try to give any warning that I had been carried away against my will," she disclosed.[29] "I concluded that my own safety would be best promoted by appearing to be entirely pleased with their scheme."[30] In Santa Barbara, she said, she planned to make a break for it.

But the escape she plotted the evening they arrived in Santa Barbara failed, she stated. The three attended a vaudeville performance, where she encountered some acquaintances. She alleged that Boxley "instantly ordered me not to speak to them. I wanted to, so he got up right away and rushed us out of the [theater]."[31]

The morning of January 3, after they spent the night at a Santa Barbara hotel under the names Mr. and Mrs. Clark and Miss West, Boxley learned of the warrant for his arrest. He stormed into their room, white-faced and waving a newspaper, according to Reatha. Anxious to be rid of her, he agreed to let her go. He drove her to the train station, gave her money for a ticket to Los Angeles, and instructed her to tell a story that would absolve him and Violet of the kidnapping charges.

By Reatha's account, she was then "hastening to mother, ill with fatigue and excitement, confused with doubt, and pained with an awakening sense of the grief I had caused at home." She continued, "It wasn't till I got home that I fully understood about my sister" and "saw the whole plot to kidnap me." Her parents, she said, "asked me if I didn't suspect—why, I couldn't suspect my own sister. I'm through with her now, and I wish I were through with my fright, but it won't go away. I'd cried myself to sleep every night I was away and now that I'm home I can't forget those terrible,

Violet as she appeared in the *Los Angeles Evening Herald,* January 6, 1913, with the caption "Police patrol roads to block escape of Boxley and Mrs. Ake."

Five

terrible nights and days. I'm so glad and happy to be home again and to be with my parents."[32]

William, basking in his daughter's safe return, told reporters he would fulfill Reatha's most cherished wish: he would buy her a pedigreed Persian cat.

After Reatha's harrowing depiction of her experience hit newsstands, Violet and Boxley, aware that police were still raking the state for them, returned to Los Angeles and surrendered January 6. They were arraigned and released after each paying $1,500 bail. At the arraignment alongside their attorney, C. W. Pendleton, the couple declined to answer reporters' questions regarding Reatha and the charges against them. Pendleton, however, warned that the complete truth would be told and "throw an entirely different light upon the case."[33]

Mrs. Boxley, accusing her husband of eloping with another woman, filed for divorce.

The Watsons refused contact with Violet, wanting nothing to do with her. Reporters were eager to hear her side of the story. In subdued, anxious tones, she broke her silence the day after the arraignment, delivering a considerably different account than the one Reatha gave.

Learning of the charges against her through the Santa Barbara newspapers, she told the *Los Angeles Evening Herald,* had been the shock of her life. With a muted laugh, she dismissed the allegations as "absurd," adding, "the child implored me to take her away—she was so unhappy at home—and I know so well what that meant, because all my life I have been unhappy at home, too."[34] According to Violet, Reatha's desperation to leave her parents went beyond typical teenage rebellion. She stated that attempts were being made to marry Reatha to a man she didn't want to marry, and that Reatha didn't want to be married at all.

Telling the reporter that Reatha was like her own child, Violet admitted that she could not help but rescue her. William, she said, was away when Reatha was born and Rose "had much to do," so she herself had assumed the role of Reatha's caregiver—despite the sacrifices that entailed. "I was only sixteen and should have been in school," she continued, "but I no more hesitated to go without an education for her sake than I later hesitated to marry a man I did not love in order to support that little sister of mine, and my baby—the child of my first marriage. There was no love between the man and myself, but my first thoughts were the two girls, and so I consented. So long as I live, even if I starve, I will never again marry without love. The price is too great." Acknowledging that she had made mistakes in her life, Violet expressed a desire to help Reatha benefit from them. She indicated that her sister had always been closest to her heart: "From the time I was a little girl I have wanted some happiness without trouble and responsibility, and my companionship with Reatha has been the nearest and only approach to obtaining that in my whole life. My baby I could not be with much—she has been kept in the best school I could find and carefully brought up. And all my mother love has expressed itself on sister."

Violet insisted that, even before reading of the kidnapping charges in the papers, she and Boxley had tried to persuade Reatha to return home. Whenever the matter was brought up, Reatha became "hysterical," she claimed. Violet next alleged that, when they discovered they were being sought by the police, Reatha offered to take full responsibility. She described Reatha wrapping her arms around her neck and quoted her as saying, "It is all my fault, and when I get home I'll explain all about it: that I insisted on coming."

Despite Reatha's rejection of her, and the supposed lies she told about her, Violet purportedly ached for the deep affection she said existed between them. "I hope," she said, "after she's thought the matter over, she'll remember what we mean to each other and come back to me."

The morning of January 18 Reatha approached the police courthouse for the preliminary hearing, scrutinized by a gathering of reporters. Her face was ashen. She held fast to Rose and William.

Violet waited outside. For the first time since the sisters were together in Santa Barbara, their eyes met. Reatha stared evenly at Violet, tossed her head slightly higher, and continued past her. William and Rose likewise ignored her. Violet wept.

Tailed by reporters, Violet followed her sister, mother, and stepfather into the courtroom of Judge Frederickson, taking a seat directly in front of them. At no time during the hearing would Violet speak to her relatives. Boxley, who arrived alone, sat apart from Violet, fretfully gnawing a pencil. Violet glanced tearfully at him throughout the proceedings.

Deputy district attorney Veitch and defense attorney Pendleton got down to business. Reporters took notes. New facts were unearthed.

First in the witness box was P. V. St. Clair, owner of the Los Angeles

Five

garage where Boxley kept his automobile. Queried by Veitch, St. Clair reiterated that he saw Boxley, Violet, and Reatha drive away from the garage the morning of Reatha's disappearance. St. Clair originally reported that neither Boxley nor the sisters mentioned where they were going. He testified, however, that Boxley told him he was driving to Riverside for a few days, and perhaps to San Francisco. Boxley, he further stated, instructed him to inform Mrs. Boxley "as nicely as I could" that he had been summoned away on business.[35]

Rose took the stand next. Under cross-examination by Pendleton, she contradicted her earlier assertion to reporters that she and Reatha had never been apart, conceding that Reatha had run away from home a few months earlier. Reatha had gotten "in a temper," Rose admitted, fled to a girlfriend's, and remained away several days.[36]

Pendleton questioned Rose about Reatha's employment history. Rose mentioned Reatha's position in the Fresno candy store and her recent motion picture work. These, she maintained, were the only jobs she remembered. Pendleton offered to refresh her memory, inquiring if Reatha had ever been a model. Rose stated that she had, "for a lady."

"No men?" Pendleton interposed.

"Yes—once—twice for men," Rose replied.

Pendleton asked what her daughter wore during these engagements.

"She always wore garments," Rose answered.

"Did she never pose in the nude?" probed Pendleton.

"Yes," Rose confessed.

Additional testimony from Rose revealed that Reatha had posed as a nude model on four different occasions.

Court was soon adjourned for the day. The case was set to continue the following week. Pendleton wasn't through yet.

Ever since photographs of Reatha began appearing in newspapers following her disappearance, she had taken on mythological dimensions throughout Los Angeles. "Has the Ake-Boxley-Watson kidnapping case revealed a new world beauty?" asked the *Evening Herald* as the preliminary hearing was underway. Rob Wagner, a local painter and self-proclaimed "priest of beauty," decided to find out.[37] Skeptical, he visited Reatha at her parents' apartment to render his expert opinion.

What Wagner encountered in the Watsons' parlor threw him off guard. He studied Reatha's "refined, clear cut features, small mouth and

January 25, 1913, *Los Angeles Evening Herald* image of "California's Venus," Reatha Watson, frolicking in the sun at Venice Beach.

chin, low forehead, [and] slender neck." He observed her "rich brown" hair, which she wore "in a simple Greek coiffe." He analyzed her "tall, lithe figure," noting her "long legs"—like those "of the classic sculpturer," he said. "Perhaps her most alluring beauty," he rhapsodized, "lies in her eyes, for they are large and slate blue with a quiet, dreamy sensuousness that is a fitting accompaniment to the long, graceful, and pantherine lines of her body."

Reatha's tender age of sixteen confounded Wagner. "Her beauty is not simple and girlish," he declared. "It is the mature, conscious beauty of the woman of thirty. It is not the bud with the promise of fulfillment, but the beauty of ripened womanhood."

Wagner presented his assessment to the *Evening Herald*. "It is a remarkable thing to find in one person all the plans and specifications of a perfect model," he concluded. "The nearest approach to such perfection I witnessed today in the physical form of Miss Reatha Watson." The *Herald* took his pronouncement a step further: "Miss Watson Hailed as California's Venus," announced the paper in a headline.[38]

Reatha, flanked by William and Rose, made her second appearance at the courthouse January 22. Asked by a reporter how they were holding up, Reatha and Rose responded that the strain of being in court was immense, mainly due to the presence of Violet, with whom they still refused to speak. Reatha needed all the strength she could muster.

Deputy district attorney Veitch called Reatha to the witness stand. She reaffirmed that Violet and Boxley had held her captive against her will and released her after William instigated a statewide hunt. She stated that she had desperately wanted to return home and had asked Boxley to take her. He refused, she said, telling her it "would be dangerous to return, having incurred the displeasure of her parents." She testified that Boxley instead promised to get her a job as a "demonstrator" when they reached San Francisco, adding that he didn't explain the type of demonstrating he had in mind.[39]

Defense attorney Pendleton moved in. Under cross-examination, Reatha admitted she made no attempts to flee Violet and Boxley, nor did she approach anyone for help—even though, at one point, the three of them dined with a deputy sheriff. Pendleton, referencing her desperation to return to her parents, asked her to account for the eight hours that elapsed between the time she reached Los Angeles and her arrival at home.

"From what I had read in the papers," Reatha said, "I was afraid there was a warrant out for me." She mentioned meeting a male friend and walking with him to the Hotel Angelus. She recounted remaining with her companion in the hotel's parlor several hours, having dinner and telling him of her ordeal. They then took in a picture show, she continued, in order that she might "collect her nerves before returning home."[40]

The judge, noting Reatha's drained condition after she was quizzed for over two hours, ordered an adjournment for the day.

Pendleton pressed ahead with a fierce cross-examination of Reatha January 29. Reatha told the court that Boxley had forced her to write the letter received by Rose and declared by William to have been written by Violet. She testified that she disguised her handwriting. Pendleton suspected otherwise. He approached the witness stand with a piece of paper, placed it before her, and instructed her to write a series of names on it. He then challenged her to write the same names—with disguised handwriting.

Pendleton hovered expectantly; Reatha hesitated. The stares of Judge Frederickson and the court bored into her. She trembled and her eyes rimmed with tears. Rose leapt from her seat, dashed to the stand, and caught her daughter in her arms. A "sensational climax" in the courtroom, newspapers would report: "California's Venus Faints as She Tells [of] Kidnaping."[41]

Veitch interceded, requesting that Reatha be excused from the remainder of the day's proceedings. The court allowed it. Reatha, assisted by Rose and with her face "deathly white" against her wide-rimmed black velvet hat, wobbled into the corridor, moaned, and again crumpled into Rose's arms.[42] Upon regaining consciousness she became hysterical, shaking violently, sobbing, and groaning incoherently. A police matron escorted Reatha and Rose to the city jail hospital, where Reatha received medical aid until she composed herself. Rose then took her home.

Back in the courtroom, Pendleton called to the stand Clara Wright, owner of the Palmdale hotel where Reatha, Violet, and Boxley had stayed while en route to Santa Barbara. Mrs. Wright testified that Violet took ill at the hotel and became lost; Boxley went searching for her, leaving Reatha unsupervised for over an hour. In Violet and Boxley's absence, Wright said, Reatha freely came and went from the hotel but didn't try to board a train that passed through.

Pendleton questioned Wright about a discussion she had with Reatha. Wright quoted Reatha as telling her, "I am running away from home. My parents and I do not agree. My sister is helping me to escape. She will accompany me to San Francisco and then return to Los Angeles . . . I came away on this trip dressed in my kimono, carrying my clothes in my arms. I do not want to return home, but both [Violet] and Boxley want me to."[43]

Wright next described hearing snatches of a telephone conversation in which Reatha seemingly discussed meeting her husband in San Francisco.

Five

Wright confessed, however, that she was waiting tables at the time and therefore missed parts of Reatha's conversation. Prior to Wright's revelation, George Gee, operator of a Palmdale gas station where Reatha, Violet, and Boxley had stopped, cited Reatha as telling him she was going to San Francisco to join her husband. Gee said Reatha was unguarded by Violet and Boxley when she spoke with him.

Boxley was summoned to the stand. He asserted that Reatha hadn't wanted to return home. She told him, he testified, "her parents were trying to marry her to some man whom she did not love."[44]

During her testimony, Violet again contended that Reatha told her Rose "was going to force her to elope with a certain man for whom she did not care," and that Reatha begged to accompany her and Boxley. Violet insisted, "I took Reatha with me because I felt sorry for her."[45] During cross-examination by Veitch, Violet admitted to deliberately concealing her intentions from Rose the morning she took Reatha.

Reatha returned to the courthouse February 11, undoubtedly aware of what she was up against. Under Judge Frederickson's order, she took the stand for further interrogation. By her own admission to Frederickson, at no time had she been forcibly held against her will by Violet or Boxley.

"I was told by them that I should talk to no one," she stated concerning her stopover with her sister and Boxley in Palmdale, "that I should not wander around and be seen and that I was not to leave. They did not command me but gave me to understand that they wanted me to stay."[46]

Asked by Frederickson why she didn't escape on the train in Palmdale, Reatha replied that the only money she had was Boxley's and she hadn't wanted to use it. She claimed she asked Boxley to drive her home that same night, but he told her the automobile's lamp was broken and that he was unfamiliar with the road. It was then that Violet became ill, she continued, adding, "my sisterly love for her prevented me from leaving her at such a time."[47]

Satisfied, Frederickson permitted Reatha to return to her seat. Citing a lack of evidence against Violet and Boxley, he pronounced his verdict. "'Reatha Watson Kidnapped? No': Case Is Dismissed by Judge," reported the *Los Angeles Examiner* February 12.

Reatha's struggle to cope with the tremendous tension the trial and ensuant publicity wrought in her intensified throughout February. Six mysterious letters, anonymously written and addressed to her, were delivered to the Watsons' apartment. Each contained the same fearsome threat: "Beware!"[48] With the receipt of each letter, Reatha edged closer to a nervous breakdown.

William and Rose grew desperate. They decided that the only way to ensure their daughter's protection and restore her peace of mind was to remove her from the city. They were, however, powerless to do so.

A court injunction forbade it. Frantic with fear when Reatha was missing, William and Rose were willing to employ any means necessary to bring her home. They submitted an application of delinquency against her; the court approved it. Their parental authority had thereby been revoked. Reatha was a ward of the juvenile court.

William entered a juvenile courtroom at the end of February, his distraught daughter by his side. Presenting the unnerving letters and stating his wish to take Reatha out of Los Angeles, he implored the judge to withdraw the delinquency order against her. His request was granted.

William and Rose had reclaimed their parental authority. Reatha was instructed to submit to it.

Six

Reatha, William, and Rose hustled out of Los Angeles. William had acquired a fieldwork assignment from the *Los Angeles Times* in El Centro, a remote town adrift in the scorching southeastern California desert.

It was a jarring change for Reatha. Slightly over six years earlier, El Centro had emerged atop a barley field. The introduction of irrigation in 1901 enabled a small but developing agricultural industry, which William began reporting on. Around the time of the Watsons' arrival, the population of El Centro was under one percent that of Los Angeles. With its rows of brick buildings separated by wide, dirt roads, the settlement was a work in progress. El Centro Chamber of Commerce commissioner Don C. Bitler exalted that El Centro is "a place . . . where life may be enjoyed in its fullness."[1]

Reatha was miserable. She longed for Los Angeles and her friends. Her family's nomadic lifestyle had cost her dearly: a childhood devoid of enduring friendships and no sense of ever truly belonging anywhere. Los Angeles, Reatha was convinced, was where she belonged. She begged to be allowed to leave the smothering heat of El Centro and return to Los Angeles. She vehemently argued that she was capable of living on her own and supporting herself. Unbelievably, William and Rose let her go. Possibly, Reatha gave them no choice: perhaps she simply left.

Back in Los Angeles that summer of 1913, Reatha secured a job in a department store, alternately staying in friends' homes and living in an apartment. She once more struggled to launch a film career. Before long she found employment as a bit player. She also fell in love.

Wallace Reid—twenty-one years old, blond, blue-eyed, and with a smile that made many a woman's knees buckle—was already smashing hearts nationwide as an up-and-coming film idol. Reatha would tell Robert Carville, her future dance partner, of working on the same studio lot as Reid. "It was love at first sight," she said. It was more than that; Reid was, according to Reatha, her "first sweetheart." He might also have been her first heartbreak. She would explain to Carville that the relationship ended over "a misunderstanding."[2]

That misunderstanding may have involved the long-standing torch

Reid carried for actress Dorothy Davenport. He had been trying to persuade Davenport to accept his marriage proposal for nearly two years. He finally resorted to attempting to make her jealous. He evidently succeeded: that October, Davenport became Mrs. Wallace Reid. Reatha ultimately forgave "dear old Wally" and remained on friendly terms with him and his bride, who also frequently worked at the same studio.[3]

At the same time, Reatha's dissatisfaction with her life and the hopelessness she felt regarding the film career that eluded her grew.

When Reatha rejoined her Los Angeles friends after leaving El Centro, she made an astonishing declaration: she had been married.

Newspapers caught wind of it. Given her popularity from what the press called "one of the strangest kidnapping episodes ever recounted," Reatha was asked about her marriage during an interview in her Los Angeles apartment November 16.[4] Her story—which she proclaimed involved a second kidnapping—was transmitted nationwide by the wire services.

The kidnapper in this instance, Reatha explained to a reporter, was a wealthy Arizona rancher named Jack Lytelle. Jack wanted to marry her, she began, and she liked him. There was just one hitch, she said: "I was so young that I could not make up my mind to marry."[5] According to Reatha, Mr. Lytelle, a ruggedly handsome man in his thirties, pursued her relentlessly. "He followed me from place to place," she continued, "wherever I went with Mother and Father." Eventually, he apparently followed her and Rose on a trip to Yuma, Arizona, just east of El Centro, shortly after they left Los Angeles.

It was in Yuma, said Reatha, that Jack, unwilling to be without her any longer, resorted to drastic measures. She next described taking a horseback ride along a dusty desert road and seeing him approach in his automobile; as he drove up alongside her, she pulled her horse to a stop to speak with him. What followed was deemed by one newspaper to be a romantic tale "worthy of a poet's fancy."

"He dragged me from the horse and into the automobile," Reatha declared, "and drove like mad for the Mexican border. He said he was determined to marry me and that our wedding day had arrived."

She claimed not to put up much resistance. "I thought I might as well make the best of it," she maintained, "and besides it was rather nice to have the man you were fondest of take such desperate means to get you."

She told the reporter that he drove her deep into Mexico, to a tiny village—she didn't know the name, she contended—and there they were wed. Jack was a wonderful man and husband, she affirmed, adding, "I never regretted that he made me marry him."

Reatha then related that, two months into the marriage, Jack left to attend to some business on one of his other properties. Several days later, she said, she received a letter from a mutual friend informing her that her loving husband wouldn't be returning. Jack had been stricken with pneumonia and had died suddenly.

When the reporter asked Reatha why she hadn't made an effort to claim her husband's property, she insisted she had no interest in it. "He had a divorced wife and child," she answered, "and I considered, in view of the short time that I had been his wife, that his child was entitled to the property rather than I."

Reatha's account of her marriage left many wondering. At least one reporter questioned why she announced her marriage and widowhood at the same time. Other reporters, unable to dig up any information about the man some of them referred to as the mysterious Jack Lytelle, dismissed her report as fiction. Verification of Lytelle's existence in the form of birth, marriage, death, and census records, directory listings, and newspaper articles, indeed appears to be lacking. Over time, Reatha would alter her story radically when presenting it to friends.

Reatha's objective in spreading such a story can only be guessed at. She unquestionably gloried in the opportunity to regale and impress her friends. She might have hoped the exposure given her by the newspapers would boost her career. That she was attempting to take control of her life is another possibility. Under California law at this time, females were bound by parental authority until age eighteen—unless they were married. Reatha doubtless felt compelled to justify her unaccompanied reappearance in Los Angeles. She likely also wanted to ward off the trouble that had been agitating around her since. She may have believed a marriage entitled her to autonomy—even though her assertions were unverifiable and she now presented herself as a widow.

Reatha Watson, married at sixteen, widowed at seventeen, newspapers reported. And she was Reatha Watson no more. Mrs. "Beth" Lytelle was the name she used now (she reclaimed her childhood nickname). "Should a third kidnapping occur with Mrs. Lytelle as the heroine," one paper speculated, "no one can possibly imagine what sublimation of romance will surround it."[6]

Reatha—a.k.a. Beth Lytelle—answered to yet another name. Around the cabarets she frequented, she was called Folly. She earned the name, she later confessed, "through my drinking and my not caring about life and other mad escapades." Frustrated over her stalled ambitions, wanting to be loved, and caught in the lure of what she termed "thrills" and "bright lights," she found refuge with her friends amid the amusements of Los Angeles nightlife.[7]

By 1913, America was swept up in the whirl of a dance craze that played out in the cafés, restaurants, and hotel dining areas of most major cities. These cabarets, purportedly "hotter than a Russian bath" and with "everything . . . sacrificed for dancing space," teemed with all classes of people intermixing in public for the first time.[8] Dimly lit chandeliers, luxurious décor, and plentiful alcohol offered the added inducement of a romantic, unpredictably informal atmosphere. As the craze reached fever-pitch, the cabarets instituted dansants—afternoon dances—to enable the masses to hoof it nearly all hours of the day and night.

Reatha, with her beauty, astonishing energy, and inborn talent for dancing, had emerged as a desired presence in the most popular cabarets in Los Angeles. By day, she graced the dansants, gliding fluidly across the satiny floors as live orchestral music swirled around her. Come evening, she joined the throbbing revelry at such film-star haunts as the Alexandria Hotel, the Vernon Country Club, and Al Levy's, amazing patrons with her natural inclination for both the classic waltzes and the latest steps.

If William and Rose had only a partial inkling of Reatha's secret life as Folly, they were soon enlightened. As Reatha's popularity blazed brighter among the cabaret crowds, so did accounts of her activities. Concerned family friends in Los Angeles sent alerts to El Centro, apprising William and Rose of the danger they believed their daughter to be in.

Newspapers, magazines, government officials, and religious leaders nationwide had been sounding an alarm against the dance craze, warning of a "menacing condition" infesting the dance halls. Their emphatic sentiments were echoed in the battle cry of moralist Ethel Watts Mumford: "The evil influence is inevitable," she admonished. No mother or father in their right mind, said Mumford, would allow a daughter to cavort in the dance halls; "they are luring young girls into a worse environment than blind parents would dream could ever reach their little girls."[9] Cabarets, so far as reformists were concerned, posed an outright threat to traditional, Victorian-based morals, and everything about them was fodder for their attacks.

The popular dances, such as the tango, one-step, and turkey trot, were among the first targets. "These dances are a reversion to the grossest practices of savage man," the *New York Sun* charged, and "are based on the primitive motive of orgies."[10] Questionable men of ill repute, the reformers pointed out, danced "cheek by jowl" with decent, unsuspecting girls, often gripping them so closely that "one vertical sweep of a sword between them must inevitably kill both."[11]

These innocent young ladies weren't the only ones said to be on the path to ruin. Married men without their wives and married women without their husbands also visited the cabarets to partake of the dancing. According to *Variety*, the dancing establishments in New York "caused more family disturbances in the time they have existed than happened among an equal number of people of the same caliber for five years preceding the dancing fad."[12]

With their unsupervised daughter over two hundred miles away, William and Rose received reports from their Los Angeles friends and imagined the worst. The hours Reatha was keeping were inconceivable: "From noon one day until almost noon the next," it was claimed.[13] These same friends warned that Reatha's constant dissipation would destroy her health—a monition William and Rose undoubtedly took seriously, after having nursed Reatha, three years prior, through her prolonged affliction.

Surely, when Reatha took to the dance floor, spinning in the arms of a partner, she hardly felt more alive. She adored dancing and was coming to regard it as "the most perfect form of expression."[14] As a celebrated beauty in the Los Angeles nightclubs, Reatha never lacked for dancing partners. Some of them were married men, William and Rose learned from friends, and others were likewise deemed unacceptable escorts for a respectable girl.

One such married man, twenty-four-year-old attorney Constantino Riccardi, was so desperate for Reatha's company that he slugged it out with his office clerk to determine which of them would be her dinner companion one evening. Shortly thereafter, the debonair Riccardi became embroiled in scandal when embezzlement charges prompted him to flee the country. His wife, discovering his incorrigible appetite for "wine suppers, women, and other frivolities," filed for divorce.[15] Indeed, the smooth-talking charmer, enticing in his custom-made suits and with his gold monogrammed cigarettes, was soon dubbed "The Love Pirate" and "idol of the cabaret girls" in the press. Divorce proceedings went ahead without him. Several attractive women, including Reatha, came forward, accusing him of exploiting his position as an attorney in order to seduce them. Citing Riccardi's fistfight over Reatha, newspapers insinuated that she factored into his marital troubles. Riccardi later insisted he had no memory of Reatha or any of the others who charged him with attempted romance. "But," he added—no doubt with his usual rascally laugh—"I have a bad memory."[16]

In addition to the suggestive dances and shady patrons, moralists condemned the cabarets as places where young girls were swallowed as easy prey by "the insidious habit of the cocktail."[17] Given an environment where uninhibited self-expression reigned supreme and "release, not restraint, was prized," it's little wonder *Variety* reported that "everything in and about the cabaret commences and stops with liquor."[18]

In 1913, California's minimum drinking age was eighteen. Reatha's ability to look and act older than her seventeen years may have fooled cabaret managers, but her growing fondness for alcohol caught the attention of authorities. According to her son, Donald Gallery, she had at least one run-in with the law over her underage drinking during this time.

Down in El Centro, William and Rose had heard more than enough about Reatha's escapades. Their ardent pleas hadn't swayed her to come home. Desperate to save his daughter from what he believed to be imminent destruction, William was through taking no for an answer.

In January 1914, when Chief Juvenile Officer Leo Marden received a letter postmarked from El Centro, he needed no introduction from the sender—or to the sender's daughter. Reatha Watson was a name Officer Marden was already well acquainted with. A year earlier, Marden and his Juvenile Bureau of the Los Angeles Police Department orchestrated a massive manhunt to capture Reatha's accused kidnappers and bring her home. Now her father called upon him again. In the letter, William poured out his anguish and concern. As before, he urged Marden to bring Reatha back to him.

Marden and his Juvenile Bureau tracked Reatha to the Rockwood Apartments, where she lived alone. They conducted an investigation and, so far as they could tell, everything appeared to be in order. But Marden knew danger when he saw it. Reatha, six months shy of eighteen, was constantly followed by men.

Mashers—relentless male flirts who stalked the streets and cafés aggressively "copping the Janes" (accosting beautiful females)—were ongoing hazards.[19] Complaints inundated Los Angeles police stations, offenders were jailed, and concern mounted for unsuspecting victims.

Marden gave Reatha a choice: she could either return to her parents in El Centro or be placed under arrest. He warned that should she choose the latter, she would be taken to juvenile court and imprisoned in an institution. Reatha stood before him, sorrowful. She voiced her decision.

Newspapers declared: "Too Beautiful for City, Girl Sent to Country for Safety."

Marden admitted to a reporter, "There is no charge against Miss Watson unless it be that she is dangerously beautiful." He continued: "We believe that, despite the oddity of threatening to arrest a girl because she is beautiful, we are taking the right steps. We would rather find her guilty of being beautiful than anything else."[20]

Seven

He caught his first glimpse of Reatha one evening shortly before the juvenile officers forced her out of Los Angeles. From the moment he saw her, across the apartment parlor through an array of partygoers and a haze of cigarette smoke, he wanted to meet her. The party's free-spirited hostess, Birdie Hughes, an older, widowed motion picture actress, introduced them. "Lawrence," she called him, and left them alone.

Almost twenty-five years old and boyishly handsome with dark eyes and sleek, dark hair, he told Reatha he owned a cattle ranch in Mexico. "[He] was a good-natured, happy-go-lucky boy," she recalled, "and talked in a way that gave the impression that he was wealthy."[1]

Their paths crossed a few more times over the ensuing week. "He professed to admire me very much," she divulged.[2] On their last encounter, he told her he was going away to Mexico. Then he disappeared.

In March 1914, around two months after Reatha was sent back to El Centro, newspapers announced her return to Los Angeles. She refused to live in El Centro. Prohibited from living in Los Angeles without her parents—"who," wrote a *Los Angeles Evening Herald* reporter, "can deny her nothing"—she had persuaded William and Rose to desert their lives in El Centro and relocate with her.[3] The three of them settled in the suburb of Burbank on San Jose Street, and William continued working for the *Los Angeles Times*.

Much to her disappointment, Reatha, now recognized as the "Too Beautiful Girl" since Officer Leo Marden's widely publicized pronouncement, discovered that life in Los Angeles wasn't the same. She vented her anguish to the *Herald* a week after her arrival. She resented being unable to live in the city without her parents. The unfavorable attention she encountered was also hard on her, she said. It was impossible for her to dine at a restaurant—"even if I am with a man my family knows and likes," she added—or walk the streets without causing a scene. Prying eyes and incessant gossip likewise confronted her at the Hollywood film studio where she had obtained employment; "everyone's tongues buzzing with the latest 'adventure' of mine," she stated, "which, after all, merely consists of letting myself be seen." So great was the commotion swarming her on the lot, she had almost lost her job, she declared. Reatha's newfound popularity had, according to her, stolen her freedom: "Lately I have taken to staying at home every minute except when I am going to and from work." She attributed her misery to a single cause. "Beauty," she contended, "is certainly no blessing, when it is too great." She insisted, "I am absolutely persecuted because of my fatal beauty." [4]

Notwithstanding the sensation she created at the studio, Reatha was again confined to being cast as an extra. Brushing off the stares and hushed chatter that accompanied her, she assuaged her despondency over her stagnant film career on the dance floor and with her old friends who knew her as Folly. She was sidestepping her parents' orders and the radar of the juvenile authorities and returning to the cabarets at night.

By the end of May, Reatha was avoiding her parents. She took up quarters with Birdie Hughes at the Faust apartments in downtown Los Angeles. "I didn't know Reatha very well," Hughes said. "[She] asked me if she could stay here, as she didn't want to go home . . . She was so pretty, that we all liked her, but thought of her rather as a kid."[5]

On May 30, Reatha was among the usual all-night gathering of theatrical bohemians at Hughes's apartment. Along with a burst of incoming revelers came a familiar face: the man she had met there several months prior, whom she knew as Mr. Lawrence. On this occasion, according to Reatha, he drank heavily and, as they rekindled their acquaintance, she asked his first name. "Max," she later quoted him as answering, further relating that he told her he had been on his ranch in Mexico. "He was very entertaining," she recollected. "He told wonderful stories of his experiences in Mexico."[6]

The next day, Reatha again saw him among the lively congregation at Hughes's apartment. Somewhere in the midst of the chatter and laughter, he openly dared her to marry him. An uproar of voices erupted in Reatha's ears, daring her to do it. She silenced them by telling her would-be suitor she wouldn't take a dare.

Later that night, when Reatha was alone in Hughes's kitchen, he approached her again. Unlike the previous evening, he appeared entirely sober to her. He told her he was completely serious about marrying her. "I loved you at first sight," he was later said by her to confess. Reatha laughed.

"You don't know me and can't love me," she claimed to have pointed out. "And of course I don't love you."[7] Eventually he left.

As night brightened to dawn in Hughes's apartment, he returned and implored Reatha to marry him. When she declined a third time, he sweetened his proposal. "He said he would send to Mexico for his automobile and I should have the use of that," Reatha said of their exchange. "He said I could have an apartment anywhere in the city that I wanted it and that he would be a kind, loyal husband." Again she warned him she didn't love him and plainly added, "If I should marry you, it would only be because you are wealthy." He was said by Reatha to reply, "Don't worry about that. I'll be such a good husband you will soon learn to love me."[8]

That afternoon, Reatha telephoned William. She told him she would be getting married the following day—to Max Lawrence, she said. She asked to have Rose present at the ceremony.

At the Watsons' that evening, William and Rose became acquainted with their daughter's husband-to-be. William had first heard the name Mr. Lawrence several months earlier, when Reatha told him of meeting a wealthy cattle rancher at a party. Now he listened as his future son-in-law spoke of being the son of a distinguished Chicago merchant and of owning properties in Chicago and New York in addition to his ranch in Mexico.

His stories continued the next morning as William and Rose walked him to the Burbank trolley station. Reatha, after a stop-off at Birdie Hughes's apartment to borrow wedding clothes, was to meet him later for their marriage ceremony. After seeing him off, Rose turned to William. Something about the young man was unsettling, she told him, especially the "vacant look in his eyes."[9]

If Reatha shared her mother's trepidation, she cast it aside. She was waiting alongside her bridegroom with a taxicab when Rose stepped off the Burbank trolley in Los Angeles that afternoon. The couple had secured their marriage license under the names Beth Lytelle and Max Lawrence.[10] Reatha listed herself on the license as single (not widowed), the marriage as her first, San Diego as her place of residence, and her age as twenty instead of seventeen. The trio combed the city for a minister, finally locating Reverend James Geissinger at his home. He welcomed them inside and performed the wedding.

The next afternoon, after a quiet wedding dinner spent at home with her family the night before, Reatha joined her groom in Los Angeles. He

Seven

had left her at her parents' that morning, alluding to an important business transaction. They rode to Hollywood in a taxi, stopping by Reatha's studio to collect her theatrical makeup suitcase. After they visited Birdie Hughes in her apartment that evening, Reatha arranged to rejoin her husband later and went alone to the Alexandria Hotel to keep what she described as a "business engagement with a friend."[11]

As she sat across from her companion in the Alexandria's dining room, a message was delivered to her table. A telephone call had come through for her. Reatha left the table and took the call.

"A friend," she later explained, "said if I would call a certain number I would get important information."[12] Bewildered and unable to resist the caller's urging, Reatha tried the number. The voice that answered gave her news about her husband. Shocked and fearful, Reatha darted from the hotel.

Six miles away, Amelia Converse was also reeling from shock. Home alone with her two baby boys, she had received a flurry of alarming reports by telephone from an unknown woman loosely identifying herself as living in the same apartments as "the notorious Reatha Watson."[13] In a panic, Amelia called Gerald Doyle, a family friend and attorney.

Following up on the informant's tip-offs, Amelia and Doyle, accompanied by a private detective, raced to Reverend Geissinger's residence. The woman who answered the door, Mrs. J. W. Van Cleve, a member of the household, informed them she was indeed aware of a wedding that had taken place there the day before; she herself witnessed it. She was next shown a photograph of a man she identified as Max Lawrence, the groom in the ceremony.

The man in the photograph was Lawrence Converse—Amelia's husband.

Lawrence Floyd Converse was born December 17, 1889, in Oakland, Iowa—not Washington State, as he listed on his marriage certificate the day he wed Reatha. His parents, recorded on the certificate as Mary French and John Lawrence, were Flora and Charles Converse, a farmer and, by 1910, an orange grower and well-regarded attorney in Glendora, outside of Los Angeles.

Lawrence Converse first became known to the American public in February 1911, as, by his admission, "sort of a soldier of fortune."[14] His military education at Harvard School for Boys in Los Angeles and a stint with the California National Guard had, he believed, sufficiently prepared him for the job.

The Mexican Revolution, waged by democracy advocate Francisco Madero against the dictatorship of President Porfirio Díaz, was raging along the Texas-Mexico border and throughout Mexico. After meeting a Madero revolutionist in Los Angeles in January 1911, Lawrence left his family and headed south, entering Madero's rebel army as a captain in the command of Pascual Orozco. He then operated as a courier, purportedly holding the rank of major general and under orders of Madero himself. Throughout February, he slipped back and forth across the border, transporting messages between Madero's agents in El Paso, Texas, and Orozco's forces as they encircled and prepared to attack the neighboring city of Juarez. The risky manner in which he carried out his missions landed him in frequent trouble; he was reportedly held up multiple times by U.S. authorities and once arrested by Mexican police while making a reconnaissance of Juarez.

On February 20, Lawrence's luck ran out. He was conveying a message to El Paso, riding north along the Rio Grande River with fellow American Edward Blatt, whom he had recruited for the Maderistas. After dismounting their horses for the night and while warming themselves by their fire, they were surrounded by a band of armed men claiming to be American deputy sheriffs. They were under arrest, the men told them, for breaking the U.S. neutrality laws. By the time Lawrence and Blatt realized they had been snared by Mexican secret service men and not American authorities, they were already being hustled to the Mexican side of the Rio Grande. Delivered to Díaz's awaiting cavalrymen and accused of aiding the rebellion as spies, they were taken to the Juarez prison.[15]

The arrest of the young men made headlines in the United States. Lawrence's parents rushed to him. "I had heard the news of the terrible thing my boy was doing," his mother told a reporter before departing California. "I intended to join the Red Cross society as a nurse. As long as he stood in possible danger of being wounded I wanted to be somewhere near him. He is just an irresponsible child, anyway, and if I had known it before he got across the border I would have had him arrested and brought home."[16]

"He ought to be spanked, and maybe I'll spank him," his father added to El Paso reporters.[17]

Seven

Lawrence and Blatt, charged by the Mexican government with sedition, were arraigned in Juarez on February 26. Both pleaded not guilty. U.S authorities, powerless to intervene, informed Lawrence's parents that their son would have to stand trial.

Lawrence was forced to endure what he called "a living death."[18] In his squalid prison cell, he suffered brutal beatings, death threats, and starvation. A gentle reprieve from his agony came when pretty, seventeen-year-old Amelia Spencer, an El Paso hardware store stenographer, entered his life. They met when Amelia accompanied his mother to see him in prison. Something about Lawrence compelled Amelia to continue crossing the border. As dismal days became weeks, her compassionate heart and kindly smile soothed him far more than the flowers and food she sneaked into the prison. By April 21, the day Charles Converse arrived in Mexico for a meeting with President Díaz and a final attempt to save his son, Lawrence and Amelia were in love.

Lawrence and Blatt were liberated April 22. President Díaz's decision was likely tactical; American authorities had verified Lawrence and Blatt's claim that they had been captured on U.S. territory. With Madero's armies dismantling his regime, Díaz was wary of incurring animosity north of the border. He ordered Lawrence and Blatt to leave Mexico and never return.

Lawrence and his elated parents returned to Glendora, California. That summer, when Amelia, then eighteen, was visiting family in nearby Santa Monica, she and Lawrence eloped and married in San Bernardino August 16. A son arrived less than a year later.

Lawrence continued making appearances in the nation's newspapers as he sought recompense for wrongful imprisonment. His $25,000 and $50,000 demands, the former initiated by his father before his death in a smash-up involving his car and a train, were rejected by the Mexican government and the U.S. Congress. It was ruled that Lawrence temporarily nullified his U.S. citizenship by joining the insurrectionists and that he violated U.S. law by carrying arms across the border.

Lawrence's doings were again set into printing presses in July 1913 when he "created a sensation" in El Paso.[19] He had recently returned from Mexico City and an aborted tenure as secretary for an Aguila Oil Company manager. Madero's victory over Díaz had been fleeting; a bloody standoff in Mexico City in February had resulted in Madero's execution. Lawrence, Amelia, and their son, narrowly escaping the crossfire of artillery shells and rampant destruction, had fled to Cuba. Three weeks after welcoming a second son, Amelia discovered that her father was ill, and the family departed for Texas. Lawrence, forced to leave Amelia in a hospital when she fell ill in Alabama, arrived at the El Paso train station with a baby in each arm. His mother-in-law insisted they stay at her home until he and his sons continued on to his mother's in California.

As Lawrence prepared to depart for the station two days later, Amelia's mother, forbidding him to take the children, seized him by the throat. Lawrence broke free, grabbing his youngest son, as a gunshot rang out behind him. He charged to the back of the house, crashed through a door, and tore down the street with his infant. After exhausting himself, he ducked into a house and sent the bewildered occupant for the police. The baby was soon delivered to Amelia's mother. Lawrence was locked in a cell.

A reporter visited him. "You see, my mother-in-law doesn't care for me," Lawrence explained when asked about his mother-in-law's kidnapping charge against him. "She thinks I am a highbrow. I attended the University of Southern California—took a law course there."[20] He added that he wed Amelia without her parents' consent, and that his in-laws had been hostile toward him since.

Lawrence was released from custody July 16, the day Amelia arrived in El Paso. Lawrence, Amelia, and their sons settled in Los Angeles, where Lawrence, despite his law studies, managed a garage his mother had funded.[21]

Following her husband's bigamous marriage to Reatha, Amelia was ravaged by unanswered questions and Lawrence was nowhere to be found. The anonymous woman who apprised her of the marriage had warned that Lawrence intended to escape to Canada and send Reatha money to join him. After leaving Reverend Geissinger's home, Amelia and Attorney Doyle went to Central Police Station, where Doyle charged Lawrence with bigamy. Police sent telegrams to California's major cities, instructing officers to monitor trains, arrest Lawrence, and take Reatha into custody.

Doyle had a theory regarding Lawrence's bigamous marriage and disappearance. For weeks, Lawrence had been running amok. He had rendered Amelia and their sons nearly destitute. With his garage in the red and Doyle attempting to save it, Lawrence had written about a dozen bad checks. Doyle suspected that Lawrence had wed Reatha as a "last act of bravado and 'high time'" before dodging forgery charges.[22]

As police spread their dragnet, reporters swooped in. "I know Law-

Seven

rence Converse better than Reatha Watson knows him—or better than he knew himself," Amelia insisted to one newsman. "He never would have sent her a cent if he got [to Canada]. He would have sent me enough money to come to him and bring the babies, but she would never have seen him again."[23]

The morning of June 4, Lawrence, per his version of events, awoke alone somewhere in the vicinity of his boyhood home in Glendora. As his eyes focused, he found himself looking up into the branches of an orange tree. "My mind was clear," he would soon recount. "I felt better than I had for weeks." Beneath his head, as a pillow, was a suitcase containing theatrical makeup and a few feminine garments. "I never saw it before, to my knowledge," he later related.[24] Gripping the suitcase handle, he walked to the closest town and hitched a ride to his mother's house in nearby Claremont.

When Flora Converse laid eyes on her son, his name was already splattered across California newspapers beneath such headlines as "Reatha Watson Bride Again; Husband Accused of Bigamy" and "One Wife Too Many."[25] Flora had been apprised of her son's marriage to Reatha by her overwrought, lawful daughter-in-law the night before. Flora and Lawrence agreed there was only one course of action available.

Later that afternoon, Lawrence stepped off a trolley car in Los Angeles and stood before Amelia. Tears streaked her face; he took her in his arms. Standing behind her was Attorney Doyle and a police deputy, holding his arrest warrant. He was taken directly to court, where his mother and Amelia posted $2,500 in bail.

When Lawrence exited the courthouse, reporters were waiting, pelting him with questions. He didn't have answers. "I came to this morning under an orange tree," he told them. "That is the first recollection I have of what has happened since Sunday." Surely astounded, reporters queried him further about Reatha Watson. "I met Reatha Watson some months ago, but I cannot recall being with her within the last week," he said. "I was drinking a good deal because a lot of troubles came on me in a bunch, and I think I must have been drugged somewhere, or I would have some recollection of all these things." When asked about posing as Max Lawrence, he replied, "I don't remember getting the license as 'Max Lawrence' at all, and I never heard the name till today." And Reverend Geissinger? "I used to attend his church when I was in law school," he responded. "But I remem-

Lawrence Converse poses with his sons for a *Los Angeles Examiner* photographer the evening he returned home. The photo ran the next day, June 5, on the paper's front page.

ber nothing of standing up before him to be married." Nor, apparently, did Lawrence recall falsifying his place of birth, state of residence, occupation, and parents' names on his marriage license. He also had no memory of being the guest of honor at the wedding supper in the Watsons' home. "I wouldn't know Mr. Watson from Adam," he proclaimed.[26]

For the sake of their sons, Amelia allowed Lawrence to return to their home that evening. She hadn't forgiven him. When a *Los Angeles Examiner* reporter and photographer arrived, Amelia refused to be photographed with Lawrence.

"I have not made up my mind what my attitude will be in his trial or if I will ever consent to live with him again," Amelia told the reporter. "Tomorrow morning, he will go to his mother's home."[27] Battered by the maelstrom of Lawrence's bigamous marriage to Reatha and the "wild life" he had been leading, Amelia conceded, "I do not believe he was himself when he did this."[28]

William and Rose had neither seen nor heard from Reatha since she left home the day after her wedding to join Lawrence in the city two days previously. As Rose lay face down atop her bed, convulsing with sobs, William

Seven

scoured Los Angeles for Reatha. He was also out for blood. "If I set eyes on Lawrence Converse," he vowed, "there will be no occasion for a trial of the bigamy charge."[29]

Likewise hunting for Reatha was a pack of juvenile probation officers. The day police commenced their search for Lawrence, Amelia let loose a startling contention: that Reatha and Birdie Hughes had known Lawrence was married. Referring to Hughes as an "old friend," Amelia told a reporter of storming over to Hughes's apartment after learning of Lawrence's bigamous marriage and demanding that Hughes explain why she introduced Lawrence to Reatha under a phony name. Hughes protested that she hadn't. "Then if Miss Watson knew that was his name," Amelia concluded, "why did she consent to marry him under another unless she knew about me?"[30]

Why indeed? a *Herald* reporter wondered while questioning Hughes that same day. Prostrate in bed from the shock of the speedily escalating situation, Hughes declared, "[Reatha] had only met him a few times, and knew him only as Lawrence. She did not know that he was married and neither did I." Alluding to the day Reatha asked to stay with her, Hughes also stated, "She said that she wanted to get married very much indeed and that she would marry anybody to get away from home and from the probation officers. She mentioned several fellows whom she knew as possible bridegrooms but said nothing about Lawrence Converse . . . She told one friend of mine that if he would marry her, she would never see him or bother him again, as she only wanted to be free from restraint."[31]

Authorities arrested Hughes June 5. Subjected to a severe interrogation, she reportedly contradicted herself. "I knew that Converse was a married man and Reatha knew it," the *Los Angeles Examiner* quoted her as saying. "But she was determined to marry someone—she would have married anybody—and so she married Converse." She emphatically swore, "I don't know where she is, and I don't want anything more to do with her."[32]

Aware that Reatha was without funds and therefore likely still in Los Angeles, officers redoubled their search. If in fact Reatha knew Lawrence's marital status, she, like Lawrence, could be charged with bigamy. Bigamists faced a $5,000 fine (approximately $118,500 today) or up to ten years' imprisonment.

Eight

Sometime after nightfall on June 5, 1914, three days after she married Lawrence, Reatha gathered her courage, bracing herself for the awaiting onslaught. She walked toward her parents' house, bolstered by an unidentified attorney and a family friend. Having been persuaded to emerge from hiding, she wept from fear.

The sight of Reatha unleashed a torrent of mixed emotions. Rose erupted in tears of joy. William wanted answers. "You're back home," he acknowledged, "but I don't know yet whether it's your home or not." Reatha wept harder, clutching her father. "I'm a naughty, naughty girl, I know, Dad, and I don't want to hurt you," she pleaded, "but won't you please hug me just as if I were a little kid again?"[1]

She poured out her account of the past two days, first to her parents, then to the inescapable reporters who rushed to the Watson residence that night. She asserted that, until she received the telephone call at the Alexandria Hotel, she had no idea she had wed a married man. She retorted, "Whatever she may say now, Mrs. Hughes did not know that he was married." Reatha swore she left Lawrence when she found out about his wife and children. Then, terrified that William would turn her over to juvenile authorities, she had bolted for the Los Angeles home of a former neighbor of the Watsons'. There she had remained until she was persuaded to return home. Regarding Lawrence's claim to have no memory of their wedding, Reatha certified, "It is false that he was drinking and irresponsible when he proposed or when we were married. If he was under the influence of any drug I did not suspect it. I am sure the Reverend Geissinger would not have married us if his appearance or conduct had indicated that he was not in a normal mental condition."[2]

When the *Examiner* photographer's flashbulbs began popping, Reatha was perched happily beside William on the arm of his chair. Owing to his change of heart, William smiled contentedly. "She was duped by [Lawrence] and he ought to be punished," he said. "But I am too happy to have her back to care much about that tonight."[3]

Eight

June 6, 1914, *Los Angeles Examiner* photo of Reatha and William the evening of Reatha's return.

William averred that the marriage had not been consummated. Reatha and Lawrence, he said, slept in separate rooms on their wedding night. (Reatha later concurred: "I was a wife in name only.")[4]

William issued a plea: "We ask nothing but that Reatha be left with us here." Reatha, it seems, was in agreement. "Of course, I intend to stay here if the Juvenile Court people will let me," she entreated to the officers who would be reading the paper. "I ask only to be let alone."[5]

Two days before his preliminary hearing, Lawrence defended Reatha. "Reatha Watson did not know I was a married man when she married me," he announced to a reporter. Referring to the night he met Reatha, he confessed, "I was in a lot of financial and family trouble that I wanted to forget for a little while, but didn't want the family dragged in, so I said I was single." He maintained: "I do not know how I drifted into the marriage, but I do remember distinctly that I told both Reatha and Mrs. Hughes that I was not married." He also admitted to falsely claiming to be a wealthy rancher from Mexico. "I am not willing to keep still and let someone else be punished through my wrong-doing," he concluded.[6]

Juvenile authorities nonetheless deliberated as to what should be done with Reatha. "We do not believe," Assistant Juvenile Officer Aletha Gilbert stated to a reporter, "that Reatha Watson should be allowed to cause any more trouble for men, as she has for Converse."[7] While preparations were made to annul her marriage, Reatha remained compliantly at her parents' home. A juvenile officer was scheduled to meet with William and Rose to determine if she could be left in their custody and kept out of trouble.

When the *Los Angeles Times* conducted its own assessment of conditions in the Watson household June 6, Reatha was on her best behavior. No longer would she attire herself in fashionable evening wear, the reporter surmised, beholding the pink-striped and blue-checked gingham aprons Reatha had supposedly spent the day stitching for herself. Rose informed the reporter she would henceforward confine Reatha to their home, permitting only the occasional diversion: "perhaps a picture show now and then, and once in a long time a run into the city for shopping and possibly a matinee, but that is all." Rather than protest her mother's rules, Reatha appeared to the reporter to have accepted home life. She apparently promised to take over much of her mother's housework and had several embroidery projects in mind. "Mother and daughter," observed the reporter, "[are] very happy together."[8]

By June 9, the day of Lawrence's preliminary hearing and four days after she returned home, Reatha had disappeared.

Deputy District Attorney Ralph Graham surveyed the courtroom in front of him. Only the upturned faces of Lawrence, Amelia, and Attorney Doyle looked back. "Where are the witnesses?" he demanded of Doyle. "I expected you to have Miss Watson and the minister who married her and Converse."[9]

Eight

"How should I know?" Doyle countered. "I am here as counsel for Converse."

Graham turned to the judge. "This is outrageous," he spat. "How can this man come into the district attorney's office and secure a criminal complaint against the man he afterwards seeks to defend?"

"I can explain the whole thing very simply," Doyle interjected. "When I came to your office I represented Mrs. Converse whom I still represent." Initially, continued Doyle, he and Amelia were certain Lawrence had committed a crime—but they had since seriously reconsidered. "I am satisfied," said Doyle, "that he was not in his right mind." Doyle proposed a cessation of the prosecution.

Prosecutor Graham was unmoved. He asked for a continuance to subpoena Reatha and Reverend Geissinger. The judge granted it, chastised Doyle for immoral conduct, and advised Lawrence to find a new attorney. "We will demand that Converse be held to answer in the Criminal Court on a charge of bigamy," Graham promised.

Forced to testify against Lawrence, Reatha reemerged. She, too, had been tormented by misgivings and had hoped to escape the hearing. An encounter with Amelia was gnawing at her. The two wives had met to discuss the bigamous marriage. Afterward, with sincere admiration for Amelia, Reatha attested to the press, "I am convinced now that he was not in his right mind . . . I am sure that Converse would not have thought of injuring her had he known what he was doing."[10]

Reatha had forgiven Lawrence. "Poor fellow," she sighed to another reporter, "I haven't the slightest feeling of resentment toward him; no, I don't love him any more, but I will say we are good friends. I am sorry for his wife and for his mother and for my mother and my father, and, as for myself, I don't think I need any sympathy."[11]

Amelia, acknowledging that she bore Reatha "no ill will," also aired a statement: "Miss Watson and I agree perfectly that this case should not be prosecuted."[12] Like Reatha, Amelia was being forced to appear as a witness against Lawrence.

The press had struck gold. As the preliminary hearing loomed, Reatha consented to another interview in the Watsons' parlor.[13]

She spoke of forging her destiny while treading precariously upon a pathway riddled with "promise givers." This breed of men, she said, has one overriding aim: possessing a beautiful girl. When a beautiful girl goes forth into the world, Reatha explained, she is watched rather than watched over. "People have kindly said that I am beautiful—too beautiful," she stated. "If a pugged [sic] nose may be considered a mark of beauty, then I must live up to the name." Then she grew solemn. A beautiful girl, she continued, "must keep a cool and level head if she would avoid the snares set for her." Reatha admitted that her professional life had also been fraught with men seeking to possess her. She warned that beautiful motion picture actresses must be particularly vigilant, lest they be seduced by hollow assurances of wealth and stardom. As for herself, Reatha insisted, "I have always advanced on merit and hard work."

When the reporter interposed the subject of her turbulent matrimonial ventures, Reatha said she would still consider marrying again. "I believe that a girl cannot do better in this life than to have a nice little home and some good man to take care of her," she mused. Still uppermost in Reatha's heart, however, was her career. "I plan to go back to theatrical work when this affair is over," she avowed. "I have practically dedicated my life to that work and I would still act whether or not I was worth a million dollars."

"I believe that the beautiful girl has rare opportunities to succeed in life," she concluded. "Her dangers may be greater than her less favored sister, but her opportunities will also be greater." A woman's destiny, Reatha believed, is in her own hands: "It really depends on the girl after all as to whether she wins or loses."

Reporters, christening Reatha the "dangerously handsome bride," the "Bigamy Bride," and "an enchantress of fatal beauty," were among the multitude thronging Justice of the Peace Sidney Reeve's courtroom June 22.[14] Not a seat stood empty; onlookers lined the walls. Reatha entered with Rose.

The first witness to be called, Reatha took her place on the stand, glancing into the assembly of probing faces. Lawrence's eyes averted hers; he wouldn't look at her once during the proceedings.

Prosecutor Graham came forward. He instructed Reatha to state her name. She answered that it was Mrs. Beth Lytelle. He directed her to describe the events of June 2. She briefly stated that she married Lawrence Converse, otherwise known to her as Max Lawrence, and that she was unaware that he was married. She testified that, in looking back upon Lawrence's behavior that day, he seemed "dazed," like an "automaton" or "a person who does something without realizing its nature or consequences."[15]

Eight

Amelia, weighted by strain, was the second witness summoned by Graham. She verified her own marriage, quickly and concisely.

"The testimony of the two 'wives,'" the *Los Angeles Examiner* reported, "was given with automatic precision."[16]

Judge Reeve had heard all he needed to hear. The case against Lawrence was going forward to the Superior Court.

With the trial set to begin the following week, the press hankered for insight into the defense strategy. Attorney Fred J. Spring, representing Lawrence and Amelia in Doyle's stead, broadcast it to reporters: "Matrimonial aphasia."[17] Simply put, Lawrence married Reatha while in the throes of amnesia, he stated. As proof, Spring offered the fact that, before awakening beneath the orange tree the morning of his arrest, Lawrence had abandoned Reatha in Los Angeles and roamed aimlessly about.

Lawrence, Spring revealed, had been mentally compromised for over a year before he met Reatha. A miscalculated dive into a swimming pool had resulted in a serious injury when his skull collided with the bottom. Little by little, the man Amelia married drifted off into a fog of debilitating headaches, unpredictable stupors, and peculiar behavior. Lately, his symptoms had escalated. According to Amelia, Lawrence married Reatha during one of his "flighty periods."[18]

"He looked too long at the beautiful face of Miss Watson," said Spring, and "was in no condition to withstand the allurements of so handsome a young woman—in fact, he should not have been permitted to be at large in his condition."[19]

Amelia and Spring believed there was only one solution.

When Lawrence lay before doctors after his swimming accident, the outlook had been grim. Brain trauma; immediate surgery required; daunting risks involved. Some of his family members voiced concerns and fervid protests. The operation was halted.

Now, as Lawrence faced imprisonment on a bigamy charge, Amelia cleaved to hope. "I know he [is] not morally responsible for his marriage," she said. She believed Lawrence still loved her and their children "when his real self was in control."[20]

Somewhere beneath the scar on his head and his bizarre behavior, Lawrence seemingly believed it, too. When doctors reexamined him following his arrest, they reaffirmed the need for an operation, attributing his bigamous marriage and other irrational acts to pressure in his brain. By alleviating the pressure, they concluded, Lawrence would become as he once was. Their theory wasn't new. Some of the more astounding effects of trepanation, a procedure involving sawing or drilling into the skull to relieve stress upon brain tissue, had been documented in the nation's medical journals: alcoholics achieved sobriety, epileptics were cured, delinquent youngsters became model citizens, and the mentally ill were restored to sanity. Lawrence decided to have the operation. "He wanted to prove to anyone who may have doubted that he did not do a criminal thing," Amelia recalled of his decision. With the operation scheduled, a sense of peace enveloped Amelia. Her bond with Lawrence strengthened. Joy returned. "I think it was the happiest period of our lives," she remembered, "because we both knew the blow on his head had caused it all." Though likely unaware of it at the time, Amelia was pregnant with their daughter.

On June 27 Lawrence was readied for surgery at the Clara Barton Hospital. Amelia stood by his bedside. "It will be alright, dear," Lawrence promised.

When the three surgeons emerged from the operating room following the surgery, Amelia was waiting beside Lawrence's mother. The operation, the surgeons said, was successful. They had removed a small, triangular section of bone from Lawrence's skull. As they suspected, the piece of bone, located beneath Lawrence's scar, bore the jagged seam of a fracture on its underside. The surgeons explained that this spiked fragment of bone had caused inflammation in his brain. They had scraped the excess bone away and secured the segment of skull back into place. They declared Lawrence's postoperative condition to be favorable.

Amelia and Lawrence's mother remained at Lawrence's bedside throughout the afternoon, encouraged. Once, Lawrence's eyes fluttered open and he gazed upon the same face that had comforted him in his Mexican jail cell. "It seemed to me that he recognized me," Amelia said later. Then his eyelids grew heavy and closed.

They did not reopen. Later that day, as Amelia sat holding his hand, Lawrence faded away. One of his puzzled surgeons deduced that a blood clot had formed in an artery leading to his brain, halting blood flow.

"My husband had to give his life to prove he was innocent of a crime," Amelia wept to the inevitable reporters. Shocked and deeply saddened, Reatha agreed. "The really tragic feature," she stated during her own interview, "is that he could not have proven his innocence in a mortal court."

The next morning, newspapers reported, "There is no longer the

Eight

image of Reatha Watson, the 'too beautiful girl,' upon the brain of Lawrence Converse."

In one resounding blow, Reatha had arrived at another dead end. The storm of publicity generated by what newspapers considered her "lurid" escapades over the past year and a half struck fear into the Los Angeles film studios. Censorship coalitions had been encroaching upon the film industry, and studios were bracing themselves for proposed censorship legislation. Studio managers weren't taking chances. Film studios throughout Los Angeles barred Reatha from appearing in their films. "We don't want public characters or limelight beauties in our pictures," one manager explained. "It may be a fine thing for stage folks, but it is ruinous for men and women who pose for the movies; it's hard enough to get things by the board of censorship as it is; there's more morality demanded in picture dramas which are seen by young children than is required from stage people."[21]

Reatha, blaming her notoriety, rendered no defense. "The managers say perhaps when people have forgotten that my beauty made Lawrence Converse forget he was married," she said, "and also when the public has ceased to think about some other matters which have caused my name to be printed in the papers, then I can get back to work—and not before."[22]

William left California for the home of his brother Chandler in Ashland, Oregon, a few months later. The *Ashland Tidings,* announcing his arrival, blamed his departure from Los Angeles upon "the enervating effects of the southern climate."[23] Since William would return to the Los Angeles area several years later and remain there the rest of his life, he evidently left for a different reason. For the third time, his name had been dragged into Los Angeles newspapers in conjunction with his daughter's scandalous activities. Once in Ashland, he immediately assumed a visible role in the community, helping the Ashland Commercial Club promote the town and encouraging local businessmen to support Ashland's newspapers with advertisements. Possibly, William had wanted a fresh start.

Reatha's celebrity, however, preceded him to Ashland. Beginning months earlier, Reatha, after being branded as too beautiful to stay in Los Angeles, had achieved legendary status in certain pockets of the country. In May 1914, the *Ashland Tidings* had jumped on the bandwagon, ballyhooing her as "the most beautiful woman in the world" and a champion

Reatha, circa 1914–1915. Courtesy of Virginia Jauregui.

swimmer capable of "buffeting the highest of tides that sweep the Pacific and Atlantic."[24] Amazingly, a rumor developed that Reatha and Mary Pickford, a screen superstar, were the same person. The *Tidings* fueled the rumor in Ashland by reporting "Pickford" to be the niece of William's brother Chandler.

William, apparently compelled to address the rumor, did so with an odd declaration in February 1915. He justified the confusion, stating that Reatha and Pickford once worked for the same (undisclosed) film studio, "exchanging work at times without indicating it on the show-house bills." He also claimed Reatha and Pickford bore such a resemblance to each other that their role swapping was rarely discovered, even in Los Angeles. "Thus it occurred," he said, "that Reatha has frequently been seen on the screen as Mary Pickford."[25]

Reatha and Pickford might have worked for the same studio while in Los Angeles concurrently (Pickford worked for Biograph in 1910 and 1912 and Majestic and Laemmle in 1911); they might even have appeared in the same films. Given the level of fame Pickford had achieved by the time Reatha arrived in Los Angeles in 1910, however, it seems unlikely that they would have swapped film roles without it being indicated. Although Biograph's actors were uncredited in 1910 (and, thus, actors' names couldn't have been switched), Pickford was widely recognized and regularly featured on exhibitors' advertisements as "The Girl with the Golden Curls" and "Blondilocks." Studios capitalized on her drawing power, using her name to fill theaters from 1911 onward. By 1914, she was arguably the world's most beloved actress. What's more, it appears that neither Reatha nor Pickford ever mentioned working together during this period.

In the wake of the abhorrent publicity surrounding Reatha's marriage to Lawrence—publicity that, to all appearances, had not migrated to Ashland—it's plausible that William was attempting to bolster his daughter's image. Regardless of the motive behind William's comments, Reatha's reputation in Los Angeles was now beyond redemption.

III

Terpsichore

I'm Barbara La Marr . . . and I've been born again.

—*Barbara La Marr*

Nine

In 1911, Americans considered the act of dancing in a public place to be shocking. By 1914, they couldn't get enough of it. As dancing consumed the nation's cabarets, the public was captivated by a new brand of celebrity. Raucous social reformers opposing the dance craze were stifled as the press eclipsed them with a rising phenomenon: ballroom dancers.

Ballroom dance teams, professional dancers hired by cabaret owners to entertain, inspire, and instruct their patrons, became role models to Americans of all ages. Perhaps the most celebrated of the cabaret stars were Vernon and Irene Castle. Even moralists were enchanted by the Castles, who, along with epitomizing grace and sophistication, were a wholesome married couple. With their youthful, innocently romantic image, the Castles elevated the physical expressiveness of dance beyond societal taboos. In so doing, they "legitimized pleasure, sexuality, and expenditure of impulses" for a public ready to writhe free from Victorian dictates.[1]

Americans swarmed the cabarets to view and emulate dance teams. Every afternoon and evening, a dance duo waltzed and trotted across the dance floor, winding among tables and showcasing the latest dances. After a performance, an orchestra struck up a new number, patrons sprang to the floor, and dinners grew cold.

As "the chiefest magnets for luring the public," ballroom dance teams came with a price, earning, in modern terms, an average weekly salary of $1,500 to $3,000; some commanded over $10,000.[2] The wages were warranted. Female dancers were expected to appear in extravagant, outrageously priced gowns and often made as many as six costume changes a week. Dancers performed multiple times a day, at all hours, and were required to maintain a constantly evolving repertoire. The closeness of the dance floor to the audience demanded dancers with substantial talent, riveting good looks, and enough magnetism to make one swoon.

Robert Carville had all three. Born Robert Hobday in Wisconsin in

1891, he was the son of a British physician and spent part of his boyhood on a Kentucky plantation and in Nevada before arriving in California. There he took up the stage name of Carville and began dancing professionally in San Francisco and Los Angeles. He was twenty-two at the end of summer in 1914. He and his dancing partner and wife of two years, Marjorie Milner, were performing at Café Nat Goodwin, a gathering place for film luminaries and high society on the Santa Monica Pier.

Before Robert and Marjorie began a performance one evening, Reatha and a handsome young doctor were escorted to a table along the dance floor's rim. Robert watched her from his table. The entire dining room, he would remember, fixated upon her, intrigued by her beauty and presence. During his performance, when he and Marjorie whirled past Reatha's table, she captured his gaze again. She was watching him intently, smiling at him. "Bravo," she called out.[3]

He was, after all, an exquisite young man. His face, framed by light brown hair, was a mixture of masculinity and elegance. His physique was trim, limber, powerful.

After his set concluded, Reatha saw him approaching. Strains of the "Destiny Waltz" floated from the orchestra. He paused before her table, bowed smoothly, and introduced himself. She cast her champagne glass aside and told him she would love to dance. Caught off guard, he led her onto the floor.

Robert's visit to Reatha's table had been for another purpose. For the moment, however, he was transfixed by her beauty, which to him was even more staggering at close range. She gave her name as Folly Lytelle and told him she was a film actress. Jolted back to the task at hand, Robert informed her he had come to her table to deliver a warning.

From a seat near the floor's periphery, a portly man glared at them. Robert's memoir, written years later, suggests that this man was director Hal Gale. Following Reatha's banishment by the studios several weeks earlier, she had been given a chance at an unspecified studio in pictures directed by Gale. She had also made an enemy; after rejecting Gale's advances, she was apprised by Wallace Reid of the director's vow of revenge against her.[4]

Gale had arranged for the café manager, a friend of his, to throw Reatha out of the café. Actor Nat Goodwin had taken pity on her when he learned of the scheme. But, blighted by financial troubles and no longer possessing authority in his own café, he was powerless to stop it. He enlisted Robert to foil the plan.

As they continued dancing, Robert explained to Reatha that she needed to leave the café. "The filthy, diseased beast," Reatha seethed, referring to Gale. "He's tried every way he could to queer me in pictures, in fact, he has queered me." She issued a promise: "Oh, but my day will come and I know it."[5] The waltz concluded and Robert walked her to her table. She and her date slipped out of the café.

Robert looked on as she went. Years later, with the "Destiny Waltz" drifting through his mind, he recounted: "A still, small voice seemed to whisper in my ear, 'She's the one.'"[6]

Reatha could no longer remain in Los Angeles. Nor could she sit idle with her smoldering ambitions. At eighteen, she traveled with Rose to San Francisco. As the First World War clenched Europe in a stranglehold, San Francisco was awash in merriment as it prepared to welcome the world to the 1915 Panama-Pacific International Exposition.

The exposition, also known as the San Francisco World's Fair, commemorated the completion of the Panama Canal and promised to be a marvel unlike anything the world had known. Premier architects and artists spent over $25 million transforming 625 acres along the bay into a thrill-seeker's paradise. Over eighteen million attendees would burst past the turnstiles, wondering at $50 million worth of exhibits. Fairgoers would be entertained by performers from around the globe and treated to appearances by film stars and such celebrities as Henry Ford and Thomas Edison. The fair would showcase the most spectacular of the latest inventions: the first transcontinental telephone call and airplane rides made available to the public. The grounds would also provide a dizzying panoply of rides and rousing simulated adventures. To experience it all would be impossible.[7]

San Francisco's hotels and restaurants readied themselves. Establishments without dance floors installed them. Entertainers of all kinds flocked to the area to secure employment in theaters and cabarets. With the countdown to the fair's February 20, 1915, opening underway, the city was primed for nearly ten months of ceaseless revelry.

As 1915 approached, Reatha and Rose were staying in an apartment near the city center. Reatha worked as a modestly paid fashion model at the City of Paris, a luxurious department store. She had also been promised work in one of San Francisco's most popular cafés, pending completion of the new dance floor. She was to appear as a chorus girl, dancing in musical revues alongside other girls.

Through a chance encounter on New Year's Eve, however, Reatha altered the course of her life.

In the final hours of 1914, Robert Carville stood in San Francisco's Pavo Real café, watching the dancers. He had recently returned to California from a dancing engagement in Oregon. Following a disagreement, his wife Marjorie had left him and their dance partnership for a wealthy Portland lumber trader. Minus a dancing partner, without prospects of a dancing engagement, and in need of funds, Robert had sailed home to his mother in San Francisco.

Out of nowhere, a gorgeous blonde gowned in white approached, took him in her arms, and kissed him passionately. "Bob Carville," she exclaimed, "I've been looking for you everywhere." She tugged him onto the dance floor, chattering animatedly while he vainly tried to determine who she was. Suddenly, a new song lilted from the orchestra: the "Destiny Waltz."

"That's our dance," said the blonde in his arms, reminding him of their waltz at Café Nat Goodwin. Robert looked closely at her. She had bleached her dark hair, but in that moment he knew her instantly. "Folly," he whispered.

As they danced, Reatha decided to give up her modeling and chorus girl jobs. "I'm going to be a dancer, a famous dancer," she told him, "and I'm going to dance with you." She explained that she had long admired his dancing, reminding him of the time when, as a teenager in Los Angeles, she served him coffee at the Elite Cafeteria after seeing him perform at the Auditorium Theatre. As recollected by Robert in his memoir, Reatha had prayed for another meeting with him. Whether influenced by his desperate circumstances, her obvious dancing talent, a deepening infatuation, or all three, he consented to her declaration of a partnership.

Along with her new appearance, Reatha wanted a new name—a Southern name, she told Robert. She confided that, although she had been born in Yakima, Washington, she envisioned herself as being from Virginia. Robert related in his memoir that she asked him to think of a name for her. As he glided her across the floor, images of childhood days spent on his family's Kentucky plantation converged in his mind. He thought of a genuine Southern belle, near to his heart: his grandmother, Barbara.

Nine

Then his memory lighted upon the La Marr family, elderly aristocrats who lived on the plantation next door. Barbara La Marr, he said, would be her new name.[8]

The orchestra fell silent. He mentioned that "Destiny" had concluded.

"No, darling," murmured the newly christened Barbara La Marr, "it has just begun."[9]

Rose was asleep when Barbara ushered Robert into her apartment later that evening. Leaving him sitting in the living room, she put his hat and stick away.

She reappeared wearing a purple silk robe. A belt of pearl strands dangled from her waist, and a pearl headdress adorned her head. She set down a tray with a bottle of wine and two glasses, positioning herself atop a pillow near Robert's feet. "Allah, be praised," he later quoted her as saying in his memoir. "Drink to your Cleopatra's health," she toasted, as incense from a nearby table sent ribbons of fragrant smoke into the air.[10]

Robert listened in rapt silence into the morning hours as Barbara poured out her innermost sorrows and desires. With an abiding sadness and tears in her eyes, she denounced her beauty as a curse and spoke of men who wished only to possess her. What she wanted more than anything, she said, was to be loved. She told him she was "sick of the casting directors, sick of the casting couches," and unable to bear the "hell" she had experienced in Hollywood.

According to Robert's memoir, Barbara presented her own version of her scandalous past. She said that the sordid events of her life had been the fault of a male relative—a blackmailer—whom she (or Robert) opted not to name. Robert recounts her saying that this relative falsely charged Boxley with abducting her when he and Violet merely took her on one of their weekend trips to Santa Barbara. She is also said by Robert to claim that Violet, too, "lived in constant fear of blackmail" and therefore disguised her Santa Barbara excursions with Boxley by saying she was visiting a girlfriend. Barbara supposedly explained to Robert that the case of her professed kidnapping never went to trial not because the judge dismissed the matter for lack of evidence, but because Boxley paid off the blackmailer, and thus the charges against him were dropped.

Barbara, Robert states, accused this same family member of threatening Lawrence Converse at gunpoint after catching him kissing her on the Watsons' porch one evening. Barbara's story continues with her relative strong-arming Lawrence into a bedroom for the night and forcing him to marry her the next day. She apparently cited Converse's parents' money as the motive.

Barbara, according to Robert, also blamed her unnamed relation for her marriage to rancher Jack Lytelle. She was "practically sold" to Lytelle, he quotes her as saying. Her narrative to Robert included Lytelle promising to leave his assets to her before he died—a fortune consisting of "a palatial ranch in Arizona, lots of Chinese servants, a swimming pool, fine horses," and beautiful furnishings. In her 1913 newspaper interview, Barbara gave Lytelle's cause of death as pneumonia and told the reporter she forfeited Lytelle's assets to his child from his first marriage. Robert's memoir has Barbara saying that Lytelle died "mysteriously" of food poisoning. She also seems to have told him that when it was discovered that the marriage hadn't been legal (no details are given as to why), certain members of her family (that is, her mysterious relative) were disappointed because she couldn't inherit Lytelle's fortune.

As Robert continued listening, Barbara disclosed her torment over the discrepancy between her life as it was and as she longed for it to be. "I want so awfully to live," he recalled her saying, "to make something out of myself, to do things, to give vent to this passion of expression . . . this pent up restless force that continually urges me on." Her aspirations were impossibly high. But so was her determination. She had already convinced him she would one day return to Hollywood and become a star.

For the time being, she wanted him to teach her to dance. Together, she said, they would become famous dancers. No longer would she allow the person she had been to hold her back. "I'm Barbara La Marr, your partner," she said, "and I've been born again."

Around 4:00 a.m., Rose called out from the bedroom, asking her daughter to come to bed. Barbara explained to Robert that her mother was staying with her, retrieved his hat and stick, and walked him to the door.

She asked if he was going to kiss her goodbye. "I kissed her lightly on the lips and hurried through the door," he remembered. "I felt like I had committed a sacrilege to even touch her. She seemed like an angel, like some creature from another world."

Robert returned to his mother's apartment and lay down in his bed. Sleep escaped him.

Barbara and Robert celebrated New Year's Day 1915 with dinner and dancing. It was after 3:00 a.m. when he escorted her home.

Nine

As they walked the darkened streets, he mentioned he had told his mother about her. With a burst of impetuosity, Barbara suggested going to meet her. If her proposal struck him as odd, he gave no indication. "I was in the clouds," he later confessed, "and madly and divinely in love."[11] Clasping hands, they walked through the slumbering city to his mother's.

Ann Hobday, Robert's mother, appeared at her apartment doorway in her robe. Barbara lunged at her, covered her face with kisses, and exclaimed that she had never had a real mother. While Robert puzzled over the identity of the woman at Barbara's apartment the previous evening, Ann fell under the spell of Barbara's charm. Refusing to send Barbara back into the cold, she prepared a bed for her on the living room divan and handed Barbara her robe. The three of them wished each other good night.

A short time later, Barbara rose from the divan, creeping through the shadowy stillness to Robert's bedroom. At first sight of her, he swore he was dreaming. Then she was beside him, kissing him. "My love, my life, my very existence," she whispered. Then, he recalled, "Our lips met again and Barbara was mine."[12] Sometime before his mother awakened, Barbara tiptoed back to the living room, leaving him with the scent of her perfume.

In the basement beneath Ann Hobday's apartment building was a ballroom with a piano. Each day, Ann played the piano while Barbara and Robert traversed miles of flooring, practicing their dancing. As Barbara's teacher, Robert admitted to demanding much, but Barbara met rehearsals with eagerness and resolve. Their dance act emerged.

Their budding repertoire blended classic and innovative styles. They prepared a traditional "Fascination Waltz," rhythmically raising and lowering themselves from the balls of their feet as they spiraled hand in hand through the empty ballroom. They included an old-time cakewalk, linking arms and kicking forward and sideways while strutting playfully about. They later incorporated a new dance known as the fox-trot. In their variation, the "Zone Promenade," they held each other close, sauntering and rotating gracefully in what Barbara described as "a flirtation one-step."[13] Another of their one-steps, "Tipperary," involved circling the space, executing long, quick steps in military fashion.[14] As Barbara progressed, Robert took her through bending lessons, training her for the dramatic dips and backbends that would accompany certain of their numbers. "She was a born dancer," he later wrote in his memoir.[15]

Barbara professed that she never had formal dance training. When not rehearsing with Robert, she practiced on her own, losing herself in the unrestrained, inspired movements of interpretive dance. She dreamed of traveling to Europe to study ancient dances. Her evolving style was akin to that of Isadora Duncan, an illustrious interpretive dancer of the time. Considered the founder of modern dance, Duncan drew inspiration from the art and drama of ancient Greece and the undulating ocean waves near her childhood home. She shattered tradition, expressing a dance form "which might be the divine expression of the human spirit through the medium of the body's movement," and urged her students to "listen to the music with your soul."[16] In this same spirit, Barbara formulated a solo repertoire.

Barbara and Robert worked into the evenings refining their routines. Rather than return to her apartment, Barbara stayed at Ann's. Ann was happy to have her and marveled at her ability to sleep on the divan without rumpling it.

Robert attributed his mother's reverence of Barbara to the hold Barbara seemed to have on everyone. "Barbara vamped everything that came near her," he said. "Old men, young men, women, children. Even for animals she had a smile and something more than beauty to offer for their adoration—some magnetic force that drew everything to her."[17]

Barbara and Robert were eager for a dancing engagement. Robert landed them a tryout at San Francisco's exclusive Techau Tavern, but there was a problem. Barbara required costly outfits to perform in. She assured Robert she would get them.

When Robert arrived at her apartment the day of their tryout, he was rendered speechless. Strewn about her bedroom were four exquisite gowns, accompanying accessories, four shoe boxes, a pile of expensive undergarments, and an exorbitantly priced, ermine-trimmed evening wrap. Barbara even presented him with a New Year's gift: a platinum watch. A wealthy friend had allowed her to charge the items to his account, she explained. They could reimburse him, she said, once they secured a dancing engagement. Robert wrote in his memoir that Barbara, sensing his uneasiness, added, "Now don't ask me any questions. I love you. That's all you need to know."[18]

Their tryout at Techau's was successful. They were hired to begin performing the following week.

Robert recounted that, before he and Barbara began work, he received a telegram from an acquaintance, sportsman and socialite Phil Band. In

Nine

the telegram, Band vaguely requested his presence that evening at the Palace Hotel and instructed him to bring Barbara.

Believing the meeting to be about a dancing engagement, Barbara and Robert met Band at a secluded divan in the hotel lobby. Robert recalled that Band, clearly agitated, spoke first. Telling Robert that he hadn't thought him capable of underhanded behavior, Band handed over a meaty roll of cash. Robert, thunderstruck, begged to know what Band was talking about. Band, according to Robert, accused him of posing as a relative of Barbara's, calling a certain millionaire the night before, and demanding $5,000 in hush money. Robert's account continues with Barbara, strangely quiet throughout the exchange, leaping from the divan. "Oh, it's him again," she railed, referring to her mysterious relative who ostensibly caused much trouble in her life.[19] She violently denounced her relative for following her to San Francisco and blackmailing the millionaire. She explained that the millionaire was the same man who had provided the expensive outfits. She asserted that, although she had visited him in his mansion, their relationship was innocent.

Band informed them the blackmailer warned the millionaire that, unless he paid up, his wife would be apprised of his activities with Barbara. Band told Robert and Barbara to take the money and get the blackmailer out of San Francisco. Robert sat, flabbergasted; Barbara slid the bills into her purse.

Outside on the street with Robert, Barbara beamed. Incredibly, she told him she would appease her blackmailer relative with $500 of his $5,000 demand. "Darling, we've got a bank roll," Robert quoted her as singing out before hailing a taxi and promising to see him later.[20] (Exactly who blackmailed the millionaire, if he was Barbara's relative, and whether Barbara was his accomplice cannot be determined. Nor can the amount of truth contained in the stories Barbara is credited with telling Robert regarding this supposed blackmailer.)

With a portion of the money, Barbara sent her mother to Oregon to rejoin William, and she and Robert moved into their own apartment. Barbara told Robert that, through their dancing engagements, she planned to become acquainted with more millionaires. Robert cringed; he asked her not to take money from men. Barbara, he said, protested, "I don't do anything wrong. I'm just young and beautiful and they're rich. They just give it to me."[21]

The San Francisco World's Fair was in full swing, and Techau's Tavern swelled with crowds. Clustered around Barbara and Robert in the tavern's luxuriant dining room were the world's elite. Film stars (including Charles Chaplin and Edna Purviance), European nobles, and others whom Robert described as having only read about were among those applauding their dancing on any given evening.

"Our success was instantaneous," recollected Robert, "and Barbara's beauty the talk of the town."[22] Each week, Robert watched Barbara blossom as a dancer, their love for one another deepened, and their popularity increased. They soon accepted offers to perform at exclusive parties and engagements at the fair.

The Old Faithful Inn, located alongside an erupting scale model of the perpetual geyser Old Faithful on an amusement street known as the Joy Zone, was an exact replica of its Yellowstone National Park namesake and the largest restaurant on the fairgrounds. Private banquets were staged within its wooden walls, and entertainment was brought in for such occasions. By the summer of 1915, along with their Techau's engagement, Barbara and Robert made appearances at the Old Faithful Inn. Fairgoers continued adoring them.

Their act had expanded. After Barbara performed with Robert, she slid onto the polished floorboards alone. She had shed her evening gown, shoes, and stockings. Her willowy figure, in one of her costumes, was draped from the waist down in flowing fabric panels, cascading from a beaded belt and exposing her thighs. About her bust was a halter top with dainty bead strands that swayed over her bare midriff.

She doubtless heard gasps ripple through the dining room. Her scanty costume and exotic dance were a complete deviation from the style of the period's unrivaled dance icon, Irene Castle. Girlish and genteel, Irene wore skirts that grazed her ankles, and her dances with her husband, Vernon, were choreographed to avoid even the slightest revelation of her stockings. Conversely, Barbara titillated audiences with her sensual, impassioned movements in an interpretive "Spring Dance" of her creation.[23] Reputedly, her barefoot dancing was unlike anything the West Coast was accustomed to and ignited a craze among restaurant shows.

One evening in July, after Barbara and Robert finished a performance at the Old Faithful Inn, a waiter excitedly approached Robert, explaining that a gentleman had requested to speak with him. As Robert arrived at the man's table, the man rose from his chair. Bypassing introductions, he asked Robert how much money he and Barbara made as dancers. Robert

Nine

Barbara and Robert, 1915. Courtesy of Virginia Jauregui.

informed him they received $300 a week from Techau's and had earned $100 that night at the Old Faithful Inn (a total of about $9,400 today). The man insisted they could make a fortune in New York City. He instructed Robert to deliver photographs of himself and Barbara to his office the next day. Then he introduced himself.

He was William Randolph Hearst. Shrewd, wealthy, and powerful,

Hearst had acquired possession of the *San Francisco Examiner* in his early twenties from his father. His knack for inflaming the public with provocative stories, combined with the best reporters money could buy, resuscitated the failing paper. At the time of Robert's meeting with him, Hearst was a publishing magnate with thriving newspapers in several cities.

With the photographs Robert provided, Hearst launched a publicity campaign as only he could, featuring the images in the *San Francisco Examiner* alongside spiced-up articles promoting Robert and Barbara's performances. Likening Barbara to the Greek muse of dancing, one headline trumpeted, "Terpsichore Never Appeared in Stockings! Fair Dancer Prefers to Trip it Barefoot." In the article, Barbara affirmed, "I like interpretative [sic] dancing best. Yes, I mean the barefoot kind. I am one of those who think shoes and stockings never were made for dancing." Certainly relishing the freedom of her new identity, Barbara presented herself as a Southern girl and told Hearst's reporter that she and Robert were dancers from New York. They had come to the fair, she said, seeking inspiration for new dances. The article proclaimed that since arriving in San Francisco, Barbara and Robert were "smashing into little bits all records for creating and composing new dances" in both their collaborative and Barbara's solo efforts.[24]

Offers of dancing engagements flowed in. Barbara and Robert performed at impresario Sid Grauman's San Francisco theater. Hearst then hired them for an extravagant party he hosted at one of the city's foremost hotels.

The delight Hearst's guests took in the pair confirmed his instincts. But Barbara and Robert were apprehensive when he suggested they go to New York City. Barbara recalled, "I frankly told him that we would like nothing better, but that we didn't have enough money to pay our railroad fare and keep us going while we were making a try for favor on Broadway."[25] As his party concluded, instead of paying Barbara and Robert their usual fee, Hearst presented them with $1,000 (around $23,500 today). He wished them well in New York.

Barbara and Robert were exhilarated. They were certain, remembered Robert, that they were on their way to fame.

Ten

Male and female dancers performing together in the United States in 1915 faced a challenge when they were unmarried. Travel was part of their business, prompted by cabaret and theater owners eager to oblige fickle patrons with novel acts. Yet unwed dance teams roaming from city to city encountered more than raised eyebrows. Denial of shared lodging and refusals of jobs were common. Barbara and Robert wished to avoid complications. They began posing as man and wife.[1]

Among the engagement offers generated for Barbara and Robert by William Randolph Hearst's *San Francisco Examiner* publicity were several from some of the nation's more widely known cabarets. While traveling to New York City, they accepted a lucrative invitation to appear at Chicago's Midway Gardens.

After he and Barbara settled into a palatial suite at a high-class Chicago hotel, Robert, with their *San Francisco Examiner* write-ups under his arm, visited Hearst's *Chicago Examiner* offices. The reporters ran multiple articles, hyping their August 28 opening at Midway Gardens.

"Seen in Chicago for the first time," declared one article, the latest dances from the West Coast performed by "Miss Barbara La Marr, 'the most beautiful girl in California.'" The paper gave readers an eyeful: two images of Barbara, barefoot in a revealing costume. "It has been very cool for the last few days, but it doesn't bother Miss La Marr," the caption read. The article gushed about Barbara's dancing, Barbara's opinion of dancing as a superior health aid, and how impressed Barbara was with Chicago. Then, slipped into the middle of the piece was a lone sentence: "She will be assisted in her performances by Robert Carville, her dancing partner."[2] Robert shrugged it off. "I was glad for Barbara's sake," he said, "and I loved her."[3]

Barbara and Robert debuted at Midway Gardens in what Robert described as "a blaze of glory," remaining in the management's lineup six weeks.[4] But beneath the spirited music and applause, trouble lurked.

Barbara and Robert hadn't received the considerable salary they had

Barefoot and in costume, as Barbara appeared in the *Chicago Examiner*, August 27, 1915.

been promised. Week after week the management evaded them with empty assurances. Their reserves dwindled to nothing. "We had been spending our money most carelessly," Robert confessed.[5] The hotel was insisting that their bill be paid. Then Barbara and Robert's worst fears were confirmed. When they arrived for work at Midway Gardens during the week of October 4, the door was padlocked. The establishment, debilitated by weighty expenses, was under foreclosure.

Gathering their *Examiner* publicity from their hotel room, Robert, driven by desperation, made a bold move. He went to the Café Royale—

Ten

fully aware that superstars Vernon and Irene Castle had been headlining there nightly—and asked to speak with the management. He made a strong impression; the management hired him and Barbara.

On October 9, after applause for the Castles' performance quieted down, Barbara and Robert stepped onto the dance floor. They had a brutal act to follow. Yet, when their routine concluded, the crowd's reaction convinced them they had been a success.

Later that night, however, the management gave them $100 and informed them their services were no longer required. No explanation was given, but a waiter privately tipped them off. According to Robert, the waiter overheard a conversation between the manager and Mr. Castle. Mr. Castle, the waiter said, insisted that either Barbara and Robert or he and Irene had to go.

Any thrill of satisfaction Barbara and Robert felt, despite being jobless again, evaporated when they returned to their hotel suite. The door was bolted. With their belongings inside, they appealed to the clerk to open the door. The clerk explained he would do so when they paid their outstanding bill. Robert handed over their $100 check (approximately $2,300 today), all the money he and Barbara had; but the clerk refused it. Their bill exceeded $1,000 (over $20,000 in today's terms), and the clerk wanted all or nothing.

The morning brought a stroke of luck. A dance team appearing at the Palace Music Hall was sidelined because of injury. The establishment's manager wondered if Barbara and Robert would fill in for four days. That same day, the afternoon and evening of October 10, Barbara and Robert gave their first performance on a big-time stage. A *Chicago Examiner* critic deemed them "a very likely and likeable pair" and described Barbara as "piquantly beautiful and as lithe as green bamboo."[6]

After their Palace engagement, Barbara and Robert were among the new acts hired by esteemed songwriter Joe Howard to help revive his musical comedy, *The Girl of Tomorrow,* at the La Salle Opera House a few blocks away. The additions supplied the needed boost. The *Chicago Examiner* confirmed: "new songs, dances, and effects make for a bigger and better play."[7]

Barbara and Robert returned to the hotel with their earnings, hoping to gain access to their room and clothing. The management permitted them to enter their room, but withheld their clothes.

During the night, the clerk slipped upstairs to their suite. The manager, he told them, planned to have them arrested in the morning. Barbara and Robert still owed more than half their bill, and the manager had made unrequited advances toward Barbara. The clerk warned that the vindictive man intended to use his political connections to have them jailed. He urged them to leave.

Barbara, for reasons unfathomable to Robert, suggested they flee to Detroit. Hurriedly wrapping their dancing garments in paper, they were on their way, arriving, Robert recalled, the next morning. A distressing realization wasn't far behind. In the fall of 1915, the dancing fad had barely begun in Detroit. Even the city's first-class Tuller Hotel, boasting Detroit's largest ballrooms, had yet to employ dancers.

With his businesslike charm, Robert changed that. The Tuller engaged him and Barbara. As compensation, they were given a room, meals, and a salary Robert considered so lamentable he declined to disclose it in his memoir. At least, he reasoned at the time, he and Barbara would have a breathing spell.

That spell was brief. According to Robert, three days later, in the stillness of the morning, forceful knocking rattled their door. On the other side were police officers with a warrant for Robert's arrest. The hotel in Chicago had found them. Barbara wept helplessly as the officers led Robert away.

In court the following morning, the judge gave Robert the option of paying the hotel bill or facing the authorities back in Chicago. As recorded in Robert's memoir, he was still standing before the judge when Barbara charged into the courtroom. Trailing behind her was a gentleman he and Barbara had met in San Francisco. The gentleman had introduced himself as a Swedish noble and was a regular guest at their Old Faithful Inn performances. Then he had vanished. Weeks later, Barbara and Robert recognized his picture in the San Francisco newspapers; he was sought by police in connection with a swindle.

Still running from the law, the man had learned of Robert's arrest and contacted Barbara at the hotel, Robert wrote. To Barbara and Robert's relief, he presented the judge with money for their hotel bill. Robert's attorney—a man he met in the courtroom—took possession of the money and Robert was released into Barbara's arms. The Swedish swindler, once more, had vanished.

Back at the Tuller Hotel, Barbara and Robert were again out of a job and place to stay. Jailbirds, the management told them, weren't welcome in the establishment.

Despairing, tired, and starving, they explained their predicament to

Ten

the manager at the nearby Hotel Cadillac that evening. The kindly man took pity, ordering them a marvelous dinner, offering up the "Bridal Chamber" for the night, and giving them breakfast the next morning.

That afternoon, Robert secured an engagement at the Café Frontenac, beginning that night. Their salary was paltry, but the proprietor, William Moebs, allowed them to move into the café's stag hotel upstairs.

Barbara and Robert soon learned the breadth of Moebs's generosity. Five days after their opening at the Frontenac, Robert was arrested again. His attorney from the Detroit courthouse had pocketed the money donated by the Swedish con man, and the Chicago hotel bill was still unpaid. Moebs paid the bill in full.

Barbara and Robert's dream of success in New York City drifted farther away. Broke, indebted to Moebs, with scarcely more than one dancing costume apiece (the Chicago hotel never returned their belongings), and earning little at the Frontenac, they now had another problem. Barbara was unwell. Buckling from their financial woes, overwork, and late hours, she was on a drinking binge. As Robert's concern for her grew, so did their determination to get out of the hole that was swallowing them.

One December evening at the Frontenac, two female regulars had a proposition for Robert. They wanted him and Barbara to dance at their gambling house. Robert accepted the offer. Later that night, he and Barbara stood on the porch of a baronial house. Darkened windows masked the interior from the watchful eyes of law enforcement, Robert remembered, but jazz music and gales of laughter escaped.

After performing for an audience of wealthy men and their female escorts, Barbara and Robert ascended a staircase to the gambling room. A millionaire who had been eyeing Barbara staked them each $50 at the roulette table. Barbara's money slipped away; Robert won $1,000. Robert offered half to the millionaire who had staked him, but the tipsy man was only interested in Barbara. He leaned into her, overturning his wine glass and drenching the front of her blue silk gown.

A brunette seized the opportunity to divert Robert from the room. Barbara soon followed and found the woman on Robert's lap, her wine glass to his lips. Livid, Barbara snatched up a pair of ice tongs and stalked toward them. "I don't like brunettes anyway," she snarled. "I'd just as soon kill one of them as look at her."[8] Robert hastily intercepted Barbara, quelling her with a kiss while the woman ducked out.

Barbara and Robert were ready to call it an evening. When the boozy millionaire insisted upon driving them back to the hotel, they left with him.

At the Frontenac the next morning, Robert used his roulette winnings to pay off their debt to Moebs. Winning $1,000 had brightened their spirits, Robert admitted, but they were still broke.

Barbara neared a breaking point. Moments before 11:00 that evening, with café guests awaiting the beginning of their act, Robert tensely scanned the dining room, looking for her. They had last spoken in their dressing room an hour earlier, before the millionaire from the gambling house arrived and barged past Robert to see her.

Robert raced upstairs to their room. Barbara was packing their suitcases. "I can't stand this place any longer," she told him.[9] They were leaving that night, she declared, for New York. Robert reminded her that they had no money. She presented $500. The millionaire had given it to her, she said, and he planned to return later and meet her in the café.

As they loaded their suitcases into a taxi after their performance, the millionaire reappeared, realized he had been duped, and demanded his money back. Robert knocked him cold. Barbara and Robert caught a 12:45 a.m. train for New York City. "Barbara would have nothing but a drawing room on the train," Robert recounted, "so drawing room it was."[10]

Robert feared for Barbara. Her health was rapidly declining, and she was still drinking excessively. When their train paused in Buffalo, nearly four hundred miles from their destination, he told her they were getting off. He checked them into a hotel and summoned a doctor. Barbara was diagnosed as anemic—a side effect of malnutrition, heavy drinking, or both—and riddled with nervous tension. The doctor insisted she consume raw meat and take a lengthy rest.

By evening, Barbara was worse. So much so, Robert wanted to send for the doctor again. Barbara, however, ached for something else. Years earlier in Fresno, she had credited Christian Science modalities with restoring her health. She begged Robert to find a Christian Science practitioner.

In the hotel room that night, the practitioner spent hours at Barbara's bedside, praying with her. Little by little Barbara's fears diminished, driven

Ten

off by an otherworldly peace. By morning the change in her was pronounced. To Robert she looked like a sleeping angel. "I never realized her beauty more," he remembered, "than this particular morning."[11]

Robert crept out of their room, returning with a beautiful dressing gown and a matching cap and slippers from a nearby shop window. Barbara rose from the bed and put them on. She began dancing, assuring him her strength had returned. His love, she told him, had cured her.

Religion and spirituality, Robert noted, profoundly affected Barbara. According to him, her religious proclivities ran the gamut, from Christian Science to Catholicism. She also dabbled in reincarnationism, sometimes entering trances and purporting to relive past lives. Robert described her emerging from Mass at a church—shortly after her healing in Buffalo—euphoric, nearly hysterical, and declaring she would become a nun. A kiss from Robert changed her mind; she told him she would continue dancing with him instead.

Yet again Barbara and Robert's money was nearly gone, depleted by living expenses, medical fees, a Niagara Falls retreat, and a week's worth of daily treatments from the Christian Science practitioner. They remained in Buffalo and began working at a prominent café, earning a minimal salary and a cramped room upstairs. Robert remembered that the room contained little more than a bed alongside a radiator. Following their opening performance, he went to bed drunk and was startled awake that morning by uproarious laughter from Barbara. Scorched into his back were the words: "American Radiator Company, Made in Buffalo."[12]

The tiny room didn't hold them long. With the New Year came the anniversary of their partnership and a new adventure. They left Buffalo the evening of January 18, 1916. At last, they were going to New York City.

Dawn was breaking when their train sighed into the station the next morning. Hailing a taxi, they asked to be taken to the 42nd Street and Broadway corner of Times Square, the pulsing center of the cabaret district. They stepped out of the cab, taking in the bustling streets, the hulking buildings, the vibrant sea of billboards—all of it bathed in sunlight. Toting their suitcases, they drifted, gaping, down Broadway, swept along in the rush that streamed past. It "seemed like heaven," Barbara wrote in a small leather diary she began keeping that day.[13]

They stopped at the foot of a ten-story brick building. Above their heads, seventy feet in the air and spelled out in electric lights, was a name Barbara and Robert—and every dancer—knew well: Rector's.

George Rector, intent on bringing Paris to Broadway with his exquisite French menu and glorious European décor, had set the precedent for Broadway nightlife. Moneyed crowds arrived nightly. Hordes were turned away once the two-story cabaret hit its 1,500-person capacity. Inside, it took famous dance acts and four thirty-piece orchestras, playing nonstop in relay fashion, to satiate the demand for dancing that raged from early afternoon until closing time at 3:30 a.m.

Peering through the front window, Barbara and Robert saw the main dining room, magnificently ornamented in green and gold, reminiscent of the style of Louis XIV. Legions of professional dance teams aspired to dance in that room. Barbara and Robert were no exception. But it seemed impossible, Barbara would remember. Barbara and Robert continued down the street. They checked into the crumbling Hotel Markwell, a cheap place from which they would plan their next move.

With their publicity scrapbook, laudable courage, and nothing to lose, Robert headed back out, striding down the street toward Rector's. George Rector was eating breakfast in the dining room when Robert introduced himself, spread his and Barbara's pictures and newspaper clippings on the table, and asked for an audition. Rector was uninterested. The dance teams that performed in his cabaret were booked through agents, he said. Robert begged him to make an exception. All he and Barbara needed, he told him, was a chance.

That night, Barbara stood alone on a remote side of Rector's packed dining room, awaiting her cue from the orchestra. Across from her on another side, Robert did the same. Earlier that day, when Robert returned to the hotel and told her Rector had granted them a tryout, they were both thrilled and brimming with confidence. After sitting through the five acts that preceded them, however, Robert later admitted that his bravado had been trampled by fear. But Barbara, he said, was "brave as a lion."[14]

Barbara was terrified. The men in the audience were outfitted in formal evening attire; the ladies were gorgeously arrayed in the height of the current dancing fashions. Barbara felt painfully self-conscious in her only dancing outfit—her soiled blue silk gown (professional cleaners had been unable to completely obliterate the Detroit millionaire's wine stain). She was also certain the female dancer who had just graced the floor—a mar-

Ten

vel at toe dancing and handsprings and attired in a stunning costume of silver scales—had ruined her chances.

The orchestra began playing. Barbara thought she would faint. She willed herself toward Robert and the center of the floor. "I never tried harder to dance well," she said later, "and I never was under a more severe nervous strain than on this occasion."[15] Her face was pale.

The music enveloped her as Robert took her in his arms. She executed the initial steps of their trademark dance, the "Fascination Waltz." Then everything seemed to disappear. She felt transported, she later remembered, oblivious to all but the music and her dancing. She and Robert continued through their routine, sliding, spinning, kicking, separating into backbends. Time seemed to Barbara to stand still.

Their act concluded; the music evaporated. Into the silence arose such booming applause, Barbara felt weak from shock. Surely, she thought, they're applauding out of sympathy. But as she and Robert took their bows, shouts for an encore rang out. They obliged the crowd with two encores before the orchestra leader hustled them to the marble staircase leading to the upper dining room.

Upstairs, Barbara and Robert repeated their waltz for the fourth time and took another encore, then another, and still another. Barbara's legs wobbled uncontrollably and she grasped Robert's arm as they breathlessly gave their final bows. They were immediately summoned to a table by the cabaret's owner, Paul Salvain (Rector was merely lending his name to the establishment at this point). Salvain engaged them at a weekly salary of $600 (around $13,000 today).

Beginning January 24, their names joined the scintillating lights on Broadway. By this time Barbara had purchased new gowns and other dancing necessities, billing them to Salvain, per his request. She and Robert exchanged their cheap hotel room for a pricey apartment at the Peter Stuyvesant along the Hudson River on Manhattan's elite Riverside Drive. Barbara employed a maid to cook and clean for her several times a week. She and Robert undoubtedly felt exhilarated to be alive.

Their stay at Rector's lasted until mid-February. As well as performing in the evenings, it's probable that they supplied dance instruction during the cabaret's afternoon dansants. When not performing or instructing, Barbara assumed the role of the cabaret's hostess.

Soon after she and Robert opened at Rector's, Barbara's "Court of Honor" assembled.[16] Apart from other admirers who congregated around her each night, she was joined at her table by a select group of men—including, it was later alleged, a count and nephew of a duke. As part of her job, she granted them the pleasure of being in her presence, amusing them with social banter. In return she received displays of their affection. One demonstration involved a purported marriage proposal from the duke's nephew—even though she had everyone believing she was married to Robert.

An older, heavyset, mild-mannered British gentleman, also apparently unconcerned with Barbara's marital status, invited both her and Robert to dine with him February 13, the night they closed their Rector's engagement. He introduced himself as Alex Sandberg, and Robert formed the impression that he had come abroad to purchase war supplies for the British Munitions Commission. After dinner, Sandberg thanked Barbara for the honor of one dance with her—with, according to Robert, a gift of $5,000 (a whopping $108,000 today). The next afternoon, when Barbara and Robert were back at their apartment, Robert bristled when Barbara unwrapped a delivery from Tiffany's: a diamond bracelet from the same man.

According to Robert, if Barbara ever saw Sandberg again after the night they dined with him, she never mentioned it. What Barbara kept from Robert, however, she divulged in her diary in coming months.

Barbara and Robert's appearance at Rector's opened the way for employment in other celebrated Broadway venues. They worked long hours at Healy's. They were snapped up to perform at the Winter Gardens. Lee Schubert hired them to dance in his musical *Alone at Last* at the Schubert Theatre. While making a hit at the Hotel Knickerbocker, they received an offer to appear at Castles in the Air, Vernon and Irene Castle's rooftop garden cabaret. The Castles had been headlining there. Now Vernon had returned to his native England to assist the war effort, and their career was on hold. Barbara and Robert agreed to fill in for them.

Barbara and Robert's Castles in the Air performances were attended by Rudolph Valentino, one of Broadway's most sought-after dancers. Enraptured by Barbara, Valentino confided to Robert what an extraordinary dancer he thought she was and that she was the most beautiful woman he had ever seen. Valentino also mentioned his intention to get into films and encouraged him and Barbara to do likewise.

Robert had more pressing concerns. Barbara was once more tottering

Ten

on the brink of collapse. Straining herself to the limit in dance performances and playing hostess until the morning hours were merely part of the problem. Her drinking was out of control. "I tried every way to stop her," Robert acknowledged, "but it was no use."[17]

During their leisure time, Barbara and Robert had been authoring a play together. Noticing the happiness writing brought her, he enrolled them both in a playwriting course at Columbia, hopeful it would snap her out of her downward spiral. It didn't. They withdrew from the class shortly after beginning it. Barbara was simply unable to continue.

Eventually, Barbara suffered a nervous breakdown. She and Robert canceled their Castles in the Air engagement. At the urging of a doctor, Robert checked Barbara into a sanitarium.

Eleven

Barbara's eyes darted apprehensively about. Fair Oaks Sanitarium, secluded atop a hill twenty-five miles away from Broadway in Summit, New Jersey, specialized in nervous disorders and alcoholism, providing modern treatments in what its brochure depicted as a "first-class," "home-like" environment.[1] Ten years later, Barbara would still recall the strange-looking invalids and sharp smell of iodoform that permeated the rooms and prickled her nose. Her uneasiness ran deeper than the sanitarium's sights and smells. She had an extreme fear of doctors and nurses, a fear that may have originated during her illness in Fresno. Fair Oaks admitted only willing patients; Barbara hadn't wanted to come. She was coaxed into it after the staff bent their rules, permitting her to bring her Pomeranian, Pom-Pom.

Robert also stayed on at the sanitarium, perhaps to soothe Barbara. After three days, Barbara's doctor told him Barbara would benefit from resting alone for a time. As darkness descended that night, Robert bid Barbara good-bye. She began crying and held on to him. "Don't let me die at twilight," she begged.[2] With her pleas tugging at his heart, he reconsidered staying. The doctor persuaded him to go.

Barbara spent the next two days consuming nothing but raw, whole milk, the sanitarium's mandatory treatment for nervous conditions, anemia, and exhaustion. Instructed to lie down and rest as much as possible, she found refuge reading the sanitarium library's books.

At night, her blackened bedroom and unyielding imagination afforded no comfort. Exceeding her fear of doctors and nurses was her self-admitted phobia of sleeping alone (one reason she brought her dog). Her mind raced. Her fears ran rampant, consuming her.

Three days after returning alone to Manhattan, Robert received an urgent long-distance telephone call from Fair Oaks. It was Barbara's doctor, telling him to come immediately.

Barbara, Robert was informed upon his arrival, had been raising Cain. "I've never seen such a hell cat," the doctor said. "All she's done is scream

Eleven

and rave and say you are with some other woman."[3] The sanitarium refused to keep her. The harried doctor suggested that Robert take her to Matteawan, a New York insane asylum. Robert took her back to Broadway.

Barbara was later said to write of her experience at Fair Oaks: "Never again will I indulge in any 'rest cure.' If that was rest, then let me work!"[4]

True to form, Barbara had barely left the sanitarium when she decided she and Robert were going dancing that night at famed impresario Florenz Ziegfeld's cabaret, the Danse de Follies. Ziegfeld's show, *Ziegfeld Midnight Frolic*, an extravaganza of sensationally staged variety acts, was deemed one of Broadway's best. Even the intermission provided a thrill: Ziegfeld invited spectators to the dance floor to entertain the house. Taking notice of Barbara and Robert's dancing as they twirled across his floor, Ziegfeld offered them a place in his show. Barbara, despite her precarious condition, was adamant that they accept it. Against his better judgment, Robert consented.

Later that night, when Albert Kaufman, studio manager of Famous Players Film Company in New York City, expressed interest in giving them both a screen test, Barbara again seized the chance.

On May 17, Barbara recorded in her diary that she believed the test had gone well; she expected to begin work on a Famous Players film the following week. A second diary entry, however, reveals that she was still waiting for word from Kaufman nearly two weeks later. The ultimate outcome of the test, assuming Barbara was informed of it, was doubtless a sting. The studio was interested in Robert—but not in her. Given Barbara's physical and emotional state at the time, it's hardly surprising.

As Robert anticipated, Barbara's worsening condition forced him to cancel their *Ziegfeld Midnight Frolic* engagement, three days after it began. Ziegfeld, nonetheless, invited them to perform at a cabaret ball down South, a single performance that would get Barbara out of New York City's fast pace for a few days. She and Robert accepted Ziegfeld's offer.

Oddly, accounts of the trip as documented in Robert's memoir and Barbara's diary differ vastly. Robert places the event at a Richmond, Virginia, country club. Compounding Barbara's health woes as they rode down on the train, he began, was a throbbing tooth and steadily swelling jaw. He wrote that she had been terrified to visit a dentist (it would be months before she did) and, to anesthetize her pain, "drank brandy like a sailor" throughout the entire trip. "She was a wreck," he added.

Barbara's jaw was bulging when they reached Richmond, recalled

Robert, but she cheerfully greeted their hosts at the train station. He describes the two of them being showered with spring rain as they were conducted to an awaiting limousine. As they cruised past a palatial, columned building, Barbara, who had told their escorts she had been born in Richmond, remarked that she believed the building to be her ancestral home. One of their hosts explained that the building was the state capitol. Peals of laughter rang out in the limousine.

Robert stated that Barbara stumbled through their engagement that night but, to his relief, no one seemed to notice but him. According to Barbara's diary, the 500-plus spectators were enchanted by their paired performances and her playful, solo rendition of a humoresque (a short whimsical piece). But the house came down, Barbara noted, when she presented her temple dance, complete with a smoking bowl of incense.

In Barbara's version of the trip, the ball occurred in Washington, D.C., not in Virginia, on May 18. Robert's memoir places them in Washington, D.C., after Richmond. He wrote in his narrative that while in Washington, during a visit with British ambassador Sir Cecil Spring-Rice, an acquaintance they made through their Castles in the Air engagement, they received an invitation to meet President Woodrow Wilson.

At the White House, remembered Robert, he and Barbara were greeted kindly by the tall, silver-haired president. When Wilson learned they were dancers, he asked if they might indulge him with a performance. Robert related that he and Barbara accompanied Wilson to the East Room of the White House, a stately space with a wooden floor and chandeliers dangling from a high ceiling. A piano-playing member of the president's staff took his place at the grand piano in one corner. Robert and Barbara performed a minuet and a waltz. When they finished, Wilson gifted Barbara with a signed photograph of himself.

Barbara and Robert entrained for New York City that night. "Somehow I'm glad I'm going back," Barbara wrote in her diary in the swaying passenger car. "There's no place quite like Broadway."

Back in New York, Barbara and Robert's finances were evaporating. Barbara's health was still shaky. Dancing engagements were few.

Barbara turned to Alex Sandberg. Due to a three-month gap in Barbara's diary, the extent of Sandberg's involvement with her after she and Robert met him at Rector's in February is unclear. What is certain is that he remained in her life.

Eleven

Shortly after they first met Sandberg, Robert confronted Barbara, pointing out that their money left her hands as quickly as they earned it. Barbara sent some of their earnings home to her parents; the rest was lost to exorbitant shopping sprees, Broadway shows, and, according to Robert, a Renault roadster Barbara insisted upon owning. Barbara told Robert not to worry and assured him Sandberg would send more.

Barbara explained Sandberg's generosity, telling Robert she reminded him of his deceased daughter and that he wished to adopt her. There was nothing more to his feelings for her, she said, than a "fatherly affection."[5] Robert nevertheless felt better when a cablegram from Sandberg arrived the day Barbara entered the sanitarium; in it, Sandberg announced his marriage to an upper-class Englishwoman. (Barbara had already told Robert that Sandberg had returned to England.)

Barbara's diary tells a different story. Beginning in mid-May, her entries reveal constant contact between herself and the Englishman, who was at this point splitting his time between Baltimore and New York City. Sandberg indeed gave her money whenever she asked for it. His financial gifts, ranging from around $50 to $100 at a time, often arrived in letters and wires from Baltimore. Whenever business brought him to New York, Barbara met him in person.

The two rendezvoused half a dozen times between May 14 and June 4, according to her diary. Several times, Barbara wrote that she met him at the Claridge Hotel, not far from her apartment at 307 West 98th Street (she and Robert had relocated). They typically went out for dinner and dancing or a show. Three times Sandberg took her on brief excursions. They took an afternoon ride to Long Beach May 14 for tea at the Hotel Nassau. The evening of May 29 they rode through the countryside in a limousine to Hill Island Inn for drinks and dancing. They spent the day together June 4, motoring past Norwalk, Connecticut, for lunch and coffee. Sandberg concluded each meeting with a gift of money.

In Barbara's possession, the money quickly vanished. Powerless against the lure of Fifth Avenue, she usually hit the shops the next day. Lord and Taylor, the city's preeminent luxury department store, was a favorite of hers. She recorded her purchases in her diary: a coat . . . a wrap . . . gloves . . . hats . . . skirts . . . dresses . . . What she didn't spend in the shops, she used for dinners and shows with Robert. On May 16, after a spending spree involving $100 Sandberg gave her on May 14, she wrote, "We are broke again—but happy."

Barbara's relationship with Sandberg, as outlined in her diary, appears to be relatively innocent. Her notes of their correspondence, telephone calls, and meetings don't mention sexual relations or romantic love between them. She referred to him as a true friend whom she loved "very dearly" for his generosity.[6]

Clearly, she enjoyed their time together. Once, after meeting for tea to say good-bye before he left for Baltimore, she talked him into taking a later train so they could go for a drive. She commented in her diary on the delightfulness of their outings and the fun she had; "never enjoyed anything more than the motor trip," she jotted on May 14, "made 69 miles on speedway coming home."

It's possible Barbara used her time with Sandberg as a temporary escape. Aside from her joblessness and unpredictable health, she was regularly distraught over Robert. Their relationship during this period was punctuated by heated quarrels followed by mutual remorse and reconciliations. Certain arguments were sparked by trivial matters (in one instance, a hat Barbara wanted to buy), while others were more serious (such as when Barbara procrastinated getting ready, causing them to be hours late for a dancing engagement). Nearly every other day, Barbara recounted their ongoing clashes in her diary, likening them on several occasions to a "war" between them.

A particularly volatile row erupted May 28. Before leaving Robert to meet Sandberg, Barbara asked Robert to call her at their apartment at midnight so they could, as indicated in her diary, "play a little" afterward. After awaiting Robert's call for over an hour, Barbara, nearly insane with worry, phoned every café in town. Robert walked in around 3:30 a.m., explaining that he had been with a friend. Barbara demanded he pack his bags. He requested to wait until morning to leave. At 6:00 a.m. sharp, she ordered him out and crawled into bed. She awoke around 2:30 that afternoon to him lying beside her—and with her own change of heart.

Sandberg's presence in Barbara's life contributed to the friction between her and Robert. While Barbara apparently succeeded in concealing her rendezvous with Sandberg from Robert, he was aware of the money Sandberg gave her, and he distrusted Sandberg's intentions. The morning of May 26, when Robert inadvertently intercepted a long-distance telephone call Sandberg placed to their apartment, Barbara braced herself; "Oh Lord!" she later scribbled in her diary. She likely attempted to smooth things over, as she often did. "If I mentioned a word about [Sandberg]," recalled Robert, "she said there was nothing to it . . . and smothered me with kisses and said she loved me better than her life."[7]

The only way to salvage Barbara's health, she and Robert decided, was for her to return to her parents' home for awhile. Her sporadic appetite, precipitated by nervous tension, had resulted in noticeable weight loss. Her continual bouts of lethargy were exacerbated by the hours she kept. Most days, she stayed out all night, going from club to club, drinking and dancing. She frequently slept during the day, too tired to get out of bed—even after sleeping into the afternoon—and longing to spend an entire day asleep.

Although the context is unclear, her May 27 diary entry contains an illegible word appearing to resemble "abortion." Since an abortion in 1916 involved a recovery period lasting up to a few days, and Barbara maintained an uninterrupted social schedule in the weeks surrounding this entry, it seems implausible that she herself had one.

On May 31, she broke down. "Oh what a night!!!" she related in her diary. A "lovely" evening with Robert at the movies ended with an argument during dinner at a café. "The war was on," she scrawled, one thought spilling into the next, "I thot [sic] for awhile was [sic] that I was going wild Oh the agony took a taxi fainted—got home at last . . . I certainly was ill—nearly mad, too." Robert eased her into a rocking chair and rocked her until daylight. Barbara's entry concluded, "He was so very sorry."

The episode may have further prompted Robert and Barbara's decision to leave New York City for her parents' home. By this time, William and Rose had relocated to the isolated placidity of Medford, Oregon. Barbara and Robert needed to settle their numerous bills and finance their trip. Robert acquired a few thousand dollars by selling their Renault roadster and the diamond bracelet Sandberg had given Barbara.

Barbara obtained additional funds from Sandberg. She received $300 from him June 3. The next night, over the telephone, she appealed for more by telling him a lie: she said she had received a wire from her mother. "I told him Dad was dead," she divulged in her diary. Sandberg left his hotel, pulling up in a taxi just down the street from her apartment. Barbara met him. He gave her $250 "to go home to Mother."

On June 5, before leaving town, Barbara raided the shops one last time. She spent the day buying gifts for her parents—a watch, chain, and cigar cutter for William and a diamond pin and ring for Rose—and clothing for herself: shoes, hats, silk suits, undergarments, sporting clothes, and a riding outfit. After burning through the $250 she received the night before, Barbara hurried to the apartment to pack.

With minutes to spare, she, Robert, and their Pomeranian arrived at Pennsylvania Station. The train surged forward and their journey began. "Can hardly wait," Barbara jotted in her diary, "it seems so long."

She had no plans to remain in Oregon, however. "I wonder if [Sandberg] really will send me some money in Medford," she wrote on June 8 as the train clattered west. "God it would certainly be awful to be marooned in that place—even if my folks are there!" She and Robert reached their destination the morning of June 10, flat broke.

At the Medford station, William and Rose wrapped their arms around their daughter. Back at the house, the family began catching up. William had been writing for the *Medford Mail Tribune,* pushing for irrigation of the Rogue River Valley, the growing of certain cash crops, and the implementation of various farming practices. William and Rose had struggled financially; Rose had again marketed her dressmaking services.

As Barbara settled in at her parents' house, her health improved. She slept regular hours and regained some weight as she feasted on Rose's cooking. When she didn't oversleep or lack money for the collection plate, she accompanied her parents to church. Some days she donned riding breeches, mounted a horse, and rode through the cool, evening air.

But tensions were brewing. Rose, disdainful of Barbara's peroxided hair, criticized her appearance and her taste in men. Potentially operating from a common assumption that male dancers were gigolos, Rose disliked Robert and resented his presence. "Mother is going to be selfish about me, I'm afraid," Barbara penned in her diary. "Poor dear—she has been awfully lonely though." Five days into her visit, Barbara jokingly accused Rose of being on a mission to split her and Robert up. It's doubtful Rose laughed. For some reason, she and William distrusted Robert's feelings for Barbara. Rose informed Barbara of their suspicions, inflaming her insecurities.

It was a thought that weighed heavily upon Barbara's heart. Once, during a moment of loneliness, she scrawled in her diary: "There seems to be no one in all this whole world who really cares for me but Bob and I doubt him." When their spats continued in Medford, Barbara and Robert decided a few weeks apart might help them better appreciate each other.

Barbara accompanied Robert to the train station June 19, willing herself not to cry. *Is this separation the beginning of happiness, or the beginning of the end?* she wondered. Tears blinded her as she watched him board a train for San Francisco. Back at home that night, she became hysterical. In a ten-page letter, she poured out her love for him.

Four days later, she sent a wire to Robert's San Francisco hotel. She would join him immediately to work if he wanted, it read. Her wire was returned; the forwarding address provided was his mother's new residence in Los Angeles. Barbara hadn't expected him to leave San Francisco. Alone with her diary that night, she was convinced he was up to no good. "Dirty little sneak—I'm thru [sic]!!" she wrote. "I don't want him nor any liar!!" She also wrote Robert a scorching letter. "This is final," she told him.

In Robert's absence, Barbara sought distractions. William, despite his strained finances, somehow procured a Studebaker. The car pulled up to the house, bearing him, Rose and—as Barbara pointed out in her diary—"a young Apollo" named George behind the wheel (since apparently neither William nor Rose had learned to drive). When the handsome young man offered to teach Barbara to drive, she was thrilled.

George encouraged her efforts. "I was some good little driver," she bragged in her diary after one lesson. "George says so." Barbara encouraged his attraction to her. They met at eight one evening, drove forty miles to Hornbrook, California, and started back for Medford around midnight.

During their journey home, Barbara yielded to some unmentioned form of temptation. "What happened on the way will never be written," she recorded in her diary. "I cannot afford the luxury of regret or remorse—I must be very careful." It was nearly 5:00 a.m. when she slipped inside her parents' house. She never mentioned George in her diary again.

True to his word, Sandberg provided financial support to Barbara in Medford. "I know it's awful," Barbara acknowledged in her diary, "but I must have some money." She presented much of it to her bill-laden parents who, unaware of where she obtained it, gratefully accepted it. She set aside $100 for a return trip to New York City. One week later, she had gone through it. A good portion had been given to her parents. Barbara had also purchased tickets for Violet and Violet's fifteen-year-old daughter, Mona, to travel from San Francisco to visit her.

The animosity Barbara had toward Violet regarding the latter's role in her alleged kidnapping in 1913 was gone. William and Rose's hostilities had also subsided; Violet and Mona were put up in their home.

Violet (now going by her middle name, June) was on her fourth marriage. She wed actor Charles Inslee in February 1914, two weeks after they met. The couple soon separated, and June filed for divorce that July, charging cruelty and accusing Inslee of rejecting her kisses and caresses by striking her. Inslee defended his actions, claiming she had "received affectionate letters from other men."[8] June's petition for temporary alimony was denied. The judge's decision was based on the fact that June, said to be working as an actress, was supposedly earning as much money as Inslee.

Now the wife of Arthur Marr (a man whose identity cannot be verified), June arrived with Mona in Medford June 27.[9] June's fortune had shifted considerably since 1914. "Poor dears," Barbara remarked in her diary, "they are absolutely destitute as far as clothes."

Barbara's heart went out to them. She gifted them some of her clothing and borrowed money back from William to send to June's husband in San Francisco. With William broke again, Barbara wired Sandberg for $25; he sent $50. Half of it went to William. Barbara spent the other half doting on her elated niece. The happiness the money brought her family swelled Barbara's heart with joy. William and Rose, now aware of the money's source, expressed disapproval. Barbara brushed it aside. "God never punishes one for being loving and kind to others," she stated in her diary, "and I know that as for money—everything will come."

Barbara and her sister made up for lost time. June talked Barbara into letting her henna her hair. The result was a flaming red mess, but Barbara, although horrified, allowed her to try again. June salvaged the abomination with a dark dye, producing a deep brown shade. Barbara admitted she preferred the color to being blonde.

The sisters formed a plan. An outbreak of family squabbles had left them both anxious to leave Medford. Barbara had begun longing for New York City within days of arriving in Oregon. She and June decided they would leave for New York together as soon as possible. When a $50 bill arrived in a letter from Sandberg July 1, their goal seemed within reach.

While Barbara had been yearning for New York, she had also been pining for Robert. She had, her diary reveals, received some "awfully sweet" letters from him, reassuring her of his feelings for her. She wired him $25, asking him to come to her so they could return to New York.

Sometime after Robert's arrival July 4, the Watsons' home descended into mayhem. According to Barbara's diary, six fights broke out between her and Robert alone (likely because Barbara had spent her remaining $25, plus the $100 she was to have saved for their trip). "Mother and Dad almost sick because he is here," Barbara fumed in her diary. "Oh Lord, whoever said we were in love? I haven't any feeling but one of repulsion." Robert was at a loss to understand why Barbara sent for him. Rose declared she would kill Robert unless he left immediately. When his mother wired him $15, Robert left for San Francisco.

Barbara's heart went with him, her animosity suddenly softening to sympathy. Robert's heart remained in Medford. He wired Barbara the next day; he was waiting for her, he said.

Any prayers Barbara may have uttered that night were answered the following morning. The mailman delivered an envelope from Sandberg; inside was $100. Barbara said nothing to her family. She left the house that afternoon, walked to the train station, and bought a ticket. Her bags were already packed.

With her ticket in hand, some of Barbara's happiness faded. She felt sorry for June; their trip to New York wasn't to be. Back at her parents', she made June an offer: if she were willing to leave Mona in Medford, Barbara would purchase a second ticket.

That same afternoon, Barbara and her overjoyed sister departed for San Francisco.

Barbara and Robert undertook to rebuild their lives. Their quarrelling had ceased. In her diary, Barbara expressed the bliss she felt. She also wrote of wiggling into her best gowns and spending entire nights back out on the town in clubs. Robert later recollected days spent on the screened porch of their Oakland apartment, nursing Barbara's frail frame with raw eggs and malted milk.

Barbara's health continued fluctuating, despite her high spirits. Although her diary doesn't offer specifics, she mentions fatigue and loss of appetite on several occasions throughout July, and feeling "sick" July 12.

June, who had rejoined her husband, possibly had a theory regarding Barbara's condition. "June began talking syphlus [sic] to me," Barbara recorded in her diary after they dined together at the Pig 'n' Whistle tea room July 11. "Good God! If she keeps that up I [sic] go nuts!" Without knowing the context within which syphilis was discussed, however, June's motive for mentioning it cannot be determined.

Barbara's happiness temporarily fizzled July 28, 1916, the day she turned twenty. "Damned rotten birthday I call it!!!" she penned in her diary. With a lighter spirit, she added, "Oh well, we should care—this is one thing we can always depend upon to come to us regularly, our birthday! So I have plenty coming."

In actuality, she had nine birthdays left.

Barbara and Robert still lacked money. With Barbara not yet well enough to perform again, Robert considered alternatives. He knew his way around a boxing ring, having fought practice rounds with lightweight champion Johnny Kilbane and boxer Frankie Burns. Robert used his connections to book his first professional fight. He hid the fact from Barbara, probably to avoid worrying her.

The evening of Robert's fight, Barbara spent hours in the kitchen preparing a roast chicken dinner, the first meal of that kind she had ever prepared on her own. Knowing nothing of Robert's plans, she beamed when she sprung her surprise. Robert, unable to tax his system with so large a meal before entering the ring, confessed only that he had eaten earlier. Barbara's tears were too much for him. He pulled up a chair and, to her delight, consumed the entire meal, down to the trimmings and bottle of wine she presented.

His fight was disastrous. A punishing blow to his overfilled stomach during the third round finished him. He staggered home with a pair of black eyes, an inflated nose, swollen lips, and $100 in his pocket. The one bright spot, Robert noted in his memoir, was being kissed and tended by Barbara when she learned what he had done—and after he reassured her he hadn't been out with another woman. Barbara's deep concern for his welfare, he recalled, had a highly restorative effect on her health.

Barbara still longed for Broadway. Impatient to hop a New York-bound train with Robert and resume their dancing career, she told him she had completely recovered. Robert, wishing to confirm that her health had stabilized, arranged a local engagement.

By mid-August Barbara and Robert were appearing at the Saddle Rock, a trendy Oakland restaurant minutes from the town's college. After they thrilled the college crowd with their novel dances from New York, Barbara tantalized them with her solo barefoot dancing. Once again, Robert later remembered, Barbara was a sensation. On one occasion, she even quashed her fears and sang for the audience. Money rolled in, and Robert's misgivings about Barbara's health faded. He and Barbara started planning their return to Broadway.

Eleven

On September 5 it all came crashing down. Hostilities reignited between Barbara and Robert at the Saddle Rock. According to Robert, it was sparked by an innocent gesture. After their performance concluded in front of a table of lively women, one of the ladies leapt up and embraced him. Barbara stormed away.

She reappeared later that night in a rage. Their partnership, she told him, was over. She would remain at the Saddle Rock as a solo artist, she said. Robert tried to explain that the lady was an old acquaintance of his and her gesture meant nothing. Barbara refused to believe it. She caused such a commotion in the café, Robert recounted, that he became furious with her.

"Goodbye, little girl," he said. "Good luck and God bless."[10] That same night, he stepped aboard a train and headed to his mother's new residence in Oxnard, near Los Angeles.

Barbara received a letter from him on September 19. "I want you," he had written in closing. She remained impassive. "Why do men always want what they no longer or never have possession of?" she pondered in her diary. "It came—that desire—it came a trifle late."

Twelve

His name was Philip Ainsworth, but they called him "the dancing fool," the "Sheik of Spring Street."[1] He wore his auburn hair slicked straight back. He dressed impeccably. His classic good looks were, on occasion, set off by a larkish grin and a subtly devilish twinkle in his blue eyes.

As autumn 1916 neared, Philip, almost twenty years old, was a chorus dancer in vaudeville headliner Trixie Friganza's hit musical comedy *The Canary Cottage* in Oakland, California. Following a performance, he and some friends from the cast headed to the Saddle Rock for the after-theater supper show. Soon after Philip and his friends arrived, music filled the dining room. The spotlight cascaded down, alighting on Barbara—the most glorious creature Philip had ever seen.

After that night, he couldn't shake Barbara from his thoughts. He returned to the Saddle Rock and asked the manager for an introduction to her. Barbara accepted Philip's invitation to have dinner with him.

Seated in the dimly lit café, they became acquainted. Philip was born in Michigan in November of 1896, the same year as Barbara. His parents owned a tube and tire company in Los Angeles, but he aspired to a show business career. After graduating from military school with athletic honors in 1913, he began dancing professionally, performing his award-winning dance numbers with various partners and alone.

Among Philip's motives in meeting Barbara may have been the formation of a dance partnership with her. Barbara evidently had something else in mind.

Robert stared at the telegram in his hand in disbelief. It was from Barbara. He knew she was angry with him, but he never dreamed she would do *this*.

Robert later wrote in his memoir that Barbara placed a long-distance call to him early one morning at his mother's in Oxnard. She had been drinking, he related, but he was "pleased to hear her sweet little drunken voice." She insisted, through sobs, that Robert return to Oakland immediately. When he dismissed her inebriated demands, she became hysterical,

Twelve

Philip Ainsworth, 1916. Los Angeles Herald Examiner Collection/Los Angeles Public Library.

he recalled, and accused him of not wanting her. He further recalled that, before Barbara hung up on him, she swore she would make him sorry for not coming—by marrying "the first man that comes in the door tonight."[2]

Robert didn't believe a word of Barbara's marriage threat. He later stated that she had turned down his marriage proposals. Among her reservations, according to Robert, had been her idea that marriage ruins romance and her fear that she would destroy his life. Her abrupt change of heart stupefied him.

Yet, as her telegram informed him, on Friday, October 13, 1916, Barbara married Philip Ainsworth.[3] To commemorate his joy, Philip opened Barbara's diary several days after their wedding, went back to the page inscribed October 13, and penned his own entry. "I married Barbara and thought it was the happiest day of my life," he wrote, "but since then I have been made to love her more each moment that I am with her."[4] His passion was still raging a month later. "I love my wife, as she wanted to be called now, as I never have," Philip wrote in Barbara's diary November 17. "Babs has lots to learn of [illegible word] love and she will learn it from me even if I am only 20."

The dance team of Philip Ainsworth and Barbara La Marr Ainsworth, billed as Mr. and Mrs. Ainsworth, debuted at the Portola-Louvre in San Francisco on December 3, 1916. The engagement was merely a stepping-stone. Their next move, they decided, would be to use Philip's vaudeville connections to arrange appearances in first-rate vaudeville shows. They would then go to New York, where Barbara was already well-acquainted with the proprietors of some of Broadway's most revered venues. Philip's unfaltering ambition was on a par with Barbara's own.

So was his emotional intensity. Barbara found herself on the wrong end of it in the predawn hours of December 7. Philip later claimed that his anger was caused by her having "contracted a large number of bills without his consent."[5] (Barbara's diary indicates she had ceased receiving money from Alex Sandberg but had since managed to acquire funds from another man.) Philip and Barbara exchanged heated words in their apartment in the King George Hotel. An explosive argument erupted and spiraled out of control. Barbara fled the hotel. At the local police station soon after, a policewoman documented the bruises on Barbara's body.[6]

Philip was jailed the same day and escorted into a courtroom December 9. Standing in front of the judge, he was asked to account for Barbara's charge of cruelty against him and her allegation that he "chased her from their apartment scantily clad" after threatening to kill her.[7]

Barbara skipped the court proceedings. Local newspapers reported her missing. Her whereabouts had last been confirmed at the Portola-Louvre when she stopped in alone and collected her salary.

After being run out of the apartment by Philip, Barbara secretly took refuge with Robert's aunt, Lenore Curran, who was renting Robert's Oakland apartment during his absence. While Philip was in jail, Barbara returned to their apartment and packed her belongings. Philip contended that she reappeared after he was released on bail, begging him to forgive her. He stated that he gave her some money. Then, he said, she disappeared again.

After her second disappearance, Barbara made her way to Robert at

Twelve

his mother's home in Oxnard. According to Robert, she arrived on their doorstep three days after her fight with Philip. She was "black and blue from head to foot," he said.[8]

Barbara declined to prosecute Philip. She took an apartment with Robert in Los Angeles and reinstated her dance partnership with him.

In late December, Barbara and Robert opened an engagement at Harlow's cabaret in downtown Los Angeles. Their opening had been postponed a week, Robert recounted, due to Barbara's injuries. An unexpected guest appeared among the crowd opening night: Philip had found Barbara. Boiling with rage, he confronted her and Robert. He "made a scene," Robert remembered, "and I socked him."[9]

Philip then filed a divorce suit against Barbara, citing desertion and a deluge of other contentions. He claimed she "threatened to kill him by taking the breath from his lips with her own when he protested against her visiting with other men" in various hotels at night "without [a] waist [a long-sleeved, high-collared blouse] or hat."[10] He declared that he had been unable to restrain her "large appetite for intoxicating liquors," adding that she "insisted on nine and ten highballs and cocktails evening after evening." He accused her of having an "ungovernable and violent temper" and abusing him with name-calling. He charged her with saying she merely wed him because she was lonely, asserting that she both scratched his face and insisted the "only man she loved was Robert Carville."[11] Philip named Robert as corespondent in his divorce action.

Robert retaliated with an accusation of his own, causing Philip's arrest in Los Angeles January 5, 1917 on an auto theft charge. The automobile in question was a 1915 Buick, purchased by Robert and Barbara in Oakland on August 9, 1916. Barbara, after wiring Sandberg that she was returning to New York and asking for money to buy the vehicle, had received $200. Robert put $100 down on the $500 automobile; and Barbara, by relinquishing her Pomeranian to the seller, acquired a $50 credit, covering the first monthly payment. A month later, on the night of her falling out with Robert at the Saddle Rock, Barbara wrote in her diary that Robert had taken the car. The car remained in an Oakland garage, where Robert presumably made payments on it before Barbara somehow acquired it. Philip, believing the car belonged to Barbara, sold it two weeks after their marriage to procure much-needed funds for himself and Barbara. Proceeds from the sale had been spent. Robert claimed he had never received compensation from Barbara for the money he paid on the car; he believed the car to be his and that Philip had no right to sell it.

Philip proclaimed he had had every right to the automobile. Barbara, he argued, had presented it to him as a wedding gift. He maintained that he sold it for $300 with the understanding that she owed $50 on it. Upon giving her $50 to pay it off, he alleged, she informed him $50 was the amount she had paid—not what she owed.[12]

The case, with its attendant complexities, proved impossible for the court to adjudicate. An Oakland judge dismissed it, absolving Philip of the auto theft charge against him.

Philip pushed forward with his divorce suit against Barbara.

Barbara and Robert continued their Harlow's engagement in Los Angeles. Success, once again, was theirs. They began dreaming of their return to Broadway. Robert, protective of Barbara's health, promised her they would depart for New York when warmer, spring temperatures arrived. They bided their time at Harlow's during the winter by saving money. As April dawned, Barbara and Robert were ready to bid farewell to Los Angeles. Broadway, and the thrill of the big-time, was finally calling them back.

Then another call beckoned. In the wake of Germany's indiscriminate deployment of submarine warfare and attempt to rally Mexican support against the United States, President Wilson's stance of armed neutrality had buckled. The United States entered World War I, declaring war on Germany April 6.

Robert enlisted in the National Guard the same day. The American military was, at this time, a far cry from the formidable German war machine. Robert was among the small percentage of American men to enlist before Wilson, faced with a staggeringly low number of volunteers, instituted a draft.

Robert was ordered to report for duty the next day. That evening, entwined in each other's arms on the gleaming floor at Harlow's, Barbara and Robert performed the final waltz of their partnership. The tumultuous emotions Barbara held in check came flooding out later that night in their apartment. For three years, American newspapers had reported on the gruesome reality of contemporary warfare in Europe: machine guns, poisonous gases, soldiers waging battle from corpse-laden trenches. Barbara, Robert remembered, cried hysterically, convinced he would be killed.

They said their good-byes a short time later in a Los Angeles recruiting office. Robert had been assigned to the office and given the task of recruiting soldiers before his imminent voyage overseas. Barbara had secured a solo dancing engagement in a Salt Lake City hotel. She and Rose—who had traveled from Oregon to accompany her to Utah—were to depart Los Angeles at noon. Robert arranged for the finest army Cadillac at his disposal and a nine-man military escort to transport them to the train station. He instructed the soldiers to bring Barbara by the recruiting center first.

She appeared in his office, Robert recalled, accompanied by her soldier escorts, doing her best to keep back her tears. He drew her into his arms and unabashedly kissed her. As they pulled away from each other, she pressed a note into his palm. She told him not to worry about her. She would pray for him, she said, each night until he came home. She raised her hand to her forehead in a salute, then followed the soldiers out of the room.

Alone in his office, Robert unfolded the note. "Darling," it read, "You are the only man I have ever loved, or ever will. God bless and keep you—BARBARA."

A realization gripped him: *Barbara is gone, gone out of my life.*

"I dropped into a chair," he remembered, "my head in my arms, sobbing."[13]

Less than two months later, on June 1, Reatha Watson was back in newspaper headlines. Philip's divorce suit, initially delayed while evidence was sought by Philip's attorney, Gerald Doyle (who, ironically, had represented Lawrence Converse at his bigamy hearing before Fred J. Spring took the case), was going forward. Whether or not Barbara's departure for Utah was influenced by Philip's suit against her is unclear. It seems, however, that pains were taken to prevent her court appearance.

While Doyle was preparing for the hearing, he received a mysterious report. According to unnamed sources, the defendant had sustained a fatal back injury from a fall she took while dancing. Doyle investigated, contacting the Salt Lake City health commissioner. Newspapers presented the commissioner's findings: "Watson Girl Is Alive."[14] The false account of the "too beautiful" girl's death, papers further announced, had allegedly been circulated to halt Philip's divorce suit; had her death been confirmed, the suit would have been dropped.[15]

The case went to court that August. Philip and Barbara, both reportedly out of state on show business, were absent from the courtroom. Doyle, however, was able to present his key witness. He called Robert's aunt, Lenore Curran, to the witness stand. Curran testified that Barbara, after her fight with Philip and before leaving Oakland, had stayed several nights at her apartment. Since the apartment belonged to Robert (Curran was renting it while Robert was in Oxnard), the judge granted Philip's divorce from Barbara "on the grounds of over-friendly relations with Robert Carville."[16]

The conclusion of Philip's divorce suit was, to newspapers, the latest episode in the scandalous life of Reatha Watson. The "too beautiful girl" forged ahead—still unbeknownst to many—as Barbara La Marr.

Thirteen

Sometime during the turbulent summer of 1917, Barbara landed back in Los Angeles. Her life, it seemed to her, had stalled again. Though she had earned good money performing as a solo dancer twice a day in Utah and making additional appearances elsewhere, her dancing prospects were drying up. Prohibition, which would go into full effect in 1920, was making its presence known throughout America. Increasing numbers of cabarets were barred from serving liquor past certain hours. Deprived of the revenue generated by continuous liquor sales, these establishments could no longer afford to sacrifice dining space for dance floors, let alone pay dancers' salaries.

Lacking gainful career opportunities and without a sense of direction, Barbara reportedly sank into depression and yearned for change.

It came in the form of a six-foot-two, dashing Irishman named Nicholas Bernard (Ben) Deely. Born in Folsom, California, the sixth child of a constable and a housewife, he was eighteen years older than Barbara and a commanding presence with his chiseled features, jovial brown eyes, full head of thick, white hair, and hypnotic charisma.

Ben was a veteran performer, a master of many talents. Early in his career, he cracked jokes and sang with a roaming band of minstrels, often performing songs he composed himself. By the early 1910s, several ragtime tunes he wrote, including "Alamo Rag" and "My Heart's Way Out in California (With My Girl of the Golden West)," had become published hits. He funneled his magnetic intensity into drama for a while, trouping the country with a theater ensemble. His acting prowess then netted him roles on the silent screen; he starred in several comedy shorts and appeared in two features, *The Patchwork Girl of Oz* (1914) and *East Lynne* (1916), the latter with the Fox Film Corporation opposite Theda Bara. Long before this, however, Ben had debuted in vaudeville, singing and dancing his way into regular bookings and esteemed acts by 1905, earning praise as a "genuine riot" who "brings down the house."[1] In 1912, he co-authored his most critically acclaimed vaudeville skit, "The New Bell Boy," and had since been presenting it throughout the United States and Canada.

Ben Deely in *Kazan* (1921), with Jane Novak.

Then Ben's career, like Barbara's, stalled suddenly. The female component of his act took a leave of absence in the middle of his 1917 vaudeville tour. As the days stretched on, it appeared to Ben that her leave might be permanent. He was detained in Los Angeles pending word from her.

When Barbara encountered Ben at a Hollywood party one night in early summer, her mind went back to the spring of 1916, when she and Robert were at Healy's café in New York. Robert had introduced Ben to her and, as Ben later confessed, it was in that instant that he fell in love with

Thirteen

her. At the time, he had just been released on bail following his arrest the week before. His second wife, actress Marie Wayne, had charged him with nonsupport; Ben divorced her soon after, claiming abandonment.

Now his life had again intersected Barbara's, and he wasn't going to let her slip away. He asked her if she was interested in joining his vaudeville act. The money was good, and they would tour the nation and return to New York, he said. Barbara accepted immediately. Their partnership became official when the other actress dropped out of the act.

Ben's booking agent arranged tour dates, Ben began rehearsals with Barbara, and Barbara made preparations to leave Los Angeles. Her career once more glistened with possibility and excitement.

Her personal life was tearing her apart. In August, before departing California with Ben, Barbara met with Robert. Recently discharged from his duties as a first sergeant after "picking up a bit of shrapnel" overseas, he had returned to Los Angeles.[2] His life had moved on without her. His dancing career over, he was working as a magazine salesman. With him when Barbara visited him and his mother was his girlfriend, Myrtle Wooten. Barbara vaguely mentions in her diary that a baby was also present. Myrtle would give birth to Robert's daughter Virginia in May 1918, and she and Robert would eventually marry and have another daughter, Betty. Perhaps Barbara was referring in her diary to Myrtle's pregnancy.

After meeting with Robert, Barbara pulled out her diary for the last time. Her feelings spilled onto the pages in uncharacteristically large handwriting. She wrote of wishing to erase her love affair with him and of seeing in his eyes what she believed to be his heart's unspoken longing. She thanked god that Myrtle had been with him, that his "pride and honor" silenced him; "for those things," she added, "must remain unsaid between us forever."

Her diary entry reveals that she had moved on with her own life. She had become romantically involved with Ben shortly after encountering him in Hollywood. Alluding to instability in their relationship, she nevertheless wrote of her desperation to remain with him. "Will you do what Bobbie did I wonder and then regret it always—will you kill my love for you too?" she scribbled. "No! No! No! Please God—don't let him—I want to love him so! But he is always hurting me—always distrusting me—will he go to [sic] far? I wonder." She next writes that, should she and Ben separate, she would marry a man she refers to as "D" and resign herself to "misery" and a "childless, loveless existence."

She expressed her desire for genuine happiness, adding, "surely I deserve it—I have surely been wretched long enough." She closed her entry with a quote, a rumination on a future she feared: "'For my song of songs will never be sung again.' Dead—forever!"[3]

When Barbara joined Ben's troupe, Ben Deely & Co., vaudeville was in its heyday. For ten to seventy-five cents, Americans of all ages could view an ever-changing program of independent acts in a reputable environment. America's involvement in the war triggered an intensified yearning for laughter and fantasy, resulting in higher wages for acts that delivered them. Comedy routines, magicians, animal acts, and musicians packed theaters with soldiers, anxious families, pining fiancées, and others seeking to unwind, have fun, and forget.

Vaudeville performers continuously looped their acts across the United States through a network of theater circuits. Acts usually received at least forty weeks' worth of bookings per year and played as long as a week in a given city. For headliners like Ben Deely, weekly salaries on the big-time circuits—the Orpheum circuit, which managed theaters west of Chicago, and the B. F. Keith circuit, which governed eastern theaters—averaged into the thousands.

The evening of September 12, 1917, theatergoers coursed into the Salt Lake City Orpheum. Appearing that week, alongside half a dozen other acts, were Ben Deely & Co. in "The New Bell Boy," a one-act "vaudeville absurdity."[4] As patrons settled into their seats, Barbara prepared to give her first performance with her new company. Her cheeks and lips were probably heavily rouged, as was typical for vaudeville stage makeup at the time. Ben, who performed the skit in blackface, had darkened his face with burnt cork.

Unlike Barbara, Ben knew what to expect from the audience when he stepped onstage that night. His act was now in its fifth season, and critical response was generally uniform. Papers hailed him as a first-rate comedian, "a scream forever" who "keeps the audience in roars of laughter."[5]

Ben starred in the act as a weary, put-upon bellhop who shirks the "one hundred and one things he is supposed to do."[6] Added to the mix were a hotel clerk and a telephone operator. Barbara, as the telephone operator, helped set up the action and further entertained in a comical song-and-dance number with the hotel clerk (alternately played by various actors, including Billy DeVore, Barbara's brother). Ben threw in a solo

Thirteen

performance of two of his most popular ragtime tunes before the act's finale: he scooped a mannequin clad in bellhop garb into his arms and flopped about the stage with it, dancing a tango.

After concluding their week at the Salt Lake City Orpheum, Ben Deely & Co. hopped a train and hustled east for a week's stay at the Denver Orpheum. For fourteen weeks, the pattern remained virtually unchanged. At the end of each week, the trio took their final bows on a stage in one city, packed their things, and dashed to the next. "Jumps," as vaudevillians called the hurried—occasionally overnight—crossings from one locale to the next, were par for the course. Barbara found herself in a different city each week, often presenting the standard two or three shows per day, seven days a week. From Denver, the company barreled into Lincoln, Kansas City, Omaha, and Minneapolis before heading south to Memphis and New Orleans. Next, they zipped north to Illinois for shows in Chicago and Bloomington. They remained in the area the entire month of December, making appearances throughout Illinois and Indiana.

Having not acted regularly onstage since her early teens, Barbara was honing her acting skills. Ben helped strengthen her sense of comedic timing and develop her stage presence. She began to assume a distinct character type that came most naturally to her: sultry, intense, and with an exotic bearing.

Critics took note of Barbara. The *Denver Post* remarked, "Each week there comes a girl who wears her frocks a trifle shorter and a trifle lower than others have dared. Barbara is that girl on this bill."[7] Other reviewers mentioned her beauty and the artful support she furnished the act. As she refined her work, she became a decided hit. "Ben Deely and Barbara La Marr in 'The New Bell Boy,'" a New Orleans critic would soon report, "have stopped each show at the Palace Theater."[8] Barbara eventually received equal billing with Ben in advertisements.

Then, in January 1918, as Barbara and Ben debuted a humor-packed hospital routine authored by prolific comedy writer Herbert Moore, their vaudeville tour ground to a halt. Barbara's health, strained by a strenuous work schedule, was deteriorating again. She and Ben settled into a New York City hotel. Ben filled the gap in their vaudeville appearances with film work, obtaining a role as a crook in a mystery, *The Face in the Dark* (1918).

Barbara's suffering is later described in the *Movie Weekly* account of her life. Without ascribing a name to her sickness, Barbara allegedly wrote in the article of being "really ill this time. Nothing 'nervous' about it." Her condition worsened, aggravated by years of punishing dance routines that had compromised her bones and joints. Apparently, pain tore at her body, her temperature spiked to 106 degrees, and depression set in. "I kept getting lower and lower," the article states, "until I didn't care whether I ever moved again or what became of me." A doctor's prescription reportedly called for three months of bed rest and an operation. Barbara evidently decided she would rather die. It is said that she stayed in her hotel bed, ravaged by intense pain and fear of being taken to a hospital against her will. It seemed to her, the article continued, "as if the bottom had dropped out of the pitiless universe."[9]

But it hadn't. Slowly, her vitality increased and her strengthening will prevailed. For a time, so would her body.

By spring, Barbara and Ben were back on the vaudeville circuits. Barbara was pushing herself to perform.

Her display of courage on April 27 was mentioned in *Variety*.[10] Before the curtain went up on the first act that night at the Majestic Theatre in Paterson, New Jersey, the management addressed some business with the audience. With the war on, the U.S. government had turned to entertainers such as Charles Chaplin, Douglas Fairbanks, and Mary Pickford for assistance with selling Liberty Bonds; theaters enlisted the charms of vaudeville performers. And who better to persuade patrons to reach for their wallets, the Majestic Theatre management reasoned, than a beautiful woman? Yet when a pair of performing sisters who sold bonds the previous two nights refused, without explanation, to sell more, the manager was in a quandary. The only other woman in the evening's entertainment lineup—Barbara—was so sick he thought it best to excuse her from the task. Barbara wouldn't hear of it. Determined to do her part for Americans overseas, she feebly took the stage and appealed to the audience to do their part.

Around three months later, Barbara's thirty-two-year-old brother, Billy, left his vaudeville career to do his part. He shipped out to Europe to serve as a cook with a tank battalion commanded by George Patton. Billy's wife, Rose (he was on his second marriage), joined the Red Cross as a nurse.

Barbara and Ben continued lifting spirits on the home front. They per-

Thirteen

formed their zany hospital act in Cleveland that June before stepping down from the boards for a while. The vaudeville season had closed until fall.

Barbara was already known to many as Mrs. Ben Deely. The lovers shared quarters wherever they traveled and, when they weren't bickering, generally conducted themselves as loving marrieds. Ben, however, was itching to make it official.

Something stood in the way. Philip Ainsworth had merely been granted an interlocutory divorce decree in the California courtroom that past August; California law imposed a one-year waiting period before a final decree could be issued. Philip would ultimately apply for, and receive, a final decree in September 1920.[11] In the spring of 1918, therefore, Barbara was still Mrs. Ainsworth. Ben hit upon what he believed to be the perfect solution. They would, he explained to Barbara, "slip one over" on Philip.[12]

For disgruntled spouses seeking fast freedom from their significant other, Illinois was a virtual haven. There, most final divorce decrees were given and in effect as quickly as a case was tried. Enough vaudevillians took advantage of this fact that *Variety*'s vaudeville pages devoted periodic columns to the litany of names and charges filling the Chicago court dockets. Ben's name had even been among them when he divorced his second wife.

Barbara and Ben put their plan in motion while they were performing in Chicago that March. On the morning of March 15, Barbara walked into a Chicago courtroom, petitioned the judge for a divorce from Philip on a cruelty charge, and won. Her final decree was awarded May 22, 1918.

Although Barbara and Ben considered themselves free to marry, they held off until September 12. On that day, the U.S. War Department, expanding the scope of President Wilson's Selective Service Act, ordered all men up to age forty-five to register for military service. As an unwed, able-bodied forty-year-old, Ben now fell into the first conscription category, those who would be called first. The second category, consisting of married registrants with a dependent spouse, would be tapped only if the first was exhausted. When Ben was asked the name of his nearest living relative by the New York City registrar filling out his draft card, he answered that it was his wife, Mrs. Ben Deely.[13] Hours later, at eight o'clock that evening, Barbara and Ben married in Fort Lee, New Jersey.[14]

Barbara would later profess that she and Ben were unaware that her divorce decree was worthless. Illinois divorces were contingent upon something Barbara lacked: a minimum one-year residency in the state. She was also seemingly unaware that remarriage within one year from the time an Illinois divorce was granted was prohibited and punishable by law.

Barbara could hardly imagine, as the reverend pronounced her Ben's wife, the extent to which her actions would return to haunt her.

The onset of the vaudeville season that September sparked the usual flurry of bookings for the big-time theaters. Barbara and Ben (with another 1918 film, *In Pursuit of Polly,* to his credit) began the season with appearances in New Haven, Connecticut, and Grand Rapids, Michigan. They had reinstated Ben's popular act, "The New Bell Boy."

By the end of September, three weeks into their tour, Barbara fell ill again. She and Ben were in Chicago, scheduled to play the illustrious Palace Theater. This time, she couldn't compel herself to perform. On opening night, Ben informed the manager they were unable to go on. They were absent the entire week. *Variety* joked that their Palace cancellation was likely the result of being assigned the "No. 2 spot" on the bill—a disdained assignment for vaudevillians, since first and second acts commonly served as openers for bigger stars.[15] *Variety* was perhaps making light of a more serious situation.

As Americans battled one enemy a continent away, another had invaded U.S. soil. Spanish influenza, a lethal type of pneumonia, surfaced throughout the nation in a matter of months. To quarantine the epidemic, health officials ordered all public gathering places closed.

Region by region, vaudeville houses went dark. Less than two weeks after Barbara and Ben canceled their Palace performance, Illinois theaters were ordered vacated. Panic swelled within the vaudeville industry. Hundreds of performers traveled into cities for scheduled appearances only to encounter unpaid layoffs. To offset financial losses, some vaudevillians presented their acts along roadsides.

Outbreaks of the flu continued leaving thousands of victims in their wake until the spring of 1919. As vaudevillians made their way from city to city, fears of exposure to sickness and of possible death were their dismal companions. The exact nature of Barbara's illness the week she and Ben canceled their Palace appearance is unknown. Given her fragile health and depleted immune system, however, she surely risked her life by continuing to travel and work.

Thirteen

After leaving Chicago, Barbara and Ben stayed afloat for the remaining months of 1918 with spotty appearances. These irregularities were probably due to either Barbara's ill health or influenza-induced theater closings. From October until the end of December, Ben Deely & Co. took work when they could get it, with engagements in Kentucky, Ohio, and Indiana. When they arrived in Indiana to perform in Indianapolis the first week of December, one quarter of the state's theaters were closed. Vaudevillians in Indianapolis around this time performed to sparse audiences and muffled laughter from theatergoers, whose faces were partially concealed behind mandated gauze masks.

Variety encouraged entertainers to take heart. On November 11, 1918, the Great War had ended. The magazine predicted that Americans would soon flock to theaters, no longer to quell their fears but for honest-to-goodness entertainment. Around the nation, Americans joyously embraced world peace and their country's returning soldiers. Like Robert Carville, Barbara's brother Billy had also made it through. He resumed appearing alongside Barbara and Ben in their act, but would for years afterward battle the occasionally incapacitating effects of the gas attack he had suffered overseas.

Vaudeville was indeed seeing happier days. Theater patronage picked up at the outset of 1919, and success attended Barbara and Ben. They received excellent reviews as they performed in the South, shuttling around Tennessee, Alabama, Louisiana, Georgia, North Carolina, and Virginia for solid bookings throughout January, February, and the first week in March. From mid-March to mid-June, they performed nonstop, circling continuously between Michigan, Illinois, Missouri, and Indiana.

They must have known it couldn't last. According to Barbara, she was in South Bend, Indiana, when she was forced to abandon her beloved career. "I wasn't so strong as I thought," the *Movie Weekly* version of her life story quotes her as saying. "I couldn't stand the strain of dancing."[16] In addition to acting and dancing with Ben Deely & Co., she was presenting her barefoot solo dance. After dislocating her hip (not for the first time) during a performance, she was examined by an Indiana doctor. He spoke severely to Barbara, telling her to take a long-term rest. Her future, in fact, depended upon it. He may have pointed out that she courted permanent nerve and bone damage should she continue dancing.

Barbara took heed this time. She struggled through the company's final bookings of the vaudeville season, performing throughout Wisconsin in June. She then made a heartbreaking decision. She stopped working and gave up dancing as a profession.

As Barbara's career unraveled, her marriage to Ben faltered. After concluding their vaudeville tour that June, she contemplated her imploding life from a New York hotel room. She was unable to continue in vaudeville. She and Ben were forced to cancel performances that had been arranged for them in London that fall. That Ben's career hung in the balance with hers was merely another blight on their already shaky relationship.

Although they were in love, they had been driving each other apart. Separations and reconciliations were frequent between them. Barbara could no more tolerate Ben than live without him. An avid gambler who allegedly slapped their money onto gaming tables as fast as they earned it, he also shared Barbara's fondness for stiff drinks. There was, too, the question of Ben's fidelity. Barbara wanted to believe he was faithful to her, but she nonetheless harbored doubts. For Ben, the honeymoon had similarly given way to what he later described as Barbara's "uncontrollable fits of temper" and constant cigarette smoking.[17]

Holed up with Ben in their New York hotel room, Barbara reputedly believed her world to be shattered and decided to end her life.[18]

But between her purported sobs and her appeals to heaven evidently came a glimmer of hope. There apparently arose within Barbara a knowing that she had yet more life to live. The knowing grew stronger.

IV

Screenwriter

I could never be idle. I could never be merely a rich man's wife. I could never make my life out of the fabric of society.
—*Barbara La Marr, "The True Story of My Life"*

Fourteen

On the advice of the doctor who attended her in Indiana, Barbara returned to the idyllic sunshine of Los Angeles. Ben, as unable to live without her as she without him, went with her. At Barbara's request, William and Rose traveled from Sacramento and moved into their apartment.

Like Barbara, William was starting over. He had launched at least two publications since she left his home in Medford, Oregon, the summer of 1916. Both collapsed in the face of increasing competition among Oregon newspapers. He and Rose then relocated to Sacramento, where he worked briefly for the *Sacramento Bee*. He arrived in Los Angeles with hopes of taking up a career as a novelist.

Barbara spent her days reclaiming her health. She made frequent trips to the beach, swimming, lounging on the sand, and losing herself between the covers of her favorite books.

Barbara and Ben seemingly made at least one more vaudeville appearance. *Variety* announced that Ben Deely & Co. would perform for a week at the San Francisco Orpheum that summer. Their act wasn't mentioned in reviews of the show, so they may have canceled their booking. Around the same time, in Los Angeles, Ben acquired a supporting role as a fortune-seeking outlaw in Paramount's South Seas drama, *Victory* (1919). By then, Barbara and Ben needed the money. "I was dreadfully poor," Barbara recollected of this period in her life.[1]

At the apartment with her parents, Barbara sought a way to pass the days. Nudged by what she described as sheer instinct, she felt a desire to write. Her reflections first took the form of poetry. Then a story formulated in her mind. Characters emerged, taking on life.

Flooded with emotion and seeking to channel it, Barbara recruited the assistance of a writer for whom she professed deep admiration: her father. She set the mood by darkening the apartment with drawn curtains, lighting candles, and burning incense. Positioning herself cross-legged on the floor, she closed her eyes. William sat nearby behind a typewriter, his fingers poised above the keys. Barbara began speaking, her ideas flowing amidst the clacking of the keys and the dinging of the typewriter's carriage bell.

Barbara's story consumed her. "I loved it. I lived in it," she is said to recall.[2] Between dips in the ocean, she kept at it. "I would write until I nearly dropped from fatigue—smoking cigarettes and drinking coffee all the time," she remembered.[3] Side by side, daughter and father worked for days; the stack of completed pages William pulled from the typewriter thickened. Barbara decided her story would be a novel. For weeks, she dictated the foundation in synopsis form.

One can imagine that Barbara and William welcomed this time together. Frequently at odds throughout Barbara's life, they now sat upon common ground, unified by their love for writing. Perhaps their shared passion enlivened their relationship and William buoyed Barbara's efforts with encouragement.

When her synopsis was complete and her story had been born, Barbara spoke of it to anyone who would listen. She had not yet expanded it into a full-fledged novel. The positive responses she received from family and friends gave her another idea.

Producing as many as fifty to seventy-five films a year, studios demanded a wealth of literary material from which writers could fashion scenarios. Filmmakers initially appealed to the public, conducting contests and soliciting submissions. Weeding through their ever-growing mountains of envelopes, however, nearly always proved disappointing; writer, actress, director, and producer Mrs. Sidney Drew (a.k.a. Lucille McVey) lamented that, for every five hundred submissions that whisked across her desk, only one piqued enough interest for a second look.[4]

By 1919, writing for the silent screen was a literary form unto itself. Screenwriters began with a plot and put the idea to paper by composing a synopsis, scene by scene. The completed scenario, or "continuity," was used as a basis for shooting the film. Scenarios were supplemented by intertitles containing dialogue and descriptions that clarified the story. Positioned in front of the camera during shooting and filling the screen in the completed film, intertitles constituted around one third of the standard production, and their creation called for a unique set of writing skills. Well-crafted intertitles were succinct, augmented rather than hampered the action, and reflected characters' personas. Some scenarists wrote their own intertitles, but often a specialized writer handled the job. Writers excelling in either or

Fourteen

both of these arenas were awarded lengthy contracts in major studios' writing departments.

Among Barbara and Ben's circle of Hollywood friends in the fall of 1919 was a man in a position to potentially help Barbara. Publicist Cliff Roberts was the casting director for Goldwyn Studios, one of filmdom's prominent production companies. Studios had long since tired of sifting through worthless scenario submissions, and movie magazines discouraged all but consummate professionals from sending manuscripts. Still, hope filled Barbara's heart, and faith in her story trumped any doubts she may have had. It would be a long shot; but, perhaps, with a recommendation from Roberts, Goldwyn studio heads might be persuaded to look at her story synopsis. Barbara made a copy of her manuscript and gave it to Roberts.

Then she waited. Perhaps she never watched for the coming of the mailman with such eagerness as she did in the days that followed. Certainly, when the envelope bearing her name and addressed from Goldwyn Studios arrived, she tore into it, and her eyes anxiously flitted across the enclosed letter.

In a painful instant, her aspiration was dashed. She had received a standard letter; her story had been rejected, it stated, because the studio had no one available to play the lead female role. Disbelieving, Barbara called to mind several Goldwyn actresses capable of playing it. A realization hit her: *The studio didn't even read it.* The studio had no intention of ever reading it. Included with the letter was the copy of Barbara's manuscript.

Barbara resumed her daily routine of transcribing her thoughts to the printed page with William. Her story, she believed, showed promise. She would fulfill her original intent and make a novel of it.

As Barbara focused on writing, Ben continued appearing in films. He returned to Fox Film Corporation and began work on the first film under his new contract, *Flames of the Flesh* (1920). Despite their marital turmoil, it appears Ben supported Barbara's writing talent. He may have been instrumental in promoting her story on the Fox lot and arranging a significant meeting.

Winfield Sheehan, general manager at Fox and vice president to studio head William Fox, was a brilliant strategist whose mind chewed ideas as ceaselessly as his lips chewed cigars. In little more than five years, Sheehan had helped build Fox Film Corporation from an embryonic company to a worldwide empire. When Sheehan was invited to dinner at Barbara and Ben's apartment, he was scouting for writers and literary vehicles. He had heard of Barbara's story and, as usual, he had ideas.

Sheehan listened as Barbara enthused about her novel over dinner. Interested, he asked for a copy. Barbara explained that she was still writing it but offered him her only copy of the scenario, the one Goldwyn had returned. Sheehan was about to head east on business and promised to look it over during his trip.

Again Barbara waited. As weeks went by and she heard nothing, her faith dwindled. She stopped expecting to hear from Sheehan or the Fox studio.

Meanwhile, Sheehan had begun a quest. He loved Barbara's scenario. But, so far as the Fox studio could tell, Barbara was suddenly nowhere to be found.

Since Ben was still employed by Fox, the studio would have needed to look no farther than him to find her—except that Ben, perhaps, had no idea where she was. Barbara and Ben had separated.

Two months after her scenario went east with Sheehan, Barbara entered the Alexandria Hotel lobby in Los Angeles, unaware that her life was about to change. As she passed Fox director Emmett Flynn, he rushed to her side. The Fox studio had been searching high and low for her, he exclaimed. The studio owed her money, he continued; her story was going on the screen.

Barbara was overcome. The moment was later detailed in the *Movie Weekly* telling of her life story. "My heart went up out of my very toes and hit the frescoed ceiling," the article cites her as saying.[5] Never, the article continues, had she known such absolute joy. A single thought reverberated throughout her being: *I'm a writer!*

To her astonishment, Fox, after reportedly paying her $1,500 for her story (over $20,600 today), presented her with a contract.[6] Barbara agreed, in exchange for $10,000 (around $138,000 today), to create five more original stories for pretty, twenty-seven-year-old Fox star Gladys Brockwell over a period of a year and a half.[7]

Several acclaimed writers inked similar contracts with Fox at this time. When Fox studio heads issued the press release announcing the addition of twenty-three-year-old Barbara to their staff, they padded her credentials, reporting that she "had considerable experience in playwrit-

Fourteen

ing for both the screen and stage."[8] In truth, aside from her poetry being featured in magazines, all she had to her credit were intrinsic talent, staggering life experience, and unshakable belief in her abilities.

As 1920 unfolded, life was golden for Barbara. Her health had improved. She and Ben decided to give their marriage another chance and reunited. The salary she received from Fox enabled her to care for her family. She had a career she loved and wanted for the rest of her life.

When her contract with Fox commenced in January, she and Ben were living alone in an apartment at 106 East Washington Street in downtown Los Angeles.[9] (William and Rose occupied an apartment in the same building.) A short distance away, on the Fox lot, seven companies labored on seven productions. Ben was acting in one, *Would You Forgive?* (1920). Barbara's story was another.

Barbara divided her time between her home and the studio. In the apartment, she dictated her manuscripts to William, doing her best work, she said, "between midnight and dawn."[10] At the studio, she participated in the production of her first story. She attended meetings with her film's director, Edward J. Le Saint, and its scenarist, Charles Wilson. Entrusted with the task of creating her story's intertitles, she collaborated with the editor. She also conferred regularly with Gladys Brockwell, the film's star.

Under the studio system, writers worked closely with their respective stars. Stars were, by far, the predominant factor in drawing the public and determining a picture's success. Writers were expected to give stars ample screen time and tailor story lines to accentuate their personalities. Fox studio heads acknowledged that Barbara's story represented a departure from the usual mother roles enacted by Brockwell, but one which, they believed, suited her ideally.

When the film was screened in the studio's private projection room, Barbara undoubtedly occupied a seat. Typically present alongside writers at initial screenings were a film's major cast members, director, producers, cameraman, editor, and cutter. A censor was also in attendance. Since 1909, filmmakers had warded off government involvement in film censorship by monitoring the industry themselves. Their National Board of Review upheld morality standards by regulating crime and sex-related content and imposing edits wherever board representatives judged them necessary.

The lights dimmed and the projector whirred. Barbara's title, *The Mother of His Children,* appeared on the flickering screen. Following that, to be seen the world over, was her name: Barbara La Marr Deely.

The story opens amid upper-crust Parisian society, where Princess Yve (Brockwell), an alluring, thrill-seeking temptress, meets Richard Arnold (William Scott), an American sculptor. They fall in love—but not without complications. Richard has a wife (Golda Madden) in the United States, the mother of his two young children (Nancy Caswell and Jean Eaton). It was she and the children who helped him win a prestigious French award by inspiring his group sculpture, *The Mother of His Children.* Yve is shocked when Richard tells her of his family and that, to curtail his illicit longing for her, he has sent for them to join him. Adding to the snarl of events, Richard is charged with murder after Yve's jealous suitor (Frank Leigh) steals into his studio to shatter his sculpture and is killed by Yve's servant (Nigel De Brulier).

Without providing specifics, Barbara, per the *Movie Weekly* depiction of her life, confessed that her story contained autobiographical elements: "The people I wrote of were real people to me. I knew them all." Her life, the article explains, had shown her "all kinds under all kinds of varying conditions" and she had studied them as well as herself. She evidently formed the story from her conviction that a man can love two women simultaneously. Men, she reputedly contended, often place unrealistic expectations upon their wives by desiring a woman capable of being at all times mother, wholesome homemaker, companion, and exotic enchantress. Barbara apparently believed women to be equally guilty of seeking the impossible from a single mate. Humans are multifaceted creatures, occasionally compelled to "turn to more than one to answer all of our imperious requirements," her bylined article states.[11]

Barbara ended her story happily. Richard is exonerated and, after his wife becomes ill and dies aboard the ship bearing her across the Atlantic, Yve marries him, conforming to her roles as wife and a second mother to his children.

When *The Mother of His Children* opened in theaters in April 1920, critical reception was divided. Certain critics praised the film as "a strongly entertaining, if not powerfully dramatic story" and "one of the strongest and most interesting photodramas of the year."[12] Others believed the production suffered from "peculiar," unappealing main characters and an "unsympathetic plot."[13]

Fourteen

Barbara scarcely had time for lengthy deliberation of critics' responses to *The Mother of His Children* that spring. She had additional manuscripts to produce. The studio had also increased her responsibilities; along with creating intertitles for her own pictures, she was titling the films of Fox stars Shirley Mason and William Farnum. Besides, her second story was entering its final phases of production.

The Rose of Nome reinstated not only Brockwell in the starring role but William Scott as her love interest and Edward J. Le Saint as director. Unlike *The Mother of His Children,* which Barbara wrote before acquiring her contract and which was adapted to suit Brockwell, Barbara created *The Rose of Nome* expressly for Brockwell. For this film, Barbara was paired with a different scenarist, Paul Schofield.

As the story unfolds in northwestern Canada (it was filmed in Flagstaff, Arizona), Rose Donnay (Brockwell) escapes her abusive husband with Jack Hilton (Herbert Prior), who, unbeknownst to her, has murdered her husband. Jack takes Rose to Nome, Alaska, obliging her to work in his dance hall and mistreating her until a policeman finds them. Jack forces Rose to flee with him by taking her adopted child—a child he fathered and whose mother is dead. Miner Anatole Norss (William Scott), in love with Rose, follows them into the wilderness, where his sled dog kills Jack. Anatole frees Rose from a doleful life by marrying her.

As before, Barbara's story struck dissimilar notes among critics after the film's August debut. There were those who loved it; some referenced the action-packed sequences, "exciting turns of events," and vibrant characters.[14] Others were less complimentary.

Reviews of Brockwell's performance were mostly favorable. Critics enjoyed her characterization and the emotional depth she brought to the role. *Motion Picture News* suggested that, after thirty-one films with Fox, Brockwell "has made one of her best pictures in *Rose of Nome.*"[15]

Fox and Barbara wouldn't get a repeat performance from Brockwell. Slightly over a week after *The Rose of Nome* finished filming that spring, Brockwell asked, for reasons unspecified by the trades, to be released from her Fox contract. Her request was granted.

With only two of the six films Barbara had been contracted to write for Brockwell completed, Barbara's future at Fox was uncertain.

Barbara and Ben's marital woes came to a head the beginning of May. Barbara decided she was through. She packed her belongings and left the apartment—but not without, according to Ben, taking his money with her; in exchange, she left him an automobile.

The trouble escalated after Ben, in a temporary lull with film work and needing cash, agreed to sell the automobile to Barbara. Barbara, he said, paid him an initial $100 and promised another $100. Ben's account continues with Barbara taking the car but failing to make the second payment.

Ben retaliated by making off with the car. He happened upon it the first week of June, parked at the Venice Beach pier. Presumably, Barbara was at the nearby Ship Hotel and Café, a docked recreated Spanish galleon and favored hot spot of Hollywood's film crowd. Ben approached the unattended vehicle, fired up the ignition, and drove away. He wasn't fast enough. Barbara spied him and called the police. He was apprehended—slapped by Barbara with an auto theft charge.

Ben decided he was through. After presenting his side of the story to police and being released from jail, he filed a divorce suit against Barbara, charging desertion. His complaints continued. Barbara, he averred, not only brought her parents to live with them but "connived with them to have a girl make love to him." He additionally accused her of "threatening to kill him or have someone else do it; concealing from him the facts about her previous marriages; having him falsely arrested for stealing an automobile."[16]

Barbara, meanwhile, had filed for divorce against Ben. Her litany of accusations was just as long. Ben, she said, "persecuted, annoyed, and shamed her; called her indecent and opprobrious names; threatened to kill her; kissed another young woman goodnight; squandered the money she earned."[17]

Barbara's messy divorce action played out in attorneys' offices and newspapers. But it was principally the "too beautiful" Reatha Watson or, on occasion, Barbara Deely, not Barbara La Marr, who appeared in the headlines and shouldered the wry commentary in the columns.[18] For now, Barbara's undisclosed identity was safe.

She went ahead with her parallel life as a screenwriter.

With Gladys Brockwell gone, Fox reassigned Barbara. Louise Lovely, a spirited, Australian-born actress, had been closely watched by William Fox, proving herself in supporting roles opposite Fox leading man William Farnum. Twenty-five-year-old Lovely, Fox believed, was ready for stardom. Fox selected Barbara to deliver Lovely's first starring vehicle.

Fourteen

To spotlight Lovely's convincingly understated acting style and subtly comedic tendencies, Barbara crafted the role of Beverly Arnold in the story *The Little Grey Mouse*. Veteran actors completed the cast, and up-and-coming director James P. Hogan drafted the scenario and directed the film.

Beverly, whose quiet demeanor earns her the nickname "little grey mouse," assists her emotionally abusive lawyer husband, Stephen Gray (Philo McCullough), as he chases a writing career; she types his manuscripts—and also writes them. The manuscripts bring renown and fortune, and Stephen, drunk from his ill-gotten success, takes up with an admirer and divorces Beverly. Beneath Beverly's timorous exterior beats a brave heart, however; supporting herself with her writing abilities, she wins the adoration of publishers, fame, and wealth. Rejecting Stephen's pleas to reconcile, she marries his ex–law partner, her former suitor, John Cumberland (Sam De Grasse).

The Little Grey Mouse, released that October, made Lovely a hit with film exhibitors and moviegoers alike, particularly females. *Variety* deemed her an "excellent type" for the role Barbara wrote for her.[19]

But Barbara was feeling challenged by screenwriting. *The Little Grey Mouse* was hailed by some critics as a gripping, potent story. Others considered the story's triangle plot crude and, though convincing, unimaginative.

After completing her draft of *The Little Grey Mouse* during the early part of that summer, Barbara had three more original stories to produce for Fox. She dug deeper within herself for inspiration and got busy.

Fate, meanwhile, had other plans for Barbara that summer.

Fifteen

Barbara's position in Fox's story department was enough to grant her at least a screen test for a credited role in several of the films the studio was casting in 1920. Yet the thought of appearing in films, Barbara later insisted, had ceased crossing her mind; she professed to have no desire to leave her writing career. The fear of notorious Reatha Watson appearing before millions, betraying her identity as Barbara La Marr and obliterating any acting career to which she aspired, may have been another factor.

Perhaps, to Barbara, it was just as well. More young women than ever were vying for film careers—and were advised by *Movie Weekly* to "prepare for a long and heartbreaking battle."[1] Thousands of female hopefuls were clamoring to break into films only as extras; and those fortunate enough to be cast rarely advanced beyond such nonspeaking, low-paying, background roles. Any woman plucked from the ranks of uncredited faces and given a screen test was expected to convey an extensive range of emotions to the camera on cue and to be a "distinct type." The current trend among filmmakers, reported *Movie Weekly,* was for "striking and stunning" women.[2]

When Barbara received an offer from director Bertram Bracken to test for a bit part in his Louis B. Mayer production, *Harriet and the Piper,* that June, she purportedly thought the experience would be "more amusing than anything else." She was also apprehensive. She was said to admit, "I didn't know what the camera was going to make me look like, and I had no overwhelming desire to know, either."[3] She chose to humor Bracken. Upon the stage at Louis B. Mayer Pictures, under the lights and with the hand-cranked camera humming as it rolled, she did her best. Bracken and the studio, in reviewing her footage, liked what they saw. Barbara won the part.

Harriet and the Piper stars box office favorite Anita Stewart as Harriet Field, a wealthy couple's secretary forced to answer to the piper for her unscrupulous past with her former lover, roguish Royal Blondin (Ward Crane). To save the couple's daughter, Nina (Margaret Landis), from marrying Royal, Harriet—who is married to Nina's recently widowed father,

Fifteen

Richard (Charles Richman)—confesses her past, impresses Richard with her devotion, and is pardoned.

Barbara reportedly received $10 per day for her tiny—albeit credited—part in the film. Her decision to accept the role surely had nothing to do with financial gain. Nor could it have been prompted by a glorified position within the film's cast. Deep in her soul, Barbara yearned to act.

From the moment Bracken called "Cut!" after her final scene, Barbara waited anxiously. She hadn't seen the film's rushes (unedited footage) during shooting. When *Harriet and the Piper* premiered in September, Barbara bought a ticket, waded through the audience to a seat, and prepared for a glimpse of herself on the big screen.

It came quickly. Billed as the Tam O'Shanter girl and projected many times larger than life above theatergoers' heads, she played a fiery café dweller who is jilted by Royal.

According to the *Movie Weekly* series depicting her life story, Barbara missed much of the rest of the film. Tears of mortification blurred her eyes, the article states; she had looked hideous, she thought, and had played her part disastrously wrong. "What can be worse," she supposedly moaned, "than to try to be tragic and dramatic and to be, after all, merely *funny?*"[4] The article describes Barbara forcing herself to stop crying, sitting through another showing of the film to see it in its entirety, and feeling even worse. Certain of ridicule, she waited—per the article's sequence of events—until the last of the audience trickled through the exit; she then left the theater, battling an all-consuming urge to shatter every mirror she passed.

Barbara wanted nothing to do with any reviews of her performance. They found her anyway. People close to her thought it their place to show her. Jittery from fear, Barbara read them.

Her brief appearance, though unmentioned in most reviews, made an impression. Her talent was noted, and *Variety* wrote that her role was "played with strength."[5]

Barbara was amazed but unconvinced. The shock of seeing herself onscreen was not an experience she cared to repeat. She would never, she reputedly avowed, appear in a film again.

Barbara had become disenchanted with screenwriting. Before the release of *Harriet and the Piper,* she spent the summer struggling to write her final three stories for Fox. Original story lines escaped her; she second-guessed her ideas. Every paragraph she composed seemed to her to echo portions of plots she had already written. She nevertheless persisted and completed the stories. Fox commenced producing two of them and, citing prohibitive production costs, temporarily shelved the third. Barbara felt as though she had exhausted her creativity and was loath to write in the absence of passion. Perhaps a break was what she needed.

As summer waned, Barbara was residing in downtown Los Angeles with Marguerite De La Motte. De La Motte occupied an enviable position in Hollywood, playing leading lady to Douglas Fairbanks in Douglas Fairbanks Pictures Corporation's upcoming thriller, *The Mark of Zorro* (1920). As De La Motte readied to leave for the studio one morning, she invited Barbara to accompany her. Barbara would never regret it.

Fairbanks's film sets were an astounding amalgam of dedicated professionalism, hilarious pranks upon unsuspecting company members, and breathtaking displays of stunts and acrobatics—all compliments of thirty-seven-year-old, tanned, tautly muscled Fairbanks himself. His wholehearted laughter was contagious. His eternal optimism and enthusiasm so galvanized any gathering, no one dared utter a depressing word in his presence.

As a reigning film star, Fairbanks was defining an era. For those who knew him, there was no distinguishing between his off-screen and on-screen personas. He helped set off a global fervor in March 1920 when he married "America's Sweetheart" Mary Pickford. Together with Charles Chaplin and director D. W. Griffith, Fairbanks and Pickford presided over United Artists, a film distribution company they inaugurated in 1919 to exercise dominion over their independently produced films. Fairbanks oversaw and participated in all aspects of his productions. When his presence wasn't called for in a scene, he shadowed the director and codirected. He also cast and developed talent for his pictures.

On the set of *The Mark of Zorro*, Fairbanks was introduced to Barbara. He thought her, he later confessed, the most beautiful girl in the world.

Barbara spent her day on the set chatting with and befriending Fairbanks and Fred Niblo, the film's director. An unmistakable feeling fluttered through her. Fairbanks was, she would relate of their meeting, "sizing me up."[6]

At the Fox studio, Barbara's fourth story, *Flame of Youth*, was complete and scheduled for release December 5. Barbara adapted the drama from novelist Ouida's 1874 work, *Two Little Wooden Shoes*. The scenario was created by Frank Howard Clark and directed by Howard M. Mitchell.

Shirley Mason's girlish beauty made her an ideal choice for the leading

Fifteen

role of Beebe, an innocent, seventeen-year-old Belgian peasant in love with wily Parisian painter Victor Fleming (Philo McCullough). Inconsolable and believing Victor ill after he leaves Belgium for France, Beebe, without money for train fare, walks to Paris in her wooden shoes. Arriving at Victor's studio, she receives a shock: he's engulfed by fawning women as he presides over an orgiastic celebration of his latest masterpiece—a painting of Beebe. Beebe flees Victor's studio and is returned to Belgium by a tender-hearted woodchopper (Raymond McKee), who has followed her to Paris and loved her all along.

Filmed slightly before *Harriet and the Piper, Flame of Youth* gave Barbara what she credited as her first chance before the camera. William Fox, needing a replacement for an absentee actress, called upon Barbara one day in the middle of filming, convincing her to take the girl's place in a small, uncredited role (likely in the party scene).

Critics expressed hearty approval for the film. *Wid's Daily* declared it "one of the best pictures turned out from the Fox studios in some time."[7] Barbara's adaptation also garnered plaudits: "entertaining all the way" and filled "with suspense to the very end," raved *Wid's Daily* and *Motion Picture News* respectively.[8]

The Land of Jazz, Barbara's fifth story, was also released in December. The film had involved elements of risk. After penning four dramas for Fox, Barbara had authored a comedy. Fox writer Jules Furthman cowrote the story, adapted it for the screen, and directed it—his first directorial endeavor.

An asylum for the innocuously insane provides the backdrop for the fast-paced story. Ziegfeld girl Eileen Percy stars as Nina, fiancée of a French captain (George Fisher) and bosom pal to Nancy (Ruth Stonehouse). To remain at the asylum and help reunite Nancy with the asylum's doctor (Nancy's fiancé, played by Herbert Heyes) after Nancy is caught kissing the captain, Nina pretends to be slightly out of her mind. Events take a madcap turn as Nina mixes with the asylum's "cracked craniums"; patients chase each other and let loose to jazz music. In the course of the madness, Nina winds up in the doctor's bed. Nancy, falsely believing the doctor to be romantically involved with Nina, rejects him, and Nina marries him.

Critics and audiences were indifferent. The hurriedly produced film, failing to evoke laughs in some theaters, was branded a flop. *Wid's Daily* blamed the story's handling. The main problem, the magazine asserted, lay in making a feature from a manuscript better suited to a one or two-reel slapstick production.[9]

For Barbara—who later admitted her outright fear of critics and that failure was unbearable for her—disappointment over *The Land of Jazz* was keen. Family and friends tried to encourage her, calling to mind her prior literary successes.

All the while, life was pulling Barbara toward a monumental crossroads.

Barbara had grown fond of the jovial gang at Douglas Fairbanks's studio. As 1920 gave way to 1921, she was visiting Fairbanks's set weekly. Fairbanks was hard at play on his next film.

The Nut, directed by Theodore Reed, features Fairbanks as Charlie Jackson, a bungling Greenwich Village inventor. Hopelessly in love with Estrell Wynn (Marguerite De La Motte), Charlie goes to ludicrous lengths to woo her and support her work with ghetto children. Muscling in on Charlie is gangster Philip Feeney (William Lowery). When Philip lures Estrell to his gambling house—under the pretense that she'll acquire supporters for her cause—and forces himself on her, Charlie bursts onto the scene. Impersonating a police officer, he single-handedly takes on a band of Philip's thugs and rescues her.

During one of Barbara's visits to Fairbanks Studios, Fairbanks refused to tolerate her presence on the sidelines any longer. He asked if she would like to join in the action and offered her a screen test for a small part. Barbara suppressed her anxiety, telling Fairbanks she would try. Underneath, she believed she would be awful. She would never get over Fairbanks's reaction to her attempt: he gave her the role of Claudine Dupree, Philip's sensual, tempestuous moll.

Fairbanks was pleased with Barbara's performance. Despite playing a bit part and being surrounded by a critically acclaimed cast, she is memorable in the role and was noticed by reviewers. Following the film's release in March 1921, one critic wrote that the work of Fairbanks's supporting cast "is equally commendable, especially that of Barbara La Marr whose seductive charms add considerably to the picture."[10]

Considering what the world had come to expect from a Fairbanks picture, some critics, while praising the film's comedic elements, believed *The Nut* fell short. Critics and fans, missing Fairbanks's swashbuckling stunts and athletic displays, hungered for more of him at his best.

He was preparing to give it to them. In January, Fairbanks had chosen his next film, heralding it as his most ambitious undertaking. By February,

Fifteen

the publicity mill was grinding at top speed. Fairbanks had vaulted into the role of gallant D'Artagnan in Alexandre Dumas's classic, *The Three Musketeers*. Construction was underway on seventy-seven sets, the creation of which would bring seventeenth-century France and England to life in epic proportions. The castle of Louis XIII, the Louvre, Buckingham Palace, rural villages, the gates of Paris, the city streets (down to the cobblestones)—all were being replicated with historical precision. The film's scenarist, Edward Knoblock, an expert in French history and culture, was overseeing costume design for a cast of one hundred sixteen actors and a horde of extras. To direct the spectacle, Fairbanks called upon the man whose decisive insight helped make *The Mark of Zorro* a box office triumph: Fred Niblo. Fairbanks's business manager, his brother John, informed columnists that no expense was being spared to secure the most outstanding talent available. Excitement built for what reporters promised would be an international sensation.

When Mark Larkin, Fairbanks's publicity manager, telephoned the offices of *Photoplay* magazine, whispers of the new actress at Fairbanks's studio had already circulated among the staff. She was quite a discovery, Larkin confirmed: not only gorgeous, she had a plum role in *The Three Musketeers*. Adela Rogers St. Johns, *Photoplay*'s feisty Western editor, purportedly pounced on the story.

Perhaps indulging her habit of blending truth with fabrication, St. Johns later wrote of being introduced to her interviewee in a dressing bungalow at Fairbanks Studios and instantly recognizing her old friend: Reatha Watson. Left alone in the room together, St. Johns recounted, she and Barbara broke into a fit of giggles. According to St. Johns, they had last seen each other in January 1914, immediately after chief juvenile officer Leo Marden declared then seventeen-year-old Reatha too beautiful to remain in Los Angeles. Over the years, St. Johns embellished the story for film fans by including a courtroom scene when in fact newspapers had reported that juvenile authorities settled the matter out of court. Though St. Johns would additionally cite this courtroom incident as her first encounter with Reatha, the two friends had evidently met earlier, on the Los Angeles nightclub scene, before Marden banished Reatha to El Centro. The fun-loving duo had spent evenings in the cabarets after St. Johns, two years older and no longer underage, helped sneak Reatha in.[11]

Back then, St. Johns was a cub reporter at the *Los Angeles Evening Her-*

ald, the lone newspaperwoman among a staff of men who placed bets on when she would give up and quit. Instead she persisted, dreaming of becoming a full-fledged reporter—virtually unheard of for women in those days. When St. Johns learned of Marden's pronouncement, she made certain that Reatha stopped by the *Herald* office before leaving town. The result was a thrill for the men in the newsroom, a front-page photo spread of Reatha, and a juicy story for the paper's readership.

In the dressing room at Fairbanks Studios, as reported by St. Johns, the delighted squeals of recognition quieted down and St. Johns gazed upon Barbara La Marr. Much had changed in their lives since 1914. St. Johns had advanced from cub reporter to a weighty position within the film industry. Dubbed Hollywood's mother confessor, St. Johns, with swift keystrokes upon her typewriter, wielded far-reaching influence over the subjects of her articles. She was fully acquainted with the life of Reatha Watson. The woman before her now, St. Johns intimated in her narrative, seemed more mature—but worried.

Barbara's inescapable past as Reatha Watson had haunted her screenwriting career. It dogged her as she took her first tentative steps into the spotlight, threatening to destroy her long-held acting ambition as her performances in two major motion pictures reached the screen. Thus far, the public had failed to make the connection. Fairbanks had now given her an extraordinary opportunity in *The Three Musketeers*. Barbara apparently made an appeal to her old pal, asking that her secret be kept, if only a little longer.

St. Johns's story continues with her reasoning with Barbara, pointing out that it wasn't a question of *if* she would be recognized as Reatha Watson; it was a question of *when*. "If I were you," St. Johns supposedly told Barbara, "I'd tell it myself, right now, the way you want it told."[12] Barbara proffered a compromise, according to St. Johns, and the women made a pact. St. Johns allegedly agreed not to publicize her damning knowledge. In exchange, Barbara ostensibly promised that, should the time come when her true identity as Reatha Watson was revealed, she would give St. Johns first crack at the complete saga.

For the present, Barbara's secret was still safe.

When *The Three Musketeers* began filming at Fairbanks Studios and nearby Robert Brunton Studios that spring, the thought of her past surfacing was just one of Barbara's worries. Around mid-January, about the time she began work on *The Nut,* she and Ben had halted their divorce proceedings and misguidedly reconciled. Tensions were already rebuilding between them. Although working regularly in major motion pictures himself, Ben was, for indeterminate reasons, displeased with Barbara's venture into film acting.

Also clouding Barbara's mind were the pointed criticisms of friends who believed she would never achieve in front of a camera what she might achieve if she kept writing. Barbara's faith in her acting abilities plummeted. She questioned her involvement in *The Three Musketeers.*

On the set, an onrushing whirlwind of exuberance drew everyone along in its wake. Swords clanked frequently as Fairbanks and various male cast members squared off in any one of the sixteen scripted duels. Fairbanks had taken to embodying D'Artagnan with such dynamism, twelve rapiers would snap in his hand before filming concluded. Fred Niblo likewise embarked upon directing the picture with his usual vivacity and enthusiasm. Barbara squelched her inner turmoil, centering herself in her role.

The court of King Louis XIII (Adolphe Menjou) is ripe for scandal after the traitorous Cardinal Richelieu (Nigel De Brulier) witnesses the queen, Anne of Austria (Mary MacLaren), giving the Duke of Buckingham (Thomas Holding) a commemoration of their secret, ended affair: a brooch gifted to her by the king. Conspiring to ruin the queen, the cardinal proposes to the king that she wear the brooch to the court ball. D'Artagnan, a lowly young swordsman who has gained entrée into the brotherhood of three of the king's musketeers, charges to England, retrieves the brooch in time for the ball, and upholds the queen's honor, earning a place in the king's regiment of musketeers.

As Milady de Winter, the film's villainess, Barbara conceals a dual identity. Masquerading as a loyal member of the queen's inner circle, Milady is in fact the cardinal's spy, recruited by him to steal the brooch from the duke in England. Aboard a ship returning to France, she is ambushed by D'Artagnan while she is asleep; partially dressed, withholding the brooch, and wielding a dagger, she battles him in one of the film's most climactic scenes.

Barbara's dedication, professionalism, and kindness throughout filming astounded Niblo. He had never, he said, encountered anyone so pleasant to direct. He found her anxious to please and "so sweet, smiling, and gracious"—the same qualities he believed tempered her acting with a "vel-

Barbara and Douglas Fairbanks aboard a ship created for their battle scene in *The Three Musketeers* (1921). Courtesy of Donald Gallery.

vety sensuous softness." Recognizing Barbara's underlying vulnerability, Niblo kept his usual forcefulness in check, taking a gentler approach in directing her. "She is of a very nervous temperament," he explained, "and you must drive her as you would drive a nervous horse—with a light, but very firm rein."[13] To avoid entanglements with censors, Milady's seduction scenes were omitted and her lasciviousness was significantly subdued. What escaped censoring was Barbara's potent, inherent sex appeal in her characterization of the role. Struck by it, Niblo later marveled, "Even a bad dressmaker cannot make [her] look virtuous."[14]

In the studio projection room, as the film's rushes flicked across the screen before the assembled crew, Fairbanks was overcome by Barbara's explosive screen presence. He turned to her and made a prediction. "You are going to be one of the biggest girls on the screen," he said. "Wait and see."[15] The moment would remain one of the greatest thrills of Barbara's life.

Fairbanks's and Niblo's constant encouragement during filming had meant the world to Barbara, drowning out the objections of her husband

Fifteen

and friends and preventing her from quitting. When her work on *The Three Musketeers* concluded, there was no turning back. She acquired the management services of producer J. L. Frothingham, signing a six-month contract with him. No matter what the future held, Barbara was pursuing a career as a film actress. Stiff opposition and discouragement from Ben and others close to her would continue buffeting her; only now their words would fire her determination to achieve the greatness Fairbanks and Niblo believed her capable of.

"I made up my mind," she was quoted as saying, "that I was going to stick."[16]

V

Film Star

God makes the stars. It's up to the producers to find them.
—*Samuel Goldwyn*

Sixteen

For Barbara, acting provided a means of fulfilling unsatisfied desires. "Most [women] never have the opportunity to reveal more than one or two facets of their many-sidedness," she said. "Enacting the roles of women of many kinds, even in a make-believe world, gives opportunity for the imagination to have its fling."[1] Orchestras on the set induced the necessary mood. The director, after calling for the cameraman to *Gun it!*—the command to crank the camera to shooting speed—talked actors through a film's scenes, guiding their inner worlds. Often, it allowed Barbara to banish unwelcome personal realities as she entered the realm of fantasy.

While film fans awaited the release of *The Three Musketeers,* Barbara was cast in a supporting role as smooth-talking Lady Lou opposite Western star Harry Carey in Universal's "rip-roaring, snorting" story, *Desperate Trails.*[2] Lou has tough cowhand Bart Carson (Carey) so firmly twirled around her finger, she persuades him to take the rap for a robbery committed by her lover, Walter Walker (Edward Coxen), telling him Walter is her brother. Bart breaks out of jail after discovering Lou's duplicity and Walter's identity: he's the abandoning husband of Mrs. Walker (Irene Rich)—a decent woman of whom Bart is very fond. Along with Bart's eventual pardon comes a new husband for Mrs. Walker.

Overall, *Desperate Trails,* directed by Jack Ford, fared well with critics following its June release. Acclaim for Carey's performance dominated the reviews, and Barbara's relatively minor contribution to the film garnered only sparse, mixed remarks.

As an actress, it would be the last of Barbara's time in the shadows of obscurity.

On the evening of August 28, 1921, the sidewalks surrounding New York City's Lyric Theatre were a scene of frenzied disorder. Car horns blared for hours as thousands of film fanatics pressed toward the theater, spilling onto streets. Inside, a galaxy of stars, including Douglas Fairbanks, Mary Pickford, Charles Chaplin, and heavyweight boxing champion Jack

Dempsey, assembled for the world premiere of *The Three Musketeers*. The showing concluded to wild applause. The *New York Tribune* trumpeted, "*The Three Musketeers* is a thrilling, gripping, unadulterated success."[3]

The film exploded onto screens nationwide. The *Los Angeles Express* lauded it as "probably the greatest achievement since the birth of the motion picture industry."[4] The manager of San Francisco's Strand Theatre reported, "Tremendous crowds breaking all previous house records. People fighting their way to the box office necessitated calling for police protection."[5] Similar states of affairs erupted nationwide, and the madness continued throughout autumn. A prominent film trade publication rendered its assessment: "This [picture] Spells C-A-S-H—Loads of it!"[6] Film exhibitors everywhere paid heed, catapulting the film to worldwide commercial success.

The Three Musketeers was a defining moment in Barbara's acting career. While Fairbanks's scenes provoked whistles, laughter, and cheers, Barbara's beauty reputedly left theatergoers in stunned silence. Critics, too, were enthralled. Barbara was pronounced "dazzling" and applauded for delivering "a keen bit of character work" and infusing her scenes with "striking moments." *Picture Play*, acknowledging her as an "unusual" and "fiery" actress, declared her worthy of stardom.[7]

As Barbara's screen career ripened with promise, her marriage to Ben Deely reached an irrevocable low. On September 20, 1921, they separated again.[8] This time there would be no reconciliation. Ben continued his film career in Los Angeles and, for the time being, slipped out of Barbara's life. Neither he nor Barbara initiated divorce proceedings. Perhaps one or both of them clung to some faint hope of a future reunion. Perhaps, at the time, Barbara was unable to conceive of ever desiring to marry again and thus neglected to officially divorce Ben. Throughout her adult life, typically following a failed relationship, she often veered from yearning for marriage to shunning it. She boldly stated in coming years that her career, not men, came first and that she couldn't be content with settled, married life. But, more than likely, Barbara's decision to forgo a divorce was strategic. She had a past to keep hidden. Her separation from Ben was announced rather quietly in Los Angeles newspapers; any divorce proceedings involving her would spawn ongoing, unwanted publicity, as they had when she and Ben briefly undertook them a year and a half earlier, during her screenwriting days at Fox. She now had more at stake.

Sixteen

James A. Woodbury portrait, 1921.

Hollywood hadn't yet learned her identity. Here and there, however, certain reporters throughout the country were connecting the face of the *Three Musketeers* beauty with that of Reatha Watson, featuring her photograph beneath headlines such as "Girl of 'Too Much Beauty' Wins Fame" and "'Too Pretty for Big City,' She Becomes Movie Star."[9]

Barbara was on borrowed time.

Barbara returned to the Fox studio—this time, as an actress. Her manager, J. L. Frothingham, leveraging her recent portrayals of maleficent women, steered her into the role of a sinister stepmother in the mystery-drama *Cinderella of the Hills*. Barbara provided contrasting support to Fox's newest star, wholesome Barbara Bedford, and was directed by Howard M. Mitchell.

As Kate Gradley, Barbara is a home-wrecking seductress with a propensity for cruelty. Norris Gradley (Bedford), resolving to win her father, Giles (Tom McGuire), back for her mother, moves in with him on his ranch after he marries Kate, enduring Kate's abuse until Kate is caught romancing her old lover, ranch hand Rodney Bates (Cecil Van Auker). Furious when Giles threatens to divorce her, Kate runs from the house, falls over a precipice, and dies. Norris convinces Giles to return to her mother.

A vehicle for Bedford, the small-scale production, released October 23, was turned out quickly, generating significantly fewer box office returns than *The Three Musketeers*. Critics considered the film's story line predictable and improbable and confined their commentary primarily to Bedford's starring performance.

For Barbara, a pattern was being established. *Motion Picture News*, singling out her performance, acknowledged: "[She] makes a very nifty vampire."[10]

The vamp wasn't new to the American public. She emerged on the screen in 1915, born of increasing cultural turbulence that was culminating in greater equality between the sexes and an unfastening of established sexual constraints. She was a shocking figure, a woman who deliberately used her femininity and powers of seduction to ensnare men. To many women, she was a symbol of empowerment, a role model to be emulated. To many men, she was the embodiment of forbidden fantasies, an object of lust. To many others, she was a threat to diminishing Victorian morals, a woman to be feared and despised. She was Theda Bara, the screen's first vamp, in *A Fool There Was*, a film inspired by Rudyard Kipling's poem, "The Vampire."

Film audiences, whether loving or loathing dark-haired, kohl-eyed Bara and her manufactured image as a foreign-born, shameless temptress, were incapable of satiating their appetite for her. Bara made forty films between 1915 and 1919 and was Fox's biggest star, her weekly earnings exceeded only by the likes of Charles Chaplin and Mary Pickford.

Bara's influence persisted into the 1920s. Film fans clearly craved more than the traditional, virtuous heroine as typified by the angelic Pickford. Americans had evolved in the past decade. Little girls raised for lives of submissive domesticity had grown into freethinking women with the right to vote and had entered the workplace. The social climate, upended by Freudian literature and ways of thinking, had also changed, enabling peo-

Sixteen

ple to discuss sex more openly. The nation's youth lived for the moment, plunging into lives of self-gratification.

Americans wanted screen personas that reflected the changing times. Taking note of the trend, director Fred Niblo confirmed that "a new order of screen idol" was rising.[11] Screenwriter Ouida Bergere concurred: "The day of the sexless, goody goody ingénue is done."[12] The public demanded stars that oozed sex appeal. New vamps, such as Gloria Swanson and Nita Naldi, like Theda Bara before them, were dark and exotic, bared their legs and shoulders in figure-accentuating gowns, and sprawled invitingly before their intended victims upon chaises and sofas. *Moving Picture Stories,* considering the "hell turned loose" style of vamping that made Bara famous, recognized subsequent vamps as hell with the promise of heaven and "full of surprises."[13]

Even while skirting the censors, producers caught on quickly. In early 1921, ten production companies made a sobering observation: sixteen of their eighteen recent films "entirely devoid of sex problems, scant dress, and suggestiveness" had been box office failures.[14] Producers' shifting attitudes during this period were epitomized by a joke in which a movie mogul states, "Two and two make four, four and four make eight, sex and sex make millions."[15]

Certain studios, dismissing vamps as a fad, were wary. After Barbara appeared in Universal's *Desperate Trails,* Frothingham spoke with the studio about signing her to a long-term contract. Universal declined; "She can only do vamp stuff," they said.[16]

The prospect of playing a vamp thrilled Barbara. "I'm not silly enough to pretend I'm an ingénue," she acknowledged. "I just want to be a woman."[17] "Part of the joy in being a woman," she said, "is to exercise fascinations on the male."[18]

Rex Ingram needed the perfect vamp in November 1921, and he refused to compromise. As headstrong as he was handsome, the twenty-eight-year-old Irish immigrant hadn't become a leading Hollywood director by sacrificing his standards of artistic excellence. After setting his ambitions upon a film career in 1913, he assimilated the art of filmmaking through any job he could get—set detailing, painting stars' portraits, acting, writing intertitles, adapting scripts, and assistant directing—at the Edison Company and Vitagraph in New York. He joined Fox two years later, writing material for the studio's biggest stars, including Theda Bara. By

1916, he was a director with Universal and moved to Los Angeles with the company. Given free rein at Universal to direct his own stories, Ingram controlled all aspects of filming and, according to Liam O'Leary, Ingram's biographer, "indulged his flair for the exotic and the delineation of strange characters."[19]

While at Universal, Ingram had made a film that would have an indelible impact upon Barbara's acting career. *Black Orchids*, released January 1917, is entirely Ingram's own: written, directed, and produced by him. Summarized by a film poster as "The Love Affairs of a Heartless Woman," it's a dark tale, featuring as its heroine a diabolical sorceress, Zoraide (played by Cleo Madison). The film raised hairs at Universal—and not for its inclusion of such themes as murder and the occult. "It got murdered by the front office," explained Grant Whytock, editor of many of Ingram's films, "for being too erotic."[20] Critics were equally put off by the film's morbidity. Animosities flared between Ingram and Universal studio heads, and Ingram was eventually fired.

It was hardly the end for Ingram—or for *Black Orchids*. In 1921, while working for Metro Pictures, he solidified his destiny. The studio, on the brink of bankruptcy, was desperate for box office gold. *The Four Horsemen of the Apocalypse*, starring (then largely unknown) Rudolph Valentino and directed by Ingram, provided it. The picture became one of the highest-grossing silent films of all time and made Valentino a worldwide phenomenon. Metro awarded Ingram absolute freedom to select the stories, actors, and crew comprising his productions. Ingram's time had come.

When Barbara arrived at Metro Pictures one Friday in November, she was nervous and doubtful. A studio employee behind a barred window admitted her inside the casting office. Ingram needed one actress to appear in two of his films. The first role, Antoinette De Mauban in *The Prisoner of Zenda*, was a supporting part and, under normal circumstances, would have been simple enough to cast. But Ingram was looking for something more: an actress to play the lead in a remake of *Black Orchids*, slated to begin immediately after *The Prisoner of Zenda*. His plan was to find someone he deemed ideal for *Black Orchids* and test her dramatic ability in the role of Antoinette. He wanted a newer actress, a woman not bound by a recognizable screen persona, someone he could completely mold into his conception of his *Black Orchids* heroine. Securing a woman of the right type was also critical to him. He had even refused his own wife, actress

Sixteen

Alice Terry, when she asked for the part. Ingram's sketches of his character reflected a female of a darker nature. And he needed an actress capable of breathing life into her depraved soul.

His search thus far had been fruitless. Then he saw Barbara. He was taking a meal break while filming initial scenes for *The Prisoner of Zenda* in early November when she entered the studio cafeteria. It was her walk that seized him, the poised, flowing gait of a dancer. She was the twenty-third actress he called in to audition.

When Barbara appeared on the set, her anxiety was apparent to Ramon Novarro, a sultry twenty-two-year-old actor who, already cast in both films, was to participate in her screen test. Novarro had arrived in Los Angeles from Mexico in 1916, pulled by his dream of achieving fame as an actor, a singer, or a dancer. While dancing in vaudeville and cabarets, Novarro first saw Barbara. Her interpretive dancing had enchanted him.

Novarro wanted Barbara to win both roles and resolved to help her. Ingram suggested that Novarro rehearse with Barbara, and Novarro obliged—even though the scene called for a forcible slapping of his face. Barbara, immensely grateful to Novarro, was later quoted as saying, "It was hard work slapping the face of a boy as good-looking as Ramon, but he was a brick about it."[21] It was the start of a deep friendship between them. Their on-set chemistry was also instantaneous.

Ingram eased Barbara's remaining self-consciousness with light-hearted joking before rolling the camera and beginning her test. Barbara nevertheless went through her scenes feeling like a fool.

"The only thing I enjoyed was kissing Ramon," she is said to have lamented to her roommate that night, convinced that Ingram had been unimpressed with her.[22]

Again, Barbara had underestimated herself. She awoke around 9:00 a.m. the following Monday to a telephone call. She was asked to return to the Metro studio to sign a contract. Ingram had chosen her for *The Prisoner of Zenda* and *Black Orchids*. Barbara couldn't believe such a wonderful thing had happened to her.

She would still need to prove herself to Ingram. His decision to cast her was based in part on his opinion that her beauty would make his *Black Orchids* villainess more appealing to audiences. Her performance in *The Prisoner of Zenda* would either confirm or invalidate his hopes for her acting abilities in a starring role. It was a chance Barbara was willing to take. She turned down Fred Niblo's offer to play Dona Sol, a supporting role opposite Valentino in *Blood and Sand* (1922), and staked her dreams on Ingram's pictures.

Barbara began work on *The Prisoner of Zenda* the first week in December, working an average of six days per week through January 1922, at a weekly salary of $150 (around $2,100 today).[23] Under Ingram's direction, she surely earned every penny. Regarding his actors "as clay in the hands of the sculptor," Ingram rehearsed them relentlessly, demanding authentic characterizations and realism.[24] For many who worked with him, the results were worth it. "He was an artist and a good one," recalled Novarro. "We knew what we had to do when it came time to appear before the camera, and we did it."[25]

In *The Prisoner of Zenda*, a suspenseful tale of deceptions and ill-fated romances, Rudolf Rassendyll (Lewis Stone) travels to the kingdom of Ruritania for the coronation of his look-alike cousin, King Rudolf (also played by Stone), and becomes entangled in a coup and love affair. Black Michael (Stuart Holmes), desirous of the throne, drugs and kidnaps the king; the king's sympathizers enlist Rudolf to impersonate the king; and Rudolf and the king's fiancée, Princess Flavia (Alice Terry), fall in love. Black Michael's lover, Antoinette De Mauban (Barbara), after being informed by Michael's officer, Rupert of Hentzau (Novarro), that Michael intends to marry Princess Flavia, betrays Michael by enabling the king's rescue. Bound by duty, Flavia relinquishes Rudolf.

To employ Barbara's hypersensitivity to his advantage, Ingram moderated his explosive temperament and coaxed her through her scenes. As he had hoped, theirs was a mutually beneficial collaboration. Barbara filled her role with the human, spontaneous moments Ingram sought from his actors. The depth of her sadness as a cast-off woman near the film's end is so gripping, he captured it in close-ups.

Barbara's presence was equally affecting off of Metro's sets. During breaks in filming, she and Novarro frequently retreated to his dressing room, where they shared a special bond and secrets. That Novarro was homosexual—a fact which, like Barbara's past, needed to be concealed from the public—undoubtedly endeared them to each other. "She had a warmth and understanding that lifted you up and made everything easy," Novarro reportedly recounted to Adela Rogers St. Johns. "You could never grow tired of talking with her and she was interested in whatever you cared to talk about and responded to your thoughts and brought them out."[26] It

Sixteen

Rex Ingram directs Barbara and Ramon Novarro in *The Prisoner of Zenda* while cameraman John F. Seitz stands at the ready.

was further stated that Barbara was the only one who understood Novarro's ambition to become a singer. Seated at the piano in the privacy of his dressing room, Novarro sang and Barbara listened. She was said to sing along and astonish him with her constructive feedback. Although she professed to being unable to read music and to playing only a little, by ear, she evidently impressed him with her knowledge of music. But it was Barbara's encouragement that meant the most.

Novarro believed himself to be one of the few to penetrate what he described as the "glittering, enchanting personality" Barbara hid behind to the humble, sensitive, insecure woman beneath. The real Barbara, he said, was even more alluring and possessed a sincerity and "kindness that made her lovable." He considered her "a loyal, fascinating friend."[27]

Barbara also formed a friendship with Alice Terry. "At first I was almost a little jealous of Barbara," Terry confessed decades later, "but after working with her and getting to know her while on *The Prisoner of Zenda*, I became quite fond of her. She was as lovely in her personality as she was in her ravishing looks... She was very big-hearted and generous and loved to please people."[28]

Barbara's benevolence, according to St. Johns, brightened Willis Goldbeck's office on the Metro lot, where he worked as a screenwriter. St. Johns credits Goldbeck with saying that, on days when he sat at his desk, struggling with a script and the demands of a profession that was new to him, the sound of Barbara's approaching footsteps was enough to lift his mood. "Then she would sit down and talk over the problem I was wrestling with," St. Johns quotes Goldbeck as telling her, "and her sure dramatic instinct always found the weak spots or showed me the way out of a tangle... Her mental energy was amazing and she was never too tired or too self-absorbed to consider your difficulties as though they were her own."[29]

Filming concluded for *The Prisoner of Zenda* in mid-March 1922. Metro officials, in examining the film's initial print, unanimously predicted a colossal box office hit.

Long before this, however, Ingram finalized his decision to star Barbara in his *Black Orchids* remake.

Seventeen

During Barbara's early days at Metro, Adela Rogers St. Johns met her for lunch one afternoon at the studio and recounted years later, "I can see those magic eyes of hers, glinting with laughter, bright with emotion. What an alive person she was."[1] With her career on an upswing and the specter of her undisclosed past a seeming afterthought, Barbara was embracing life. Her attitude throughout the coming months was summarized in a statement she made to a reporter: "I enjoy every bit of life," she said. "I want to get all I can out of every bit of it."[2]

Barbara's ability to live to the fullest stemmed from a predisposition that was both liberating and risky. Friends described her as living for the moment, never considering consequences or the future when life was going well. Emancipated from fears of the past or the future, Barbara indeed sought the most from each moment.

When not on a studio lot, she hit the town. Among other nightspots, she was a frequenter of the Ambassador Hotel's Cocoanut Grove, the film crowd's preferred gathering place. Some evenings, she and a partner commanded the dance floor, swirling beneath towering papier-mâché palm trees in the pool of the spotlight.

Other times, her antics were the spice of parties she attended and hosted. Once, along the beach in a gauzy gown on a biting January night, she challenged fellow partygoers to a swim and was the first to charge into the water. A favorite party prank of hers involved switching off the lights, thereby enticing intoxicated guests to get better acquainted. Later, without warning, she would turn the lights back on to reveal partially undressed bodies and sheepish expressions.

When it came to indulging her passion for men, Barbara made no pretense. "Sometimes, in my life, I have been called something very like [a vamp] off the screen," she admitted.[3] Also attributed to her is the statement "One loves to live only because one lives to love" and the saucy confession "I take lovers like roses, by the dozen."[4]

One of her affairs involved handsome, charismatic actor John Gilbert.

In January 1922, Gilbert was reeling with anger over an imposed separation from his wife, actress Leatrice Joy. Joy, making a picture with Cecil B. DeMille, was nearly fired when her ongoing tiffs with Gilbert compromised her work. Frantic, Joy moved out of the Laurel Canyon house she occupied with Gilbert, explaining to her distraught husband that they could reunite when filming of the picture concluded.

It was during this time, according to Leatrice Gilbert Fountain, daughter of Joy and Gilbert, that Gilbert began "a short but passionate affair" with Barbara.[5] The pair was spotted together at film showings and parties. Joy witnessed them blazing around town in Gilbert's car, Barbara's scarves fluttering behind them in the breeze. Joy believed Gilbert loved *her*—not Barbara—and suspected that he was trying to make her jealous. Even so, she felt betrayed not only by Gilbert but also by Barbara, whom she considered a friend. "Several times during their separation," Fountain wrote in her father's biography, Joy drove to the Laurel Canyon house, "but her pride would not let her go in. She also knew that she might walk in on something that would be hard to put behind her later."[6]

Gilbert and Joy reconciled after a few months. He told her his liaisons with Barbara had been innocent and that he had indeed been trying to make her jealous. Joy returned with him to their house that evening. In the middle of the night, she was awakened by the jangling of the telephone. She answered it and heard Barbara's voice. "Oh, Leatrice darling, may I speak to Jack, please?" Barbara asked. "I said, 'Of course, dear,'" Joy recalled, "and then threw the phone under the bed and went back to sleep."[7]

Barbara was also seen in the company of sophisticated, soft-spoken writer and director Paul Bern. Born Paul Levy in Wandsbek, Germany, in 1889, he became Paul Bern in 1910, following his acceptance to New York's American Academy of Dramatic Arts and his decision to pursue a show business career. When Barbara met Paul in California, he was editor-in-chief at Goldwyn Studios. It is believed that a romance between them began in late 1921.

Mutual friends may have considered them kindred spirits on some levels. Both were extremely intelligent; writer Willis Goldbeck described Barbara as having the sharpest intellect he had ever come across in a woman, and Paul was regarded as "one of the most brilliant minds in the film world."[8] Both were exceedingly sensitive; Paul was said to "suffer intensely himself when ill-luck came to his friends."[9] Their generosity knew no bounds. Tales of Paul's kindness were legion. Destitute children throughout Los Angeles were fed through his efforts. An impoverished young actress was given the opportunity to attend a major industry networking ball when Paul bought a lovely gown and anonymously sent it to her. Down-and-out screen stars languishing on their deathbeds had their medical expenses paid by him. Paul had only one fault, his sister Friedericke Bern attested: "his heart was too big for his body."[10]

Paul's character has been shrouded by hearsay and contradiction since his death at age forty-two in 1932. Two months before he died, Paul, by then a producer and director at Metro-Goldwyn-Mayer Studios, wed the studio's newest star, platinum bombshell Jean Harlow. On Labor Day morning, Paul's butler, John Carmichael, found him on his bedroom floor with a fatal gunshot wound to his head. His death was officially ruled a suicide.

Certain accounts suggest otherwise. Clifton Davis, Paul's gardener, viewed Paul's body immediately after Carmichael. "I think it was murder," Davis testified to investigators.[11]

Preceding police to the grisly scene were MGM kingpin Louis B. Mayer, MGM publicity manager extraordinaire Howard Strickling, and MGM security head Whitey Hendry. "Hell, I knew the guy was murdered as soon as I saw him," Hendry was later said to relate privately. "He was lying in the closet and the gun was on the floor halfway across the room. Whoever killed him threw it there, it didn't walk there."[12] Mayer, fearing devastating consequences for the studio, allegedly wanted to obliterate any possibility that Harlow would be presumed guilty.

At least two and a half hours elapsed before police were summoned to the house. Precisely what occurred during that time is unknown. When Detective Joseph Whitehead assessed the scene, he observed a pistol on a nearby dressing table and a revolver clenched in Paul's right hand and positioned beneath his body.

Witnesses' accounts added to the puzzle. After Harlow left for an overnight visit at her mother's house the evening of Paul's death, Paul's neighbor, Slavko Vorkapich, saw an unknown woman arrive at Paul and Harlow's home in a limousine. Hours later, Vorkapich's wife saw a limousine speeding away from the house.

MGM, meanwhile, presented reporters with a suicide motive. MGM doctor Edward Jones, claiming to be Paul's physician, declared Paul killed himself because of depression resulting from a lack of marital relations; Paul, the studio reported, was impotent. Paul's family and friends thought the pronouncement absurd. Harlow never supported it, despite the studio purportedly pressuring her to do so. Dr. Frank Webb, assistant autopsy surgeon, stated that the coroner's office found nothing to suggest Paul was impotent.

But the damage to Paul's reputation had begun. He went from a man actress Estelle Taylor deemed "the only individual in Hollywood about whom *no one* ever says an unkind thing" to the subject of rumors that, even by gossip columnist Harrison Carroll's standards, were "vicious" and "[without] a word of truth in them."[13] One rumor held that he was homosexual. Others alleged that he beat and otherwise abused Harlow. All three claims were refuted by people close to Paul and Harlow.

From Paul's brother Henry Bern, reporters discovered that, until he died, Paul supported a deranged woman in New York, caring for her "as though she were his wife."[14] Paul met Dorothy Millette, a onetime actress, around 1911 and lived with her for many years. Henry stated that, although no marriage took place, Paul considered himself "morally married" to Millette.[15] When Millette became increasingly haunted by voices only she heard, Paul, heartbroken, placed her in a sanitarium. By the end of 1920, he had departed for California. Millette was eventually released from the sanitarium—not cured, but presumed harmless—and moved into New York City's Algonquin Hotel, where, under the name Mrs. Paul Bern, she remained for about ten years, paying her expenses with checks Paul sent. Henry related that Paul visited her at first, each time coming away "actually sick"; Paul's visits ceased in 1928.[16] In the spring of 1932, Millette left the Algonquin for San Francisco's Plaza Hotel.

Paul had been greatly disturbed by Millette's arrival in San Francisco. To a few friends, he confided that she was determined to see him and that she maintained a delusion that he would star her in films. Paul's cook, Winifred Carmichael, identified Millette as the woman who visited Paul hours before he was found dead. Both Winifred and Paul's neighbor said they overheard a violent argument between Paul and a female voice in the middle of the night. After hearing an "unearthly scream," Winifred emerged from the servants' quarters and saw Millette bolting from the house.[17] Millette rushed into a waiting limousine and was taken to San Francisco, reportedly begging the driver repeatedly to "go faster."[18]

The circumstances surrounding Paul Bern's death may never be unearthed. Any information police may have extracted from Millette, had they found her, remains with her. She was last seen September 6, 1932, aboard a steamship sailing from San Francisco to Sacramento. Fishermen discovered her body in a Sacramento River tributary September 14—an apparent suicide.

Seventeen

Paul's association with Millette, encompassing over twenty years, factored into his affair with Barbara. Throughout 1922, Paul and Barbara's relationship deepened and, in time, Barbara considered Paul her closest male friend. Given Paul's tendency to speak openly to those he trusted, Barbara doubtless knew of his love for Millette. Perhaps Paul told her, as he told his other confidants, that if ever Millette's mental state improved, he hoped to resume their married life.

Still, Paul and Barbara loved each other. He was aware of Barbara's past and overlooked it. She called him "the understanding heart."[19] The press noted Paul as her constant escort at industry gatherings and believed a wedding to be imminent. But when asked by a reporter about an engagement, Barbara downplayed any romantic involvement, saying, "Dear Paul is the only man I have ever known who has permitted me to love him as a friend."[20] There would be no marriage between Barbara and Paul. His relationship with Millette may have been one reason. That Barbara was merely separated, not divorced, from Ben Deely may have been another.

Years after Barbara died, in an exclusive interview with Jean Harlow following Paul's death, Adela Rogers St. Johns wrote of a confidential exchange she claimed took place between herself and Barbara. Barbara, she said, told her she wouldn't marry Paul because of his impotence.[21] Yet St. Johns's revelation—like others generated to back the impotence claim and safeguard Harlow's image—lacks support.

Paul's feelings for Barbara tormented him at varying times. Leatrice Joy related that he once waited for Barbara at a party in a hillside house, an orchid corsage and diamond bracelet in hand. When Barbara failed to turn up as promised, he hurled the corsage and bracelet into the brush out back. Party guests spent the evening combing the hill for the diamonds, but never found them.[22]

Paul's greatest torment over Barbara was yet to come. Through it, she would learn the immensity of his compassion for her. Perhaps she somehow sensed the pain he would one day endure for her sake. A silver cocktail shaker she gave him bears the inscription "TO PAUL, LIKE THE PHANTOM HAND OF MEMORY MAY I SOOTHE THEE NOW THO' TOMORROW THOU MAY'ST REGRET ME.—B. LA M."[23]

From the time Barbara completed her *Prisoner of Zenda* scenes January 30, 1922, she began a period of waiting. The picture would not premiere until midsummer. Filming of her leading role in *Black Orchids* would

Left: Barbara attends a film premiere with Paul Bern (on her left) and Lew Cody in June 1924. Wisconsin Center for Film and Theater Research. *Right:* Paul Bern, Hollywood's "father confessor." Courtesy of Laura Riebman.

commence in mid-March. Both films, when released, would give her much-needed exposure in major productions. *Black Orchids,* she wholeheartedly hoped, would help secure her launch to stardom. In the interim, she settled for supporting roles in two smaller-scale films.

The first was Fox Film Corporation's romantic adventure, *Arabian Love,* directed by Jerome Storm. Barbara worked on the production in early 1922, during her affair with John Gilbert, the film's star. Barbara plays Themar, a sheik's jealous daughter who is attempting to end a romance between Norman Stone (Gilbert)—an American who joined her band of Arabs to hide from the law after killing a man—and Nadine Fortier (Barbara Bedford)—a newly widowed officer's wife who is abducted by the Arabs while traveling to her deceased husband's African encampment. Themar tells Nadine that Norman killed her husband. Nadine ultimately learns that her husband was unfaithful to her; he wronged Norman's sister and died when his gun misfired during an ensuing confrontation with Norman. Nadine forgives Norman, and the lovers depart for the United States.

Seventeen

Barbara earned accolades in the mixed reviews that followed the film's April debut. *Photoplay, Film Daily,* and *Variety* wrote that her beauty enhanced the picture; *Variety* proclaimed, "the real punch is delivered by Barbara La Marr, who screens like a million dollars in this production."[24]

Barbara's next film, *Domestic Relations,* produced by Preferred Pictures and directed by Chet Withey, follows the parallel lives of Mrs. Benton (Katherine MacDonald), wife of a wealthy judge (William P. Carleton), and Mrs. Martin (Barbara), wife of a low-class laborer (Frank Leigh)—both wrongfully suspected by their husbands of infidelity. Judge Benton drives Mrs. Benton out of their home; Mr. Martin gives Mrs. Martin a beating and receives a prison term from Judge Benton. The women's lives intersect after Mrs. Benton, homeless, moves into Mrs. Martin's run-down neighborhood. Following Mr. Martin's release from prison, Mrs. Martin warns Mrs. Benton of his plan to enact revenge upon Judge Benton. After saving Judge Benton, Mrs. Benton likens his treatment of her to Mr. Martin's treatment of Mrs. Martin. Both men realize the error of their ways.

The film, blasted as lusterless, was a miss with most critics when it entered theaters June 4. Barbara's characterization, however, fared better. *Moving Picture World* stated: "A vivid touch is accomplished by Barbara La Marr in a drab role."[25]

Barbara shifted her focus to Ingram's *Black Orchids,* her career primed for stardom. But as she did so, her deepest fears were realized: Reatha Watson emerged.

Isolated stories of Barbara's identity had trickled through the film colony. At least one had reached Ingram's ears. On hearing of Barbara's past, worry overshadowed his prior enthusiasm for her. He reputedly informed her that, should the public learn of her identity, she would be fired from his picture.[26]

Ingram had cause for alarm. The Hollywood film industry was tumbling from public favor. The descent began in 1921, after a Labor Day party in comedian Roscoe "Fatty" Arbuckle's suite at San Francisco's St. Francis Hotel. Arbuckle was charged with raping and murdering actress Virginia Rappe during the party. Overnight, Arbuckle, a beloved film star, became a target of public outrage.

While Arbuckle's defense team fought to clear his name in court, another scandal exploded in the newspapers. William Desmond Taylor, a prominent film director, was found slain in his Los Angeles home in February 1922. In addition to a slew of potential suspects, police uncovered Taylor's true identity and secret past: his real name was William Cunningham Deane-Tanner, and he had abandoned a wife and daughter before setting off for Hollywood and a film career. Other evidence emerged, hinting at Taylor's involvement with several women. The case unleashed a fresh outpouring of public antipathy, ultimately devastating the careers of actresses Mary Miles Minter and Mabel Normand, both of whom were reported to be romantically involved with Taylor at the time of his death. Taylor's murder remains unsolved.

As the Arbuckle and Taylor scandals took on global proportions, a third scandal was in the making. Following Arbuckle's rape and murder charges, a *Variety* reporter wrote of an unnamed star, a narcotics addict whose wife was causing his suppliers' arrests. By late 1922 Wallace Reid, Barbara's former beau, was in a sanitarium. His wife, Dorothy Davenport, issued a statement acknowledging his morphine addiction and his determination to break his habit. (Reid's addiction began after he sustained a serious injury during the making of a film; a studio doctor repeatedly injected him with morphine to keep him working.) In January 1923, with Davenport by his sanitarium bedside, thirty-one-year-old Reid died.

With each scandal, animosity toward the film industry escalated. Government officials launched ongoing probes to ensure "cleanliness in [the] producing and acting ranks" and to "rid [the industry] of dopesters, degenerates, and parasites."[27] In thirty-six of the forty-eight states, censorship legislation was proposed.[28] In Los Angeles, film producers were frantic. Their sole option, they concluded, was to beat the government to the impending punch.

Filmdom's leaders established the Motion Picture Producers and Distributors of America, their own governing organization. As president, they selected former postmaster general Will Hays, and the group became known as the Hays Office. Hays assumed his position March 5, 1922, with a firm resolution: "to attain and to maintain the highest possible standard for motion picture production and to develop to the highest possible degree the moral and educational value of the industry."[29]

Hays's first move sent a wave of shock and fear crashing over the film colony. On April 18, 1922, with Arbuckle jubilant over his courtroom acquittal, Hays banished him from the screen, costing Paramount Pictures, Arbuckle's employer, an estimated $100 million in revenue. It was considered a necessary price to appease the government, the public, and film exhibitors, who warned stars to henceforth "lead clean and moral lives" or "be wiped from the screen of the country."[30]

Studios began guarding their investments, rewriting contracts to include morality clauses. One such clause mandated that performers "avoid places, circumstances, and conduct which might in any way bring themselves and the motion picture profession into disrepute."[31] Screen siren Gloria Swanson's contract prohibited her from engaging in "adulterous conduct or immoral relations with men other than her husband."[32] Producers even included retrospective clauses, stipulating that questionable behavior from an actor's past must never appear in print. Violation of one's morality clause was punishable by dismissal.

Barbara understood that Ingram couldn't allow her past to shame Metro Pictures and ruin his film. She evidently saw only one road to potential salvation: she must own up to the truth—or at least a version of it. Her hope, Adela Rogers St. Johns alleged, lay in the vow Barbara made in her dressing room during the making of *The Three Musketeers*. "I promised you that if anyone was going to print that story that I was once Reatha Watson, you should do it," Barbara supposedly told St. Johns. "Treat me as gently as you can."[33]

St. Johns pulled her chair up to her typewriter and went to work. Strategically omitting the name Reatha Watson and merging fact with fiction, she presented an overview of Barbara's past. She opened her story in a Los Angeles courtroom, with a judge beholding the face of a teenaged Barbara—"the face that launched a thousand ships, the face that lost Mark Antony the world, the face a million poets have sung"—and sending her home to her parents. Barbara's beauty was to blame for her troubled past, wrote St. Johns, for it "threw her suddenly into the whirlpool of life, quite without warning[,] . . . preparation, knowledge or protection." She glossed over Barbara's alleged kidnapping at sixteen, portraying Barbara as a frightened child who was stolen from her parents and her serene life by her unnamed sister and an unnamed male. St. Johns described Barbara being whisked atop a horse by an unnamed, lovesick Arizona rancher and riding with him to the altar—only to be widowed by his sudden death from pneumonia. St. Johns profiled garage manager Lawrence Converse as an unnamed lawyer—"cultured," "romantic," and everything Barbara had dreamed of. Knowledge of Converse's wife and children broke Barbara's heart, St. Johns continued; and her father blamed only himself for failing to protect her.

St. Johns pointed out that Barbara's tumultuous past, rather than having destroyed her, had given rise to uncommon wisdom and strength: "I am willing to salute the unconquerable soul of a girl who can beat her own destiny and with her bare hands climb back up the cliff over which life has thrown her." It was a rare actress, she assured readers, who possessed Barbara's emotional profundity and understanding of the world. "It will be interesting to see what she does," mused St. Johns, "if she goes beyond the mark set by the others who have not known life face to face as she has. And, do you know, I rather think she will."[34]

Metro's publicity department, fronted by Howard ("The Suppress Agent") Strickling, was apprised of St. Johns's article. Working in tandem with studios' publicity departments was part of St. Johns's job. Studios relied upon their relationships with journalists to protect stars from unfavorable publicity. Sympathetic journalists were rewarded with exclusive interviews and juicy story leads. Metro was pleased with St. Johns's article. Titled "The Girl Who Was Too Beautiful," it would appear in the June 1922 issue of *Photoplay*, which also, conveniently, promoted the premiere of *The Prisoner of Zenda*. Meanwhile, Metro's publicity team, in the same way that it concealed Ramon Novarro's homosexuality and upheld his Latin lover image, would work to keep Barbara in good standing with the public.

Ingram's fears subsided. He retained Barbara's services for *Black Orchids*. But as the film entered production, Barbara had more than the facts of her past to keep hidden.

She was pregnant—and without a husband.

Eighteen

Barbara reported to Metro Pictures for her first day of work on *Black Orchids* March 15, 1922. Her $200 weekly salary (around $2,600 today), a $50 jump from her *Prisoner of Zenda* salary, reflected her increased value to the studio.[1] Rex Ingram was relieved to have kept her on board. She was the only actress he believed capable of embodying both the youthfulness and the sophistication demanded by the dual role he had given her. Barbara was likewise grateful. The film, she said, "appealed to me powerfully. I threw myself into it heart and soul."[2]

The lone female in the cast, she portrayed the fiendish fortune-teller Zareda (renamed from the 1917 version) and Jacqueline de Séverac, the fifteen-year-old daughter of a French novelist. Worried that Jacqueline's coquettishness is breaking the heart of her devoted suitor, Henri (Ramon Novarro), her father, Léon de Séverac (Pomeroy Cannon), reads her his manuscript, *Black Orchids*.

Jacqueline is transported by her father's story from her French village to 1914 Paris, where Zareda plays men like pawns, seeking wealth. Newly married, yet wishing to rejoin her lover, champion swordsman Ivan de Maupin (also played by Novarro), when he returns from the war, Zareda claims that Ivan insulted her, thereby instigating a duel that she knows her husband, the wealthy Marquis Ferroni (Lewis Stone), cannot win. Mortally wounded by Ivan's sword, Ferroni discovers Zareda's treachery and, capitalizing on her belief that he is already dead, relays instructions for her to claim her inheritance in a remote tower on his estate. Alone in the tower, Zareda is confronted by Ferroni—whom she thinks is a ghost—and is dragged, terror-stricken, to the tower's snake-infested dungeon and locked inside. When Ivan arrives to rendezvous with her, Ferroni shoots him, throws his body down to her, bolts the door, attaches the black orchids she placed at his mock crypt, and dies. Cradling Ivan's corpse, Zareda awaits death.

The film, deemed gruesome in its time and, as one period magazine described it, "reeking with sex," is tame by modern standards.[3] In 1922, however, Ingram was obliged to satisfy the censors; along with Zareda

Barbara as Jacqueline (with Ramon Novarro as Henri) in *Trifling Women* (formerly *Black Orchids*).

Barbara as Zareda in *Trifling Women* (formerly *Black Orchids*). From the collections of the Margaret Herrick Library, Academy of Motion Picture Arts and Sciences.

Eighteen

Final tableau of Zareda (Barbara) and Ivan (Ramon Novarro) in *Trifling Women* (formerly *Black Orchids*). "You probably will love the shivers," noted *Picture Play* of the film, "but don't take Aunt Clara if she has a weak heart!" ("Trifling Women," *Picture Play*, January 1923, 54.)

receiving a punishment comparable to her heinous behavior, Ingram included a happy ending. The *Black Orchids* story read to Jacqueline by her father in the film accomplishes its purpose: Jacqueline desists trifling with men's hearts and weds Henri.

What Ingram was required to sacrifice in the way of a climactic ending, he made up for with pictorial aesthetics. His actors were bathed in tenebrous lighting, underscoring the sinister atmosphere. Cameraman John F. Seitz, using his groundbreaking matte technique and a black border on the camera lens, obliterated the cityscape surrounding a tower on the Metro lot. Hanging foreground miniatures were then superimposed in a double exposure, bringing a Gothic castle, shrouded in clouds, into existence.[4]

Seitz's technique was again employed when a brutal outburst nearly forced Ingram to scrap one of the film's key scenes. Barbara, in many of her scenes, was accompanied by Joe Martin, an orangutan who served as Zareda's cunning companion. Joe's gentle disposition had earned him regular film appearances. Barbara adored him; in a candid photo taken on the set, she is seated beside him, tenderly nestling him under her arm. The adoration was mutual. Joe became enamored of Barbara, recalled Seitz, and jealous of the men.

One day, something within Joe snapped. During a scene between Barbara and Edward Connelly (portraying the Baron de Maupin, Zareda's rejected suitor), Connelly playfully dangled a necklace in the ape's face before pushing him aside to place the necklace on Barbara. Joe, frayed to a breaking point by the fifteen-hour shooting day, turned violent. He shoved Barbara to the side and lunged at Connelly, trapping him in his arms and crushing him against the weight of his body. His bones fracturing, Connelly flailed a terrified hand in self-defense. Joe clamped it with his teeth. Blood spouted from beneath Connelly's fingernails as horrified crew members rushed the set. Barbara, in a near faint, was caught by Ramon Novarro. Six men attacked Joe. Three of them, by wrenching the animal's testicles, freed Connelly. After a hospital stay, Connelly returned to the set. No one blamed him when he refused to work with Joe.

Seitz managed to film Ingram's crucial scene—in which Zareda's orangutan, instructed by Zareda to poison Connelly's character at a banquet, raises a goblet in a mocking toast to his corpse—without Joe coming into contact with Connelly. He shot the scene once with Joe at the table and a bolt of black velvet over Connelly's empty chair, then a second time with Connelly alone, slumped in the chair. It was the only time Seitz used his matte technique for shots featuring Joe. Joe's remaining scenes, all involving Barbara, were captured without incident.

Exactly when Ingram may have learned of Barbara's pregnancy is unclear. It seems impossible he wouldn't have known. Clearly, he didn't fire her from *Black Orchids*. Considering that, before work began on the picture, he was evidently prepared to fire her if her past went public, filming was probably well underway when he likely discovered her secret.

By that point, Ingram and Metro had more to lose by letting her go than by keeping her. To swallow the cost of reshooting Barbara's footage with another actress would be unthinkable. It might also have been suicidal. The publicity generated by such a move would bring unwanted attention to the studio and, should the public learn the reason for Barbara's dismissal, to the film industry in general. It's also conceivable that the studio, still on shaky financial footing, couldn't afford to dismiss her. Absent from Metro's payroll at this time were big stars like Valentino, Fairbanks,

Eighteen

and Pickford. Metro was banking on its newest faces: Ramon Novarro and Barbara. Ingram devoted considerable energy to crafting Barbara's screen image. The Metro publicity department kept the trades full of predictions that she would be the next big thing. It was more than hype; as Ingram's *Black Orchids* rushes flitted across Metro's projection room screen, many at Metro believed it.

As filming and Barbara's pregnancy advanced, Ingram and Seitz were seemingly compelled to greater levels of creativity. The average woman can go as long as four or five months before exhibiting outward proof of pregnancy. For taller women and those whose abdominal muscles have not accommodated previous pregnancies, initial signs could appear up to two months later. A woman seeking to conceal a pregnancy might cheat nature longer by binding her midsection with girdles and corsets. Ingram and Seitz appear to have stepped in when Barbara could no longer hide her pregnancy herself. Ingram selected her costumes strategically. Barbara's gowns were floor length and loose-fitting. Some were fashioned from dark, monochromatic satin and velvet, elongating her body. Many had long, draping sleeves, concealing her waistline and diverting attention from her lower torso. In some of the film's stills, she is wrapped in additional layers, accented with eye-catching headpieces, and, for at least one scene, completely enfolded in a billowy cloak. Seitz's shadowy lighting and, in the case of the dungeon scene, forceful backlighting, could certainly help mask what Barbara's garments didn't. When all else failed, props and tactical staging seem to have come into play. The photos on pages 186–87 illustrate a few of such attempts likely taken to disguise Barbara's pregnancy.

Barbara worked on *Black Orchids* an average of six days per week, beginning mid-March and concluding sometime before the film's final production date of June 21.[5] When not at the studio, she doubtless kept out of sight. It was simple enough to do in the pre-paparazzi days of the silent era. "We lived two lives: our film life, and our own private one," Novarro explained of his days as a major star; "it was necessary in order to sustain the public illusion that made us stars."[6]

Novarro's statement would hardly prove more fitting than in the case of Barbara and her child.

Details of the child's birth are cloaked in mystery. It occurred in secret; exactly where it took place and who was present are unknown. In the early

Barbara pictured with Lewis Stone (*left*) and Edward Connelly in *Trifling Women* (formerly *Black Orchids*). From the collections of the Margaret Herrick Library, Academy of Motion Picture Arts and Sciences.

Barbara pictured with Edward Connelly (*seated*) and Lewis Stone in *Trifling Women* (formerly *Black Orchids*). From the collections of the Margaret Herrick Library, Academy of Motion Picture Arts and Sciences.

Eighteen

Barbara with Ramon Novarro and orangutan Joe Martin in *Trifling Women* (formerly *Black Orchids*). From the collections of the Margaret Herrick Library, Academy of Motion Picture Arts and Sciences.

1920s, it wasn't uncommon for a woman to give birth at home (50 to 70 percent of American women did), often without a medical practitioner or midwife in attendance.[7] The child's birth date is also an enigma and, for reasons that will become clear, would be unknown even to the child. Barbara must have given birth sometime after finishing work on *Black Orchids* and July 16, 1922, as Metro's payroll records indicate an extended gap in her presence at the studio during this period. (Before this, the only gap in Barbara's work schedule occurred briefly in March, and the next would not begin until August 29.) Actress ZaSu Pitts, soon to become Barbara's close friend, would nonspecifically place the date around the end of June. The father's identity would also elude the child, surfacing only in a lingering, wistful hope, the unverifiable convictions of those who knew Barbara, and rumors.

What is clear is how desperately Barbara wanted her baby. Not long after giving birth, she privately confessed to her friend, writer Jim Tully, that her child was "born in heartbreak," perhaps hinting at a marital union

187

that could never be.[8] Fully aware that entering motherhood as a single parent could destroy her career, Barbara neither aborted nor relinquished her baby. Painfully disillusioned by the love of men and unfulfilled by the world's pleasures, she contemplated her future. "There's only one person in the world you can actually count on loving you," she concluded, "when there are silver threads among the gold and you can no longer amuse or delight the world."[9] Barbara wanted her child because, in her words, "I wanted somebody to love always," somebody whom she believed would forever love her in return.[10]

Sequestered in Los Angeles in mid-1922, Barbara welcomed the love of her life: her son.

Her initial bonding with her newborn was short-lived. She had been hired for a third Metro production. She entrusted Irene Almond, her personal maid, with acting as a nurse for her boy.[11] With more than herself now to earn a living for, she began work on *Quincy Adams Sawyer* July 17.

On the evening of July 31 at New York City's Astor Theatre, Metro's faith in Barbara was substantiated. The film industry's elite and prominent critics made their way between the sky-bound arcs of two massive lamps marking the theater entrance. The occasion was the world premiere of *The Prisoner of Zenda*. The picture was declared a "sensational and instant triumph."[12] More stellar appraisals poured in and would continue following the film's general release that September.

Barbara's arresting presence in her supporting role entranced reviewers, exhibitors, and film fans. *Moving Picture World* and *Picture Play* respectively summarized the widespread sentiments: "Barbara La Marr displays that she is one of the most beautiful women on the screen and an actress of uncommon ability" and "Barbara La Marr alone is worth the price of admission."[13]

With the premiere of *Black Orchids* over two months away, prophesies peppered the trades that July. Barbara's performance in *Black Orchids*, affirmed columnists, would either make or break her chances for screen stardom.

Metro studio chiefs weren't alone in their assessment of Barbara as a viable commodity. As she worked on *Quincy Adams Sawyer* from mid-July to August 28 at a weekly rate of $300 (a 50 percent increase over her *Black Orchids* salary), producer Arthur Sawyer's certainty also deepened.[14]

One of the first postcards featuring Barbara's likeness: as Antoinette in *The Prisoner of Zenda*.

A fast-talking film industry pioneer, Sawyer quit his job as a Boston schoolteacher in the early 1900s and never looked back. His brief fling as an East Coast actor ended when he became a producer of plays and vaudeville sketches. Later, as an exhibitor of one-reelers, he owned one of the country's first theater chains. Sensing the boundless potential of the motion picture and the tremendous fortune to be made, he entered film production as general manager of the Kinemacolor Company of America. By 1914, he headed his own company (Sawyer, Incorporated), produced films from his luxurious headquarters overlooking Broadway, and experimented with revolutionary filmmaking techniques. He partnered with distributor and Metro executive Herbert Lubin in 1918 and formed S-L Pictures, merging a shared ambition to manufacture large-scale films and one day establish a major motion picture studio.

Barbara likely met Sawyer, by then a trim, dapper man of middle age, shortly before or while filming *The Prisoner of Zenda*. In addition to being the supervising director of S-L Pictures and operating the company's New York and Los Angeles offices, he was at this time in charge of Canadian distribution for Metro Pictures. In teaming with Metro to produce *Quincy Adams Sawyer,* Sawyer worked closely with Barbara.

Barbara's supporting role as a simple country girl came with a challenge: vamping the film's hero without the mandatory components of every vamp's arsenal. Stripped of the usual clinging gowns and alluring fabrics, Barbara was costumed primarily in looser-fitting country garb. It was a challenge she was up for. "A vamp in any other dress is still a vamp," she insisted. "It's the look in the eye that does it."[15] Sawyer and Metro believed her well-suited for the task; she was among the first to be cast in the film.

Surrounded by an all-star cast and directed by Clarence Badger, Barbara put her vamping to the test as *Quincy Adams Sawyer* was filmed on Metro's lot and among Washington State's Columbia River rapids. Boston lawyer Quincy Adams Sawyer (John Bowers) visits a widow's country home to prevent her lawyer, Obadiah Strout (Lon Chaney), from stealing her inheritance. He falls for the widow's brazen daughter, Lindy (Barbara)—until he realizes he loves the town deacon's blind niece, Alice (Blanche Sweet). Obadiah hatches a plan to get rid of Quincy, enlisting Lindy and the local blacksmith into his scheme. Fooled into thinking she's getting rid of Alice, Lindy lures her aboard a riverboat, but the blacksmith cuts the cables before Obadiah can get Quincy onboard. As the boat nears

Eighteen

Barbara, post-pregnancy, on location for *Quincy Adams Sawyer*. Clarence Badger and Blanche Sweet are second and third from left, cameraman Rudolph Bergquist is on far right. From the core collections of the Margaret Herrick Library, Academy of Motion Picture Arts and Sciences.

plunging falls, Lindy, guilt-stricken, warns Quincy in time for him to rescue Alice.

Premiering that November, the film reaped consistent returns and supportive reviews on average, and Barbara proved she could vamp with the best of them. Her performance, deftly interlaced with comedic touches, was selected by *Photoplay* as one of the six best for the month of February 1923. "If a girl can vamp successfully in gingham," Barbara quipped while making the film, "think of the havoc she can wreak in georgette."[16] Her fans were about to find out.

Black Orchids, renamed *Trifling Women*, debuted in October 1922 to impassioned critical responses. Some critics, repelled by what they described as a ghastly, absurd story, despised it; a *Motion Picture* writer wrote that Barbara, despite "a certain bizarre appeal," was a disappointment as Zareda.[17] Many more disagreed. *Moving Picture World* applauded the film as riveting, citing Ingram's "practically faultless" direction and the

191

cast's "brilliant performances."[18] Barbara was accorded honors; her acting was deemed "excellent" and "flawless," and she was heralded as "one of the most brilliant of the newer screen celebrities."[19] One reviewer, referring to the eerie dungeon scene in which Zareda awaits death with her dead lover, proclaimed that audiences "seldom have an opportunity to witness better acting."[20]

Arthur Sawyer needed no further convincing. By the time production of *Quincy Adams Sawyer* concluded in early October, he had already approached Barbara with a business proposal. Expressing his desire to manage her career, he offered her a personal contract with him. Aligning herself with Sawyer seemed like a lucrative proposition to Barbara. In the eyes of many, he was a force to be reckoned with. His goal of heading his own major studio was nearing fruition. Real estate mogul Colonel Ed Fletcher had gifted him twenty acres of land, investors were onboard, and construction plans had been drafted for a superstructure in La Mesa, California, just outside San Diego. When fully operational, S-L Studios, Sawyer explained, would be the finest film processing plant in the world, housing fourteen stages for his films and those of leasing companies. *Exhibitors Herald* predicted that the studio's completion would elevate Sawyer and Lubin to the "foremost ranks of motion picture producers."[21] Barbara accepted Sawyer's offer, entrusting him with her future.

On the afternoon of November 19, 1922, Barbara stood upon the grounds of the proposed S-L Studios before hundreds of Hollywood film notables, the local mayor, and over twenty thousand others. Sawyer's speech, in which he promised to turn the area into the Mecca of the motion picture industry, concluded in a roaring ovation. Sawyer's cameramen captured the scene, gathering footage that would appear in theaters throughout the country and entice additional shareholders. The cameras settled upon Barbara as she stepped forward, clasping a silver trowel. Ceremoniously kneeling to the ground, she spread the mortar for the S-L Studios cornerstone.

Barbara's future prospects had surely never looked better to her. Sawyer believed her stardom to be imminent. "Rising young publicity hound" Bert Ennis, chief press agent for S-L Pictures and former publicity man for Vitagraph, Keystone, and Thomas Ince, was given charge of promoting her.[22] At long last, Barbara was on her way.

How the matter of her secret love child would be handled remained to be addressed.

Nineteen

Barbara would look back upon *Trifling Women* as the film that made her. Following its release, life as she knew it would never be the same. Her fan base expanded; men and women alike now went to theaters specifically to see her—the latter often returning two or three times to the same picture. Her images were snipped from magazines and pinned to bedroom walls. Teenage girls attempted to paint her sensuous lips upon their faces. (To better show her lips, Barbara would adopt the habit of pursing them in photographs and films.) The fashion-conscious looked to her for inspiration, and journalists sought her opinions of the latest styles.

Despite her growing popularity, Barbara shunned fashion trends and remained true to her own inclinations. "Clothes ought to be subservient to your personality," she believed.[1] While newly emerging flappers paraded through Hollywood in short, formless frocks and bobbed hair, Barbara typically displayed her curves in long, close-fitting dresses. She rejected the flappers' practice of flattening their breasts with tightly bound cloth strips—a decision many hot-blooded males thanked her for. "When Barbara La Marr inhaled," cartoonist Al Capp reminisced over forty years later, "boys became men."[2] Eyes followed when she stepped out in public, taking in her garments; single shades of dark colors were accented with a vibrant contrasting hue in the form of a hat or jewelry. Her black hair, parted down the middle, oiled flat against her head, and loosely secured at the nape of her neck, quickly instigated a fad. Like the women she portrayed, she was enshrouded in an aura of mystery. "She is made for lurking tragedy," writer Willis Goldbeck mused in *Motion Picture Magazine*. "One feels the beat of ravens' wings about her . . . her radiance is that of moonlight in the heavy shadows of the night . . . Calypso she is, burning with the flame of subtle ecstasy."[3]

Reporters, hard-pressed to find the slightest trace of the wicked ladies Barbara enacted in films, were pleasantly startled upon meeting her. Her graciousness and wit were said to disarm even the most hardened newspapermen. When one interviewer pressed Barbara to reveal something

Photo by Hoover, 1922.

unusual about herself, she offered to stand on her head. *Los Angeles Times* reporter William Foster Elliot, struck by her sincerity, wrote, "She is remarkably straightforward and man to man in her attitude" and "really human despite the exotic bunk."[4] Journalists described the melodic, animated tones of her voice. They noted how her hands fluttered expressively, her nostrils flared slightly as she spoke, and the inner corners of her brows,

Nineteen

Photo by Hoover, 1922. Courtesy of Allison Francis.

when enlivened by emotion, quivered upward like the sides of a triangle. Many of them chuckled at her self-deprecating humor. Her intensity kept others in suspense.

Director Louis J. Gasnier saw more in Barbara than her screen characterizations had yet revealed. An esteemed French filmmaker, Gasnier had

Photo by Milton Brown, circa 1922.

begun his directing career with the Pathé Frères company in 1899. He immigrated to the United States in 1913 to head Pathé's American branch, bringing with him a talent for combining picturesque cinematography and stirring, human stories. By 1922, a string of successful films had led

Nineteen

him to a directing contract with Preferred Pictures and the beginning of the best years of his career. As Gasnier prepared to cast his third picture with Preferred, an adaptation of Gilbert Emery's acclaimed 1921 Broadway play *The Hero,* scenes from *Trifling Women* turned over in his mind. He needed to fill the role of Hester Lane, a dutiful mother and respectable woman—the diametric opposite of Zareda. Barbara, Gasnier decided, was it.

As Hester, Barbara was called upon to create the inner conflict of a woman who, although infatuated with her brother-in-law, Oswald (Gaston Glass), a returning war hero, remains true to her lackluster, kindhearted husband, Andrew (John Sainpolis), after Oswald moves into her home, taking advantage of Andrew's hospitality before stealing money, running off, and eventually reforming. In a 1924 interview in the British publication *Pictures and the Picturegoer,* Barbara credited herself with writing the film's scenario (the film was released in Britain as *His Brother's Wife*).[5] Her statement cannot be confirmed via period trade magazines, and no surviving prints of the film are known to exist. While most period trades credit Eve Unsell with the scenario, some credit Unsell with the adaptation; and, in the future, Barbara would have an uncredited hand in other film scenarios she enacted.

Barbara worked on *The Hero* from October to early December 1922, burying herself in her role. Between takes of highly charged emotional scenes, she isolated herself on the sidelines, her head cast downward to an open book upon her lap. She confided to a visiting columnist that she didn't actually read the book; she used it to ward off interruptions, remain in character, and thereby give her best for the film.[6]

As dedicated and accommodating as Barbara was, there was one line she was unwilling to cross. In the middle of filming one day, Gasnier told her she would be hit by an automobile in a particular scene. To him, the idea was reasonable. In the pre-union days of the silent era, actors were routinely placed in precarious situations in the name of art. Gloria Swanson lay as though dead beneath the paws of a roaring lion for a scene in *Male and Female* (1919); John Gilbert was chastised by a director for ruining a scene involving a fire after Gilbert extinguished flames that had leapt onto his clothing. Gasnier explained to Barbara that she was to remain in place as Gaston Glass drove the automobile up to her. Barbara refused. Exasperated, Gasnier stood on her mark to demonstrate the stunt himself. Glass, unaccustomed to the car, plowed into him. "The script flew one way and a flock of blue words flew the other," remembered Barbara.[7] Gasnier apologized to Barbara and settled for faking the scene.

The Hero, released January 1, 1923, was commended as "a quiet, sincere picture, soothing to the spectator who has been surfeited with sensation and sex."[8] The Exceptional Photoplay Committee of the National Board of Review chose it as one of the year's exemplary films. Gasnier's instincts regarding Barbara's dramatic range were rewarded. *Photoplay* extolled her as the real surprise of the film. "She was always a beauty," the magazine raved, "but now she is an actress. And she proves beyond a doubt that she is not dependent upon slinky gowns."[9] Other reviewers agreed. "She does some marvelous emotional acting," wrote a *Dallas Morning News* critic, "and really is the outstanding figure in the picture."[10]

Before *The Hero* wrapped, Gasnier was already eager to work with Barbara again. *Poor Men's Wives,* developed as a companion to Gasnier's *Rich Men's Wives* (1922), depicted how the other half lived. Gasnier chose Barbara for the role of Laura Maberne, the film's heroine.

Best friends Laura and Claribel (Betty Francisco) marry for different reasons; Claribel ropes a millionaire, and Laura weds for love. Laura's life in the ghetto with cab driver Jim Maberne (David Butler) and their twins is trying, particularly after she borrows a pricey gown to attend a ball with Claribel, her children destroy it, and she depletes the family's savings to pay for it. Jim, mistakenly believing Laura is involved with Claribel's playboy husband, Richard (Richard Tucker), orders her from their home. Later, finding her at Claribel's, he realizes the truth and forgives her for taking the money. Laura returns with Jim to the slums, wanting nothing more than their love.

As filming took place throughout December and into January, Barbara often left the set after midnight. Without a car of her own, she hitched a ride home with her costar David Butler in his Buick. "She was a lovely girl," Butler recalled. "Paul Bern was very friendly with her," he added, reliving his nightly jaunts to Barbara's apartment on Wilshire and Vermont. "The bell would ring and he'd be there with his big bunch of roses, and I'd go out the back way."[11]

Poor Men's Wives, premiering in New York City January 28, 1923, was a nationwide hit, particularly with women. Again, Barbara was a winner with critics. *Picture Play* contended that she "does excellent work as the drudge" despite her beauty. *Moving Picture World* concurred, adding, "She is natural and convincing in a role that tempts overacting." A *Dallas Morn-*

Nineteen

As Laura Maberne, with Muriel McCormac (*left*) and Mickey McBan, in *Poor Men's Wives* (1923).

ing News reviewer remarked that she "gives one of the finest portrayals of mother love for small children the screen has ever seen."[12]

Portraying Laura seemed to strike a chord with Barbara, causing her to examine her conceptions of marriage and home life. In an article entitled "What I Would Do if I Were [a] Poor Man's Wife" (which may or may not have been written by Barbara as claimed), it is stated: "[Laura] has taught me a lesson that I will carry in my heart for a long time, that I won't have to be reduced to poverty to appreciate." Barbara's reputed desire to be the type of wife who is an asset to her husband, a woman who inspires and encourages a man to succeed, is revealed. Her purported yearning for children, referenced in the article as "the essence of every home," is also discussed, and her supposed intention to make her home a happy one for her future family is declared.[13]

Barbara's dream of happiness and her private reality were worlds apart. The joy she had known since giving birth to her son was indescribable.

Her child, she later stated, had made her life worth living. Thoughts of him awaiting her at home gave her work deeper meaning. Amazed by his pleasant disposition and tendency to cry only rarely, she nicknamed him Sonny.

Barbara ached to share her pride in her son with the world. But the world Barbara inhabited with him was dreadfully small. It included, apart from her family and Irene Almond (her maid and Sonny's caregiver), a handful of persons Barbara trusted most. Paul Bern was one such person.

Virginia (Hobday) Carville, Robert's younger sister, was another. Barbara met the winsome, auburn-haired beauty in Oakland, when she and Robert began their partnership in 1915. A gifted dancer herself, Virginia had occasionally joined Barbara and Robert in their performances. The girls became so close they often presented themselves as foster sisters. By the end of 1922, Barbara counted twenty-eight-year-old Virginia as her dearest friend.

Barbara also included writer Jim Tully among her confidants. Tully later related how Barbara lovingly presented her son to him. "He's mine, Jim," she said. Tully remembered, "I can still see her magnificent eyes melt as she looked at him." But sadness welled beneath her joy. "And they want to deny me that," she sighed.[14]

Along with Barbara and her child, her manager, Arthur Sawyer, had much to lose if scandal annihilated her career. Sawyer and Barbara's press agent had a hand in a certain scheme in the making. A scheme that, if successful, would enable Barbara to live openly with Sonny. A scheme that would allow for the continuation of a film career which, judging by its trajectory, promised to be nothing short of stupendous. A scheme that would safeguard the anticipated millions of dollars resulting from that career, thereby ensuring a secure future for Sonny.

A scheme that would require Barbara to live a painful lie.

After taking the helm of Barbara's career, Sawyer adopted a strategy. He decided it would be in her best interest to avoid long-term studio contracts at the outset. A far more profitable course of action, he believed, was for her to contract for one picture at a time, apportioning her services among many studios. In this way, studios would be compelled to compete to obtain her, and her earning potential would increase. Sawyer additionally reasoned that demand for her services would escalate as Barbara, rather than being restricted to a single studio and distributing organization, was seen on screens worldwide.

Nineteen

Barbara followed her two films with Gasnier and Preferred Pictures with Goldwyn's *Souls for Sale*. Written and directed by Rupert Hughes (uncle of aviator and business tycoon Howard Hughes), the picture commenced filming in December 1922 and would give movie fans a behind-the-scenes glimpse into the motion picture industry. Shots of stars' hillside homes, aerial footage of Hollywood studios, and appearances by a few dozen of filmdom's finest are interspersed throughout the story of a young newlywed, Remember ("Mem") Steddon (Eleanor Boardman), who is running from her husband, Owen (Lew Cody), a man who marries, insures, and murders women. Traveling with Owen through the desert, Mem, suspecting his true character, jumps from the train while he sleeps and is rescued by a film company making a picture. She goes to Hollywood to become an actress, is given a break by Frank Claymore (Richard Dix), director of the company that saved her, and rises to fame. She also finds herself in a love triangle between Frank and the company's leading man, Tom Holby (Frank Mayo). Owen, meanwhile, recognizes his runaway bride on the big screen and confronts her in Hollywood. In the film's dramatic conclusion, pandemonium ensues after lightning sets fire to the company's circus tent; Owen attempts to run Frank into the rotating blades of a wind machine, but kills himself when he leaps in front of it to save Mem. Free from Owen, Mem takes up with Frank.

Barbara appears in the supporting role of Leva Lemaire, the company's vamp. Although derided as the screen's leading home wrecker, Leva, actually benevolent, remains faithful to her deceased boyfriend, a stuntman killed in a plane crash. Tragically struck down by the lightning bolt that sets her company's set aflame, she dies anticipating their reunion.

Rupert Hughes believed Leva's tenderheartedness to be a direct reflection of Barbara's nature and admitted to casting her for that reason. Barbara was true to Hughes's estimation of her throughout filming. "There isn't a girl in the picture business who is kinder to all the extra girls than Barbara La Marr," he observed. "She practically lets them help themselves from her wardrobe and she does other equally kind things all the time."[15]

As production of *Souls for Sale* continued that January and February in Los Angeles and one hundred miles east in Palm Springs, Hughes was forced to deal with a minor catastrophe. The majority of his cast, Barbara included, were stricken with klieg eyes. Klieg lights, powerful carbon arc lamps, were the scourge of filmmakers throughout much of the silent era. The intense heat they emanated, often melting makeup from actors' faces,

Playing with two of her castmates during a break in filming *Souls for Sale*. Courtesy of Allison Francis.

was one disadvantage to using them. Far worse was the ultraviolet radiation they emitted. Day after day, the glare of anywhere from three to eight banks of kliegs bore into an actor's eyes, eventually bringing on klieg eyes: inflammation and unrelenting pain, accompanied in severe cases by temporary blindness. To protect his afflicted crew, Hughes temporarily halted production of *Souls for Sale*. Barbara and her castmates were confined to darkened rooms, salving their throbbing eyes with ice bags until they recovered. As a precaution against future injury, Barbara soon heeded a producer's advice and insured her eyes for the modern equivalent of around $100,000.[16]

The loss the studio took from the production delay was briefly forgotten when the film opened that April to packed theaters and wonderful reviews on both coasts. The long lines at box office windows soon disappeared, however. Hughes had a theory on the matter: filmgoers, he said, expected a film that would expose "the terrific wickedness of the modern

Nineteen

Gomorrah." Yet "when they found instead a story emphasizing the hard lives of the toilers and the merely human and normal procedures of their love affairs, they warned their friends to stay away."[17] In reality, the film was an attempt by Hughes to help fade Hollywood's recent scandals from public consciousness.

Mary of the Movies, another film intended to offer an inside look at the industry, was released by Columbia the following month. Directed by John McDermott, the film chronicles the adventures of a young woman, portrayed by Marion Mack, who arrives in Hollywood to become an actress. Barbara, along with an array of stars and several directors, made a cameo appearance. Sprinkled with comical situations, the film, like *Souls for Sale,* depicted film folk as normal, congenial human beings. Box office returns were modest.

At the studios during filming of *Souls for Sale* and *Mary of the Movies,* hidden from meddling eyes, Barbara's burning secret found another outlet. Actress ZaSu Pitts, appearing as herself in both films, had first met Barbara when she played a small role in *Poor Men's Wives.* The doe-eyed twenty-nine-year-old had endured a strenuous climb into Hollywood's ranks. While other girls from her Santa Cruz High School graduating class settled into futures as housewives, ZaSu bid a tearful farewell to her mother at the local station and, lugging a tin suitcase, walked aboard a train for a three-hundred-fifty-mile journey south. After arriving in Los Angeles, the timorous girl with a brow-raising name—an amalgam inspired by her Aunts Eliza and Susan—scoured the city for film work. Her first break came when screenwriter Frances Marion noticed her in a casting office. Bit parts resulted, and ZaSu received honors for a minor role opposite Mary Pickford in *The Little Princess* (1917). Pressing through the setbacks that attended each victory, she continued taking any role offered, no matter how insignificant. Her inimitable manner of infusing comedy with pathos was noticed by directors, producers, and the public. By 1923, life was looking up; she worked steadily as a character actress and had a devoted following. She was the wife of a handsome actor, Tom Gallery, and the mother of a baby girl, also named ZaSu, but whom she called Ann.

ZaSu didn't permit her work to prevent her from mothering her daughter. Having given birth in April 1922, ZaSu was still nursing and, as she worked on *Souls for Sale* and *Mary of the Movies,* little Ann was a daily visitor at both studios. During breaks, in a secluded area away from the set, ZaSu lovingly collected her infant from her nanny for feedings.

It might have been ZaSu's affability that first drew Barbara to her. Maybe it was her compassion and tenderness that won Barbara's trust. Perhaps, too, the sight of ZaSu blissfully cuddling a baby nearly the same age as her own was more than Barbara could bear.

Barbara took a substantial risk. Each day around lunchtime, Irene Almond, Barbara's maid, entered the studio gates with a large picnic basket. Fielding any queries the basket aroused with the falsehood that Barbara was on a special diet, Almond made her way inside the studio to Barbara. Then, seated beside ZaSu and Ann, isolated from the rest of the cast and crew, Barbara received her son.[18]

In many ways, Barbara and ZaSu were polar opposites. ZaSu was described by one film magazine as being "as wholesome as milk"; she had an impeccable reputation, disdained drinking and smoking, and preferred her quiet home to Hollywood parties.[19] Her beauty was downplayed in the majority of her roles, affording her a career not contingent upon sex appeal. Yet, despite the women's differences, motherhood and a deepening friendship united them.

The mothers savored their private times together, nursing their babies and anticipating their futures. Barbara avowed that her son would receive a fine, character-building education, first in a religious school, then in a military academy. She envisioned exploring the world with him. She pondered various occupations for him, deciding she would support whatever he chose, even if he became an actor. Closest to Barbara's heart, however, was her pledge to make a good man of him. She promised she would bring him up to be the kind of man she always wanted to marry, but had yet to find.

Upon the bright horizon envisaged by Barbara hung a dark cloud of uncertainty. She confided her fears to ZaSu, mentioning the scheme whereby she would soon introduce Sonny to the world. ZaSu, who, like Barbara, had once entertained thoughts of becoming a nun, encouraged her to have faith. She brought to Barbara's mind the story of the infant Moses, another boy hidden in a basket. She assured Barbara she would be praying for her.[20]

Twenty

As Barbara prepared to reveal Sonny to the public, she wrestled with a quandary. Although she and Ben Deely had been separated nearly a year and a half, they had not divorced. As long as they remained married, Ben was, per California law, entitled to half of her earnings. Barbara sought to protect her son by preventing Ben from laying claim to her assets.

She took her concerns to her old friend, Constantino Riccardi. Their association spanned back to 1913, when she was called Folly and he—a suave, wealthy, young attorney—was an eminent man about town. He had since relocated to San Francisco and, sometime around January 1923, Barbara went north to meet with him and his associate, attorney Frank Drew. She conveyed her wishes concerning the settlement of her estate should anything happen to her. A generous sum was to be given to her parents. She wanted the remainder of all she had and would ever have placed in a trust fund for her son. Barbara also expressed her desire to be free of Ben and her apprehension regarding a divorce suit. Financial considerations aside, the resultant publicity—at a time when Arthur Sawyer was relying on her box office pull to negotiate contracts for her—would be damaging. Riccardi and Drew assured her they would investigate matters and notify her of her options.

Their findings must have seemed to Barbara almost too good to be true. They told her that, since she was not an Illinois resident when the Chicago judge granted her divorce from Philip Ainsworth, she had remained Mrs. Ainsworth until Philip's decree was finalized in 1920. Her marriage to Ben, taking place two years before she was officially divorced from Philip, they asserted, was therefore null and void. Barbara was also informed that a statute of limitations forever protected her from prosecution for fraud.

The solution to Barbara's problem, they determined, was thus relatively simple. They would present the facts of her two marriages to the Illinois court and obtain an annulment of her marriage to Ben. There was a potential hitch, however: they needed the cooperation of Philip Ainsworth.

Philip received a visit from Riccardi in Los Angeles February 7, 1923.[1] He was told that Barbara desired an annulment from her current marriage and that his signature, verifying the facts of his marriage to her, was required before proceedings could begin. Explaining Barbara's fear of unfavorable publicity, Riccardi told Philip that they needed him to sign the papers in San Francisco and that Barbara would give him $300 ($4,100 today) for helping her.

Philip, by his account, balked at the idea of leaving Los Angeles. That August, he had narrowly escaped imprisonment in San Quentin after passing a worthless $35.00 check off on a department store. He had begged the judge for leniency, blaming a handful of other bad checks he had written on the hard times that followed his show business career. His second wife and their son, born in 1918, were set to return to him if he would care for them. For the sake of Philip's family, the judge reluctantly released him on a two-year probation. Philip had maintained a job with a realty company since the hearing. Worried that a trip to San Francisco might constitute a parole violation, he allegedly told Riccardi he would have to consult his parole officer. Riccardi, Philip later contended, assured him there was no need to do so.

Philip related that he soon received a second unexpected visit from Riccardi. On Saturday afternoon, February 10, Riccardi presented him with a train ticket. Both men boarded a train for San Francisco that night.

After signing the papers in Riccardi's office on Sunday, Philip requested the $300 owed him. Riccardi told him he had not yet cashed Barbara's check. Since all banks would be closed the next day in observance of Lincoln's birthday, he promised Philip he would deposit the money to the bank of his choice Tuesday morning.

It was an empty promise. Philip was arrested on Thursday, after writing a useless $25 check for his hotel bill the night before. His frenzied attempts to reach Riccardi were unavailing; Riccardi had departed for Los Angeles. Philip was forced to plead his case alone in a San Francisco courtroom, avoiding prosecution by borrowing money to make the check good. He rehashed his ordeal with the hotel manager as he paid his bill. When the manager heard the name Riccardi, he proceeded to disclose all he knew about the man.

Twenty

Riccardi's career had been no less shocking in the years since 1914, when Los Angeles newspapers reported on his extramarital affairs (one of which, as mentioned previously, Barbara was implicated in) and embezzlement charges against him. After dodging criminal action when the prosecution's star witness mysteriously moved out of state, he left Los Angeles, elevating himself into powerful circles wherever he went. (He had earlier even worked alongside Thomas Marshall, vice-president of the United States from 1913 to 1921, during Marshall's successful campaign to become Indiana's governor in 1908.) He also amassed a criminal record. After Riccardi set up a law practice in St. Louis, the city's bar association pursued multiple allegations against him, which landed him in jail for swindling in 1916. Incredibly, he surfaced in Colorado that same year, similarly incensed the Denver Bar Association, and fled to San Francisco. There he joined a frame-up ring, later admitting to bribing judges and fixing juries. Following multiple accusations of corruption, Riccardi was disbarred by the San Francisco Bar Association in 1921.

Philip never saw his $300. Riccardi ultimately told him Barbara decided to forgo an annulment. In truth, her annulment was approved by an Illinois judge; she would receive official confirmation that April.

Riccardi, despite his disbarment, apparently continued servicing certain clients. After leaving Philip stranded in San Francisco and reaching Los Angeles, Riccardi went to Texas.[2]

Barbara would already be there by the time he arrived.

On January 27, Morelle Ratcliffe, publicity director for the third annual Southwestern Automobile Show and Food and Home Exposition in Texas, received an anxiously anticipated telegram from Los Angeles. Its contents gave him and the show's planning committee cause for celebration. When Ratcliffe and Dallas Automotive Trades Association officials initially discussed the entertainment line-up for their 1923 show, they were unanimous in their choice of a star to headline it. An invitation was enthusiastically dispatched to Los Angeles, negotiations proceeded, and an official acceptance was now in hand. Ratcliffe issued an immediate press release to local newspapers: Barbara La Marr to Appear in Dallas.

On a rainy evening the second week in February, Barbara slipped away to the train station after a farewell dinner attended by dozens of her film friends in a Los Angeles café. She had accepted her friends' well wishes with a smile, undoubtedly restraining a churning anxiety. Her appearance at the auto show was merely a ruse, masking the true motive of her trip. In reality, Barbara was preparing to wage her greatest gamble. From the time the idea of appearing at the auto show was presented to her, a secondary plan was afoot. Concealed in a private railroad car, Barbara, her son, Irene Almond (her maid), Bert Ennis (her press agent), Arthur Sawyer, and Virginia Carville rolled toward Dallas and an indeterminate future.[3]

The sight from the cabin windows as the train hissed to a stop at Union Station in Dallas the afternoon of February 11 surely quickened Barbara's heart. A sea of thousands jammed the platform and exits, waiting to welcome her. Her emergence from the train was met with thunderous cheering and winking flashbulbs. "Barbara La Marr is beautiful in front of the camera," a *Dallas Morning News* reporter would remark in the following morning's paper, "but no glass lens could hope to depict all her gorgeous appearance."[4] Accompanied on the platform only by Sawyer, Virginia, and her maid, Barbara was eagerly received by the auto show's organizers and a sizable cluster of prominent Dallas citizens. The foursome was escorted through the boisterous mob and whisked to the opulent Adolphus Hotel.

In her hotel suite, Barbara held court with her hosts and reporters. She told them her visit was a vacation. "I came here because I've never been in Texas before and I heard so much about Dallas," she said. "Then your committee was so insistent that I just couldn't refuse." Overwhelmed by the reception she received at the station, Barbara demurred, "I'm afraid you people will be disappointed in me."[5] Profuse objections erupted from her audience.

That evening, Barbara was shuttled to radio station WFAA to deliver a live broadcast. The first official radio broadcast in the United States in 1920 had generated a radio craze and, by 1923, millions of Americans tuned in daily for music, news, and advertising. Shortly after 10:00 p.m., Barbara leaned timidly toward the microphone. "This is Barbara La Marr speaking," she began, her voice crackling into living rooms throughout much of Texas, "and as this is the first time I have ever had the opportunity of speaking over the radio I hope that my audience will not be too critical."[6] Expressing her newfound love for the Lone Star State, she extended an invitation for her listeners to meet her at the auto exposition.

Barbara's voice rang out over the WFAA airwaves again the next night, formally opening the week-long 1923 Southwestern Automobile Show in a live broadcast from the Fair Park fairgrounds. Along with perusing the

Twenty

rows of gleaming automobiles, Barbara met her fans upon a courtyard stage each afternoon and evening. The flood of people anxious to shake her hand and have a friendly word never slackened—housewives, polished businessmen, bashful children gripping their mothers' skirts, factory workers, teenaged aspirants to fame and fortune, the elderly... There were so many, she couldn't meet them all.

Barbara cut her afternoon appearance short February 15. Assuring her fans she would return that evening, she explained that she had accepted an invitation to visit Hope Cottage, an orphans' home.

A labor of love undertaken by Emma Wylie Ballard, the cottage had opened in 1918, during an era when the disgrace of illegitimacy resulted in a distressing number of abandoned infants. Soon in dire straits with more babies than her makeshift location could handle, Ballard relocated to a Presbyterian mission home, but continued struggling with overcrowding and limited finances. Though Hope Cottage had secured permanent homes for hundreds of children, its future looked bleak by 1922.

But February of 1922 brought a reversal of fortune. Zebina E. ("Zeke") Marvin, Dallas businessman, millionaire, and charity organizer, intervened. Marvin and the Dallas chapter of the Ku Klux Klan—of which he was grand titan—donated $50,000 to construct a spacious, permanent site for Hope Cottage. Marvin was made president of the cottage, and a grateful Ballard would take possession of her new location in October 1923.

Barbara's visit to Hope Cottage had been masterminded, in part, by Marvin. Upon her arrival at the cottage, he introduced her to Ballard. He and Ballard then guided her, followed closely by Sawyer and Ennis, through a tour of their orphanage.

Barbara walked among the babies' cribs with tears in her eyes. Ballard, perceiving her tears to be those of a "childless woman with a big mother heart," was overcome with sympathy. As they continued through the rooms, Barbara held some of the babies, expressing her love for children and appreciation to Ballard and her staff for their dedication to their cause. Her "gentle, unaffected manner" and genuine concern for the infants, Ballard later related, "won the hearts of all the nurses and attendants."[7]

Barbara scanned each tiny face, then she saw him: a blue-eyed seven-month-old with tufts of blonde hair. Her precious Sonny. Reaching down, she took him in her arms. She sat with him on the nursery floor, playing and laughing with him, calling him Sonny. Ballard and her nurses certainly detected the mutual adoration between them. Barbara eased him back into the crib—and steeled herself for a monumental performance.

She announced her firm intention to adopt him. Her plans for him were "as high as the blue sky," Ballard recalled.[8]

Marvin conducted Barbara to the orphanage's office and closed the door. Adoption papers were already waiting. Barbara signed them.[9]

Four months after Barbara's death, Bert Ennis, attempting to circumvent the "unkind rumors" that asserted that Barbara adopted her own son, wrote "The Truth about Barbara's Baby" for the June 1926 issue of *Pictures* magazine. He stated in the article that Barbara and Sonny bore no blood relation and that he himself engineered the adoption as a publicity stunt. He offered a copy of the adoption papers to support his assertion. Was he attempting to preserve Barbara's memory and, along with it, the profitability of her films, which were still circulating at the time? Absolving from blame those who facilitated the scheme? Deflecting a sorely unneeded industry scandal? Safeguarding Barbara's son against the burden of stigma? Ennis, who remained Barbara's publicist and business confidant until her death, was clearly protecting someone.

Yet contained within Ennis's article are underpinnings of truth. Sawyer, Ennis stated, feared the effect motherhood would have on Barbara's career. He worried that her fans, who worshipped her as a vamp, would reject her as a mother.

Sawyer's fears were warranted. Image was everything for 1920s film actors. Writer Peter Kobel has compared silent era stars to godlike beings in a supernatural realm, stating, "There were not yet paparazzi photos of actors going grocery shopping without makeup, bringing them down to earth, or ritualized televised confessions, like those with Barbara Walters."[10] After the Roscoe Arbuckle scandal, *Motion Picture News* writer William Johnston implored actors to guard their screen images. "You belong to the public. You have given them an illusion," he wrote. "They think of you not as you are but as they dream you are." For the sake of those depending upon that illusion to fill theaters, Johnston admonished: "Let only your screen personality be seen and known . . . [or] the same forces that made you will rise up and put you out of business overnight, destroy you in the same magic way you were created."[11]

Barbara later informed a friend that she would one day tell her son she was his real mother and that, for professional purposes, she led the world to believe he was adopted. Ennis may have come up with the idea to stage the adoption. Sawyer, in contemplating possible public reaction to Barbara as an unwed mother as opposed to that of her as an adoptive mother, doubtlessly preferred to take his chances with the latter.

Barbara, Sawyer, and Ennis knew what they were up against. In 1923, California law prohibited single women from adopting within the state. Pulling off their plan required greater assistance than any of them had at their immediate disposal. That Constantino Riccardi, Barbara's attorney, went to Texas at the same time she did suggests that he had a role in connecting her to Zeke Marvin—a man who, like Riccardi, had strong political ties. According to Barbara's son (who met with Virginia Carville before her death in 1982), Marvin was instrumental in orchestrating the staged adoption and putting it through. Virginia's role in the plot was to ensure Sonny's placement in Hope Cottage by secretly delivering him to Marvin.

All involved anticipated that, once news of the adoption hit, reporters would turn out in full force. They were ready for them. The adoption papers bearing Barbara's signature were filed at the Dallas county courthouse the morning after she signed them. A document contained in Sonny's Hope Cottage file, typed on Marvin's personal letterhead and titled "Barbara La Marr Baby," presents the boy's (falsified) date of entry to the cottage: August 11, 1922. A Hope Cottage intake form for an infant purported to be Sonny includes an alleged birth date, the name of a local hospital, and the names of two Texans—his supposed birth parents. This same infant is said, per Hope Cottage records, to have had his birth name changed by the staff to simply "Marvin" upon his arrival. Also in the boy's Hope Cottage file is a medical exam report, reputedly conducted at the cottage September 21, 1922, when Sonny would have been around two and a half months old—and recording him as weighing a mere eight pounds and eight ounces.[12]

Those involved in the scheme awaited the breaking of the story.

With Virginia by her side, Barbara returned to Hope Cottage the morning after her visit. She left with her son. Dallas reporters were already on their trail. No longer compelled to hide her beloved boy, Barbara proudly introduced him as Marvin Carville La Marr (his middle name was chosen in honor of Virginia). She told reporters he was born on her birthday, July 28, in 1922. (Decades later, in order to enlist in the Army Air Corps, he requested a birth certificate from Hope Cottage and received three different birth certificates—all with conflicting dates of birth and all guaranteed to be correct.) Apparently attempting to throw off suspicions by justifying the adoption, Barbara told a fib: "He will take the place of my own baby who did not live," she stated. She then mentioned her intention to make him her sole priority. "I shall never marry again," she insisted, "and Marvin will have the best of everything and a mother's love." Engulfed by a wave of maternal adoration, she declared, "He is just the cutest and sweetest baby in the whole world."[13]

At the auto show the same evening after reporters seized the story, a particularly electrifying ovation accompanied Barbara when she walked onstage for her regularly scheduled appearance. One of the largest crowds of the week had turned out to see her.

Come Sunday, the final day of the show, Barbara had, according to the *Dallas Morning News*, taken the city by storm with her adoption of "the luckiest boy in Dixie." The paper likened her to a "queenly mother" who rescued a destitute waif "in no less a fairy fashion than was wont in the days of good King Arthur."[14]

Barbara stood upon her auto show stage for the last time that Sunday evening, her eyes rimmed with tears of gratitude. Below, an expanse of adoring faces awaited her farewell address. Her week in Dallas, she began, had been the most thrilling of her life. She thanked the Dallas auto dealers for inviting her to Texas and enabling her to meet her son. Overpowered by an upsurging of emotion, she kissed her fingertips to the crowd and descended the stage amidst tremendous applause.

Following a three-day stop in San Antonio for personal appearances at the Princess Theater, Barbara and her companions left Texas. The reactions of Barbara's Texas fans were encouraging; motherhood had seemingly enhanced her public appeal. There was still no way of knowing, however, how the rest of the world would react to the news.

After exiting her railroad car at the station in Los Angeles, cradling her son in her arms, Barbara would find out.

Twenty-One

Most of Hollywood was no less astounded by Barbara adopting a son than Texans had been. Columnists credited her with providing the biggest surprise to come out of filmdom that year. Reporters vied for interviews but were temporarily disappointed. Barbara's so-called vacation ended the moment she returned to Los Angeles; she headed back to work.

Arthur Sawyer's strategy for increasing Barbara's earning capacity and star power by spreading her services among multiple studios had resulted in several contracts. Though Barbara had proven herself an actress of substantial emotional depth in movingly "human" roles in *The Hero* and *Poor Men's Wives,* Sawyer was taking a different route. While many critics praised her acting in these roles, not everyone believed they showcased her at her best. *Picture Play* deemed her "atrociously miscast" in *Poor Men's Wives,* adding, "if anyone is fit for velvets and brocades it is the exotic Barbara."[1] *Movie Weekly* and *Photoplay* concurred: "she is at her best with a background of gorgeous gowns," said the former, while the latter felt she was "not so impressive in shabby frocks."[2] Sawyer had reached a similar conclusion. He was determined to capitalize upon Barbara's beauty and her ability to embody seductive, iniquitous types.

Temptress-turned-murderess Camille Lenoir in *The Eternal Struggle,* a Louis B. Mayer production, seemed an ideal match. Barbara was prolific Canadian director Reginald Barker's first choice for the role, and what had been planned as a minor part was enlarged after she agreed to play it. Her weekly salary was reported as $2,500; in reality, she received $800 per week (about $11,000 today).[3] (The higher figure might have been planted by publicist Bert Ennis to assist Sawyer as he negotiated contracts for Barbara elsewhere.)

Filming of *The Eternal Struggle* was underway by mid-March in Los Angeles and Alberta, Canada. The film's heroine, Andrée Grange (Renée Adorée), believing she has killed fur trader and drunkard Barode Dukane (Wallace Beery), flees north through the Canadian wilderness. Two Northwest Mounted Policemen (played by Pat O'Malley and Earle Williams), both in love with Andrée, pursue her, one intending to arrest her, the other to help her escape; eventually Andrée is brought back to account for Barode's death. Barbara, as Barode's fiancée, Camille Lenoir, fuels the conflict and enables the requisite happy ending. Admitting that she secretly witnessed Barode assaulting Andrée and that Andrée merely knocked him unconscious, Camille confesses to jealously murdering him.

Between takes, Barbara shed Camille's licentiousness, becoming the image of tenderness. Waiting for her off the set with his nurse or his grandmother Rose was Sonny. Paraded around the studio in Barbara's arms, the child made many friends with his perpetual cheerfulness. He "never cries as long as there is anything to see," Barbara explained.[4] A visiting reporter captured one of the first official glimpses of mother and son.

The Eternal Struggle, released that September, encountered moderate success and mixed reviews. Many critics faulted the film's clichéd story line.

The impact the film had upon Barbara's career was negligible. *Film Daily* insisted she was "shoved into more or less obscurity in a role that gives her very little opportunity to overshadow the work of Miss Adorée."[5] There were, of course, the usual disagreements; several reviewers saluted her performance and *Movie Weekly* proclaimed that "no picture requiring a dark-eyed adventuress is complete these days without Barbara La Marr."[6] Sawyer's formula was holding, at least.

One spring morning after Barbara finished filming *The Eternal Struggle,* *Movie Weekly* journalist Grace Kingsley ascended a winding road, between Highland Avenue and Cahuenga Boulevard, into the hills of Hollywood. The city sprawled beneath her as her car rolled through a majestic subdivision. Luxurious homes fanned out along the hillside, linked by white, palm-tree-lined avenues. Near the center of the community, a row of colossal electric letters, visible at night from over five miles away, towered above the most exclusive real estate in Los Angeles: WHITLEY HEIGHTS.

The pièce de résistance of real estate magnate Hobart Johnstone Whitley, the area was masterfully replicated from Spanish and Italian hillside architecture. Standing two or three stories high, the dwellings, most topped with red tile roofs and finished with cream-colored stucco, featured arched entryways, secluded courtyards, hanging balconies, and ornamental iron detailing. Vibrant gardens encircled each villa, roses clung to fences, and bougainvillea twined upward along exterior walls.

Cuddling her boy during a break in filming *The Eternal Struggle*. Photo by J. C. Milligan.

Spectacular views accompanied each residence, sweeping outward in all directions. Occupants gazed upon immaculately manicured lawns, lush shrubbery, and, in the distance, the gleaming Pacific Ocean. In planning for the vistas, telephone and power lines had been placed underground—an innovation in development. To maximize views of the glittering cityscape just beyond the foothills, the boulevards were lit each evening by the gentle glow of gas streetlamps.

By 1923, Whitley Heights was host to a colony of screen idols. Their glamorous lifestyles imbued the area with elegance; tales of their lavish parties grew to mythical proportions. It was rumored that a grand ballroom—accessible only through a secret passageway within various homes—existed inside one of the community's hills. On a bright afternoon, a bus crammed with star-struck sightseers might be found looping along the hillside, the names of the neighborhood notables rippling through the air from a megaphone: Eleanor Boardman . . . Eugene O'Brien . . . Francis X. Bushman . . . Marie Dressler . . . Blanche Sweet . . . Rudolph Valentino . . .

Kingsley's car stopped in front of a two-story sienna house, partly shaded beneath eucalyptus trees, at 6672 Whitley Terrace. It was the recently built home of one of the subdivision's newer residents, Barbara La Marr. From the road, Kingsley descended the steps leading to the entry. It's possible she noticed Barbara's red Paige-Daytona convertible roadster—direct from one of the auto dealers Barbara met in Dallas—along the roadside.

The joyful pride Barbara felt for her house—the first true home she had known—was evident to Kingsley. The journalist hardly blamed her. "It's a dream of a home," Kingsley gushed.[7] Inside the front entryway, a vaulted ceiling arched high above the living room. A fireplace and paintings adorned one wall. A domed window, inset with the letter "B" and French doors, extended across another. Through it, one could look down and see Valentino's house; in another direction, gigantic letters spelling out HOLLYWOODLAND would soon be visible on the hill. The room was beautifully furnished, yet comfortably inviting. A baby grand piano stood in one corner, for the increasingly rare evenings when Barbara had time to play.

In keeping with the unconventional floor plans characteristic of Whitley Heights, three of the house's four bedrooms were on the ground floor. Barbara's bedroom was at the end of a hallway leading from the living

Twenty-One

View of Barbara's Whitley Heights home in the 1920s, from the top of the staircase leading from the street.

room. Her haven after a trying day of filming, it was decorated in soft shades of blue and green. Her single bed was positioned beneath an airy window, and a chaise lounge—perfect for reading her books—rested at its foot.

As with other film stars' houses in the area, whispers of outrageous opulence swirled around Barbara's. Her bathroom (one of two in the

Russell Ball photograph of Barbara beside her piano.

house) was fashioned entirely from onyx, it was said, and boasted a massive sunken tub with solid gold fixtures. Whether this was true is debatable; when her son visited the house in the 1980s, he found no evidence of such extravagance.

Upstairs, a special room was in progress. When finished, the bright space would be painted baby blue and white, with Mother Goose figures along each wall. Barbara explained to Kingsley that the room was her son's nursery.

Barbara's house had a component Kingsley was likely unaware of. Barbara's son, during his 1980s visit to the house, paused beside a section of hallway connecting the living room to Barbara's bedroom. A vague memory of being placed behind a secret door somewhere along the hallway wall flickered through his mind. He voiced his recollection to the house's owner (at that time, an Arco executive), and the man eyed him curiously. When a remodeling of the house occurred, the executive explained, the renovators discovered such a door. Proceeding inside, the workers followed a narrow, dusty staircase to a small room containing a bed and

Twenty-One

heaps of old booze bottles. Evidently, earlier occupants had used the space to house their drunken mother. Barbara intended it for a different purpose. Threats from would-be kidnappers were an ongoing source of fear for stars with children. Sonny's nanny was well aware of the hidden door and room. "Guard Sonny with your life," Barbara admonished Sonny's caregivers.[8]

As charmed as Kingsley was by Barbara's home, it wasn't the reason for her visit. Seated in the living room, she turned her attention to the subjects of her interview: Barbara and her baby. Seeing Barbara clad in a matronly apron and fretting over the temperature of a baby bottle, Kingsley would relate in her article, "World's Wickedest Vamp Adopts a Baby," was a sight to behold. (In truth, Kingsley was touched by Barbara's maternal devotion. She later remarked that, despite Sonny's dutiful nurse, "Barbara can never hear that baby cry without rushing to him.")[9]

Kingsley's interview with Barbara drifted into a conversation about child rearing. Always one to eschew rules, Barbara confessed to following her own parenting practices. Common schools of thought in the early twentieth century, warning against spoiling children, advised parents to minimize affection in favor of a strict, regimented approach. Barbara dismissed the methodology, refusing to raise a "system baby." She informed Kingsley that, while she wouldn't abide thumb sucking, she rocked her son and sang him lullabies. In a subsequent interview with Kingsley, Barbara reiterated her stance on comforting her child whenever she felt he needed it, adding, "Hang take the old systems that won't let a blessed baby do anything he wants to!"[10] Barbara was also unopposed to waking him in order to show him off to friends she entertained certain evenings. The little fellow enjoyed it, she assured Kingsley, and had no trouble going back to sleep.

Shifting the topic to the adoption, Kingsley innocently veered into sensitive territory. She inquired about Sonny's birth parents. Barbara initially turned away as she answered, diverting her eyes to her compact mirror. "His mother is a college-bred woman, a lovely girl," she began, "and his father is of good blood, too." She told Kingsley that the birth parents were separated at the time of Sonny's placement in Hope Cottage. His mother, she continued, lacked the means to give him a quality life, and the father "didn't wish to do anything unless he could own the child."[11]

Kingsley had no further questions regarding the adoption; Barbara knew, however, that others did. That May, *Photoplay* would run an article entitled "Why I Adopted a Baby" by Barbara La Marr. In the article, Barbara swallowed her motherly pride and, in her poetic fashion (and doubtless with guidance from publicist Bert Ennis), told the story the way she wanted it told. "I took this little, trusting man-child that nobody wanted out of a foundling home," she wrote, "because my heart was empty and my soul needed an altar upon which to sacrifice." She needed him, she explained, to fill the void in her lonely life.[12]

Melding invention with reality, Barbara charted the depths of that loneliness. Restating her oft-repeated falsehood that she herself had been adopted, she professed a yearning for something that was hers alone. She also repeated the untruth she had presented to Dallas reporters: that she had had a boy who died (in another newspaper interview, she places the death of this fictitious child as occurring two years earlier). His silenced voice still haunted her, she related, and not a day had passed since his death that she hadn't longed to clutch a baby to her breast.

She then ventured closer to the bone, detailing her unfulfilled longing for genuine love from a man. "I am sick of men," she proclaimed. "The admiration of men. The so-called love of men . . . Men's love is most unsatisfactory, the most disillusioning thing in life. The little girl who has only one beau, who grows up and marries him, and keeps her ignorance and her faith in men, is the lucky girl. Not the woman whom the world may call fortunate because men flock to her feet . . . The desire of men leaves you stranded on a sea of fear and loneliness and self-loathing."

She addressed those who questioned a screen vamp's suitability for motherhood. Mother love, she wrote, "doesn't belong exclusively to any little circle of women who look blonde and spiritual and perfect. You can't put a fence around [it] and say—this kind of women shall have it, and this shan't. No. I have seen it in the gutter and I've seen it in palaces. I've seen it shining in the eyes of some worn, flat-chested spinster. I've seen it still glorified in the eyes of women who had sold or sacrificed or been robbed of every other glory . . . I'm not willing to admit that because I've got black hair and green eyes and what they call beauty, I'm not going to make a good mother to my son."

Barbara asserted that her son was hers, so far as she was concerned. "I shall never tell him that he isn't, either," she added. "And I think I'd kill anyone that did."

While Barbara's article succeeded in winning many over to her cause, she had her detractors. "Not a real mother," "publicity adopter of orphan

Twenty-One

"There is more motherhood in my little finger than in the whole body of the majority of mothers," declared Barbara in the *Oakland Tribune*, April 17, 1924.

babies," "unfit mother"—were but a few of the gibes she endured.[13] Many times, she countered such insensitivity with grace, relying on her sense of humor. When a young flapper inquired at a party, "Oh Miss La Marr, what in the world will *you* do with an adopted baby?" Barbara responded, "My dear girl, what did you think I'd do with it—put it in a bird cage?"[14] Barbara was unashamed to admit, however, to losing her temper on other occasions. She once unleashed her wrath upon a journalist during an interview after the woman, giggling, remarked that she found Barbara's adoption of a baby to be funny. "Nobody can say to me that they think my baby is funny," averred Barbara when she recounted the incident later.[15]

Alone with her son in their home, Barbara discarded the illusion of his adoption and enjoyed her secret reality. Collecting Sonny in her arms, she often sat on her sun porch after dinner. There, with the cool evening breeze ruffling through the canyon, she sometimes encountered her neighbors, Hobart Whitley and his wife, out for their walk. Mrs. Whitley recalled, "She was always so happy holding the baby, a beautiful smile gracing her face."[16]

Barbara's career and screen image showed no indications of being adversely affected by motherhood. The contracts Sawyer secured for her before their Texas trip remained in place. Bidding for Barbara's services increased, Sawyer continued negotiations on her behalf, and additional contracts poured in. Barbara had never been busier.

Concurrent with Barbara's *Eternal Struggle* contract with Louis B. Mayer was a contract for a second Mayer film, *Strangers of the Night*. She arrived at the studio with Sonny when filming began in April 1923, receiving $600 per week for the film.[17]

Directed by Fred Niblo, the story, a rousing fusion of satire, mystery, and action, begins along a desolate stretch of English coastline (in reality, California). Faint-hearted aristocrat Ambrose Applejohn (Matt Moore), aching for excitement, gets more than he bargained for when Russian thieves—Anna Valeska (Barbara) and Borolsky (Robert McKim)—arrive at his mansion one night, seeking the hidden treasure of Captain Applejack, Ambrose's pirate ancestor and onetime occupant of the mansion. Temporarily evading them, Ambrose falls asleep and dreams he's the gallant Captain Applejack (also played by Moore) aboard a ship, quashing a mutiny and winning the affections of his captive (also portrayed by Barbara). Emboldened by his dream, Ambrose outwits the thieves and finds the treasure.

Strangers of the Night was released that September to general adoration. Niblo was thankful to have had Barbara; he enjoyed directing her in *The Three Musketeers* and was adamant that she play Anna Valeska. Critics, pleased with the results of their collaboration, consistently affirmed the greatness of Barbara's work; *Moving Picture World* remarked that it was some of the finest of her career to date.[18]

Before completing *Strangers of the Night*, Barbara began work at United Studios on *The Brass Bottle*, a Maurice Tourneur production. Her role, though minor, was evidently demanding: the *Dallas Morning News* reported that she had the "hard job of vamping a king with a thousand jealous wives as competition."[19]

Her acceptance of the role was certainly strategic. French-born producer-director Maurice Tourneur, following the tremendous success of his film *The Last of the Mohicans* (1920), was regarded as one of the world's top directors, his ingenious filmmaking considered on a par with that of the prodigious D. W. Griffith. Struggling to kowtow to the demand for assembly-line films at his Hollywood-based production company, he remained

Twenty-One

(*Left*) Barbara as Anna Valeska (with Matt Moore) and (*right*) as the "haughty wench" in Ambrose's dream, from *Strangers of the Night* (1923). Photo at right from the collections of the Margaret Herrick Library, Academy of Motion Picture Arts and Sciences.

true to his matchless artistic vision and his infatuation with the bizarre and outlandish.

The Brass Bottle, a comical tale well suited to Tourneur's inclinations, was richly enhanced by his superlative camera effects and elaborate staging. Partially set in the distant past during the reign of King Suleyman (Sam De Grasse), the film opens with Suleyman's genie (Ernest Torrence) conspiring to run away with his illicit lover, the Queen (Barbara). Suleyman imprisons the genie in a bottle and casts him into the sea. Thousands of years later, Horace Ventimore (Harry Myers), a hapless London architect, finds the bottle, frees the genie, and unleashes bedlam as the grateful genie goes to extremes fulfilling Horace's every desire.

The Brass Bottle provoked strong reactions following its July 1923 release. Some critics, crediting the actors' performances and Tourneur's exquisite composition, applauded it. Others pronounced it a freakishly preposterous fiasco.

Although Barbara received respectable notices from certain critics, her brief appearance was largely unreferenced in reviews. Her association with Tourneur would nonetheless pay off; she would work with him again in a much larger role.

(*Left to right*) Nigel De Brulier, Barbara, John Gilbert, and Warner Baxter in *St. Elmo* (1923).

Barbara completed an additional film that spring, rushing from the set of *The Brass Bottle* to the Fox studio for *St. Elmo,* a film derived from Augusta Jane Evans's 1867 best-selling tale of passion and infidelity. Director Jerome Storm, banking on the story's success as a novel, selected leading screen lover John Gilbert, Barbara's former beau, for the role of plantation owner St. Elmo Thornton. Barbara was cast opposite him as Agnes Hunt, St. Elmo's lustful fiancée.

Using St. Elmo's love to her own selfish end, Agnes agrees to marry him in order to obtain his money and elope with his best friend, Murray Hammond (Warner Baxter). Discovering their betrayal, St. Elmo kills Murray and roams the world a broken man, his faith in humanity destroyed. Eventually returning to his plantation, he learns to love again, becomes a minister, and marries Edna Earle (Bessie Love).

Released that August, the film didn't translate to the modern generation—although many grandparents enjoyed it. Critics panned it, citing an "old fashioned" story and lack of action.[20] Barbara's heated characterization of Agnes, by contrast, drew positive notices. Her performance was

Twenty-One

praised as exceptional, "an impressive portrayal of a woman who gives herself with impassioned vehemence from one man to another."[21]

Barbara's career was progressing according to Sawyer's plan. Newspapers nationwide were likening her quick rise to Valentino's. It was said that she was encroaching upon Gloria Swanson's reign as the screen's eminent vamp. The hype generated by Barbara's recent string of films was exactly what Sawyer needed. He entered into secret negotiations for various contracts for her—one of which, if successful, would cinch her stardom.

Barbara had never been happier in her professional life. The constant work had been arduous, but entirely worth it to her. She was pleased with Sawyer's efforts. "I have had one great director after another," she related to fellow actress Helen Ferguson. "I love every moment of the work I have done—love every inch of the progress I have made."[22]

Barbara's private life was another matter.

Twenty-Two

By the time Barbara returned from Texas in late February 1923, her romance with Paul Bern had cooled. His feelings for her hadn't. He remained in her life as one of her closest friends, fostering her faith in her abilities as her career ascended. After he joined Louis B. Mayer's writing staff that March (around the time Barbara began *The Eternal Struggle,* the first of her two Mayer films), mutual friends swapped stories of the great lengths to which he often went for her. One rumor held that he raked Hollywood in the middle of the night to secure bootleg liquor for one of her get-togethers, even though he hadn't been invited to attend. Some questioned his continued concern for her. Paul justified his actions. "Barbara has a lamentable taste in lovers," he said, and "needs protection."[1] Be that as it may, Paul's empathetic ears hadn't borne the last of Barbara's romantic woes.

The first week in March, a surprising report surfaced in a rash of newspaper articles: Barbara was engaged. Less than two weeks had elapsed since she exited Hope Cottage and voiced her intention never to marry again. Reportedly, her groom-to-be was Wallace Beery, Hollywood villain and her *Eternal Struggle* costar.[2] A marriage never took place between them. Their engagement (assuming that news of it was not in error) was soon broken.

At some point that spring, Barbara plunged into a relationship with Hollywood newcomer William Haines. By the late 1920s, at the pinnacle of his screen career, Haines would rule the box office with his captivating looks, vivacious wit, and swaggering charm. In 1923, his stardom was a few years off. Less than a year earlier, the twenty-three-year-old Virginian had stepped off a train from New York to claim his prize for winning a "new faces" contest: a $40-a-week contract with the Goldwyn studio. He walked into Goldwyn's Los Angeles branch—his nose swelled by a dreadful cold, his lips singed from traveling through the desert—and, standing on wobbling knees and with as much valor as he could rally, announced, "I'm your new prize beauty." He was in for a rude awakening. Contest win-

Twenty-Two

ners, he later related, were as common in Los Angeles "as coal miners in Pennsylvania."[3] Shoved into uncredited roles and eking out an existence, Haines despaired.

It's believed that Haines met Barbara through Paul Bern, although Haines worked with her in February when he played a bit part in Goldwyn's *Souls for Sale*. As the three friends socialized at various public events, Barbara and Haines formed an intense connection. He was, like her, deeply sensitive, a lover of excitement, a dreamer. His impish humor made her laugh; his underlying pain called to her. "She encouraged me and made me believe in myself," remembered Haines. "She was a wonderful woman."[4]

Though Haines's homosexuality was an open secret among his friends, Barbara fell in love with him. Haines, entranced by her mesmerizing persona and intoxicated by her feminine magnetism, seemingly returned her feelings.

It was the second time Haines had fallen for a woman. During his days in New York as a bookkeeper for an investment banking company, a wealthy society woman nearly two decades his senior became his friend and, months later, his lover and sole support. By the time he left for California, however, they had drifted apart. Haines had, he said, grown "restless."[5]

It seems probable that Haines had a sexual relationship with Barbara. "Oh, yes, I think so," Haines's employee and "surrogate son," Ted Graber, conveyed to Haines's biographer, William J. Mann. "She was a great, great beauty. There was something between them for a while."[6]

That "something" came to a shrieking halt in early May. Their relationship ended, according to Haines, "in a quarrel."[7] Any possibility of a friendship shattered with it; they would never speak to or see each other again. While Haines provides no further insight into their breakup, Barbara possibly offers a clue. The pain of their terminated affair likely lingered in her heart when the *Movie Weekly* chronicle of her life story was published a little over a year later. "I don't have violent dislikes," it is written in the article, presumably by her. "Someone has to humiliate me to make me dislike them. And I never forget a humiliation. NEVER. When I say I'm through, I'm the *most* through person you've ever seen."[8]

Haines intimated no such bitterness toward Barbara. "He always spoke highly of her," said Ted Graber.[9] In a 1929 interview after Barbara's death, Haines credited Barbara with being one of three women who would always

William Haines, 1925.

mean the most to him. The second was the woman he had loved in New York; the first was his mother.

Losing the closeness he shared with Barbara was painful for Haines. "Romances are interesting, but friendships are better," he said. "They seem to last longer."[10] Minus Barbara's companionship and unsure of career success, he considered returning to New York. Providence stepped in: lacking money for train fare, he stayed in Los Angeles, determined to remain as long as it took.

Barbara dealt with the pain in another way. What Haines couldn't give her, she would get somewhere else. On May 5, three days after the quarrel that destroyed her relationship with Haines, she did something rash.

Jack Daugherty had had a hell of a day. As an actor and stunt man in two-reel westerns at Universal, the strapping twenty-seven-year-old regularly

Twenty-Two

defied danger. In one film, he plunged from a plane and landed on a speeding motorcycle. He exercised by galloping down the road on his horse, balancing atop the saddle on his hands and performing other rodeo tricks. An on-set accident Saturday, May 5, 1923, however, almost killed him. The horse he was riding reared up and fell backward on top of him. Somehow Jack managed to walk away from the scene. But as the adrenaline faded and the day wore on, pain gripped him. All the same, he kept his dinner date with Barbara. He arrived at her house just after six and limped down the stairs to her front door. His day was about to get better.

Barbara greeted him with a bombshell. "You're going to be married tonight," she said. His mouth fell open. A lone word escaped his lips: "Huh!"[11] It was the moment he had been dreaming of.

The first time Jack saw Barbara was in Chicago during her dancing days, after he had left his Missouri hometown and settled in the city as a stockyard clerk. He served as a Marine in World War I, performed with theater companies, and began working in films before finally meeting her in Los Angeles in late 1921.[12] They met, according to him, while engaged in their respective film work. After their meeting, he was officially a goner. "I was insane about Barbara," he said, declaring her the most charming woman he ever met.[13] He resolved to make her his wife, but had quite a time of it. I "was so deeply in love, I couldn't even think of the [films] I was doing," he said, "—and was desperately trying to marshal up enough courage to propose."[14]

Only Barbara knows what prompted her sudden decision to marry Jack Daugherty. She later confessed to being intensely attracted to the freckle-faced, six-foot-one-inch Irishman at first sight. It was his head of wavy, blazing-red hair that initially did her in, she said. He was, according to her, a refreshing change from other men she had known. Not once had he resorted to idle flattery to win her. Nor did he have misgivings about taking charge when he believed it was in her best interest. "He is able to boss others in the nicest way," she conceded. "Perhaps I was looking for a good boss all the time. All the others took the obvious way of trying to please me . . . But being petted like a wax doll was probably the wrong thing for me. And Jack understands." There was something, too, about his blue eyes and his concern for her well-being that was reassuring. "He has been shoulder to all my burdens," she related.[15]

As Jack regained his senses and the import of Barbara's announcement sunk in, all thoughts of dinner likely flew from his mind. Barbara had reportedly been notified by her attorneys five days earlier that the annulment of her marriage to Ben Deely had been authorized. She instructed Jack to make arrangements for their wedding that very evening. He hobbled off to attend to the details; she telephoned her mother and a few friends, sharing her news and swearing everyone to secrecy.

Jack, meanwhile, encountered his first hindrance. He was unable to secure a marriage license in Los Angeles, doubtless because the courthouse was closed. Paul Bern stepped in. With Paul's assistance, a license was obtained in Ventura, an oceanside town roughly seventy miles north. Rousing a leading Hollywood jeweler from sleep, Paul also bought Barbara's wedding ring. Purportedly, Jack lacked funds to purchase the ring himself. Paul additionally procured bootleg liquor for the postwedding merriment.[16]

It was necessary for Barbara and Jack to stop by the Ventura County clerk's residence to pick up their license. It was past 10:00 p.m. when they arrived. A *Los Angeles Times* reporter, somehow learning of their elopement, had beaten them there. Barbara candidly admitted all. "I had made up my mind to marry Jack some day," she divulged, "but at noon today I had no more idea of marrying him than—well—than of marrying you. Then—well—I just decided."[17]

The couple drove to the parsonage of the Reverend T. W. Patterson. Shortly after 11:00 p.m. Barbara, dressed in a deep blue sport suit and matching hat, became Mrs. Virgil Ashley Daugherty (the name "Jack" was adopted for the movies). Paul served as best man. Rose and Barbara's brother Billy—aside from the reverend, the *Los Angeles Times* reporter, and their wives—were the only other witnesses.[18]

Barbara and Jack departed the reverend's home alone, driving northward to Santa Barbara. Reservations had been made for them at the Hotel Samarkand, a Persian-themed resort whose name meant "land of heart's desire" in ancient Persian. Reaching the hotel around 1:00 a.m., they went directly to their suite for their own private celebration. They returned to work that Monday.

In the months following her marriage to Jack, Barbara would face other reporters; many reminded her of her avowal to never marry again. "I certainly was through that time," she admitted to one. "But any woman who says she won't marry again is just a plain fool—of course she will, when something like Jack's adorable hair strikes her."[19] To another, she asserted, "No girl should get married before she is twenty-four; those that

Twenty-Two

Barbara, Jack, and Sonny on the porch steps of their Whitley Heights home. Russell Ball photo.

do don't know what their real ideal at that age will be. Divorce may be an evil but it certainly makes one appreciate a good husband afterwards." She confessed to waiting a long time and enduring tremendous suffering, scandal, and bad publicity to find her ideal. "I certainly have found it in Jack," she declared.[20] "This time it's going to stick."[21]

While news of Barbara's elopement was being printed nationwide, another report was spreading. On April 30, Philip Ainsworth was again hauled into a courtroom. His trip to San Francisco that February, to sign papers enabling the annulment of Barbara's marriage to Ben Deely, had cost him. The judge asked Philip to account for violating the two-year probation granted him following his issuance of a bad check in 1922. Philip's explanation—that Barbara wanted to avoid negative publicity in Los Angeles, and that Constantino Riccardi, her attorney, tricked him into going by assuring him he would not be violating parole—garnered no sympathy. Nor did a $15 check he forged that January. Philip was sentenced to a term in San Quentin.

231

A reporter sought Barbara out, eager for a comment. Apprised of the bad checks Philip had written, she remarked, "That's one of his favorite outdoor sports."[22]

Philip's term in San Quentin was one of several prison stays. Released on probation after serving eighteen months, he laid carpets by day and hoofed across Los Angeles dance floors at night until he was arrested again in 1926. He had forged his mother's name to a $15 check, five days before his parole expired. After a year, he was discharged from Folsom Prison and found work as a salesman, but his attempt in 1928 to cash a $25 check upon which he had signed his employer's signature landed him back in prison. In 1934, he began his last and lengthiest prison sentence in Folsom after forging two $10 checks; he had done it, he said, to buy food for his elderly mother. He passed away in 1962 at age sixty-five in Los Angeles, a free man.

After the San Quentin warden escorted Philip to his cell in 1923, Barbara—to her abject consternation—discovered he was spending his time behind bars writing a tell-all account of their marriage. *Motion Picture Magazine* offered a preview, obtained from an unnamed visitor to the prison: "Barbara," Philip said, "is a nice girl, but she just can't stick to anything—not even to a husband."[23] Barbara and her business associates did everything within their power to stop him. It appears they succeeded. At present, Philip's memoir—assuming he completed it—has not surfaced, its possible whereabouts unknown even to his descendants. Given Barbara's connections, one can merely wonder what possible financial and legal benefits Philip might have received in exchange for his silence.

As Barbara and Jack attempted to settle into married life, Barbara's reputation took another hit. The uproar began when a woman named Mildred Gray Maryatt filed her second amended divorce complaint against her husband, Oscar Maryatt, a cameraman at Douglas Fairbanks Studios. In it, Mrs. Maryatt named Barbara as the other woman in her husband's life. As proof of her accusation, she submitted letters her husband had written her, telling of Barbara's alleged love for him. "I love Barbara more than I do you," he wrote in one. Mrs. Maryatt also claimed her husband told her, after coming home late one night, that he had been on a date with Barbara and, on another occasion, that if she didn't like his behavior, Barbara was waiting and "would stand for anything." It was purely wishful thinking on Mr. Maryatt's part; he answered his wife's complaint with a sworn affidavit,

Twenty-Two

admitting that he hardly knew Barbara and that he invented the entire affair "just to tease [his wife] a little."[24] The allegations nevertheless horrified Barbara. She feared some unknown party was conspiring to smear her character and thus ruin her chances at the new starring contract Arthur Sawyer was negotiating for her. "I have some right to happiness," she told a reporter May 9, "and these continuous slanders are making a nightmare of my life."[25]

Although Sawyer's negotiations of Barbara's various contracts survived the hubbub surrounding Philip's sentencing and Mrs. Maryatt's complaint, a degree of damage was done. For weeks, as Sawyer had worked toward signing Barbara to a lucrative long-term starring contract, he also sought roles for her in different studios' films. Several deals had been made, and more were in the works. Of utmost importance to Sawyer as he secured these roles was the way Barbara was to be billed in them. Billing her as a star at this point would create the impression that her commitments were spread too thinly, therefore disrupting contracts already in place and greatly lessening amounts of money offered for her exclusive starring services. Accordingly, as a condition of each contract, Sawyer mandated that Barbara be referred to as a featured player, rather than a star. On April 13, a violation of Sawyer's stipulation and a false announcement resulted in the withdrawal of multiple contracts and nearly cost Barbara the most incredible opportunity of her career to date. The general manager of Universal, following a verbal agreement with Sawyer to hire Barbara for a single picture with an option for a second (an agreement that ultimately was not fulfilled), issued a press release stating that Universal had entered into a long-term contract with her.

The news shocked Samuel Goldwyn. For months, he had envisioned Barbara in the large-scale production he was filming that summer, and he had just finalized her contract through Sawyer. Universal's declaration had him fuming; a long-term contract with Universal would make it impossible for Barbara to fulfill her obligation to him. Sawyer acted swiftly. He issued a press statement explaining that Barbara had not signed a long-term contract with Universal. To further pacify Goldwyn, Sawyer announced Barbara's plans for the summer.

Barbara, from the moment Goldwyn's proposal was proffered, had been so thrilled by it, she was willing to forgo other appealing offers. She was to appear as the leading female in a stellar, otherwise all-male cast, enacting a choice role in a celebrated story. Reputedly, she was to receive

$3,000 per week for her services. The picture involved an unprecedented trip to Europe, where filming would take place among the famed landmarks of ancient Rome. She was scheduled to depart from New York the first week of June to make *The Eternal City*.

Twenty-Three

As the train transporting Barbara and Jack bustled into the station in New York City at the end of May 1923, Barbara pulled her hat over the sides of her head, rendering herself unrecognizable. Her trip to Italy, although for business purposes, would also serve as her honeymoon—and a desperately needed vacation. Months of working the standard twelve-to fifteen-hour workday had taken a toll. "I scarcely seem to have had time to breathe," she told a journalist before departing California.[1] The honeymooners slinked from the train, meandered unnoticed through the station, and taxied to Goldwyn's New York headquarters. For Barbara, there were to be no more treasured moments of anonymity.

Sucked into the spotlight, she was thrust into the most eventful, hectic four months of her life. Her week in New York was a frenetic blur of interviews, business meetings, and obligatory appearances, a constant battle between giving the public her genial, charismatic best and containing her swelling inner tumult. In the rare moments she and Jack had alone, in the seclusion of their hotel suite, Barbara's composure crumbled. Nervous exhaustion assailed her. She cried herself to sleep at night.

Jack, Barbara related to one of her New York interviewers, was "worried to death" over her. Unwilling to allow Barbara's professional demands to compromise her health, he comforted her in the evenings and insisted she stagger her appointments. "I never knew what love was before," Barbara said, her face aglow. "It's wonderful to have someone taking care of me like that."[2]

Yet there were aches in Barbara's heart that Jack could not salve. She missed her baby dearly. Still under a year old, he was deemed too young to travel abroad, and Barbara had been forced to leave him at home with his nurse. She wept for three nights straight after bidding him a tearful goodbye and couldn't get him out of her mind. She thought of his sweet smile and the way his little face, when the discomfort of teething became too much, wrinkled into an "adorable" expression of "pained surprise."[3] Sometimes her mind raced with thoughts that harm would come to him in her absence. After viewing a play in which an infant died, she immediately wired the nurse, begging for a lengthy report on how Sonny (whose name she had changed from Marvin to Ivan) was doing.

Barbara was also distressed that her career commitments and popularity were coming between her and Jack. Wanting to be a good, supportive wife, she tried to offset the various insults he had encountered since marrying her. For her sake, he did his best to bear them. He stood by dutifully as she was swept away from him by the enthusiastic crowds that swarmed her at each of their New York social engagements. "I was so darn proud of her and so happy for her," he later recounted, "that I hardly noticed that nobody realized I was alive, except Barbara. God bless her!" Other slights, however, were impossible to disregard. At one dinner party, Barbara was ushered to the seat of honor while Jack circled the table searching for his place card. He didn't find it; the hostess had forgotten him. During another party, he endured what he described as the most miserable moments of his life. Utterly ignored at one side of the drawing room, he tried to look confident and composed as each guest was presented to Barbara. He tried even harder to smother his rage after the hostess, finally acknowledging him, introduced him to the distinguished room as "Mr. Barbara La Marr." Barbara, too, was mortified. Knowledge of Barbara's love for him, Jack later admitted, was the only thing that helped him endure such slights and the men who flirted with her right under his nose. "Barbara always turned to me with some open word of love or some demonstration of affection," he said, "which made them know that we loved each other and that no one else really mattered."[4]

Compounding Barbara's anxiety during her week in New York was the sheer magnitude of her upcoming undertaking, the biggest film she had yet done. "I don't mind admitting that I am simply scared to death," she confided to a journalist.[5] Expected to carry *The Eternal City* as the head of a notable cast and opposite the illustrious Lionel Barrymore, Barbara worried that she was unworthy of the faith that had been placed in her. But she was, as always, determined to give her best. Considering what succeeding in the role would mean for her career, as her publicist, Bert Ennis, readily acknowledged, she had to try. Barbara's fortitude subdued some of her self-doubt, and the idea of creating a stable future for Sonny alleviated a fraction of the guilt she felt for leaving him behind.

With a cascading bouquet of flowers on her right arm and Jack's arm under her left, Barbara walked up the gangplank of France's most opulent ocean

Twenty-Three

Left to right: Bert Lytell, Barbara, Lionel Barrymore, and Montagu Love aboard the SS *Paris* in 1923.

liner, the SS *Paris,* June 6. Joining them as they sailed to Europe were Lionel Barrymore, Bert Lytell, and Montagu Love, Barbara's *Eternal City* castmates.

While Barbara and her costars chatted over delectable cuisine in the ship's first-class dining room and luxuriated in lavish staterooms, George Fitzmaurice, their director, attempted to end a battle of wills. On May 26, accompanied by his wife, screenwriter and *Eternal City* scenarist Ouida Bergere, the Paris-born Irishman had departed for London to meet with Hall Caine, author of the book upon which the film was based. Fitzmaurice and Goldwyn had encountered a significant problem and urgently needed Caine's cooperation to move past it.

Set in Rome and primarily a love story, Caine's hugely popular 1901 novel, *The Eternal City,* involves the creation of a socialist state through the efforts of its hero, David Rossi. In 1923, under fascist leader and Italian prime minister Benito Mussolini, Italy was a markedly different place. While the formerly struggling country was benefiting from Mussolini's social reformation and public works, democracy and free speech had been outlawed, an army of black-shirted men maintained tight control over the populace, and socialists were considered enemies of the state. When initially apprised of Goldwyn's intention to film Caine's story in Rome, Mussolini forbade it.

Goldwyn and Fitzmaurice had then made an appeal to Caine. Informing him of the fortune they had already spent in preparing to shoot many of the film's scenes in Italy, they proposed what they believed to be their sole option. They asked that Caine's story be altered, substituting Mussolini and fascism in place of Christian socialism. Appalled, Caine refused. Then, unable to pull out of his contract with Goldwyn, he was forced to compromise. He agreed to allow Bergere to write a separate scenario, under her name alone, and pair it with his book's title. Before Fitzmaurice and Bergere left London for Rome, Caine had approved the scenario they had shown him.

Two months later, Caine would charge that he had been tricked. Stating that the script he approved was further twisted into fascist propaganda, he would attempt to stop the film from being made. He would not succeed.

Eternal City cameraman Arthur Miller, upon meeting Mussolini, perceived the fascist leader's character to be in opposition with the man he became in later years. In his memoir, *One Reel a Week,* he wrote of Mussolini's cordial treatment of the film's cast and crew, his willingness to pose for photographs, and the way his softly spoken English belied his imposing physique.[6]

Mussolini was so pleased with Bergere's scenario, he placed himself entirely at Fitzmaurice's service, granting complete access to restricted areas such as the Coliseum and Capitol building, as well as streets in the city's center and small mountainside villages. A troop of Mussolini's Blackshirts attended the company during filming, restraining crowds, blocking off streets, and escorting the filmmakers (including thousands of extras) between locations. Mussolini, his men, and Victor Emmanuel III, king of Italy, additionally obliged Fitzmaurice by appearing as themselves in the picture.

Barbara, accorded a glowing reception by locals at each location, threw her heart into her character, Donna Roma. In love with David Rossi (Bert Lytell), Donna endures the heartbreak of his presumed death in the Great War; leaves her Italian village for Rome; and, assisted by the wealthy Baron Bonelli (Lionel Barrymore), becomes a famous sculptress. David, meanwhile, having survived the war, has joined Mussolini's Fascisti move-

Twenty-Three

As Donna Roma in *The Eternal City*. Russell Ball photograph.

ment against the Bolsheviks and is searching for her. Donna's heart is again shattered when David, believing she is Bonelli's lover, rejects her. To prove her love, she confesses to Bonelli's murder when David kills him for aiding the Bolsheviks. Mussolini saves the day; after David exonerates Donna, his service to the fascists vindicates him. Donna and David reunite.

Though Barbara was a continent away, stateside tongues continued wagging about her. A story circulated, propelled by the press, that she had

With Lionel Barrymore in *The Eternal City*. "He gives you the consciousness that you are the weaker, the dominated being," Barbara said of Barrymore's characterization of Bonelli. (Quote from Barbara La Marr, "My Screen Lovers," *Photoplay*, November 1923, 63.)

adopted another child in Italy. The lucky waif, according to *Movie Weekly*, was a five-year-old Italian girl named Rosa Siccardi.

The announcement was news to Barbara. "I find my hands full with one baby," she remarked, "not to mention a husband."[7] The rumor nonetheless persisted in certain newspapers. Rather than visit an orphanage in what little leisure time she had in Italy, Barbara attempted to have a honeymoon.

Months later in the film magazines, Barbara and Jack's honeymoon would read like a romantic fairy tale. One journalist, after visiting the couple in their Whitley Heights home, wrote of Barbara sitting beside Jack on the arm of his chair, the two of them sharing details of their Italian adven-

Twenty-Three

tures like blissful lovebirds. Barbara spoke of gripping Jack's hand as they descended damp, chilly tunnels into the bowels of Rome, winding their way through the city's narrow catacombs. They recalled a carriage ride over ancient Roman cobblestones, past picturesque greenery, quaint roadside vendors, and centuries-old monuments, along the legendary Appian Way. Barbara described a harrowing escape from Mussolini's Blackshirts. Visiting the Coliseum one day, she was unable to resist the urge to snap a photo of it from the top—even though the public was prohibited from entering it. She teetered up the side in a pair of heels and obtained her shot before being spotted. With armed guards in pursuit and her heels fraying, she scuttled toward the bottom, fell down, and dove back into her carriage, finally speeding to safety with Jack. A highlight of the trip, according to the honeymooners, was sliding through a moonlit canal in a gondola in Venice.[8]

The reality, however, wasn't so picture-perfect. "Our honeymoon," Jack later revealed, "—and, after all, a man does feel some rights to privacy and happiness and romance on his honeymoon—was about as private and romantic as Madison Square Garden." Excited mobs, clamoring for Barbara, followed them wherever they went. Jack retreated to the periphery, longing to rescue his wife and have her to himself—if even for a short while. "I don't think I had ten minutes alone with her while we were there," he said.[9]

By the first week of August, with some minor scenes remaining to be shot, Fitzmaurice and his crew had overstayed their welcome in Italy. Mussolini had viewed Fitzmaurice's *The Man from Home* (1922)—a film that he believed lampooned Italian nobility—and was livid. Fitzmaurice fled for New York before the Blackshirts could seize him. Cameraman Arthur Miller concealed some two thousand feet of developed negative in his wardrobe trunk, smuggling it first to Venice, then to Cherbourg, France. Miller and the film rolls made it aboard the *Aquitania* with the film's cast and crew, departed Cherbourg August 11, and arrived in New York August 18. "If the black-shirt boys had gotten their hands on the film that would have been the end of it," he later recalled.[10] The rolls were delivered to Goldwyn's offices; the cast and crew then began a month of shooting the film's interior scenes in New York City.

The risk involved with making *The Eternal City* was ostensibly justified by the initial reception it received following its December 1923 pre-

With Bert Lytell in *The Eternal City*. "Things have certainly become modern when a siren can vamp with short hair!" *Movie Weekly* quipped. ("Whispers from the Studios," *Movie Weekly*, November 24, 1923, 21.)

miere. A nonstop flood of thousands squeezed into New York City's Strand Theatre on opening day; standees numbered in the hundreds at every showing. Opening-day records were similarly smashed in theaters nationwide.

As patrons and critics exited theaters, mixed reactions went with them. The *St. Louis Star* summarized the overriding reason: "[The film] is not bad if one has not read the book. It is a mockery if one has."[11] Other critics—cheering the story, acting, and settings—responded more positively.

Barbara, who debuted a new look in the film (her hair had been bobbed to accommodate a blonde wig she wore in certain scenes), also prompted a divided response. Critics and many of her colleagues, including her costar, Bert Lytell, praised her performance, specifically mentioning her outstanding emotional work. Certain reviewers, however, several of whom were unable to look beyond what they considered

Twenty-Three

a lifeless film lacking a story and centering on Italy's political turmoil, dismissed her.

Yet there was a point upon which most critics converged: they couldn't take their eyes off of her. "She is one of the most beautiful women of the cinema," *Motion Picture Classic* lauded, "and let her but once flicker across the screen and it becomes instantly vital with beauty and glamour."[12]

Accounts of the film premiering to overflowing houses soon tapered off in many areas, commingling with reports of limited attendance. *Variety*, observing that the majority of the Strand's opening-day audience consisted of patriotic Italians, had predicted capacity audiences followed by diminishing returns for exhibitors nationwide.[13] *The Eternal City* had indeed exhausted its primary market.

Barbara hadn't exhausted hers. When she disembarked the *Aquitania* in New York that August, about a month after her twenty-seventh birthday, Arthur Sawyer was there to meet her. He presented her with a contract, the culmination of her childhood aspirations and his management of her career. Barbara signed it the same day; she was officially a star. Under her new contract with Associated Pictures Corporation (the production company with which Sawyer and Lubin superseded S-L Pictures), she was to make four starring pictures per year for five years. Sawyer contracted on Barbara's behalf with Associated First National, regarded at that time as the industry's leading distributor, to distribute the first four, and granted them the option of distributing Barbara's succeeding films. Per her contract with Sawyer and Lubin, Barbara was to earn $1,000 per week for the first year (about $14,000 today) and would receive a $500 weekly increase each ensuing year. She would also collect a portion of her films' profits, plus half of any supplementary sums Sawyer negotiated for her services. Her contract, according to an announcement made by Lubin, would net her a projected amount in excess of $3 million (over $42 million today).[14]

On September 28, after filming of *The Eternal City* concluded in New York, Barbara and Jack arrived in Los Angeles. Barbara exited the train to a heroine's welcome. Awaiting her among the crowd of friends, business associates, and reporters were her father and her son. Squeezing past a profusion of floral offerings, she went directly to her boy and held him close. It would be a long time before reporters persuaded her to hand him off to pose for pictures.

Never, Barbara vowed, would she allow her work to separate her from Sonny again. It was a vow she would keep.

Twenty-Four

Barbara's elevation to star status came as little surprise to many in filmdom. Yet although it was easy for her colleagues and admirers to explain her achievement of stardom, they were rarely in agreement. One writer, unable to define the mysterious combination of elements behind Barbara's enormous appeal, simply credited "her ability to keep us guessing."[1]

Barbara's physical allure was undeniable. Some concurred with the pronouncements of Douglas Fairbanks, Rudolph Valentino, and Buster Keaton that she was the most beautiful woman they had ever seen.[2] The children of Whitley Heights, enchanted by her beauty, beseeched their nurses to walk them past her house.[3] (Once, when columnist Jimmie Fidler arrived at her home to interview her, he found her roller skating with these same children.)

Director Fred Niblo believed she possessed "the most tremendous sex appeal of any woman on the screen."[4] She had a certain, unexplainable aura, attested others, which magnetized men, yet somehow nullified women's jealousy toward her.

That Barbara had talent to match her physicality and incendiary sultriness was also acknowledged. Running deeper than her sex appeal, according to actress Helen Ferguson, is the enigmatic look in her eyes, an innate "primitive fire" that infuses her roles.[5] Fueling that fire, and enabling Barbara to surprise audiences with diverse characterizations, were her manifold life experiences—experiences for which she now expressed gratitude. She wouldn't change the people, surroundings, and events of her life, she told Ferguson, because they had made her who she is. Barbara's inherent sensitivity and vast storehouse of emotional experiences prompted Adela Rogers St. Johns to liken her versatility to the genius of Italian actress Eleonora Duse. Even Barbara's style of vamping frequently defied expectations. Capable of engrossing subtlety, Barbara surpassed the conception of the vamp as a dimensionless caricature, incorporating comedic touches and, often, a gripping, underlying sadness into her portrayals.

This sorrowful undercurrent was, for many, the most compelling aspect of Barbara's characterizations. Asked to account for it, she replied, "Every woman has in her life more tears than laughter. Some are able to forget, but for those of us who are not, sadness is an ever-present emotion."[6] While other actresses used glycerin drops to produce tears, Barbara pleased directors with her ability to cry on cue. Rather than allow her inner pain to inhibit her, she relied upon it to stoke her creativity. "When I am happy I am like a cat, sleek and purring, quite useless," she said. "It is when I am unhappy, with an ache perhaps in my heart, that I do my finest work."[7] Yet, paradoxically, in giving her characters life, she simultaneously drained it from herself. "Every characterization I give the screen takes a chip off the edge of my very soul," she admitted, and "makes me just a little older."[8]

St. Johns asserted that, as considerable as Barbara's talent was, her personality outshone it. Others who knew Barbara likewise testified to her abundant energy, her propensity to freely speak her truth—often in a "shrewd . . . clever and not infrequently racy" manner—and her utter *aliveness*.[9] Perhaps it was Barbara's aptitude for lending so much of her soul to her screen personas that caused some to wonder about her acting abilities. "Her performances are triumphs of sheer personality," proposed journalist Malcolm H. Oettinger.[10]

At no time would Barbara's stardom go to her head. "When she was at the top, she was at her sweetest," an unnamed friend told a columnist. "She was less vain, more lovable than at any other time in her career."[11] Reporters continued commenting on Barbara's genuine kindness; one described her as a "regular girl," devoid of affectations, who "radiates good-fellowship."[12]

She was still a pleasure to work with. Only once did she reportedly lose her temper on a set. Upset over Ouida Bergere's superiority toward her following a disagreement between them during filming of *The Eternal City*, Barbara admonished, "Be yourself, Ida Berger."[13] Many stories exist of Barbara's pleasant, accommodating, and considerate ways. "Artistic temperament is bunk," she contended, making it a point not to hold up rehearsals or filming.[14] Prone to overwork and put others first, she admitted, "I get so interested in a picture that I'll go down to the studio any time of the day they want me, no matter how I feel or how late I have been up the night before."[15] Directors extolled her work ethic and willingness to both follow their instructions and offer intelligent input. Cast and crew alike sought her company between scenes, often congregating in her dressing room.

Cameraman Gregg Toland attributed Barbara's sex appeal to her "softness of expression—not to be confused with the softness of innocence—her smolder, her tremulous reserve . . . and her undulating movements of locomotion." (Helen Haskin, "Glamor [*sic*]? All Just My Camera's Magic," *Portsmouth Times*, December 13, 1936.) Photo by Russell Ball, 1924; courtesy of Donald Gallery.

"She has personality plus something equally intangible that induces you to linger a little longer. Then she has sufficient charm to make you glad you did stay," observed columnist Malcolm H. Oettinger. (Oettinger, "The Studio Lorelei," *Picture Play*, March 1924, 74.) Photo by Melbourne Spurr, 1924; courtesy of Donald Gallery.

Journalist Helen Klumph considered Barbara a woman of contrasts: "Silken, alluring, exotic . . . she likes to wear gingham aprons and romp around on the floor with her baby." (Klumph, "When Is Barbara Sincere?" *Picture Play,* September 1923, 62.) Photo by Witzel, 1923; courtesy of Donald Gallery.

Barbara's eyes reminded actress Louise Fazenda of women at tombs. "Sometimes I seem to get outside of my own sadness and look at it," Barbara said, "and I know then what she meant." (Joan Drummond, "Beautiful Barbara," *Pictures and the Picturegoer,* April 1924, 44.) Photo circa 1923.

"The atmosphere of her 'star' quarters," noted a reporter visiting the New York set of *The Eternal City*, "had the same spontaneous camaraderie that marks the dressing room of a college football team. First names were the rule, informality the expected thing, and gayety predominant."[16]

Barbara's goodwill was, as before, not reserved for the higher-ranking members of her productions. When an admirer sent her a grandiose assortment of orchids on another film set, she distributed them among the cast's extra girls. She also brought struggling extra girls into her home to live with her until they got on their feet. An account circulated that she won a bet by inducing two producers to offer one such girl screen tests; Barbara had dressed the girl in a dazzling outfit, taken her to a Hollywood party, and presented her as a famous New York stage actress.

Privately, among her household help—which now included, in addition to Irene Almond (Barbara's housekeeper and Sonny's nurse), a cook and chauffeur—Barbara was the same compassionate woman. She eschewed the word "servant" and regarded them as friends. She avoided nagging and wasn't above pitching in if she noticed a bit of dust. She was repaid with loyalty and empathy, especially when she came home haggard and testy after long hours at the studio. Barbara declared such kind treatment to be "worth a lot more to me than just being sure that maybe there isn't a speck of dust underneath a rug somewhere."[17]

Barbara freely distributed the fruits of her success among her family, friends, and the less fortunate. She was quoted as saying, "I never could let anyone near to me want for anything," and later added, "I am absolutely sure that if I were a pal to some man or woman and they should come to me and say that they had to have two thousand dollars the next day and something happened and I didn't have it on hand to give them, I would put in all my personal possessions in order to get it for them."[18] Her father, William, told reporters after her death, "She gave away more money than she ever spent on herself."[19] Barbara supported her parents financially, enabling William to write his novels. Her widely publicized shopping sprees typically centered on others; female friends reported receiving gifts as exorbitant as ermine coats; Valentino received a traveling bag containing solid-gold toilet articles; Barbara's costumer for *Sandra* (1924) would be given an automobile. It was also Barbara's habit to indulge her friends with evenings of extravagance by renting entire dining rooms in the glitziest hotels in Los Angeles.

She recurrently donated large portions of her earnings to charities, but

Twenty-Four

Barbara helping a young girl with the drinking fountain during one of her Hollywood Orphans' Home parties.

she didn't stop there. On a sun-drenched Friday in early spring 1923, she and Sonny hosted a playground party—complete with balloons, games, prizes, and ice cream—for the youngsters at the Hollywood Orphans' Home. The reporter covering the event remarked how Barbara lavished her love upon the children. One young boy, recently left at the home following his mother's death, found comfort in her arms as he cried himself out on her neck. The neediness of the children, particularly those who were never taken out on Sundays, visitors' day, pierced Barbara's heart. She arranged to return with a caravan of cars the following Sunday to take all the children who had been left behind on a beach trip. So began her ritual of hosting monthly parties and outings for orphans.[20]

While seeing parentless children suffer was heartrending for Barbara, turning her back on a relative or friend in need was unthinkable. Robert (Carville) Hobday discovered this firsthand five years after their relationship ended. While Barbara was in New York filming *The Eternal City*, Robert's life took a tragic turn in Los Angeles the rainy night of August 21, 1923. After accidentally (and unlawfully) entering an intersection, his car collided with two others and flipped over. His female passenger, nineteen-year-old Fern Reeder, was killed. Robert, deeply remorseful, was charged with manslaughter. When the case was tried in 1924, Barbara saw to it that his defense team included Milton Cohen (her attorney at that time and one of the men who had defended Roscoe Arbuckle after Arbuckle was charged with rape and murder in 1921). The court, beleaguered by a recent wave of deaths resulting from reckless driving, was initially unsympathetic. Robert reportedly fainted when the judge pronounced his sentence: seven years in San Quentin. His attorneys submitted an application for probation, providing proof of his commendable record and industriousness, and pointing out that, although he and his wife were separated at the time of the accident, he had continued supporting her and their daughters and had since reconciled with her. The judge ultimately suspended the sentence, granting Robert probation.[21]

Robert indeed did well with his second chance, eventually becoming a supervisor for the Veterans of Foreign Wars and establishing various non-profit organizations. One of these organizations, the Thomas A. Edison Foundation, promoted exceptional contributions to the arts and sciences; another, the George Washington Carver Institute, headquartered in Washington, D.C., encouraged the strengthening of race relations. Robert was also, according to his youngest daughter, Betty, "the best father ever."[22]

When relatives and friends expressed alarm over Barbara's liberal generosity, she assumed her fixed stance: that "money was made to spend."[23] She was also unconcerned whenever anyone warned of the potential impermanency of success in the film business. "I don't care!" she replied. "I have it now. Whatever happens I shall have had my taste of it. Nothing can take that away."[24]

Perhaps Barbara's acknowledgment of the relative temporality of fame and fortune figured into her tendency to downplay her stardom. She often signed her photographs, "Lest you forget." Averse to being gaped at in public, she told a journalist, "A movie actress may be interesting, but so is the zoo—so you see what a doubtful compliment it really is."[25] Another writer recounted how, after she and Barbara passed a table of society women as they left a New York café, one of the ladies exclaimed that she had just seen Barbara La Marr. "I dare you," Barbara laughed, "to go back and say to them, 'Well, what of it?'"[26]

Certainly Barbara's inclination to disparage her success stemmed from her underlying insecurity. "I am just as lacking in self-confidence now as when I made *Harriet and the Piper*," she is said to confess in *Movie Week-*

Twenty-Four

ly's account of her life. "I just can't believe that these things happen to me." She still abhorred seeing her work onscreen and avoided doing so. "I go to see rushes of my pictures sometimes when it is absolutely necessary," she purportedly said, "and come home and go into my room and sit there for half an hour, *all in*. I seem to have given so much and it seems to come out so *little*."[27] Barbara acknowledged that, while her work never tired her, it often made her anxious. "I lie awake at nights and wonder whether I am really progressing," she admitted, "whether I am really giving the best of my soul to my art, whether I am really satisfying my public."[28] Evidence of public approval surrounded Barbara; her image appeared regularly on the covers of major magazines, her fan mail arrived in bushels, and she was selected to endorse such high-end products as Lablanche cosmetics, Vivaudou perfume, and later Richelieu pearls. Still her doubts remained. Extremely sensitive to reproach, she feared reading newspapers the day after her films premiered.

She furthermore detested the way she looked on film and dismissed her physical beauty. As an adult, Elaine St. Johns, Adela's daughter, recalled a visit Barbara made to her childhood home in Malibu. "She was dressed in white and was truly a gorgeous vision," she said. "Everyone stared at her. She was indifferent to this attention."[29] Barbara was similarly unmoved by those who proclaimed her the most beautiful woman in pictures. "Everybody is beautiful to someone," she countered.[30] She had no reservations about pointing out her perceived flaws to interviewers: "I have none of the marks of beauty. I am too long-waisted. My nose is too sharp and pointed. My head doesn't fit my body. My eyes are crooked."[31] Nor did she conceal the fact that stars' photographs were periodically retouched. The allure of a film star for the public, she insisted, is personality, not beauty.

Yet, as she did with her talent and beauty, Barbara also discounted her personality as being enough to intrigue her fans. Harry Reichenbach, Samuel Goldwyn's publicist throughout production of *The Eternal City*, later recounted a discussion between Barbara and his wife, distinguished fashion consultant Lucinda Reichenbach. Barbara asked what sort of off-screen persona would best complement her vampy screen counterpart. Lucinda advised her to simply be her kind, sweet self. Barbara protested, saying, "The public expects eccentric things from stars," and, according to Harry Reichenbach, henceforth wore heavier makeup and exotic clothing.[32] Barbara embellished her image with invented tales of her childhood and parentage, even presenting different versions of both to various interviewers and friends. Continuously upholding the illusion that the Watsons had adopted her, she alternately presented her fabled birth parents as a French actress and an Italian of noble blood, an Italian mother and French father, and a beautiful Virginia aristocrat and European wine dealer. The story credited to her in *Movie Weekly*'s depiction of her life, that she was sent to America at age five and taken in by the Watsons, contrasted with an earlier account of hers that she had been an orphan, "thrust out into the world at the age of four to earn [her] living as a dancer," and had subsequently danced onstage until her teenage years.[33]

Rather than try to overcome her lack of faith in herself, Barbara professedly embraced it. "It is good for me," she is quoted as saying in *Movie Weekly*'s version of her life story. "Whenever you think you are essential, you are, usually, through . . . No one likes a conceited personality. And the screen will pick out conceit as it picks out other flaws, every time."[34]

Just as Barbara's stardom amplified her insecurities, it dominated her life. Days spent before a camera gave way to endless hours of costume fittings, business meetings, interviews, sessions with photographers (followed by time spent autographing photographs), work with scripts, and obligatory social and publicity appearances. "There's no such thing as after-hours for the movie actress," she noted. "Sometimes I think I'd give anything for an eight-hour job, with the luxury of spending my leisure hours as I wish."[35]

She nonetheless endeavored to be a good homemaker and lead a normal life. She kept Sonny with her as much as possible, leaving him with his nurse only when she had no choice. Kept apart from her husband, Jack, by their respective film work, Barbara made the most of the time they had together. "Parting in the morning we make a real little farewell," she said, "and meeting at home in the evening we give the importance of a homecoming from a journey."[36] She stayed home with Jack and Sonny in the evenings as often as her schedule permitted, usually retiring by ten. She arose between five-thirty and seven o'clock when she and Jack were working, either to prepare for her own early call or—without waking her cook—to make Jack's breakfast before he left for his. She also arranged delectable dinners for Jack, even forgoing her own favorites and stomaching his much-loved corned beef and cabbage.

Barbara's life was anything but normal, however. This fact was apparently driven home for her at a tea party she attended with Jack after returning to Hollywood from abroad. According to *Movie Weekly*'s account of her life, she arrived at the gathering with her recently bobbed hair and was conservatively dressed, so as not to attract undue attention to herself; in honor of her husband, she presented herself as Mrs. Jack Daugherty.

Supposedly, a curious thing happened. "No one tried any clever repartee," she is said in the article to recount. "None of the men flocked about to pay me compliments, obvious, subtle, or any kind at all. They didn't even notice me. They just treated me like an average woman, and very average at that."

Evidently, a chance remark from Jack, in which he referenced her last picture, suddenly unhinged the floodgates. The article continues with the eyes of the crowd turning on Barbara. A cacophony of voices, enquiring if she was in pictures, arose. Barbara admitted she was. The voices persisted; people wanted to know her screen name. Barbara provided it. Shock registered on the faces of the party guests, causing her to silently question whether she was being complimented or insulted. Then a mob merged around her. "I stake my sacred word of honor," the article cites her as stating, "that no one spoke to anyone else for at least an hour. They all, every man and woman of them, talked directly to and at me."[37]

Barbara seemingly deferred to her sense of humor; rationalizing that the partygoers were thrown by her new hairstyle and had merely expected her to behave in public as her screen characters would, she is said to have chalked up the incident to human nature and later joked about it. Still, a thought lingered in her mind: Who would notice her if she were not Barbara La Marr?

Twenty-Five

On October 16, 1923, two weeks after Barbara returned from New York with her starring contract, a summons was placed in her hand. Ben Deely was suing her for divorce, citing infidelity and naming Jack Daugherty as corespondent. He further charged her with committing adultery with various unnamed men. The complaint was signed by Ben's attorney, Herman Roth.

The spindly fifty-nine-year-old Roth had argued high-profile cases in New York and California throughout his thirty-year career, drawing the majority of his clientele from the theatrical crowd. Specializing in divorces, he promised his clients high settlements and often delivered—for a price.

Ben later stated that he was not seeking a settlement from Barbara. He did, however, have an ax to grind. During his initial consultations with Roth, he vented his anger toward Arthur Sawyer, accusing the producer-manager of both "alienating" Barbara's affections and using industry connections to prevent him from obtaining acting work for over a year.[1] Ben therefore believed himself entitled to around $150,000 in damages from Sawyer. He asked Roth to prepare a second complaint. If the wily attorney drafted such a complaint, he evidently didn't file it.

The shock Barbara felt after receiving Ben's divorce complaint temporarily receded when she consulted her lawyer, Frank Drew. Drew reiterated what he and Constantino Riccardi told her before her Texas trip: in his estimation, her 1918 marriage to Ben had not been legal. Drew next met with Roth, explaining that, since Barbara was not legally divorced from Philip when she wed Ben, she was thus never married to Ben. He likely also pointed out that an Illinois judge had already annulled the apparently bogus marriage on these grounds. Drew commanded Roth to drop Ben's complaint.

Roth had another plan. He drew up an amended complaint, naming seven men—many of them members of the film industry—with whom Barbara had allegedly been intimate during her marriage to Ben. Roscoe Arbuckle was listed. Sawyer was also included. Roth asked Ben to sign the document. Ben refused, later asserting that he never authorized Roth to amend his original complaint and that he objected to the inclusion of some of the men.

Unflinching, Roth divulged the details of the amended complaint to three newspapermen: Edward Doherty of the *Los Angeles Times,* Harrison Carroll of the *Los Angeles Times* (and, later, of the *Los Angeles Herald Express*), and R. D. Knickerbocker, former *Los Angeles Examiner* reporter. Roth presented the complaint and purported evidence of his allegations against Barbara to Knickerbocker, permitting him to photograph the documents. As the men left his office at the conclusion of their interviews with him, he knew where they would be headed.

When Doherty, Carroll, and Knickerbocker asked to meet with Barbara regarding new developments in Ben's divorce suit, her fears undoubtedly resurfaced. Seated alongside Sawyer in her home, she listened, horror-struck, as the three reporters told her what they learned from Roth. Knickerbocker pulled out his copy of the amended complaint and discussed two other documents he had also photographed. One of them, an affidavit, contained a statement supposedly provided by actress Jacqueline Dyris, a roommate of Barbara's when she resided at the Christie Hotel (probably sometime around late 1921 or early 1922). According to the statement, in a conversation said to have occurred between Barbara and Dyris, Barbara described Sawyer as a "perfect lover, although you'd never think it to look at him."[2] (The contents of the other document, a reputed letter from a girl named Rose, were seemingly never publicly revealed and are therefore unknown.) The reporters informed Barbara and Sawyer of Roth's intent to file the amended complaint. Barbara and Sawyer, both highly alarmed, denied Roth's accusations.

Roth, confident his bomb had landed, called Sawyer to his office. Brandishing the amended complaint, affidavit, and letter, he told Sawyer that, to prevent the complaint from being filed—and all three documents from thereby becoming public property—it was going to cost him. He threatened to publicize an allegation that Barbara, supposedly seeking privacy, rented a house at which Sawyer had regularly visited her and, in one instance, spent part of an evening with her. Aware that a morality clause in Barbara's starring contract with Sawyer prohibited her involvement in scandal, Roth named his price: $25,000 (almost $350,000 today).

Threatening Sawyer with a claim that Ben wanted a slice of Barbara's success and the assurance that he could get it, Roth demanded that Sawyer pay up or he would "ruin [Barbara] overnight in the eyes of the public."[3] Sawyer told Roth that he would discuss the matter with Barbara.

The thought of losing her career and livelihood brought Barbara to her knees. So did the thought of the alternative. Capitulating to Roth's demands, she reasoned, would finish her as surely as scandal; so long as she remained in the public eye, he would own her. After a night of hellish deliberation, she announced her decision to Sawyer and Jack: Roth wasn't getting her without a fight.

Barbara and Jack headed to Drew's office; Sawyer went to the district attorney. While the district attorney launched a probe, Roth learned of Barbara's meeting with her attorney. Furious, he telephoned Sawyer. "I'm going to go through with the case now," Sawyer quoted him as saying, "and have her jailed for bigamy."[4]

Sawyer, following the instructions of the district attorney's detectives, told Roth he would pay the $25,000 to halt the case. Pacified, Roth insisted Sawyer pay $500 up front, explaining that he needed to pay off the girls who signed the affidavits.

Roth then contacted Ben. Without providing specifics, Roth asked if Ben was interested in settling out of court. "Yes," Ben later said he answered. "Anything within the law will be satisfactory with me."[5]

The afternoon of November 14, Sawyer entered Al Levy's Spring Street café. Seeing Roth seated alone in the dining room, Sawyer joined him at his table and handed him a $100 installment.

The district attorney was ready to act. In the district attorney's office November 15, investigator John Dymond counted eight $50 bills into Sawyer's hand. The serial number on each bill had been recorded. When Sawyer walked into Roth's office a short time later, Dymond and his men, one of them posing as a janitor, were in place outside.

Sawyer handed the $400 worth of marked bills to Roth. Placing them in his wallet, Roth prepared an agreement between himself and Sawyer. At Sawyer's request, Roth wrote a telegram to First National, distributor of Barbara's starring films, assuring them he would not be filing the amended divorce complaint.

Dymond and his men moved in. Roth was arrested and charged with extortion. The officers, ruling Ben out as a participant in Roth's scheme, made no further arrests. The November 16 issue of the *Los Angeles Times* heralded, "Miss La Marr Jails Lawyer." Newspapers throughout the world carried similar headlines.

Twenty-Five

For Barbara, the worst of the ordeal was still ahead. Roth's trial would begin in February. That she would be subpoenaed as a witness against him was a certainty. That his accusations against her would appear in newspapers was also guaranteed. That intimate details of her past would be elicited from her as she sat upon the witness stand was highly anticipated. Still unknown to her, however, was the scope of the damage that would result from it all.

In addition to Roth's trial, Barbara had yet to face her own. The California Superior Court was uncertain whether Ben and Barbara were husband and wife. Thus, Ben's original divorce complaint remained in place. Maintaining that she and Ben had never been married—and therefore denying she committed adultery with Jack or any other man—Barbara continued consulting her lawyer while a hearing was scheduled.

From mid-October through December 1923, as Barbara endured Roth's blackmailing tactics and awaited her time in court, she sought solace in her work. *Thy Name Is Woman*, a Louis B. Mayer film Sawyer had secured for her the spring of 1923 (before her Associated Pictures and First National contracts), again partnered her with two of her favorite people: Ramon Novarro and director Fred Niblo. The film also gave her the opportunity to embody a character who fascinated her: a torn, multidimensional woman who, in love for the first time, summons the strength to follow her heart.

The heartbreaking story is set in a Spanish Pyrenees town and is centered largely around Pedro (William V. Mong); his much-younger wife, Guerita (played by Barbara); and youthful Juan Ricardo (Novarro). Juan, hopeful of earning sergeant's stripes, seduces Guerita in order to obtain incriminating evidence against Pedro, a smuggler. Aware of the Spanish army's plot, Pedro instructs Guerita to outmaneuver Juan; but Guerita, tormented by her loveless marriage, and Juan, sensing her sadness, succumb to love's pull. Their feelings deepen in scenes interposed with such intertitles as "Frailty, Thy Name Is Woman," "Hope, Thy Name Is Woman," and "Sacrifice, Thy Name Is Woman." Guerita begs Juan to run away with her. Pedro, unwilling to lose her to Juan, kills her.

Barbara evaded her real-life fears and pain by channeling them through Guerita. "I lost myself so completely in the part," she said, "that I would come home night after night, drag myself to my room and without eating a bite of dinner, sob myself to sleep."[6] Guerita was, she added, the most exhausting part she had ever played. Seventy years after the February

Barbara as the lovelorn Guerita in *Thy Name Is Woman*. Courtesy of Robert S. Birchard.

4, 1924, release of *Thy Name Is Woman*, reviewer Kevin Thomas attended a Los Angeles screening of the film and remarked, "The world weariness, the pervasive sadness that La Marr brings to her role seems palpably real, especially in her single, startlingly revealing close-up."[7]

Donning a wig and Guerita's peasant dresses at Mayer's Mission Road studio and giving her all for the film was one of Barbara's escape methods.

Twenty-Five

Barbara with Ramon Novarro at the tragic denouement of *Thy Name Is Woman*.

Excessive drinking was another. Harry Reichenbach grew wise to her problem months earlier while promoting *The Eternal City* for Goldwyn. He related how, during production of *The Eternal City*, Barbara dropped to the floor of New York City's popular Beaux Arts restaurant one night, "unconscious with drink." He explained to her that such a public spectacle couldn't happen again. She promised it wouldn't. "It happened every night thereafter," he said. Exasperated, Reichenbach insisted she sign a pledge to abstain from alcohol until filming wrapped. "She signed," he recalled, "but drank."[8] Barbara's benders were likewise a source of concern throughout production of *Thy Name Is Woman*. Irving Thalberg, Mayer's production supervisor, was a regular presence on the set, keeping a prudent eye on her. Paul Bern, still on Mayer's writing staff, also maintained watch; according to Paul's friend Samuel Marx, Paul had set aside his own career to assist with Barbara's, and he conceivably influenced Mayer's decision to hire her.

Thy Name Is Woman netted generally favorable notices. Some critics denounced what they believed to be a feeble plot and an awkward handling of the film's dramatic scenes. Many felt differently. *Motion Picture*

Magazine rhapsodized, "[The film] could have been played before black velvet or cheesecloth and been just as gripping."[9] The production yielded steady box office returns overall—largely, it was presumed, because of the performances of its three leads.

As she had in *The Hero* and *Poor Men's Wives*, Barbara shone outside of her usual vamp mold. The *San Francisco Chronicle* likened her portrayal to "having the soul of a woman on the dissecting table, where the scalpel has been used ruthlessly." *Motion Picture Magazine* was still applauding her nearly a year later: "one of the most potent and subtle performances of the year."[10]

Seated next to Novarro, Barbara viewed a completed print of the film. Typically contemptuous of her work, she was actually proud of her performance. She believed it, in fact, to be the best thing she had ever done. She would always consider the role among those she enjoyed most.

After the closing fade-out, she turned to Novarro. She told him of her certainty that he would have a glorious film career. "But your career will be as great as mine," he assured her. Her reply surely startled him. "Oh no," she said. "In two years I will be forgotten."[11]

Besides Barbara's drinking during the making of *Thy Name Is Woman*, Novarro seemingly detected an additional change in her. After her death, he warmly recounted their days on the Metro lot in early 1922, when they were two hopefuls working together on *The Prisoner of Zenda* and *Trifling Women*, both excited by what the future might hold. Attributing his success in those films largely to the fact that he had been working with her, he spoke of what an inspiration she was to him and contended, "There was never anyone else like Barbara to work with." He was also said to remark, "And it was the greatest happiness to work with her then."[12] After making *Thy Name Is Woman* with her, however, he acknowledged a "curious fatalistic strain" pervading her life and personality, her underlying "feeling of an overwhelming Fate against her"—a feeling "of which she has a dread."[13]

Unknown to Novarro and just about everyone else, Barbara's internal turmoil throughout production of *Thy Name Is Woman* ran considerably deeper than her legal troubles with Herman Roth and Ben Deely. Possibly, her drinking while filming *The Eternal City* in New York had its roots in the same cause.

About five months previously, sometime around August 1923, Barbara was dealt the blow of her life. A doctor's examination had unearthed a

Twenty-Five

grave reality. Months before her death, Barbara would entrust a confidant with certain vague details of the devastating news her doctor delivered. Her lungs, the doctor informed her, were deteriorating. Nothing could be done. Then the prognosis had come: she wasn't expected to live beyond twenty months.[14]

Perhaps Barbara, having received such a diagnosis, felt she had nothing to lose by exposing Roth. But, in all probability, her determination to fight him didn't originate from a sense of resignation toward her illness. It came from a place deep within her. From this same place, in the coming months, would emerge a mounting resolution.

After the doctor's diagnosis, while groping through the morass of her fear for a source of strength to cling to, Barbara undoubtedly confronted her beliefs. She had, due to her intractable inquisitiveness, explored many of the world's spiritual doctrines throughout her life, yielding—as noted by Robert Carville and mentioned in her *Movie Weekly* serial—to "one of the deepest rooted instincts of mankind to find out all that can be found out about the Hereafter and the Maker of the cosmic scheme."[15] Her studies, involving the Bible, the Koran, Confucianism, Buddhism, and the philosophical writings of Rabindranath Tagore, had led her to a central conclusion: to live by the Golden Rule. Her life, meanwhile, had instilled in her a concurrent conviction: "that the fates alone determine [one's] happiness."[16]

Considering Barbara's apparent belief in an outside force at work in her life, it's not surprising that she often felt victimized by it; less than a year earlier, she confessed in an interview, "It's only life," never work, "that makes me tired."[17] And yet, running counter to her recurrent fears of powerlessness had been her inherent, self-proclaimed lust to enter fully into life. Faced with the reality of impending death, Barbara was again at war with these same opposing aspects of herself.

In the end, her characteristic willfulness, brought to the fore by her love for life, won out. She was nowhere near finished living yet. If Fate truly was against her, she would beat it. *I won't let my body give in,* she resolved.[18]

Aside from initial confessions to a few of those closest to her, Barbara kept her illness to herself and got on with living.

Twenty-Six

Barbara's career remained one of her top priorities.

Her next assignment, *The Shooting of Dan McGrew,* another film Arthur Sawyer had arranged for her prior to her Associated Pictures and First National contracts, is an adaptation of Robert William Service's poem of the same name. In Service's Yukon verse, a woebegone gold miner staggers into a saloon, draws his gun, and resolves his grudge against Dangerous Dan McGrew over "the lady that's known as Lou." In Sawyer's hands, the well-known tale became a blatant vehicle for what he believed would sell the most tickets: Barbara's sex appeal. A considerable departure from Service's work, the film, produced by Sawyer-Lubin Pictures for release through Metro, revolves around Lou (Barbara's character), with roughly two-thirds of it involving a backstory to the poem's events.

The scenario was credited to Winifred Dunn. A *Photoplay* writer, however, let it slip in the magazine's gossip column that Barbara wrote her own adaptation. According to the writer, despite the studio supposedly hiding the fact, most of the film was based upon Barbara's version.[1]

To hype the production, Sawyer staged a nationwide contest, inviting film fans to vote for the two male leads to appear opposite Barbara. Percy Marmont was selected to play the miner; Lew Cody, a leading Hollywood scoundrel, won the much-coveted role of the cold-blooded Dan McGrew. Some anticipated that Barbara and Cody would be a deliciously lethal screen combination. When the two stars, in San Francisco that January 1924 for the annual Western Association of Motion Picture Advertisers (WAMPAS) Ball, rode together down Market Street, Cody overheard a telling remark while stuck in traffic: "Cody and La Marr!" exclaimed a female pedestrian. "Gosh, what a carload of sin!"[2]

After fans wrote letters, asking to see more of Barbara, reporters visiting Metro's lot while filming took place throughout January and into March assured them *The Shooting of Dan McGrew* would gratify their wish. "Barbara La Marr Displays Primal Lure of Vamp," wrote a *Los Angeles Times* writer; for one scene, "a one-piece garment of cheap silk is

Twenty-Six

wrapped about that vital body"; in another, "her curves [are] but partly concealed by a few wisps of gold cloth."

The reporter asserted that Barbara faced her biggest challenge yet as The Lady Known as Lou—a "woman of volcanic, impetuous disposition, with moments of rare softness and beauty of soul . . . a characterization that runs the dramatic scale."[3] Barbara wasn't taking chances. When directed to her own queenly suite of dressing rooms the first day of filming, she asked to be reinstated in the room she used when she made *The Prisoner of Zenda* and *Trifling Women* "because," she said, "those pictures brought me so much luck."[4]

That there was a particularly supportive face among the film's extras likely also bolstered Barbara's confidence. Her brother, Billy DeVore, taking time out from performances in Oakland revues, had a bit part in the film. Her husband, Jack, was also frequently present to curtail her drinking. Jack had turned down a starring role in a Broadway production to be with her.

Directed by Clarence Badger, *The Shooting of Dan McGrew* involves Lou, a dancer who is seeking a better life for her herself, her husband, Jim

(*Left to right*) Arthur Sawyer, Barbara, and Clarence Badger on the set of *The Shooting of Dan McGrew* (1924).

263

Lou (Barbara) performing in a cabaret aboard an abandoned South American ship in *The Shooting of Dan McGrew*. From the collections of the Margaret Herrick Library, Academy of Motion Picture Arts and Sciences.

Lou (Barbara) on Broadway. *Film Daily* predicted Barbara's "near-nakedness" was "quite likely to bar" *The Shooting of Dan McGrew* "where there are eagle-eyed censor boards." ("The Shooting of Dan McGrew," *Film Daily,* March 30, 1924, 9.)

Twenty-Six

(Percy Marmont), and her son (Philippe De Lacy). Lou falls prey to gambler Dan McGrew (Lew Cody), who promises to make her a star. She leaves Jim and their touring musical company in South America; later, as the toast of Broadway, she sends money to him and their son until Jim arrives in New York. Tricked by Dan into believing her son has died and that Jim vows revenge against her for leaving, Lou flees with Dan to Alaska, working for years as his gambling decoy in a saloon before Jim, now a successful miner and convinced of her faithfulness, traces her. The film then enacts the poem's shooting with an exception: instead of both men dying, Jim lives and reconciles with Lou.

Critics were at odds following the film's March 31 premiere. The *New York World* and *New York Post* reviled it as "garish, defiant, and incorrigible" and a "butchering" of Service's poem "to make a Sawyer-Lubin holiday." *Variety*, no doubt reacting to the liberties taken with Service's theme and obvious attempts to disarm censors by tempering Lou's raciness with a sympathetic story line, accused Barbara of "failing entirely to get the character over as the author wrote her." *Film Daily*, evidently overlooking the film's perceived shortcomings in light of Barbara's "highly sensuous and voluptuous performance," branded it an outright success: "S-E-X APPEAL IN BIG LETTERS. Undoubtedly a clean-up for some exhibitors."[5]

One of the proudest moments of Barbara's life occurred when legendary stage actor David Warfield praised her portrayal of Lou. She would long recall his words: "What an artist you are! Two characterizations so different as that in *Thy Name Is Woman* and *Dan McGrew*—different as the North and South poles." His compliment, it was related in *Movie Weekly*'s chronicle of her life, had her walking on air. "I don't go in for hero-worship, but I do make Mr. Warfield an exception," she is said to have admitted.[6]

As honored as Barbara was by Warfield's sentiments and critics who commended her whole-souled acting, part of her was ashamed of her performance. Before her death, she made it clear that *The Shooting of Dan McGrew* was a film Sonny was never to see. She believed it to be vulgar and Lou an inaccurate representation of her.

The trial of the case of *The People of the State of California vs. Herman L. Roth*, occurring during filming of *The Shooting of Dan McGrew*, was another chapter of Barbara's life that she would long to blot from existence.[7]

BARBARA LA MARR

On the witness stand before revealing what at least one headline deemed a "Wilder Life Story Than Barbara Ever Helped to Film." ("Trial Yields Wilder Life Story Than Barbara Ever Helped to Film," *Sandusky Star Journal*, February 18, 1924.)

Wearing a black hat and veil, black velvet coat, and black velvet gown, Barbara entered the courtroom of Judge Russ Avery the morning of February 13, 1924. Her face was drained of color. She clasped Jack's arm. Through the testimony of Ben Deely and the three reporters to whom Roth had guaranteed an exclusive story, the world already knew of her alleged intimate relationship with Sawyer and the sordid details of Roth's amended divorce complaint against her. Now it remained for her testimony to confirm or refute Roth's charges.

At the behest of deputy district attorney John Hill, she assumed the witness stand. Before a crammed courtroom, she gave an account of her entire life up to Roth's attempt to blackmail her, pausing repeatedly and weeping into her black handkerchief. Asked to identify Roth's amended complaint, she responded, "My eyes are too full of tears to read it."[8] The judge ordered a recess to allow her to collect herself.

Back on the stand for cross-examination, she was asked if her home

Twenty-Six

was Sawyer's office. "Please don't be insulting," she answered, arousing sympathetic murmurs from spectators.[9]

When another tearful breakdown occurred as the defense queried her about the morality clause in her contract with Sawyer, she was excused.

Sawyer took the stand next. Deputy district attorney Hill needed to prove that Sawyer, in paying Roth the initial $100, was motivated by fear of disgrace, rather than fear of financial loss should Ben's divorce action damage Barbara's reputation. Citing his wife of eighteen years, his son, and his daughter, Sawyer testified that he indeed feared that the publication of Roth's allegations concerning himself and Barbara would destroy him.

As the trial dragged on, and with each stymied attempt by the defense to establish Roth's innocence, Roth's health faltered. Plagued by a worsening heart condition, he nevertheless made a last-ditch endeavor to save himself.

Taking the stand in his own defense, he incited an uproar in the courtroom. Sawyer, Roth claimed, offered him $25,000 to keep him from filing Ben's amended complaint. He denied authorizing reporters to show Sawyer and Barbara the amended complaint; denied presenting Sawyer with the affidavit, supposedly signed by Barbara's former roommate, charging him and Barbara with an illicit relationship; and denied telling Sawyer he would ruin Barbara. He averred that he never accepted $100 from Sawyer in Levy's Café, and insisted that the $400 worth of marked bills were planted on him by the district attorney's investigators when he was arrested. Incredibly, however, during cross-examination, Roth admitted that he did not intend to have Ben sign the amended complaint before a notary at the time he had handed it over to the reporters. He further confessed to instructing his secretary to see to it that Ben was unavailable when one of the reporters sought his verification of the amended complaint.

Following a searing final argument, during which Hill accused Roth of being "the rottenest perjurer who ever testified from a witness chair," the jury rendered a verdict of guilty after a record eight-minute deliberation.[10]

While the Hollywood film firmament applauded Barbara's victory—particularly since a search of Roth's papers uncovered names of other screen stars he intended to blackmail—Barbara felt sympathy for the convicted man. Doubtless identifying with his ailing condition, she issued a press statement: "I am fully convinced that if he goes to jail it will be his death. I can't bear to carry the thought that I sent a man to his death."[11]

When Roth appeared before Judge Avery for sentencing February 29, a doctor testified that Roth's current condition was serious. Roth's attorney conveyed Barbara's desire for leniency, asking that probation be granted. The request was denied. The judge, commending San Quentin's exemplary medical staff, sentenced Roth to between one and five years behind bars.[12]

Roth was released on parole a year and a half later, disbarred and still in poor health. His pardon came after an intervention by his wife, who died weeks afterward.[13]

Barbara filed an amended answer to Ben's divorce complaint March 21. In her original answer, she had denied that a marriage had taken place between them and asked for a dismissal of his complaint. In her amended answer, she admitted to a marriage but refuted its validity on the grounds that her marriage to Philip Ainsworth had not yet been dissolved. She reiterated her assertion that she therefore had not committed adultery with Jack or anyone else. She asked that her purported marriage to Ben be annulled.[14]

Barbara had exchanged the legal counsel of Frank Drew for that of Milton Cohen and former reporter R. D. Knickerbocker (who apparently was practicing law at this time). Beside herself in their office, she lamented, "It is all too technical and so hopelessly tangled I don't know where I am."[15] The attorneys were unable to offer much encouragement. They advised her to live apart from Jack while they worked to resolve the matter. Barbara and Jack—the latter outraged—did as they were asked, planning ultimately to move back in together or remarry, depending upon the court's decision.

To withstand the resulting publicity blitz, Barbara held fast to her wit. A quote of hers, appearing in a *Moving Picture Stories* article entitled "The Husbands of Barbara," is indicative of her attitude on the subject: "I am different from some women. I *marry* my men!"[16] Whenever her humor may have fallen short, her "sex-magnetism," according to Bert Ennis, her publicist, at times did the job. Ennis related witnessing the phenomenon at Barbara's press conferences: "hard-boiled newspapermen" who were initially prepared to sensationalize her marital troubles, he said, "left her with a far-away look in their eyes and a handful of mimeograph drivel of the kind wise press agents always have on tap."[17]

Sawyer, meanwhile, attempted to deflect the onslaught with silence. When reporters confronted him, pressing to know if he believed Barbara had violated the morality clause in her contract with him, he refused to comment.

Twenty-Six

The media circus was but one tormenting aspect of Barbara's life. She was also heavily in debt. By mid-March, Sawyer had advanced her $38,084 of her starring salary. Legal fees consumed some of it; she would continue meeting with her attorneys over a dozen times in coming months, paying an average of $1,000 per visit.[18]

Ben's divorce complaint wasn't the only reason for the meetings. A warrant had been issued on February 18, 1924, for Barbara's arrest. Charged with contempt of court, she had failed to appear in a suit brought against her for monies owed to a jeweler. One of her attorneys prevented her arrest, explaining that Barbara thought she had three years to pay for her purchases. Two days later, while Barbara was at the studio, she wept after receiving notification from a process server that her Whitley Heights home had been attached. The amount owed plus interest would reach $14,800 before Barbara would begin making payments to the claimant eleven months later.[19]

More liens followed. A claim involving $1,423 worth of goods purchased from a furrier would soon be filed. The IRS would demand $302 and $1,143 in unpaid taxes for 1923 and 1924 respectively.[20]

Barbara carried the load of her debts, questionable marital status, brittle health, and intense emotional strain into her next film around the beginning of March, immediately after *The Shooting of Dan McGrew* wrapped.

Sawyer's self-professed "most unusual and exceptionally binding" contract with Barbara stipulated that she "accept any and all employment provided under that contract."[21] That employment included, aside from the starring vehicles she was to make with Sawyer's Associated Pictures, any additional film work he obtained for her. Like *The Shooting of Dan McGrew*, *The White Moth*, the last of the films Barbara would make before beginning her starring series, offered a taste of what was to come.

Released by First National, *The White Moth* was produced and directed by Maurice Tourneur. Whereas Barbara had worked under Tourneur in a minor capacity in *The Brass Bottle* a year earlier, *The White Moth* features her as a lead. Her character, Mona Reid—an insolvent American student in Paris rescued from suicide by impresario Gonzalo Montrez (Charles De Roche)—soars to fame as a dancer known as The White Moth. When Douglas Morley (Ben Lyon), a young millionaire, becomes infatuated with her and deserts his fiancée (Edna Murphy), his brother, Vantine (Conway

BARBARA LA MARR

For decades, Barbara would be credited with making the milk bath famous.

Tearle), endeavors to save him. Inducing The White Moth to fall in love with him, Vantine marries her, realizing by the film's finish that he loves her.

So risqué was Tourneur's treatment of Barbara's role by 1920s standards that *Variety* proposed, "Barbara La Marr, the great undressed, would be accurate billing for Barb, the vamp, in this picture."[22] In one scene, she disrobes behind a screen while Ben Lyon steals a lingering glance into a mirror, strategically angled to give him—and the camera—a peek. Later, she speaks on the telephone while luxuriating in a bathtub—a provocative scene in its time. The film concludes with Barbara entering her screen husband's bedroom in her negligee and flinging a pillow at him, prompting him to follow her into her room and close the door. Censors in certain states eliminated such scenes before allowing the film in theaters.

Sawyer and Ennis used the film to spice up Barbara's image. Titillating *White Moth* film stills of her soaking in a tub ran in fan magazines, along with stories that she spent her days chatting on a telephone while immersed in cow's milk. (The stories were false; Barbara confessed that she never took milk baths, and close friends verified her tendency to forgo elaborate beauty rituals in favor of a simple jar of cold cream.)

Twenty-Six

The opportunity to costar with Barbara was a dream come true for twenty-three-year-old up-and-comer Ben Lyon. "Every leading man would have given an arm to work with her," he later wrote in his memoir.[23] The blue-eyed, dark-haired Georgian evidently had luck on his side. In 1923, after taking his final bow on a New York stage and arriving in Hollywood to continue his film career, he was cast alongside Colleen Moore in First National's *Flaming Youth* (1923), a box office smash that defined the rising flapper movement. Intent on priming him for stardom, First National presented him with a five-year contract.

Lyon would one day concede that he did more than act in *The White Moth* with Barbara. "I fell in love," he admitted in his memoir.[24] A *Photoplay* article, purportedly written by him, alludes to why, describing his "priceless and never-to-be-forgotten experience" of being vamped by her "for screen purposes."

"No woman," he supposedly relates in the article, "can be, within one body and one mind, the things that Barbara is . . . There is intoxication in every line of her, every sound of her voice." The article further states that he found the scent of her hair, her soft skin, and her "sheer, overpowering, tender sweetness" irresistible. Said to be intrigued by her exceptional mind, he allegedly nonetheless remarks, "[A man] does not think when he is with Barbara. He can only feel . . . until sanity and he have become strangers."[25]

Barbara certainly detected Lyon's intensifying feelings as production of *The White Moth* advanced at United Studios. She was seemingly charmed by his nonchalant wittiness (mildly seasoned with his Southern accent), chivalry, charisma, and jolly manner. It would be months before newspapers printed assertions of a romance between them. For the time being, Barbara was doing her best to push through filming.

The costume Barbara wore as The White Moth, complete with diaphanous wings and a cascading, multitiered skirt of gauzy, pearl-accented fabric, presented challenges. While wearing it during the filming of one of her dance sequences in a magnificently recreated French theater, she slipped suddenly, her face whitened, and she dropped to the floor. She immediately rose to her feet and filming continued. Over three hours later, after Tourneur shot the scene for the last time, Barbara wilted, unconscious, on the stage. Lyon raced to her, sweeping her into his arms and rushing her to her dressing room.

The studio physician examined her and announced the trouble: a seri-

Ben Lyon romances Barbara in *The White Moth*. "I fell hook, line, and sinker for her," he said, "and was proud to be seen in her company." (Lyon quoted in Jimmy Bangley, "The Legendary Barbara La Marr," *Classic Images,* May 1996, 20.)

ously sprained knee, swollen to nearly twice its size. Barbara sustained the injury after slipping during her routine and exacerbated it by continuing to work. Asked why she hadn't said anything, she confessed to wanting to save the studio the significant expense of calling the extras back for another

Twenty-Six

Barbara as The White Moth.

day of work. She spent two weeks tottering about the set on crutches, setting them aside whenever she was needed on camera. The press spent months afterward extolling her dogged professionalism.[26]

There came a day when Barbara couldn't summon her tenacity. The towering wig she wore as part of her White Moth costume had become unbearable. After days of suffering silently, she explained that she was unable to work in it. A production assistant telephoned for expert assistance.

Perc Westmore was First National's director of makeup and hairstyling, a position he would hold over thirty years, long after the consolidation of First National and Warner Bros. Studios. His artistic creations, both the stunningly beautiful and the frighteningly hideous, would set new standards as they adorned movie screens throughout his illustrious career.

Westmore placed Barbara's wig over her head, removing it when she recoiled in pain. He immediately pinpointed the problem: wires encircling its base were digging into her temples, irritating sensitive nerve centers. Aware of the agonizing discomfort resulting from such pressure, he wondered how she had worked in it so long. His admiration for her courage must have shown in his eyes, he later recounted, and Barbara smiled at him. "In that glance between us, passed an unspoken understanding," he said, "that many people could never achieve in a lifetime of intimacy."

Something more passed between them. "I somehow sensed a great sadness about Barbara—a prophetic sadness," Westmore continued. "But it was more than a year before my forebodings began to come to pass."[27]

Reactions to *The White Moth*, when it opened that May, were heated. Numerous reviewers scorned it; "tawdry" with "touches of downright indelicacy," sneered *Photoplay* and *Picture Play*. That *The White Moth* indeed appealed to some critics and a significant segment of the public, however, was clear. Exhibitors provided the most noteworthy confirmation; in the Booking Guide, a report on U.S. box office business, the film rated 80 percent (of 100), signifying its classification as a "money-getter." Barbara and her contribution to the film's sex component received ample credit for the profits. The *San Francisco Examiner* raved, "Barbara is scintillating as she has never scintillated before."[28]

With Barbara's starring pictures with Sawyer and First National next on her filming schedule, Ennis was in high gear. Working with the Los Angeles Chamber of Commerce, he arranged for Barbara to represent Southern California (and the various chambers of commerce therein) on a "Southern California Message of Welcome" tour. She was to depart Los Angeles by train with a delegation of Chamber of Commerce dignitaries, traveling to New Orleans and various other cities along the way as the organization's official spokeswoman. Widely advertised personal appearances had been arranged for the party at every stop, during which Barbara would extol the virtues of Southern California, dispense brochures, and encourage tourists to visit. After leaving Louisiana, Barbara would attend an honorary reception in New York City on behalf of Los Angeles mayor George Cryer, delivering to city officials an invitation to visit Los Angeles. Ennis intended that the interviews accompanying her appearances would help promote her upcoming films.

Los Angeles Times writer Alma Whitaker, shocked that the Los Angeles Chamber of Commerce had selected Barbara to represent "the kind of girl we admire above all women in Southern California," condemned the choice as a boorish insult. "Wasn't she rather a peculiarly notorious little girl in this city before she became worth $15,000 [sic] a year?" she argued. "Weren't the recent revelations anent her five marriages, brought out in a

Twenty-Six

recent court trial, a bit staggering, even in these days?" Whitaker suggested that the Southern California chambers of commerce were duped by Ennis into a ploy to provide Barbara with free publicity. "On our prestige, our honor, our reputation she will make personal appearances and receive courtesies through us," she wrote. "And if she doesn't, if she is slighted—the slight will be ours. And we shall deserve it."[29]

Barbara and the chambers of commerce representatives departed Los Angeles the morning of April 6, 1924. Traveling with Barbara were Virginia Carville, Sonny, Irene Almond, and a Russian wolfhound recently given to Barbara by Paul Bern.

Bert Ennis was also with her to oversee publicity—though it wouldn't be the kind he and Barbara anticipated.

VI

Outcast

When you're down they don't get down and kiss your feet as they do when you're up.

—*Barbara La Marr, "The True Story of My Life"*

Twenty-Seven

Barbara's train, billed as the La Marr Special, rattled into towns throughout Arizona, New Mexico, Texas, and Louisiana. At each stop, Barbara blew kisses from the platform of her railroad car as hundreds of men, women, and children—and, in Lafayette, Louisiana, even the town's priest—cheered her.

Publicist Bert Ennis busied himself supplying reporters with copy for their papers. During the train's Lafayette stopover, the mayor unwittingly assisted him by losing his head over Barbara. Firmly fixed in Ennis's mind for years was the image of the besotted man charging down the tracks after the departing train—apparently, according to Ennis, "ready to leave his official duties to the janitor and proceed to New Orleans with our party."[1]

The throngs awaiting the train in New Orleans April 8, 1924, witnessed another unusual sight. Barbara, wearing a beige and emerald crepe dress, black opera cape, and around $25,000 worth of sparkling sapphires and diamonds (her maid had been leaving the gems around and Barbara was afraid of losing them), climbed down from the engine cab. She had helped drive the train a distance of about fifteen miles.

Ennis made the acquaintance of Meigs O. Frost, a *New Orleans States* reporter. After Barbara enjoyed a hearty welcome, the threesome convened in her personal car.

Frost's interview ran the following morning, replete with statements attributed to Barbara. There are two types of women, she was quoted as saying: those who, unable to navigate life's deep waters, "ought to chain themselves in the kitchen and the nursery and the church, and get all the thrills they want out of a guarded home life, with an occasional trip to the movies if they want to be really wild," and those "who can take everything life has to offer regardless of the conventions, and through it all rise to heights of artistry that make them world-famous."

According to Frost, Barbara asserted that the latter type must exist independently of rules. "An artist," Barbara was said to have added, "has to live her life from the bubbles to the dregs—really live it—to be able to portray her parts vividly. You can't act convincingly a passion you have never felt." Nor could any screen vamp, she purportedly stated, render her characterizations had she not "lived fierce love and fierce hate and the breaking, tearing pain of a passionate love that she has lost." Barbara next apparently took a jab at her detractors, pointing out the hypocrisy of those who pay to see artists scale the heights of human emotion, yet condemn the unconventional life that facilitated the expression of such emotions.

Asked by Frost if love helped her in her work, she supposedly retorted, "My dear, I couldn't act worth a cent if I were not in love. I've got to be in love. Love is the very greatest thing in the world, and the very greatest thing in the world can't be anything but a help to you, can it? Love is as much a necessity to the creative artist as breath and bread . . . the body keeps alive on so very little, but the heart and soul—they've got to have love to live."[2]

The same day Frost's article hit New Orleans newsstands, Barbara and her traveling companions sailed for New York. Back on the mainland, hell was breaking loose.

First National officials were staggered when the contents of Frost's article, filtered through the wire services, reached them in New York. "Only an immoral woman can play the part of a vamp successfully"; "the screen vamp must live the life of a vamp if she is truly to portray the part"; "Immorality, free love, and a double standard are the highlights in the interview"—was the essence of the inflated, fragmented reports.[3] Many in Hollywood were equally aghast. Screen vamps Gloria Swanson, Nita Naldi, and Theda Bara were reportedly outraged by Barbara's ostensible contentions. Industry representatives investigated, deducing that the interview may have been an imprudent ploy by Ennis to generate publicity. First National, harboring similar suspicions, ordered Ennis to their offices for a heated meeting after the publicist reached New York. Ennis arrived with a letter written on behalf of the Los Angeles Chamber of Commerce, expressing support for "Miss Barbara La Marr, one of the leading artists of our city."[4]

But damage was already done. On April 17, the women's council of Sacramento, resolving that Barbara "will have a demoralizing effect upon the young people who go to the movies for amusement," demanded that her films be banned from the city's theaters.[5]

A certain amount of the animosity toward Barbara soon dissolved.

Twenty-Seven

She decreed to the press that some of her statements to Frost had been distorted and that subsequent reports had misquoted her. The investigation into the matter confirmed her assertion, the Sacramento women's council forgave her, and the ban on her films was lifted.

The tumult had barely died down when another furor erupted. In June, papers linked Barbara to the murder of Count Miguel Escoto, a purported Spanish nobleman. The reports were based upon a confession made to police by Los Angeles County Jail inmate Morris Nodler. Nodler, imprisoned for robbery, stated that he drove a car for two men—one of them alleged to be a relative of Barbara's husband, Jack Daugherty—when they dumped Escoto's corpse into the sea near Oceanside, California. Escoto's affection for Barbara and her supposed mutual feelings for him, according to Nodler, were motivations for the murder. Nodler's claims were invalidated when deputy district attorney Buron Fitts discovered Escoto—alive—in Los Angeles. Escoto said he had recently met Barbara aboard a ship traveling from San Francisco to Los Angeles and, since then, had been the victim of two baffling assaults, one of which involved a near-fatal beating. Fitts determined that the beating resulted from Escoto's attention to a married woman and that Barbara had not been connected to the assault. Barbara denied ever meeting Escoto.

The Frost and Escoto incidents, along with the roasting the press gave her during Herman Roth's trial, left Barbara shaken. As she anticipated her starring films, increasing trepidation intermingled with her usual performance anxieties. "I'll do my best in pictures," she said, "if I can only be allowed to go my uneventful way in privacy out of pictures."[6]

Shortly after Barbara signed her contract in August 1923 to make starring pictures, Arthur Sawyer announced his intention to produce the films at his S-L Studios in La Mesa, near San Diego. Following the November 1922 ceremony at which Barbara laid the cornerstone for Sawyer's proposed megastudio, the first stage was completed and grandly dedicated in July 1923. But by January 1924, it was obvious to Ed Fletcher, the developer upon whose twenty acres of free and clear land Sawyer's fourteen-stage plant was to be built, that something was amiss. Construction had inexplicably stalled, creditors and S-L Studios shareholders were asking questions, and attempts to reach Sawyer were unavailing.

Fletcher initiated a probe into the books and business of Sawyer and Lubin's S-L Studios. "What I think about Mr. Sawyer," he wrote to a concerned builders' supplies company manager as his own fears were confirmed, "is not fit to repeat." Fletcher laid the results of his investigation before the San Diego district attorney. S-L Studios, Fletcher had discovered, was deeply in debt. A large number of the shares of stock sold by Sawyer and his associates to finance the studio remained outstanding. A significant amount of the money Sawyer had collected was unaccounted for. He had illegally funneled some of it into a real estate venture involving a subdivision adjacent to the S-L Studios site. His activities in the fall of 1923, however, undoubtedly infuriated Fletcher and the shareholders most: Sawyer and his associates resigned at that time as original trustees of S-L Studios; Sawyer appointed new trustees; and, through a contract with them, he absolved himself of any liability to the shareholders. By the summer of 1924, so far as Fletcher was able to deduce, Sawyer had disappeared. Indistinct rumors provided few answers: he had allegedly left California for good, was presumed to be financially destitute, and was understood by Fletcher to be in a sanitarium in the East. Doubtful of recouping losses, Fletcher and the district attorney opted to forgo criminal action against him.[7]

Sawyer's whereabouts, although unknown to Fletcher and S-L Studios investors, were noted in *Moving Picture World* June 21. Herbert Lubin, commending the original locales, access to fresh faces, and close proximity to First National's executive offices, announced that he and Sawyer had moved their recently formed Associated Pictures producing unit to New York City. Sawyer, having accompanied Barbara on her cross-country tour, had arrived in the city that April. There, he was preparing to produce Barbara's first vehicle under her starring contract with him.

That Barbara knew nothing of Sawyer's fraudulence, and was unaware that he would be financing her films with S-L Studios shareholders' money, is entirely possible.

Knowing when she departed Los Angeles that her stay in New York would be an extended one, Barbara moved into the Strathmore, a twelve-story building at 404 Riverside Drive characterized by ten-room luxury apartments with high ceilings, mahogany doors, and parquet flooring. Retaining Irene Almond as her maid, she hired Ada Slater as a new live-in nurse for Sonny; the middle-aged Englishwoman would come to adore him. Jack soon joined Barbara in New York but moved into a hotel, in accordance with their forced separation until California courts determined whether Barbara was married to Ben Deely.

Twenty-Seven

Someone else also followed Barbara to New York. Barbara was seen in theaters and nightclubs with her *White Moth* costar, Ben Lyon. The press again thrust into overdrive, circulating hearsay. It was stated that Barbara's tearful pleas in repeated, long-distance telephone calls to Los Angeles induced Lyon to come to her. Adela Rogers St. Johns later insinuated that Lyon was equally desperate for Barbara. She claimed to witness a scene while visiting Barbara's home before Barbara left California: a young actor matching Lyon's description burst in, she said, accusing Barbara of driving him mad and warning that he would kill himself; Barbara, enraged, purportedly commanded her dog to chase him out. Lyon was said by columnist Harry Carr to have been spotted in New York with a slave bracelet encircling his wrist, the current craze among lovers and a suspected depiction of Barbara's ownership of him. Reports erupted, alleging Barbara's imminent, permanent separation from Jack and engagement to Lyon. Barbara fielded reporters' inquiries with her customary wit: "I have two husbands now and I don't know which one I am really married to, so I'd hardly be thinking about another."[8] Lyon's parents, reportedly horrified that their son was implicated in a scandal, were not amused.

Neither were Sawyer, Lubin, and First National. Anxious to proceed with Barbara's first starring film, *Sandra,* they sensed impending trouble. Lyon, who was to star opposite Barbara as one of her character's extramarital love interests, was reassigned to another film. Jack, who had been given a leading role as Barbara's screen husband, was also stricken from the cast. The censors were unsatisfied; in their judgment, the film's story line bore too many similarities to Barbara's personal life. Will Hays halted the making of the picture.

Barbara took to her typewriter, working with the film's production team to produce a scenario that would appease the Hays Office.[9]

Jack, meanwhile, decided he was finished being Barbara's real-life husband. He announced in mid-July that he and Barbara had permanently separated. The press hounded them for statements.

"Jack and I just agreed that it would be better to separate," Barbara maintained to one reporter. "There really was no particular trouble, no hard feelings at any rate."[10]

In *Movie Weekly*'s rendition of her life story, Barbara was slightly more forthcoming. "Courtships are deceiving things," she assertedly wrote. "Instinctively, men as well as women are on their best behavior before marriage. A man will go a good deal out of his way to assume an interest in something a girl is doing that he couldn't possibly keep up through the long and steady pace of matrimony."[11]

Jack conveyed his feelings in his own article; it would run in *Photoplay* that October, below the title "Why I Quit Being Mr. Barbara La Marr." Barbara's stardom, he began, had separated them. "And yet no man was ever more in love with his wife than I was with mine, and it is my absolute conviction that if she hadn't become Barbara La Marr, a screen idol, we would have been a thoroughly happy and devoted married couple."[12]

A husband, he said, is a "poor second" in a star's life. "Her life is in her work, her career. The reflection of portrayals which she actually lives while she is playing them [and] the continual emotional upset . . . make a woman an entirely different being than she would be otherwise." The unrelenting demands upon Barbara as a star had furthermore left her no time for him. "I had a wife—and I didn't have a wife," he wrote.[13]

Jack admitted that his pride, wounded by the vast discrepancy between Barbara's earnings and the good living he made, also came between them. "I became so sensitive that I thought I saw sneers in everyone's eyes," he continued, relating that he had denied himself certain luxuries to avoid accusations that he was profiting from Barbara's success.[14]

He didn't blame Barbara for the failure of their marriage. "I sometimes wish the world might know Barbara as I know her—might see behind the alluring and beautiful exterior into the fine intellect and big, warm, generous heart of hers," he added. "She was the best of pals, the sweetest of sweethearts, and, insofar as her position permitted her to be a wife at all, she was a good wife."[15]

It simply hadn't been enough. "My own individuality was smothered," he said. "I became so unhappy and so unlike myself that I could no longer enjoy our life together." He concluded, "And I'm sorry and I know Barbara is sorry because—in the beginning—we did love each other very much."[16]

To the insatiable press, Barbara's official separation from Jack meant a pending marriage to Lyon. According to Barbara's son, with whom Lyon privately shared his memories years later, Lyon did indeed intend to marry Barbara. "There was only one difficulty," Lyon recorded in his memoir. "Barbara was not in love with me."[17]

The February 1925 *Photoplay* article on film vamps Lyon had known—reputedly written by him and theoretically referencing his onscreen romances—afforded film fans a speculative glimpse into the dissolution of his relationship with Barbara. He is credited with describing her as being as "fickle as the sunlight upon the water" and writing of her "poignant," recurring sadness. "[A man] cannot make her happy," the article cites him as saying, "though he sell his soul to the devil in striving."[18]

Reporters were soon preoccupied with other stories. Lyon began dating Gloria Swanson; "If any woman wants to take up my castoffs," a New York paper quoted Barbara as remarking, "I'll keep her busy."[19]

Behind her witticisms, Barbara felt ever more victimized by the ceaseless media attention and the repeated, biting criticism it generated. She avowedly acknowledged that her treatment by various reporters had resulted in "some of the greatest blows to my inherent faith in human nature."[20] She began dreading being recognized in public and despaired over what might be printed about her the next day. She professed to "worrying myself sick" over statements and actions falsely ascribed to her. "I suppose the whole thing would be funny if it wasn't tragic," she said.[21]

Jack likened the change worldwide scrutiny induced in Barbara to what occurs when criminals are forced to face a blinding light during interrogation. "It takes away their resistance and presently they lose their control and do and say whatever is asked of them," he said. "Their life force is being used up. Well, stars live in a much stronger light all the time . . . They are irritable, without much self-control and susceptible to strong influence."[22]

Twenty-Eight

Barbara's devotees, eager for the release of her first starring picture, received welcome news from fan magazines at the end of August 1924. The censors had approved the script Barbara helped rewrite. Production of *Sandra,* now six weeks behind schedule, had begun.

Impatient to distribute the film, First National organized what they touted as the most wide-ranging publicity campaign ever undertaken. Throughout filming of *Sandra,* Barbara would continuously be stopped in mid-scene, a photographer would swoop in, and hundreds of thousands of photographs would be disseminated for promotional tie-ins in theaters, storefronts, and restaurants nationwide. First National proclaimed, "We look for great things from Barbara La Marr."[1]

Barbara felt the pressure. She tethered her faith to Arthur Sawyer who, besides taking up the megaphone and director's chair for the first time, had total control of the production. Sawyer tethered his faith, as always, to Barbara's sex appeal and sacrificed no expense in showcasing it. Costumer Claire West, renowned for her elegant, provocative designs, accentuated Barbara's assets with a plethora of costly gowns, lingerie, and headpieces. Fifteen tremendous sets had been fashioned on the stages of New York's Biograph Studios, including a Paris apartment, a Russian cabaret, gambling palaces, a sweeping dining room, and a spectacular ballroom.

The story, handpicked by Sawyer, thrust Barbara into the role of Sandra Waring, a woman with a split personality. At her best, Sandra is the affectionate, obedient wife of David Waring (Bert Lytell), a loving New York architect; at her worst, she's a callous adventuress. Sandra's shadow self overtakes her and she goes to Europe, discarding David for lovers of ill reputation, becoming disillusioned when each betrays her. Notorious and broken, she returns to New York, her sinister side purified by an understanding of the pain she caused David. Before carrying out her plan to commit suicide, she visits the church David built. There she encounters the Reverend Hapgood (Leslie Austin), and asks him to

Twenty-Eight

Barbara with her screen husband, Bert Lytell, in *Sandra*.

communicate an apology to David. David overhears her and takes her back.

Sawyer staged the story as daringly as he could, featuring Barbara in various erotic circumstances—even a nude swimming scene. Placing the blame for Sandra's debauched behavior on a psychological impairment and ending the film with her reformation were likely what enabled it to scrape past censors. No credit would be given for the scenario; while it isn't known how much of a hand Barbara had in its creation, her efforts were reportedly denied recognition in order to downplay her intelligence and promote her vamp image.[2]

To columnists visiting the film's sets, Barbara appeared at her best. She gave interviews and put in long, irregular hours; due to the summer heat, the production crew worked all night and throughout the morning. Behind the scenes, she was fraying. Doubts about both her work in the film and her abilities assaulted her. She convinced herself she was a better actress when she was a child. Turning to her books for comfort at home, she caught her mind circling back to scenes she shot that day and berated herself for not doing them differently. She was also still turning to the bot-

Barbara costumed in a negligee consisting of a clinging, silver sheath swathed in fifteen yards of lavender chiffon, one of many decadent creations she wore in *Sandra*.

Twenty-Eight

tle. Ethlyne Clair, an extra in *Sandra,* would recall filming a sequence aboard a yacht and witnessing an inebriated Barbara fumble through the scene.[3]

Ever present in Barbara's mind were the devastating words her doctor had spoken the previous year: you won't endure more than twenty months. By early summer 1924, half of the time he had allotted her was gone.

Rather than submit to death, Barbara clung to life. "I deliberately burned the candle at both ends," she acknowledged to a friend.[4] That she invited disaster by disregarding her doctor's admonition to rest made no difference to her. She continued keeping her diagnosis a secret, determining to enjoy each moment to the utmost. "Eight hours of sleep out of every twenty-four—how perfectly ridiculous!" she declared. "When life is so short and so delightful, why should we spend a third of the precious hours in a coma? I seldom waste more than two hours a day in sleep and I never intend to."[5]

Since her arrival in New York, Barbara was a fixture at racketeer Larry Fay's infamous El Fey club. Here, a medley of New York City's upper crust, stage and screen luminaries, corrupt prohibition agents, mobsters, and hangers-on could guzzle bootleg booze and get their kicks watching "a dozen or so girls, wearing only a few beads and a feather" dance among tables.[6] Texas Guinan, El Fey's raucous, effervescent hostess, made certain of it. Every night, Guinan, festooned in flashy gowns and gaudy jewels, ruled El Fey from her ringside stool, rattling a clapper, tooting a police whistle, and spouting wisecracks. Big spenders received her trademark salute: *Hello, sucker!*

From the moment Barbara entered El Fey's well-guarded doorway each night, slipping $25 tips to coat-check girls, she was on a spree of reckless indulgence. Dining on sumptuous foods and bingeing on overpriced liquor were but a minuscule part of it. Her tendency to be generous with others ran riot. Bert Ennis recalled, "It was a common occurrence for her to turn over her checkbook to her nightclub pals. She signed and they spent." Barbara's weekly salary, he said, in the hands of "good fellows who acquired a big rep as heavy money tossers on the Big Alley," vanished "faster than snow on Hollywood Boulevard."[7]

Rumors of Barbara's "magic checkbook" and foolhardy behavior circulated.[8] She allegedly kept signed checks in a drawer at her apartment for various boyfriends to use at will. She was said to accompany some of these boyfriends for a night out, little realizing she was footing the bill.

Barbara rationalized her actions to her friend, film critic Harriette Underhill. "Eat, drink, and be merry, for tomorrow we die," she sang out to Underhill above the whoopee-making at El Fey one night. "This life is so short, and there are so many things to do. I must hurry."[9]

Only Barbara grasped the full import of her words.

After separating from Jack Daugherty in July, Barbara voiced her intention to enjoy her freedom for awhile. By October, however, just after *Sandra* wrapped, she professed to be in love again.

He was dark-haired, Georgia-born, twenty-eight-year-old Benjamin Ficklin ("Ben") Finney Jr.—part Southern gentleman, part man-about-town, part happy-go-lucky drifter. As an impressionable Marine recruit in 1917, Finney stumbled upon his self-acknowledged credo when his romanticized notions of army life faded in the glare of reality. "Living recklessly, plunging in feet first," he later recorded in his memoir, "became the behavior pattern of my life . . . I have never regretted it." His daring earned him a Croix de Guerre medal in France; back home in the States, it impelled him to drop out of the University of Virginia after only three years. Of his decision to tackle life without a college degree, he remarked, "I . . . never let [school] interfere too much with my education."[10]

Finney's boldness paid off. After taking possession of a 4,000-acre North Carolina plantation willed to him by his deceased mother, he turned to farming in 1922, despite knowing nothing of growing cotton, corn, and tobacco. His unwitting success with the plantation (and his father's position as president of the University of the South at Sewanee, Tennessee) granted him access to social circles in both the South and New York, where he spent half his time.

Fortune smiled upon him again in early 1924. He moved to Miami, Florida, for the winter on a whim, threw a party, and met film star Betty Compson. One encounter with the handsome Finney was all it took for Compson, in town to film *Miami* (1924), to offer him a leading role opposite her in the picture. Finney, who admittedly "didn't know one end of a camera from a light meter," uttered his typical rejoinder: "Sure!"[11] Following the film's release, he was exalted in newspapers nationwide as "the South's favorite son" and reentered the New York nightclub scene in a blaze of glory.

Sometime that spring, during an evening of jollity at El Fey, Texas Guinan introduced Finney to Barbara. Enshrined in his memory several

Twenty-Eight

decades later, the image of Barbara as he first knew her remained: her dark hair smoothed against her head . . . the way she flowed when she moved . . . that she didn't walk into a room so much as she arrived in one. "She had the charisma of Sophia Loren *and* Brigitte Bardot plus that 'star quality' most movie actresses don't know how to exude any more," he wrote.[12] The two forged a close friendship that summer.

Then Barbara fell hard. Finney had spoken to her of the state where he spent some of his school days. With time on her hands before her next starring picture went into production, Barbara proposed they go there. They set off on a crisp October day, making their way toward the still, scenic Blue Ridge Mountains of Virginia.

Under a cerulean sky in Yancey Mills, they checked into a small, antebellum inn known as the Green Teapot Hotel. In the surrounding orchard, apples hung red, ripe, and plentiful from dipping branches.

Shortly after their arrival, a jaunt to the nearby University of Virginia for a football game landed Finney in trouble. From the university's president, Edwin Anderson Alderman, Finney would one day learn of the hefty allegation that had been hung on him by University of Virginia football coach Earle Neale. The game, Neale related to Alderman the day after it took place, was a calamity. The kickoff had resulted in a great return by a Virginia player to the fifty-yard line. But then, one by one, the entire Virginia team beheld Barbara—seated front and center near the forty-yard line in a short white dress. "And while our lads were looking at Miss La Marr, *their* lads were beating the bejesus out of us," Neale continued, "and if I ever get my hands on that goddamned Finney I'll break *both* his goddamned heads!"[13]

Barbara caused another thrill the next day when she and Finney visited his former preparatory school. On the drive over, Finney spotted three boys walking toward the campus and offered them a ride. After leaping into the jump seats, one of the boys turned and noticed Barbara. Finney, peering through the rearview mirror, observed what happened next. "There was a loss of breath, heightening of color, and blood beating at the temples," he recalled; the boy "whispered his discovery to the other two . . . The boys sat in stricken wonder." The moment Finney pulled up to the school, the boys raced from the car. Excitement ricocheted through the campus. Finney went inside to say hello to the headmaster; Barbara waited in the car. "I came back to find that half the school had for some mysterious reason important business in the vicinity of the car," Finney said.

"Some boys were huddled in a group arguing over a manuscript which was being held upside down. The captain of the football team was raking nonexistent leaves. Dozens of others had decided this was an ideal place to study and, tomes in hand, had formed an academic circle around the unconcerned queen."[14]

On their way back to New York, Barbara and Finney enjoyed a stopover in Gettysburg, Pennsylvania. There they posed for a photograph perched atop the barrel of a Civil War cannon, Barbara near the front with Finney behind her, his arms encircling her waist and his head on her shoulder, their feet dangling above the ground, both of them laughing.

Upon her return to New York, Barbara confirmed to the press that she and Finney were an item. She had found, she said, "the perfect love of her life."[15]

Barbara's official marital status was still undetermined. While her attorneys petitioned the courts to have the trial for Ben Deely's divorce case advanced to the soonest possible date, an unforeseen development occurred.

Forty-six-year-old Ben died in Hollywood September 23. The end came four days after he was led, pallid and ailing, from the set of his latest film and helped into bed at a friend's house. The trades, commemorating his noteworthy vaudeville and film careers, announced the cause of death: double pneumonia. Not long before his passing, Barbara, despite their turbulent marriage and its knotty aftermath, openly professed that no malice existed between them. (She even suggested him to a film director looking to cast a heavy months before Ben's death, contending that he was the industry's best.) In light of Ben's death, his divorce suit was scratched from the courthouse hearing docket.

Ben's passing did nothing to resolve Barbara's marital standing. Without his suit to confirm or refute the legality of his marriage to her, her marriage to Jack remained questionable.

Now Barbara's love for Finney was thrown into the tangle. Jack's continued presence in New York and Barbara's life (although still separated, they were frequently spotted together) whipped the hopelessly confused press into a frenzy. A climax ensued, precipitated by a mystifying incident occurring sometime before the predawn hours of November 5, 1924.

Multiple physicians, prompted by a telephone call seemingly placed from Barbara's Riverside Drive apartment, raced to her aid. Barbara was

Twenty-Eight

pronounced by them to be "in a critical condition."[16] Her state, it was said, remained unchanged for two days. She was kept in bed, attended by Virginia Carville and, most probably, a doctor or nurse.

A story reached the press, declaring that Barbara had attempted suicide. Reporters gathered along Riverside Drive and inside her apartment building. Their observations appeared on newsstands nationwide. Finney, Jack, and Ben Lyon also rushed to Barbara, each armed with flowers and each, according to the press, believing himself responsible for her alleged act. It was reported that Virginia assured the men that there had been a mistake. Barbara, she said, merely grabbed the wrong bottle from her medicine cabinet. Supposedly Barbara had intended to drink aromatic spirits of ammonia (an anxiety remedy and antacid) but inadvertently overdosed on nux vomica (an herbal treatment derived from the strychnine tree and used for heart and lung diseases, anemia, nervous disorders, indigestion, and poisoning rats).[17]

Not everyone accepted Virginia's explanation. More stories reached the press; speculations flew. One account held that, on the night in question, Barbara had gone to a nightclub with Jack and spied Finney with another woman. Another maintained that Barbara was desperate to wed Finney and distressed that she lacked legal clearance to do so. Meanwhile, per eyewitness reports, Finney was an unremitting presence at her apartment. The press decided Barbara had indeed attempted suicide, and that her motive centered on Finney.

Convalescing in bed and greatly troubled by the allegations, Barbara acted urgently. On the evening of November 7 she allowed reporters into her apartment. She did not, she said, deliberately take poison. She insisted there wasn't a man alive worth killing herself for. Then, contradicting Virginia's prior statement, she provided her own explanation of what happened. "It is ptomaine poisoning from something I ate," she stated.[18]

Reporters didn't buy the latest explanation for Barbara's sudden illness. The next day they were given what they believed to be proof that Barbara attempted suicide because she couldn't wed Finney: Jack left New York, tacitly relinquishing Barbara as his wife.

Traveling by train through Chicago and heading into Los Angeles, Jack was met by reporters at both stations. Those hoping for dirt didn't get it. Jack stated that he had no enmity toward Barbara or Finney. "We are just three close friends and are often seen around New York together," he said. "I don't care who goes around with Miss La Marr, as I am very fond of her and would do anything in the world for her." He confirmed his plan to divorce Barbara—"just as soon as some legal red tape is out of the way."[19] He intended to charge desertion.

Barbara likewise told journalists that no ill will existed between her and Jack, that they were still friends, and that she would do anything in the world for him.

Her main allegiance, however, lay with Finney. Jack's divorce suit was being undertaken to enable her to wed again, newspapers pronounced. The day Jack left New York, Barbara and Finney were photographed walking arm and arm along the street. "Presenting," more than a few captions read as the photo appeared in newspapers, "the new Mr. La Marr."[20]

The publicity spawned by Barbara's personal life paired with the massive promotional campaigns Sawyer, Lubin, and First National had carried out on her behalf, creating the preamble for one of the most long-awaited films of the year. *Sandra* entered theaters November 16. On screens and in advertisements worldwide, Barbara's was the name above the title, her name being counted on to fill theaters. The thought petrified her. She avoided viewing the film upon its debut and, months later, would admit to still being too afraid to see it.

Because *Sandra* was the biggest blow she had sustained as an actress, perhaps she chose never to see it. Critics bewailed the film as an outright failure and were merciless in their attacks. Numerous reviewers faulted the story, denigrating the idea of a woman with the dual personality of a dutiful wife and an untamed siren. Others, such as *Film Daily*, blamed Sawyer's "poor" direction for the "draggy," lengthy production: "Eight reels of Barbara La Marr and sex appeal and not much of anything else."[21] Some castigated the acting.

Barbara confessed not long before the film's release, "I think it would kill me to fail . . . to disappoint those who believe in me."[22] Surely, it took every vestige of her strength to endure the assessments of her performance. "When it comes to playing gilded sirens, Barbara La Marr is in her element," wrote a *Boston Traveler* writer. "But it was something of a shock to find out what a rotten actress she is."[23] Reviewers accused her of resorting to mannerisms; the *St. Louis Globe-Democrat* remarked, "Miss La Marr . . . wiggles her eyebrows, purses her lips, shrugs her shoulders, and is artificial to such a degree that at the end of a few scenes we are surfeited with [her] affectations."[24] *Photoplay* commented, "Our disappointment on

Twenty-Eight

viewing this picture was the greatest we have ever felt while sitting before a screen. Great expectations were shattered."[25]

A handful of critics offered sympathetic appraisals, suggesting that Barbara had done her best with the substandard material provided her. There were those who were so taken by her sex attraction they forgave all else.

Barbara rejected such supportive comments. *Sandra,* she believed, was a disaster. Exhibitors reported loss of business. Filmgoers laughed during sequences intended to be serious; more than a few exhibitors touted the film as a comedy rather than a drama. Perhaps Barbara did not, at this time, blame Sawyer; she purportedly extolled him as one of her favorite directors and "one of the greatest producing executives we have in the film business."[26] Nor did she blame novelist Pearl Doles Bell, the story's creator; she voiced her admiration for Bell's clever writing style. It's entirely likely that Barbara's festering insecurities caused her to regard *Sandra* as a personal failure.

"Miss La Marr," predicted a film journalist, "doubtless will spend the balance of her career in pictures living down that terrible [film]."[27]

Indeed she would.

The Fox Film Corporation released a film the day *Sandra* premiered. The studio had promoted it for months, announcing that its original story was authored by none other than Barbara La Marr. Their strategy worked. Increased interest was generated for *My Husband's Wives.*

Barbara birthed the story during her nocturnal writing sessions four and a half years earlier. It was the last of the six she was contracted to write for Fox. Budgeting constraints had prevented Fox from producing it in 1920. Barbara's stardom had provided the impetus for the studio to revisit her manuscript.

Fox publicized the film's other notable aspects as well. It was the first American picture to be directed by Maurice Elvey, a prominent director imported from England to direct Fox films. Scenarized by Dorothy Yost, *My Husband's Wives* was a vehicle for Fox superstar Shirley Mason, who had earlier triumphed in Barbara's adaptation, *Flame of Youth* (1920).

Inspiration for the story, Barbara explained, was involuntarily given her by one of her friends. The woman, an unnamed, well-known actress, was wed to a man with three ex-wives; whenever she encountered her husband's past flames at social gatherings, she deftly referred to them as "my husband's wives."

From this phrase, Barbara invented the comical tale of Vale Harvey (played by Mason), a naïve young newlywed whose jealousy torments her. When her groom, William (Bryant Washburn), tries to tell her of his ex-wife, Vale forbids him to speak of her. She invites her old school chum, Marie Wynn (Evelyn Brent)—and trouble—for a visit: Marie is her husband's ex-wife and contrives to reclaim her ex-husband. Danger is averted when William learns of Marie's motives, Marie is thrown out of the house, and Vale is made by her faithful husband to see the foolishness of her fears.

Variety implied that Barbara injected at least one autobiographical detail into her story. Was it mere coincidence, the magazine proposed, that she chose the name Marie Wynn for the ex-wife and made the character "particularly catty"?[28] The writer passed over particulars, but it can be inferred that the woman referenced was vampy actress Marie Wayne, Ben Deely's second wife (and the woman from whom he was about to undergo an acrimonious divorce when he met Barbara in 1916).

Although various critics sounded off against what they classified as a silly film and lean plot, acclaim for *My Husband's Wives* predominated, and Barbara's story was recognized: "Will please those who love a good story and fine picture"; "A more delightful picture was never sat through with a plot which never allows one's interest to lag"; "Barbara La Marr's story provides food for serious thought . . . possesses dramatic force and presents some good comedy."[29] The film kept audiences in stitches as it enjoyed nationwide success.

Barbara must have counted popular response to *My Husband's Wives* among her life's brighter spots at the time.

Twenty-Nine

Barbara had been struggling with her weight for months. Measures were taken to conceal it during the filming of *Sandra*. She was laced into corsets and stuffed into girdles. Arthur Sawyer and cameraman George Clarke tried filming around it, capturing her in what some reviewers suggested was an inordinate number of close-ups. None of it worked. Barbara's fans, exhibitors, and critics were appalled by the change in her. In mid-December 1924, just before she began her second starring picture, Sawyer and Lubin raised the issue with her again. Her contract with them required that she remain below a specific weight limit; she was eighteen pounds above it.

Barbara was glorified as being ideally proportioned before her dissipation in New York nightclubs obscured her figure with surplus poundage. She had been trying to reduce, reportedly shedding twenty pounds while filming *Sandra*. But a battle lay ahead. In the past, she had maintained her weight with light breakfasts and lunches, and dinners consisting of a small portion of meat, a salad, toast, and an occasional serving of cake or ice cream. She had avoided late-night eating. She had incorporated daily body conditioning whenever she could, relying upon a combined regimen of standard and dancing exercises.

This protocol would no longer suffice. Her body's naturally curvaceous mold, once idealized, was plummeting from grace. In its place, along with the swelling popularity of films featuring flappers, a new feminine standard had arisen. The so-called perfect flapper figure—boyish and shapeless—would rule throughout the remainder of the decade.

The repercussions were enormous. In the mid-1920s, the normal average weight for a woman of Barbara's age and ranging in height from 5'4" to 5'6" was 135 pounds. By the late 1920s, *Photoplay* acknowledged that, for female film stars, that average had plunged to 119 pounds.[1] Weight clauses in stars' contracts became general procedure. Actresses were weighed before beginning a production; anyone exceeding her set limit had her contract terminated or was barred from working until she reduced.

Though the cap imposed upon Barbara is not known from available sources, period publications report permissible weights as varying between 120 and 130 pounds, although some contracts had considerably lower limits (Molly O'Day's was 108). Slender stars' weight—as well as the diets and exercise routines they relied upon to retain their weight—were broadcasted by the press. A craze, "reduceomania," took hold of American women.

On January 5, 1925, two weeks after the preproduction weigh-in for her second starring film, Barbara appeared on the set as scheduled, ready for filming. The eighteen pounds she had been ordered to lose, Bert Ennis later recalled, had disappeared.[2] Barbara's weight was soon announced in *Photoplay*: 124 pounds.[3] A newspaper article appearing shortly afterward provided a rundown of Barbara's daily food intake: eggs and spinach for breakfast; and, for lunch, a glass of tomato juice and cup of mushroom soup.[4] Concealed from the public until after her death, however, was the supplementary protocol she used to achieve and maintain her slender shape.

The national obsession with thinness had ushered in an industry devoted to capitalizing upon desperation. Those seeking to reduce quickly had their choice of a wide selection of nostrums, most of which purported to safely strip pounds almost overnight. Many such formulations were worthless; others were hazardous.

Among the more notorious was a tablet reputed to contain the pin-sized head of a tapeworm. The parasite imbedded itself in the intestinal wall of its host by means of hooks on its head, growing as many as twenty feet long and around half an inch wide, absorbing digested food through its skin. One could supposedly expel the worm by fasting and consuming a mixture of salts and extracts. Those who harbored it experienced, besides weight loss, side effects varying from ongoing diarrhea and headaches to anemia and organ damage. Though it has been suggested that the tapeworm pill belongs in the annals of folklore, Ennis and film magazine articles of the period assert that Barbara ingested one.[5]

Another method reported by period magazines to have been used by Barbara is the thyroid treatment.[6] The therapy was based on sound research that human consumption of high doses of the dried thyroid glands of certain animals (in capsule form) increased metabolism and reduced weight. The trouble was, in doses significant enough to cause weight loss, hyperthyroidism also resulted. Continual intake could produce shakiness and

Twenty-Nine

excessive nervousness; weaken the kidneys, heart, and pancreas; and hasten the development of tuberculosis. The glandular matter was also documented to produce insanity; thus, assuming Barbara indeed attempted suicide November 5, such a weight-loss program may have contributed to her compromised mental state.

Barbara's radical dieting practices would, in time, be blamed for her failing health in approaching months. It would also be declared that her fear of criticism and ridicule prevented her discontinuation of them, regardless of the potentially ruinous cost. To her, stated columnist Myrtle West, "life meant success, and, without success, Barbara didn't want to live."[7]

Barbara's trimmed-down physique probably gave her a confidence boost as she filmed *The Heart of a Siren* at Universal's studio in Fort Lee throughout January. Columnists commented on how wonderful they thought she looked, some stating they had never seen her more beautiful. Sawyer hired future Oscar-winning costumer Charles LeMaire to create eighteen ravishingly seductive costumes for Barbara—a reward, remarked one newspaper, for her weight loss. First National, Sawyer, and Lubin pushed *Sandra* from their minds and conducted a forceful promotional crusade, much of which entailed Barbara modeling her figure and costumes. Barbara's health, meanwhile, was taking a hit. LeMaire fretted over her, later recounting her on-set exhaustion and determination to give her best.[8]

Supporting Barbara in the picture is the most capable talent Sawyer could obtain. Originally intending to follow up his directorial debut on *Sandra* by directing *The Heart of a Siren*, Sawyer instead served as supervisor and abdicated the megaphone to Phil Rosen, recipient of *Photoplay*'s Medal of Honor for his work on *The Dramatic Life of Abraham Lincoln* (1924). Art director M. P. Staulcup erected fourteen extravagant sets, unveiling his groundbreaking coloring technique whereby photographed objects stood out in raised relief from backgrounds. Desirous of replicating the box office success of *The White Moth*, Sawyer reunited Barbara with her *White Moth* love interest, Conway Tearle. He also granted Barbara a favor, yielding to her insistence that Ben Finney have a minor role in the film.

With his selection of the role of Isabella Echevaria, Sawyer continued his exploitation of Barbara's typecasting. Despite the role's formulaic nature, Barbara attempted to create a warm-hearted characterization. As

Barbara bedecked in two of the ensembles she wore in *The Heart of a Siren*. "She was gorgeous, feline, and wore clothes with grace and elegance," said Charles LeMaire, designer of the garments. Upper photo courtesy of Allison Francis. (LeMaire quote from Jimmy Bangley, "Barbara La Marr: A Memorial Tribute," *Classic Images*, February 1999, 29.)

Twenty-Nine

Barbara and Ben Finney (playing a portrait artist) in *The Heart of a Siren*.

the camera rolled, she transformed Isabella from an unfeeling, wealthy temptress of dubious reputation to a woman in love with Gerald Rexford (Tearle), an English diplomat visiting France. The lovers are torn apart when Gerald's mother (Ida Darling), fearful that Isabella's notoriety will besmirch Gerald, convinces Isabella to surrender him. Gerald is apprised of his mother's doings; and Isabella, saved by her maid (Florence Auer) from suicide, accepts his marriage proposal.

Barbara's methodology for enacting Isabella struck Clifton Webb, one of her costars, as unconventional. She endured Webb's good-natured ribbing whenever she asked the on-set mood orchestra to accompany her dramatic scenes with her favorite tango tune. Her performance, complete with flamboyant outbursts and affecting delicacy, pleased director Phil Rosen; he considered her portrayal to be the best she had turned out since her masterly work in Rex Ingram's *Trifling Women*. First National, placing an elevated exhibition value on *The Heart of a Siren*, evidently felt the same.

Several of the trades had already pegged *The Heart of a Siren* as a moneymaker when it was released April 26. *Film Daily,* although anticipating that Isabella's ribald nature and Barbara's "continual décolleté" would barely slip past censors, advised exhibitors, "No question about the success of a sex angle picture if your crowd is right for it." In its element, *The Heart of a Siren* was a winner. *Moving Picture World* christened it "one of the best vamp roles of [Barbara's] career." Outside of its element, within a changing market, the film suffered. *Variety,* labeling the story "ultra-melodramatic and nonsensical," noted that the "direction, subtitling, and acting drew laughs."[9]

Before *The Heart of a Siren* reached theaters, Sawyer seemingly had little doubt of a favorable outcome. He was envisioning Barbara's next film by February, an ambitious production lifted from the titillating pages of a 1924 novel already in its tenth printing under a year later. As the film's supervisor, he retained the entire *Heart of a Siren* production staff, including Phil Rosen.

With a break in her schedule as Sawyer and Rosen attended to various preproduction details, Barbara picked up her copy of the best seller and studied the part she was to play. Her heart, however, was apparently pulled elsewhere.

Barbara's time with her son had been lacking.

Sonny, now two-and-a-half and walking, was growing before her eyes. He already showed signs of inheriting her writing talent; his scribbles could be admired throughout their apartment—particularly on the wallpaper. But Barbara, occupied with career obligations, had rarely been around to encourage his budding abilities. She relied upon Ada Slater, Sonny's loving nursemaid, to fulfill her motherly functions.

Although grateful for Slater's help, Barbara longed to mother Sonny herself. She likewise still ached to discard her pseudo image as his adoptive parent. She risked exposure by revealing the truth to Slater months earlier following a doctor's visit. Concerned by the bowed appearance of Sonny's legs, Barbara had instructed Slater to take him to a specialist for leg braces. The doctor advised Slater that the trouble resulted from rickets; the boy's mother, he said, hadn't had enough to eat while pregnant, and this had resulted in the boy having soft bones. Barbara received the report with indignation. "He lied," she told Slater. "I am his real mother and I had all the food I wanted."[10] She explained to Slater that Sonny's legs were bowed because he was born with his foot soles pressed together. (After months of wearing braces, his legs straightened.)

Considering Barbara's worsening weariness and the increased urgency with which she was living her life, she likely felt a heightened need to be with her son. On February 7, days after filming ended for *The Heart of a Siren,* Barbara, Sonny, and Slater boarded a steamship. Barbara was fulfilling one of the dreams she had had since Sonny's birth. They were off to begin exploring the world.

Ben Finney accompanied them. He and Barbara were still awaiting the filing of Jack's divorce suit and, in the interim, were living together in Barbara's apartment. They listed themselves as married on the ship's manifest.

The ship sailed from New York toward tropical climes. The foursome drifted around the Caribbean Sea for nearly a month, visiting Miami, Havana, Jamaica, Honduras, and Guatemala.

Barbara and her traveling companions returned to New York on March 3. The vacation hadn't alleviated her fatigue. As she looked ahead to her next film, uneasiness also took hold.

Barbara had reservations about the story Sawyer selected. *The White Monkey* was an intensely psychological study. Written by celebrated British novelist John Galsworthy, the story was inspired by an ancient Chinese painting. In it, a white monkey sits clasping an orange; the piece of fruit and its cast-off rinds are vibrant against a gray backdrop; the animal's face and its brown eyes reflect a futile longing, a haunted hopelessness. Galsworthy, likening the monkey to the modern generation, formulated his book's premise: "Youth forever reaching for it knows not what and unhappy because it cannot get it."[11] Intriguing as the book may have been to Barbara as she studied it during her cruise, she thought Galsworthy's work, filled with in-depth character explorations, unsuitable for the (silent) screen. "The delicate subtleties of [his] philosophy" cannot be interpreted via screen action, she believed.[12] Her conviction was echoed by columnists who expressed surprise that Galsworthy's novel had been chosen as her next vehicle.

Sawyer and Lubin were of a different opinion. Big money had been spent to procure film rights to the best seller. First National, Sawyer, and Lubin had launched their usual advance advertising blitz. Barbara began work on the film, titled *The White Monkey* after the book, at Universal's

Barbara with (*left to right*) Henry Victor, Thomas Holding, Colin Campbell, and George F. Marion in *The White Monkey*. Courtesy of Allison Francis.

Fort Lee studio March 26—wishing, she later disclosed, "my weak voice [had] been heard."[13]

Barbara's character, Fleur Forsyte, personifies the monkey, losing sight of what she has by grasping for what she has not. The coddled daughter of Soames Forsyte (George F. Marion), an English noble, Fleur is wed to London publisher Michael Mont (Thomas Holding), but yearns to taste the affections of his best friend, artist Wilfrid Desert (Henry Victor). The film ends with Fleur realizing she loves Michael and heeding the painting's moral.

Rosen shot the film's final scene around the end of April; after its June 7 release, assessments of the production reached the Associated Pictures and First National offices. The majority voiced shameless contempt. Disgruntled exhibitors held forth in the trades, warning their colleagues. "You will disgrace your theater forever if you should run this one," wrote one in *Moving Picture World*.[14]

As Barbara had foreseen, the essence of Galsworthy's novel had not translated to the screen. "The whole affair is toneless," the *Los Angeles Times* hissed—a "rather trite triangle," moaned the *New York Sun*.[15]

Twenty-Nine

Numerous critics placed blame for the catastrophe at Barbara's feet. The unpitying raking she received agonized her. The *New York Telegram* hooted, "All Miss La Marr can do in the role is close and open her eyes and purse her lips." A *Picture Play* reviewer declared that she "reached heights of hilarity that I didn't dream could exist." *Photoplay* jested, "Every time Barbara La Marr starts to act, the scene is mercifully cut."[16]

Multiple factors may have prompted such cutting of Barbara's scenes. Sawyer and Rosen were again pushing the envelope with censors. As documented by a few reviewers, some of Barbara's scenes were overtly suggestive, and at least one ended abruptly at an inappropriate place. Possibly another explanation for Barbara's truncated scenes is that she was nowhere near her best throughout filming. Critics agreed that, swathed in costly, revealing costumes, she was a vision to behold. She had kept her weight down and frequent mention was made of her beautiful, sinuous figure in reviews. Her health, meanwhile, was suffering. Reviewers commented on how tired she seemed and how, despite being as seductive as ever, her usual inner fire was much subdued. The long hours she spent fulfilling her career obligations no doubt contributed to her fatigue. Certainly, her flagging lungs and the effects of her diet regimen were hitting her harder.

More and more, Barbara abused alcohol.

Finney's concern over her drinking and the strife it caused between them had been building. One evening before he moved into her apartment, the two of them were to attend a performance of *Ziegfeld's Follies*. Finney arrived at Barbara's to pick her up and was told by Irene Almond, her maid, that Barbara was ready but had retired to the bathroom. The longer Finney waited, the more a familiar fear nagged at him. Finally, he asked Almond if Barbara had been drinking. Almond admitted that she had. Finney pushed the bathroom door open. Barbara, gowned in a body-hugging black sequined dress, was wallowing in a tub filled with water. "I made the only gesture possible under the circumstances," remembered Finney. "I pulled the plug and left by myself for the New Amsterdam Theatre."[17]

By the end of May, Finney had had enough. His attempts to curb Barbara's binges had failed. "I had long been an advocate of a system called 'beating a lady with your hat,'" he explained years later, "i.e., putting it on and departing rather than remaining to quarrel. So, as Barbara's problem with hooch became progressively worse, I figured the best thing for both

305

of us would be for me to leave for somewhere." As he dined with a friend at Dinty Moore's the night of May 22, the friend rattled off the celebrity-studded passenger list of the RMS *Majestic*, which was reported to depart for Europe two hours later, and remarked that it sounded like fun. Finney told him he would be packed in an hour. He rushed to the apartment, penned Barbara a farewell letter, hoisted his bags, and sped to the pier. At the stroke of midnight, he sailed out of New York and Barbara's life. "My sincere involvement with Barbara," he later recounted, "had ended in disaster."[18]

Finney would hear from Barbara at least once more. Although he retired from the screen that same year, his name remained in newspapers. Aboard the *Majestic*, he met actress Marilyn Miller and, after they disembarked in England, their appearances together around London sparked juicy items in British papers. Gossip flared up stateside following their return to New York. Finney, rather than risk infuriating Miller's husband, Jack Pickford (Mary's brother), or damaging Miller's career, jumped on another ship that November. It was a spur-of-the-moment trip; he told almost no one about it. But somehow, Barbara learned of it. Aboard the *President Jackson* in Seattle, while preparing to sail to China, a crewman slipped an unexpected wire into Finney's hand. Finney's eyes scanned Barbara's words: "BON VOYAGE. MY THOUGHTS WILL FOREVER BE FULL OF RED APPLES IN A LITTLE GREEN TEAPOT."[19] His mind returned to just before newspapers announced their engagement the previous fall, to their trip to Virginia, to the Green Teapot Hotel nestled among apple trees.

Finney would not get the chance to ask Barbara how she knew of his voyage. By the time he returned to the United States, after his footloose disposition propelled him around China's nightclubs and racetracks and the ancient ruins of Southeast Asia, she would be gone.

While the press hinted at a romance between Finney and Miller the spring of 1925, the trades reported that the careers of Colleen Moore and Corinne Griffith, two stars signed by First National at the same time as Barbara, had continued soaring. In other recent news, Sawyer denied rumors that First National was about to break their contract with Barbara. In the El Fey club, Barbara, amid whispers that she was washed up, drank herself into oblivion.

A relentless swarm of "Broadway playboys," "sharpshooters," and "hangers-on," recalled Ennis, served as temporary distractions from the inner demons that were crushing her—if only to help her fritter away her money.[20] It's unlikely Barbara suspected their intentions. "I am naturally very trusting," she was said to admit months before in the *Movie Weekly* adaptation of her life story. "I take everyone as they seem to be, until they have, irrevocably and for all time, proved themselves to be otherwise. It is, perhaps, my greatest fault and my best virtue." Had she suspected their motives, it's improbable that she would have cared. "I am so hungry for friends," the article further quotes her as saying. "I want people to like me. Not for what they may think I am; not for someone exotic and different. I am, really, neither one of these two much-abused adjectives."[21]

More than this, Barbara ached to be loved. "No woman who has not known love can have a soul," she insisted. "Love IS soul."[22] Time and again, she had sought for what her experience continuously convinced her was elusive. "I've always been in love," she wrote, "in love with the great ideal of love itself—something too many men and women experience; something that makes us go on seeking through personalities and the years. The world calls us fickle, but that isn't true. We are merely the idealists of love, who search and very rarely find that for which we look."[23] Through her seeking, Barbara had grown wise enough to recognize the futility of her quest. "It is rarely a *person* we truly love," she explained; "we bring from the lavender wrappings of our [childhood] memories all of those first ideals we had of the man our Prince Charming was to be, and drape them over the man before us."[24] With each failed attempt to find what she described as "heaven-sent" "real love," she abandoned her searching only to resume it.[25]

Barbara's desperation to be liked for herself (despite the facades she veiled herself with), and her ceaseless reaching for a man to quell her insecurities, were attempts to extract from others the acceptance and love she had been unable to give herself. A sampling of her poems below, written when she was twenty-five, exemplify this ongoing struggle.[26]

The Savage
Yes! I would have put away God and the World,
And, into space, Hope of Eternity hurled,
To have clasped the dream form of Love to my breast,
Forgetting all else—but the lips I caressed.

BARBARA LA MARR

For Woman's Life was Love in Life's beginning,
And the Hypocrite alone calls it sinning.
But, if 'twere the Highway of Sin I would trod—
Straight on—'till I returned unto Dust and Sod!

I would fight 'till Death! In jungle-mad fashion
For my Mate—and then, from She-Panther passion,
I would turn—to sink like a slave at his feet—
To wait—the surrender of myself. Complete!

And then—as the blood ran riot in my veins
To lips trembling with ecstasy and pains—
I would call out for death, though I know full well
I had gained Paradise through the Gates of Hell!

The Price
MY PRICE! You wish to know? Certainly.
'Tis neither POWER, nor GOLD I want.
Mine is the PRICE a fool would ask for a priceless thing—A SONG!
But like that of the Lorelei, it must so ravish my soul, that I, who
     know not of sincerity—believe it to be sincere.
That I, who know that all is a beautiful lie, believe in its glorious
     truth:
That I, whose web of dreams is not torn asunder, may live again.
That I, whose ideals—illusions—molded once by pale hands
     trembling with ecstasy of belief in their existence, may live to see
     them return to gray shapeless mounds of the wet clay half
     formed thoughts, to be molded again—though they be wet by
     the blood tears from the heart of remorse.
But NO! MAN WILL NEVER PAY MY PRICE, though the price of
     my Soul be but a Song.
I, who have always deluded, wish to be DELUDED.
I, who am but an ILLUSION, wish for an ILLUSION.
I, whose love is but a "living lie," wish for the LIVING LIE OF LIFE:
Make me believe you! YOUR LIES—YOUR DREAMS—YOUR
     FOOL'S PARADISE—all the impossible possibilities of it—the
     mad, wonderful, horrible, glorious, fantastic nothings—believe
     them with my soul—then you may buy that SOUL for your SONG!

Though if I DID believe, my Soul would then be a worthless thing—a thing to be cast aside—unworthy EVEN THE PRICE—A SONG!

The Seeker
I WHO have loved one thousand times, and yet have not LOVED at all—I who have explored the abysmal depths of love, yet have not found depths worthy of exploration—
I who have poured the oil of love on turbulent seas of emotion, and have seen its glistening multi-colored hues dull to drab, becoming a weighty, weightless slime, sinking to the bottomless bottom—
I who have gazed upon LOVE'S ETERNITY, yet unable to discover one Atom of time belonging wholly unto it—
Still seek on—striving for the unattainable, as a child attempts to reach the star it glimpses thru a rift in Life's storm clouds—
But, like the Child, yearning with tiny outstretched hands for the Star it can never hold,
I ACCEPT A TINSEL STAR, WHICH SCINTILLATES, AND GLEAMS—A-N-D—CRUMBLES AT THE TOUCH OF MY EAGER HANDS.

Moths
Moths?—I hate them!
You ask me "Why?"
Because to me they seem
Like the souls of foolish women
Who have passed on.
Poor illusioned, fluttering things
That find, now as always,
Irresistible the warmth of the
Flame—
Taking no heed of the warning
That merely singed their wings
They flutter nearer—nearer—
Till wholly consumed
To filmy ashes of golden dust.
Foolish—fluttering—pitiful things—
Moths! I fear them!

Yet I watch them fascinated
And realize—many things.
Perhaps they are not useless
Nor the message they convey
To me, a futile one.
They make me see the folly
Of seeking that which it seems
Women were created for—
The futility, the uselessness of longing—
Perhaps you do not understand,
But—
Moths!—I hate them!

Along with Finney, Barbara's illusions had again vanished. Her fair-weather nightclub companions were of no comfort. When her money ran out, so did they.

In early May 1925, Sawyer offered a possible explanation for what he called a false report that First National intended to terminate its distribution contract with Barbara and Associated Pictures. Reassuring the public of the solid relations between Associated Pictures and First National, he acknowledged the difficulty he had had in obtaining a suitable story for Barbara's next film. By June, the search was over. Associated Pictures announced that Barbara would begin filming *Florrie Meets a Gentleman* that same month.

Barbara would never make the film.

About this same time, she suffered a nervous breakdown. She left New York, her heart and career in tatters, and with, in her own words, "a broken spirit."[27]

Exactly where she went is unclear. Film magazines and newspapers offered only imprecise details: a vacation . . . an extended motor trip . . . Canada . . . parts unknown. Ada Slater believed that Barbara had gone to Quebec "for a rest." Who may have traveled with her is unknown. Sonny had been left with Slater. To escape New York City's rising temperatures, Slater took him to her family home in Newton, Massachusetts. "I always had him with me wherever I went," Slater recalled. "I was all he had."[28]

During the final days of her absence, as she passed through Pennsylvania's Pocono Mountains, Barbara was accompanied by at least one person. She arrived at Deer's Head Inn with an unidentified male, someone

Twenty-Nine

registering under the name "G. V. La Marr" and claiming to be her brother.[29]

Any therapeutic effect Barbara's trip may have had upon her was transitory. Around the time of her breakdown, she was assessed by her New York physician. He advised her to go back to the drier, milder California climate. Within days of returning from Canada, Barbara departed again, this time with Sonny.

When her train chattered into Los Angeles on July 25, three days before her twenty-ninth birthday, her parents, William and Rose, were waiting at the station. The sight of their daughter descending from the train must have shocked them. Barbara collapsed on the platform. William rushed toward her. He gathered her shrunken frame, now down to ninety-eight pounds, in his arms.[30]

VII

Butterfly

My little moment is almost over. Butterflies aren't meant to live long.
—*Barbara La Marr*

Thirty

Barbara's entire world had crumbled.

Her failing health, career woes, and shattered love life were only partly responsible for her breakdown. Although she had satisfied a portion of the claims issued against her in 1924 for monies owed, she had sunk deeper into debt. Even worse was her newfound conviction that Arthur Sawyer and Herbert Lubin were cheating her financially. According to them, the amount she owed for salary advances had soared to $60,000 (about $831,000 today) as of April 1925.[1]

The two producers were desperate for money. After abandoning S-L Studios shareholders and their partially built S-L Studios in California to make Barbara's films in New York, they conceived of another grand vision. They determined to build the most magnificent theater in existence. Drowning in debt (one reason for their indebtedness being overspending on Barbara's films), they nonetheless moved forward, dissolving Associated Pictures and forming Associated Holding Corporation. Lubin located a block of real estate in Times Square. Unfazed by the estimated $7 million required to see their venture through, the men knocked on many doors that spring. Finally, an investment firm saw merit in their proposal; and the remaining balance was produced through stock sales. The news was in print by August 1, 1925: construction of the Roxy Theatre, the "world's largest amusement palace," would begin that November.[2]

Preoccupied with their Roxy Theatre endeavor in New York City, or perhaps because of the tense relations that had developed between themselves and Barbara, neither Sawyer nor Lubin accompanied her to California. Lubin's brother, Barney Lubin, production manager at their company, had escorted her instead.

Los Angeles reporters, prepared to greet Barbara for the first time in almost a year and a half, were perplexed. She had been carried from the train station on a stretcher, was immediately taken to a room at the Ambassador Hotel, and remained in seclusion almost two weeks.

BARBARA LA MARR

From Barney Lubin, Barbara's new business manager in Sawyer's stead, reporters learned what they could. She had developed bronchitis and a throat infection en route to California, he told them, and was suffering from unspecified intestinal disorders. He informed them she was not permitted to see anyone, explaining that she was to begin her next film August 24 and needed to regain her strength. After Barbara was secretly moved from the Ambassador August 12, he withheld her location.

From Dr. Clinton E. Galloway, Barbara had learned the seriousness of her condition. Assessing her symptoms after being called to the Ambassador July 29, Galloway found cause for alarm. Barbara exhibited signs of incipient pulmonary tuberculosis.[3]

She had probably harbored the disease for some time. Tuberculosis remains with its host for life after initial (often undetected) exposure, frequently lying dormant for years and flaring up under certain conditions. Almost surely, it was the reason Barbara was given just twenty months to live two years earlier. It may even have plagued her before her suffering from an undefined illness during her girlhood in Fresno. Now her dieting, alcoholism, extreme nervous tension, and failure to get adequate rest had ravaged her immune system, precipitating a resurgence of the disease.

Galloway certainly told Barbara that, were the germ to become fully active in her, he could not guarantee her survival. In an era predating effectual drugs, half of those afflicted with active pulmonary tuberculosis died, the disease consuming their increasingly skeletal bodies from the inside out. The only hope Galloway could offer was to tell her that, with complete bed rest, ideally in a sanitarium and for a period of months, she might suppress a full-blown infection.

Barbara's temperature soared. William, Rose, and two nurses stood by. Barbara remained in bed, yearning, she soon related, to "hear the cameras clicking again."[4]

At least one person got in to see Barbara. She summoned him herself, persuading William to telephone him on her behalf.

When Barbara first met Perc Westmore, First National's makeup director, on the set of *The White Moth* a year and a half earlier, she must have sensed he was someone she could trust. He had a way about him, an underlying compassion as he readjusted the wires in her wig and sympathized with the pain they had caused.

Westmore arrived at Barbara's home. Since Barbara had leased her

Thirty

Whitley Heights house while in New York, she, Sonny, and her parents were occupying a temporary residence. *Photoplay* soon reported that she was renting Mabel Normand's house at 526 Camden Drive, but this may be false. A newspaper reporter would soon place Barbara's residence on South Bronson Avenue (street number omitted to preserve current owners' privacy), a mile and a half away from the studio where she was to shoot her next film.

Westmore was unprepared for what he saw when Barbara entered the room to greet him. Her face hollowed, her body frail and emaciated, she registered his shocked silence. "Yes," she said, "it's what I want to talk to you about." What she said next shook him to his core. "You see, Perc, I—well—I'm dead," she confessed.

He felt physically ill as she confided in him, his memory circling back to their encounter during filming of *The White Moth*, to the mournful undercurrent he had perceived in her, the unnerving presentiment he had felt. She talked of her ailing lungs and the doctor who, two years earlier, predicted she would die within twenty months. She told him of her love for life and how she purposely lived to the fullest after being told how long she had left. She admitted her debts and her desire to repay them. "You've got to help me," she implored. "I'll make myself stay alive, if you can make me lovely enough to keep on working until the end. Will you?" Westmore knew Barbara had no money to pay for his services; he wouldn't have accepted any. "I capitulated utterly," he recalled. "My heart, my admiration were hers." He agreed, as had Dr. Galloway, to keep her illness secret.[5]

Barbara informed Barney Lubin she was ready to work. William and Rose begged her to reconsider, to heed Dr. Galloway's advice.

Barbara held firm and faced her public. She told the press she was recovering from bronchitis, and that being back in California had already improved her health. To a newspaper reporter, she disclosed another reason for her determination to make her film. Citing the production as her last chance, she stated, "If this picture flops like my last ones, I will be out. And I would so much rather retire gracefully than be kicked off the screen!"[6] In a hoarse voice, she told a *Photoplay* journalist, "I'm not going to stay ruined . . . I've learned my lesson. And I'm going to work as I've never worked before."[7]

Her weakened body notwithstanding, Barbara—who had insisted upon a stage career at eight, fled her parents at sixteen to make her own way in life, resolved to succeed as a dancer and screenwriter, and vowed after *The Three Musketeers* to triumph in films—was back.

Barbara began reclaiming her life.

She conferred with Milton Cohen, her attorney, around the end of August, secretly presenting her allegations against Sawyer and Lubin. She voiced her distrust of them, maintaining that they had not paid her monies she was entitled to collect. She also charged that they had failed to produce a full account of wages owed her: an itemization including her weekly salary (currently $1,500 but scheduled to increase to $2,000 in October), film revenues due her, and her 50 percent cut of auxiliary sums Sawyer had obtained from outside production companies for her services. Cohen initiated a confidential investigation of Sawyer and Lubin's Associated Pictures Corporation.[8]

Still under contract with Sawyer and Lubin for her forthcoming film, Barbara had taken a stand. Her financial dealings with them aside, she was dissatisfied with the way they had managed her career. The uncommon stringency of her contract had denied her any say in the roles and stories chosen for her. She had been instructed to exaggerate her characterizations through mugging and posing. Her input had furthermore been unwelcome in the editing room when she attempted to assist with cutting her films. Barbara spoke candidly to the press—her voice wheezing but her sense of humor intact—of her foundering career and what she was doing about it.

She announced herself as the queen of poor films to *Los Angeles Times* reporter Barbara Miller with a chuckle, referencing the pictures she made in New York.

She explained to writer Caroline Bell, "I was put into a silken sheath and told to parade my 'fatal beauty.' . . . They wouldn't let me act. And I hold the opinion that that is something an actress should do." Barbara admitted to loving every bit of enacting the bejeweled, impious vamp at first—the money that poured in as Sawyer capitalized on the sex-picture rage and demand for her services, the blazing ascension of her career. Yet although the vamp had made her, the vamp had unmade her. Barbara had seen it coming. "Vamping is a gamble," she told Bell. "Beautiful Good is perennial, because she is an ideal that has breathed with the regularity of heartbeats, down through the ages. Beautiful Bad can never be more than a temporary exhilaration, because, though she thrills the impulse to sin which is in all mortal clay, she offends the basic and stronger instinct of decency." Barbara's producers had dismissed her insight. "My whispered protest that the public would tire of alluring ladies in clinging velvet was placated with assurances that my 'beauty' alone would suffice," she said. "It didn't." Her repeated enactments of wayward women, combined with the uncovering of her past during Roth's trial and the harmful publicity she had received since, convinced many that her real-life and screen identities were the same. Concurrently, the demand Sawyer initially stoked among production companies and exhibitors for Barbara in vamp roles had ended in overexposure. From now on, Barbara would do things her way. "I'm down, but not licked," she continued. "The pageant they put me into almost snuffed me out, but I'm fighting for a chance to forget those idiotic pearl headdresses and feather fans . . . everything that was used to put an aureole around what they called my beauty!"[9]

After losing nearly all, Barbara had faced herself. The insecurities that burdened her throughout her career had loosened their hold, shoved aside by renewed fortitude, subdued by her underlying belief in herself. This time, she had insisted that Sawyer and Lubin allow her a voice in the selection of her next production. This time, they had listened. Recognizing that a fresh interpretation could restore interest in her, Barbara had made her choice. She had settled on the type of story she had been yearning to play: a meaningful tale, she told Bell, of an authentic character. There were to be no feathers, no fancy gowns, no negligees. And, in the drama's lighter scenes, Barbara would be summoning her skills as a comedienne, something her friends and certain critics had long deemed her capable of. This was, she knew, a sizable risk; "but," she said, "I think I am holding the winning hand."[10]

Others thought so, too. Paul Bern was still in her corner. A director at the newly merged Metro-Goldwyn-Mayer studio, Paul was paying Barbara's medical bills and other expenses for her, reputedly living out of a rooming house to do so. It was also later purported that he adapted the scenario of Barbara's next film specifically for her that spring (although anonymously and seemingly without her knowledge).[11] Barbara's fans had written to film magazines, proclaiming their faith in her, calling for better material for her.

Who else, Barbara wondered as she prepared for her first day on the set, "likes me enough to start a '*Vive!*' for the new me?"[12]

Barbara motored through the gates of First National's United Studios around the beginning of September, beaming. "Tell everybody I am get-

Supported by her nurse and a walking stick, Barbara returns to work, September 1925. Courtesy of Allison Francis.

Thirty

ting along fine," she told reporters through the window of her Rolls Royce.[13] A cheery contingent, drawn together from around the lot, waited to greet her. Emerging from her car, she shuffled forward, gripping a walking stick and assisted by a nurse. Her smile scarcely left her as she met the crowd. Thrilled to be back and begin filming, she radiated enthusiasm. She declared she never felt better in her life.

Reinforcing Barbara's buoyant spirits was the team assisting her with her film. With Sawyer in New York, Barney Lubin acted as production supervisor. June Mathis, First National's editorial director, was also on the project. Cannily discerning and credited with discovering Valentino, Mathis had supervised the drafting of the film's continuity and had overseen casting. She would have final approval of the daily rushes and charge over editing and titling. Directing the film—his first with First National since contracting with them in mid-August—was Alfred ("Al") Green. In his mid-thirties and known for his work with the Lasky company and Colleen Moore, Green was regarded as a leading director. Barbara was again performing opposite Lewis Stone, star of *The Prisoner of Zenda* and her leading man in *Trifling Women*. She considered the courtly Stone one of her favorite actors to work with; his poised, multihued characterizations, in her estimation, rendered him "far more fascinating than the most dashing young juvenile."[14]

The film, a romantic adventure from the pages of Anthony Pryde's novel *Spanish Sunlight*, would be released under the title *The Girl from Montmartre*. Barbara put her soul, every ounce of her strength, and all of her disquieting, concealed emotions into the role of Emilia Faneaux.

Poverty-stricken and assisting her two soldier brothers in 1917, Emilia is a disreputable Montmartre café's main attraction: a meagerly costumed, masked dancer. Graceful and alluring, she is sketched by Jerome Hautrive (Lewis Stone), a British Army officer and artist, from his table in the audience one night. They later meet in postwar Spain, he a seeker of inspiration among Majorca's backdrops, she a peasant returned with her brothers to their homeland, her seedy dancing career behind her. Jerome and Emilia fall in love; but Emilia, discovering her dancing portrait in his sketchbook and fearing that her background may prevent their union, attempts to drive him away by dancing at the local casino, the same half-mask across her face. Jerome, now recognizing her as the dancer he sketched in the infamous café, is undeterred by her identity and eventually marries her.

Barbara with Lewis Stone in *The Girl from Montmartre*. Courtesy of Allison Francis.

Barbara struggled to work each morning, often in her bathrobe, putting on a brave face. Behind her dressing room door, the effort was painfully evident to Perc Westmore. Every day, "she rose from the [makeup] chair wearier than the day before," he recalled. He forced himself to keep his promise, telling no one, he said, "even when she'd stumble blindly off the set to faint in my arms in her dressing room."[15]

Unable to prevent his daughter from working, William accompanied her to the studio. All day he hovered near, watching her scenes with adoration in his eyes, smilingly fetching her powder puff if she called for it from the set, keeping up his own courageous front.

At the start of production only William, Westmore, Dr. Galloway, and Barbara's nurse knew the degree of Barbara's suffering. Margaret Reid, one of the film's extras, later recounted that Barbara remained her charming, considerate self. One day, as Barbara ambled slowly toward her place on the set, Reid saw a male extra, elderly and scruffy, approach timidly, telling Barbara how wonderful it was to have her back. More extras gathered,

Thirty

Barbara and her father arrive at United Studios during filming of *The Girl from Montmartre*. Courtesy of Allison Francis.

inquiring about her health, wondering if she remembered making films with them. Astounded by Barbara's treatment of them, Reid later attested, "I had never seen a similar demonstration before. She shook hands with each one, calling them by name, laughing and kidding and asking how things had been going."[16]

Despite her natural ebullience, Barbara had greater difficulty maintaining the illusion of health. Her voice—husky and, according to Reid, nearly inaudible at times on this day—was one indication. What occurred next was another.

Standing before the camera on her mark, Barbara came alive with the orchestra's tango number. Around the stage she spun in a bandeau top, executing a dance sequence, the red tulle panels of her skirt flying. Upon Al Green's directive to cut, she went to her chair, clearly drained, and flumped into it. William hastened over with her shawl, covering her bare shoulders. Reid and the others were led to believe she was still recuperating from bronchitis.

More incidents occurred. Green described filming another strenuous dancing sequence. Barbara completed the scene and drifted into the wings. Descending the steps leading to the stage, she withered to the ground in a faint. "The next day her ankles were swollen and black and blue, and the pain intense," Green stated, "but she insisted on continuing her scenes, not only on that day, but succeeding ones."[17]

Dr. Galloway soon insisted otherwise. The frequency of Barbara's fainting spells had increased. Her temperature flared, sometimes to 103 degrees. His words to her were absolute: stop making the film.

Green remembered that Barbara's physical anguish was palpable. But, he said, "she refused to quit."[18]

Green did everything he could to help Barbara finish the film, even when she could only work three to four hours per day. He rearranged his shooting schedule, prioritizing her close-ups, allowing her to rest between takes, and working around her scenes when she was unable to perform. Barbara was grateful for his patience and kindness. Green was awed by her courage.

It took all Barbara had to keep going. Westmore would one day tell of Galloway administering treatment all night long for many nights during filming. On certain days, Barbara was transported from her car to the set in a wheelchair. William walked her from her seat on the sidelines to her mark on the set; and, reportedly, when she couldn't stand on her own, she was held up through takes of scenes.

Urging Barbara forward was undoubtedly the same unrelenting force that had always called to her, an internal prompting to express all that was within her. She continued to answer it. "One good picture," she believed, "will reestablish me."[19]

Barbara knew time was running out. Rising from the makeup chair

Thirty

each morning, she turned to Westmore. "Perc, is this the last day?" she asked. It may have taken all his strength to answer. "Far from it," he said, "—not for many days."[20]

Such encouragement, combined with the faith so many had in her, surely fortified Barbara's determination. Her selflessness, perhaps more than ever, prevented her from letting down those who were counting on her, those who were doing so much for her, those who knew how important *The Girl from Montmartre* was to her. Her feelings of indebtedness were keen.

She wanted to repay Westmore, for one. "Perc," she frequently said to him, "some day soon—before the last day—I want to dance for you my Dance of the Rosary. It is beautiful."[21] Westmore, fearing that the exertion would accelerate her demise, always demurred.

Barbara's resolve predominated. They were filming on the Palos Verdes Peninsula, thirty miles southwest of Los Angeles, at La Venta Inn, a Spanish villa atop the hills fronting the Pacific. Alone with Westmore in her dressing room in the inn's tower between scenes, Barbara was supposed to be resting. She went to the phonograph in the corner. Sensing his thoughts, she warned him not to stop her. She told him she kept her promises.

With the flip of the lever, the opening notes of "The Rosary" surrounded them. Barbara surrendered to the music. "And there, just for me, she danced," Westmore later remembered. "Wearing that little tight bodice over that once beautiful breast, the flaring skirt, her bare legs white, her feet naked. Danced divinely. I can close my eyes today and see her as the last sad notes wept, sway with eyes closing, to faint dead away in my arms as I leaped to catch her."[22]

The remorse Westmore felt remained with him a long time. "I could have beaten myself for letting her do it," he said.[23] He told her as much when she regained consciousness. Barbara smiled; it had given her happiness, she said.

"A few days later," recounted Westmore, "she said simply, 'Today, Perc, is the last.'"[24]

Barbara's final impressions of working on the role she so loved were the warmth of the lights bathing the set, the gentle whir as Rudolph Bergquist cranked the camera, the loving support of her production team. Midway through the day on October 3, during the filming of a scene, she collapsed and didn't get up. Carried past her weeping fellow crew members, she was taken from the set in a coma.

Thirty-One

In her rented house on Bronson Avenue, Barbara faced Dr. Galloway. The telltale symptoms—nightly fevers around 104 degrees, chest pains, a severe cough—were present. Pulmonary tuberculosis was taking hold.

The prescribed treatment reportedly tore into her more than the physical pain. Her only chance of evading death was to retire from her career and make an indefinite retreat to the mountains. Pitifully weak and barely able to speak, Barbara was again placed in the care of two nurses, their faces likely shielded by masks, and ordered to remain in bed.

She was apparently unable to accept her doctor's advice. News of her condition reached the public when her father spoke to reporters October 5. Describing Barbara's collapse as a complete physical breakdown resulting from overwork, he said nothing of tuberculosis. Possibly, he was guarding her against the stigma of carrying an infectious disease. He may also have been complying with her wishes that he keep silent. He spoke of her hope of returning to the studio within a day or so to finish *The Girl from Montmartre* before resting. Nothing definite had been decided, he said, as to where she might go.

If Barbara had any say, she wouldn't be going anywhere.

As those at United Studios worriedly awaited further word on Barbara, studio executives weighed their options. Too much footage had been shot to warrant scrapping the film. Director Al Green had completed Barbara's close-ups, but several of her long shots remained to be done. There was too much money at stake to justify production delays. Production carried on.

With everyone in place on the set, Green prepared to call for action. Costumed for Barbara's dance sequence in the casino scene, actress Lolita Lee had nabbed what she considered her biggest break yet. Hollywood hadn't exactly welcomed the young, dark-haired former Miss San Francisco after she left the Bay Area a year earlier—without money, training, or reference letters—to begin a film career. Then her passable resemblance to Barbara was noted, Perc Westmore employed his makeup magic, and cam-

Thirty-One

eraman Rudolph Bergquist made up the difference with camera angles. Lee, shot from a distance in Barbara's dance sequences, ever hopeful that publicity would come of it, is believed to have appeared in two or three scenes in the picture.[1]

Filming ended for *The Girl from Montmartre* by October 17. An edited print of the film went to New York with Barney Lubin for a preview at First National's headquarters, arriving October 22. Barbara was taken from Los Angeles the same day.

Around Hollywood, pieces of a hazy picture began coming together. History had proven that the public avoided films featuring dead stars. A presumption arose: Is Barney Lubin making arrangements for Barbara's next picture—or rushing *The Girl from Montmartre* into theaters before death destroys her marketability?

Outside Barbara's bedroom window in the southern foothills of the San Gabriel Mountains, stillness reigned for miles. Untouched by fog and industrial exhaust, the dry air was advertised as the country's best.

Weeks of seclusion in Los Angeles had not improved Barbara's health. Reluctantly, she had come fifteen miles northeast to the rural community of Altadena. Her new living quarters, a white, rented lodge on Boston Street (specific address omitted per request of current owners for privacy) loosely enfolded by ranches, a developing middle-class suburb, orange groves, and poppy fields, was cozy and unpretentious. She had wanted it that way. She was living almost entirely on Paul Bern's good graces.

Bedridden and instructed to do nothing, Barbara was kept in isolation. Her tuberculosis, now fully active, was fairly contagious. Her two nurses had come with her, one of their responsibilities being to collect the blood-tinged mucus she coughed up into cups, thereby minimizing the risk of infection for other household members. Those members were her parents, William and Rose, and Irene Almond, her maid. Sonny, too young to occupy such a small space with a tubercular person, had been sent away.

Barbara originally entrusted her son to his nurse, Ada Slater. (Slater had come with them to California and had relatives in Los Angeles.) Word from a friend then changed Barbara's mind.

Fretful thoughts had tormented ZaSu Pitts ever since she heard the fearsome reports about Barbara. Deeply attached to her three-year-old daughter, Ann, she was well acquainted with Barbara's love for Sonny, witnessing it herself during their secret lunch breaks with their babies during filming of *Souls for Sale*. Anxious to be of service to Barbara but unaware of her address, she went to Altadena with a plan. It worked; inquiries at local flower shops turned up a vendor who had delivered roses to Barbara, leading ZaSu to her door. She was denied admittance to the house, but relayed an offer of help. Barbara accepted it.

Sonny arrived at the lovely Hollywood home of his new guardians a short while later. Barbara felt relief and sadness. She knew, in the care of ZaSu and her husband, Tom Gallery, her agreeable boy was happy. Thrilled to have a spunky playmate his age, he delighted in Ann. ZaSu and Gallery took pleasure in spoiling him a little. Barbara comforted herself with daily accounts of his activities and the twitter of his voice over the telephone.

Unverified reports of Barbara's condition appeared in newspapers, many of them all but pronouncing her dead. Arthur Sawyer and Herbert Lubin worked to quash them. Bert Ennis issued a news release at the end of October, declaring that Barbara was suffering only a slight malady from overwork. Shortly after, Barney Lubin asserted that she had nearly recovered and would soon begin her next picture with Sawyer and Herbert Lubin.

Neither statement was true. Barbara was still bedridden and prohibited from having visitors. Besides this, she had no intention of ever making another Sawyer-Lubin film.

The investigation of Sawyer and Lubin's Associated Pictures Corporation that had been undertaken by her attorney, Milton Cohen, in August evidently turned up something suspicious. On November 5, in a formal letter from Cohen, Barbara charged Sawyer and Lubin with breach of contract, accusing them of failure to comply with salary terms. She called upon them to make restitution for wages she believed they owed her. Their contract, so far as she was concerned, was voided.[2]

Sawyer and Lubin proclaimed themselves innocent of any such infringement. In their estimation, they were still entitled to Barbara's services for the three years remaining on her five-year contract. Reports arose of an impending lawsuit to settle the matter.

Barbara was not going to wait for the outcome. First National, now a producing unit as well as a distributor, had an option on her services in the event of a default by Associated Pictures. She had already inquired through Cohen whether they would be interested in exercising their option. A negative response had come quickly: her last three pictures hadn't been as successful as anticipated, they said.[3] Barbara persevered. Virginia Carville,

Thirty-One

according to her great-niece, managed Barbara's career at one point during their eleven-year friendship; perhaps Virginia was assisting Barbara at this time.[4] Barbara made inquiries to other producers, eager to obtain another screen contract.

Barbara wanted desperately to return to the life she had known, to fulfill the dreams still tapping at her heart.

There were roles she wanted to play: fascinating women consumed by sincere motivations. She would take on errant ladies gladly—so long as they be "humanly, grandly bad," not "foolishly, unnecessarily bad"—and endow them with all the raw honesty of feeling and behavior culled from her sweeping interplay with life.[5]

Barbara had often voiced her intention to one day return to writing. Feeling as though fame had smothered her individuality, she once said she would reclaim it through the pen. Only one thing gave her a true sense of independence: "sitting at my own desk, in my own room . . . writing. Because it is *mine*."[6] She envisaged herself writing into her advanced years, delving more fully into her humorous side. She desired to write a play—a spectacular comedy that would storm Broadway—and more stories and poetry. Between scenes while filming *Souls for Sale* (1923), she had written a screenplay inspired by psychoanalysis, which she titled *Pomp*. She had intended to star in it, as well as other screenplays she had written, but her overcrowded film schedule had prevented it. Perhaps she considered making these films yet. She even entertained the notion of producing a film.

Conceivably, Barbara also revisited a longing she had confessed to the previous year, after insisting she had never truly been in love: she wanted to know love. Her disillusionment with matrimony and unwillingness to sacrifice her liberty and vocation had seemingly altered her perspective on male companionship. "My ideal man would have to be—just my pal," she ostensibly stated in *Movie Weekly*'s rendition of her life story around that same time. She wanted a man who truly understood her; to her, it was said, understanding was the most vital component of friendship. She apparently arrived at a formula for a lasting union: "I would rather have a real friendship," she is further credited with saying, "something I knew I wasn't going to lose, than a mad infatuation that would last for two years and then be completely finished."[7]

Counting off the days as an early November snow settled upon the mountaintops, Barbara spoke frequently to William and Rose of her aspirations and resuming work in Los Angeles. Her hope and courage inspired her parents and, along with her rest cure, were evidently life-giving. By mid-month, Barbara's temperature had returned to normal and her cough was gone. Her appetite resumed; her weight increased to 112 pounds. Though her condition was still relatively critical, the Watsons rejoiced.

In what may have been an effort to rout reports of her encroaching death, Barbara met with a *Los Angeles Times* correspondent the second week in November. Her voice was raspy and virtually silenced, the reporter wrote, but "her spirit still flashes fire." Barbara admitted that her fight for health was wearisome, but insisted it was a fight she would win. "I'll soon be better . . . pretty soon!" she whispered. "And tell everybody 'Hello' for me!"[8] Propped upon her pillows in bed, she posed for a photograph in a lace-trimmed silk negligee, her hair smoothed loosely into place. Dark semicircles shadowed her eyes; her heavily made-up face bore the appearance of her struggle. She smiled bravely.

William provided the *Los Angeles Times* with an update November 21, stating that Barbara had overcome nearly all traces of her illness. She occasionally left her bed and walked around the house, even into the backyard on warmer days. The tranquil garden gave her great pleasure. Seated upon her wicker lounge, she considered the space her sanctuary.

Since her arrival in Altadena a month earlier, Barbara worried that those in the outside world had forgotten her. Many hadn't. Letters poured into the house daily—more than forty at once on at least one morning—expressing wishes for her health and return to the screen. Barbara read each letter or listened as William or Rose read them, all of them dear to her.

Treasured gifts of thoughtfulness from friends were placed where she could constantly see them. Flowers filled her bedroom. A photograph of Ramon Novarro was on display, together with a black fan, its feathered plumes entwined with a rosary he had given her.

When Galloway removed his ban on visitors around the end of November, friends rode up from Los Angeles, traveling (minus modern freeways) around three to four hours round trip. Barbara received them with intense joy and gratitude. Through shared stories and memories with industry pals, she reconnected with happy times. She revisited carefree days of her younger years when she reached out to one of her girlhood chums.

Around fifteen years had passed when Viola Melvill Barry was unex-

Thirty-One

pectedly contacted by her friend "Beth," the beautiful teenaged girl with a wild streak who had shared her old Figueroa Street apartment building in Los Angeles and posed alongside her for her grandmother's painting. Barry, now a mother and wife, was delighted by the invitation to catch up with Barbara.

Escorted inside Barbara's bungalow, Barry was led to the garden where Barbara awaited in her chair. The initial sight of her caught Barry off guard; Barbara's eyes greeted her from behind a black veil concealing the rest of her face. The women commenced chatting, the years that had distanced them slipped away, and they reminisced for hours.

Their warm, wonderful visit, Barry would recall, was marred slightly by a sudden pang of sadness. A light wind blew past, temporarily taking Barbara's veil with it. Barry pitied her for the toll her sickness had extracted. Yet that "something special" she had always recognized in Barbara's personality was undiminished on this afternoon.[9]

There were times when hope failed Barbara, when courage left. Liquor, men, overwork, luxuries, nightclubs—all had served as modes of escape whenever unwelcome realities intruded. Cut off from these diversions, the potential threat of death ever present, Barbara was forced to face herself again. She journeyed frequently into the shadows of her past. She often hated what she saw.

During her darker moments, Barbara leaned upon the strength of others. Paul Bern came to her faithfully, reputedly making the trek from Los Angeles every day, sometimes awakening early in the morning to visit before reporting for work at Metro-Goldwyn-Mayer. Together, they kept faith alive. "No one is really poor who can boast the friendship of Paul Bern," she said.[10]

It was one of the severest trials Paul ever underwent. In her despair, Barbara once told him she feared the cruelty of life more than death. Wounded by his own past, he empathized. Watching her suffer pained him greatly; contemplating her death was evidently intolerable. When she asked him to watch over Sonny in the event of her passing, he devotedly accepted. When she requested that he sell her Rolls Royce—a gift he had given her—he was unable to go through with it. He told her it sold and gave her the cash. But the automobile sat hidden in a garage. Paul remained hopeful that she would drive it again.

As November faded to December and Barbara's health continued strengthening, Paul took a necessary leave. An MGM megafeature he was to direct was postponed after the costumer resigned at the eleventh hour. Unable to wait until the new year before MGM assigned him another project, Paul left the first week in December to work in New York. Leaving Barbara at this time must have been difficult for him. He hadn't stopped loving her.

As Christmas hung in the brisk air, a *Photoplay* columnist came calling with a message of holiday cheer for Barbara. The message would have to wait, however. Turned away by William at the door, the writer walked off, mulling over the troubling look in William's eyes.

Barbara's temperature had suddenly shot up; she began vomiting; piercing pain arose in her lower back. Galloway's diagnosis was a blow to the Watsons: Barbara had developed acute nephritis, a kidney inflammation, precipitated, he said, by her temperamental character and failure to consume enough water.[11]

Another problem emerged. The inflammation spread to her pelvis. She became nearly comatose for ten days. Galloway administered daily intravenous injections of an antibacterial drug and dispensed a Murphy drip, consisting of water, soda, and glucose, into her colon.[12] The world discovered the seriousness of Barbara's condition via newspapers the first week of January; *Photoplay* called for prayers on her behalf. Persons described by one newspaper as near-relatives—almost surely including Virginia and possibly Robert Carville—were summoned to Barbara's bedside. William and Rose scarcely left it.

As Galloway noted subtle improvements, Barbara struggled inwardly. Only weeks before, she was told she would be able to return to work in a couple of months. Nephritis sent her back to square one. If not kept in check, the disease could become chronic and, in 1926, potentially fatal. Galloway reestablished the ban on visitors. Barbara was again indefinitely confined to bed.

Convinced she was dying, Barbara hit bottom. Regret for all she would never do overwhelmed her. "I wouldn't care," she said, "if the public had only let me come back before ill health took away my last chance."[13] She had failed in her hopes of providing for Sonny and her parents and had wasted everything she had ever had, she thought. She weathered the black night of her desolation until, finally, it broke her. William and Rose took turns beside her in her bed one sleepless evening, holding her between her screams of not wanting to die, sobs, and spent silences.

Thirty-One

Soon afterward, Barbara was done fighting. The morning of January 14, after a restful sleep, she had strength enough to sit up in bed for the first time in a while. Galloway was informed upon his arrival the next day that she had discharged his nurses and no longer required his services.[14] Barbara's situation, to her, seemed hopeless enough to require a miracle beyond what medical treatment was capable of achieving. "Barbara so willed it," William later explained. "We all agreed that mental healing could do more for her than anything else."[15]

Barbara's experiences with Christian Science had led her to accept the concept that life, truth, and love—the professed ultimate realities of God's creation—remedy sin, disease, and death. In refusing medical treatment, she was therefore renouncing a so-called false belief in herself as temporal matter, affirming the notion that cause and effect are spiritually based, and recognizing God as the master healer. Christian Science practitioners were called to the house to help open Barbara's consciousness to the transfiguring activity of Jesus Christ—regarded as divine love—and thereby, it was thought, restore her wholeness.

And so Barbara prayed. She understood, per Christian Science theory, her rightful identity to be limitless, ever-lasting Spirit. She thus regarded death to represent a transition to another stage of existence, a rebirthing of the spirit, an expansion into holiness.[16] She prayed to embrace God's ultimate will for her, whatever that might be.

Her fear of death and life departed. Serenity dawned.

Barbara's hope and courage, according to William, resurfaced. She was content and pensive, and seemed to grow stronger throughout the final days of January, he felt. She awoke on January 28 feeling well enough to leave her bed.

That afternoon, she asked to be taken to her garden. William rolled her out in a wheelchair and positioned her upon her chaise, securing a blanket around her. For a long while they sat together, Barbara absorbed by and commenting upon the beauty before them. The grass and flowers glistened in the sun. Butterflies fluttered from bloom to bloom. Barbara watched them attentively. "Are they happy, Daddy?" she purportedly asked.[17] William apparently believed they were.

As the sunlight faded, they thought it best to go inside. Barbara seemed to her father to be weary and quiet. A basket of roses had recently arrived from Barbara's *Eternal City* and *Sandra* costar, Bert Lytell, and his wife, Claire Windsor. Barbara wished to dictate a note to them before going to bed. She told them she was getting better every day. Then she closed her message: "May you always be happy."[18]

The following morning, with her mother and father sitting at her bedside, Barbara was at ease. She dozed, awakening every so often and smiling at her parents.

About noon, her strength diminished suddenly and a relapse overtook her. She drifted away. Alarmed, William and Rose sent for medical assistance, yet there was no reviving her. "I'm so tired—I want to rest," she whispered around three.[19] Her eyes closed. She slipped into a coma.

William and Rose stayed with her, keeping watch that afternoon, throughout the night, and all day the next day. But their daughter was gone. At four o'clock on January 30, 1926, Barbara ceased her faint breathing and passed away at age twenty-nine.

The end, William would recount, had come peacefully.

Thirty-Two

Reporters seized news of Barbara's death the night of January 30, 1926. William met with them, as he would many times in the coming days, sustaining his shaken composure throughout their barrage of questions, reliving his daughter's final weeks, days, hours as he detailed them again and again. Barbara's death, he loosely explained, resulted from complications following her nervous breakdown. From Dr. Galloway, reporters obtained particulars. He told of Barbara's nephritis, attributing her demise to an altered diet and the termination of medical treatment (on her death certificate, he listed tuberculosis as her cause of death and nephritis as a contributory factor).[1] "I could have saved her," he stated. "She was convalescing until mental practitioners were given the case."[2] Headlines sent shockwaves across the globe: BARBARA LA MARR IS DEAD! Telegrams of condolence from film notables and fans flooded the woeful house in Altadena by the hundreds.

William and Rose pressed through their crushing grief, arranging Barbara's funeral. Barbara's brother Billy helped. (Performing in Fresno when notified of Barbara's coma, he arrived in Altadena just hours after her death.) William announced to the press that the funeral was to take place in Los Angeles Friday, February 5. The lengthy delay, he said, was to enable Paul Bern, who was traveling from New York, to attend.

In the meantime, Barbara's dying wish that she be returned to her public one last time would be granted.

Before Barbara's passing, Perc Westmore made what he considered a sacred promise. But standing over Barbara's body in a side chamber in the chapel of the Walter C. Blue Company funeral home on West Washington Street in Los Angeles, he groped for the strength to keep it. Barbara's instructions, relayed to him by William, hung heavily in his heart: "She wants you to do what you two agreed on. And no one is to see her until you say it is time." Westmore opened his makeup kit. "I transformed her into the beauty she had once been," he said. "It took all the wizardry of makeup. And I cried, unashamedly, as I worked . . . It was the least I could do for her."[3]

When the doors of the Walter C. Blue Company parted on Monday, February 1, a procession of people over a block long had already assembled. Police officers, stationed at the entrance, waved those first in line forward. A few at a time, others were permitted to follow. Slowly, solemnly, they passed through a small foyer into the chapel, walking along a center aisle edged with potted palms. Upon a draped bier of golden velvet at the aisle's far end, softly illumined by a fringed lamp, and gowned in pink and gold, was the woman deemed by reporters "too beautiful to live."

For four days Barbara lay in state in the chapel. Lines of people stretched unabated along the streets, at times under drizzling skies, from 8:30 each morning into the evening. Visitors of all ages and walks of life streamed past the bier—those who had worked with or known Barbara intimately, obscure film folk to whom she had extended a friendly hand, and many more who had loved, laughed, and cried with her image in darkened theaters. Over 120,000 persons would pass through the chapel doors before they were closed to the public for the final time Thursday night.[4] With heads bowed and through tears, they paid their respects. Floral offerings—some extravagant and sent from around the world, others plucked from home gardens—enveloped the bier, filling the chapel.

A single red rose resting beneath Barbara's hand, placed there by a twelve-year-old schoolgirl, particularly touched William. "To my Beautiful Lady," the accompanying note read, "whom I have longed to meet in this life and whom I look forward to 'knowing' when my time is over here. May my life be as lovely and unselfish as yours has been, and may you find eternal peace and love in the 'Happyland.'" William decided to bury it with Barbara. "It is the ultimate tribute," he said.[5]

Barbara's public could not let her go. On February 5, long before 2:00 p.m., the hour set for her funeral, a mob swarmed outside the chapel. Police, anticipating its presence, preceded it. But as the afternoon progressed, the officers, on foot and horseback, snaked uneasily through the crowds, eyeing their multiplying numbers. Backup regiments arrived. Ropes were stretched across the horde's fringes. Boys and men shimmied up light poles, trees, and signposts; faces peered from upper-story windows of nearby buildings; people took to rooftops. Below, a multitude of craning heads and teary eyes witnessed the arrival of the first funeral guests, many of them film stars, and swelled forward.

Thirty-Two

Barbara, beautiful in death as in life, lies in state. Courtesy of Allison Francis.

Reverent silence suffused the chapel's interior. William, Rose, and Billy sat in the front row. Paul Bern accompanied them. June and Henry, Barbara's half-siblings, seemingly did as well. Ramon Novarro, pale-faced, sat behind Barbara's family; en route to New York when notified of Barbara's death, he cancelled a European vacation to be there. Sonny arrived with ZaSu and Tom Gallery. Consistent with Barbara's wishes, other close friends of hers completed the small, intimate gathering.[6]

Paul made an observation. Half of the chapel's seats were empty. He suggested permitting some of Barbara's fans to join the service. William and Rose consented; several grateful mourners entered.[7]

All eyes gazed forward upon Barbara, resting in an open-faced, white-lined silver casket, a spray of flowers encircling her waist. In keeping with her instructions, a Christian Science practitioner approached a podium beside the casket; the rites began. An opening prayer was offered and, as Barbara had requested, a simple service was read. Two Christian Science hymns, more prayers, Bible readings, and a closing song—"Eternity," sung by a female friend of Barbara's—followed. The ceremony, though merely twenty minutes long, was a moving one, broken only when Sonny tearfully asked why his mother hadn't come home.[8]

Barbara's family wanted to be alone with her a final time.[9] The guests left the chapel. Several minutes later, when the casket was closed and the pallbearers reemerged, Rose was inconsolable.

The lobby doors opened. On the street, around 10,000 bodies pitched forward against straining ropes. The honorary pallbearers—Paul Bern; actresses ZaSu Pitts, Gloria Swanson, Bessie Love, Colleen Moore, Pola Negri, Blanche Sweet, Gladys Brockwell, and Claire Windsor; Milton Cohen, Barbara's attorney; director Marshall Neilan; and John McCormick, chief of First National's western branch—exited the building first. In slow, even strides, the pallbearers—Tom Gallery; Barbara's past costars, Bert Lytell and Henry Victor; director Alfred Green; assistant director Henry Hathaway; and R. D. Knickerbocker, Barbara's former attorney—filed out behind them, gripping Barbara's flower-strewn casket.[10]

Barbara's family trailed the casket. Rose, sobbing and attended by William and apparently June and Henry, collapsed. She was quickly taken to a waiting car.[11]

The crowd met Barbara's casket with near hysteria. Desperate to touch it as it neared the hearse, a human wave ripped through the barricades, swallowed parked automobiles along the streets, and charged toward the cortege. Bert Lytell was flung against a wheel of the hearse. The other pallbearers scattered for cover. Several women fainted and were saved from trampling by police. Traffic along Washington Street was gridlocked for blocks. For almost half an hour, police, abetted by citizens, fought to control the multitude, driving it back toward the sidewalks. Locking hands, officers and civilians formed a human blockade. Barbara's casket was finally placed in the hearse by the pallbearers. The seven-car funeral procession, shielded by patrol cars, started down the street. With arms pulled taut and bodies bracing backward, the heaving throng was restrained until the convoy was out of sight.[12]

Around five thousand people crushed through the cordon and stormed the chapel, seeking any remnant of Barbara. But the floral displays had all been removed and heaped onto a truck in the funeral procession. It was said that only their scent lingered.

The cortege wound through Los Angeles, along Santa Monica Boulevard in Hollywood, and through the gates of Hollywood Cemetery (renamed Hollywood Memorial Park in the 1930s and Hollywood Forever

Thirty-Two

(*Left to right*) Bert Lytell, Tom Gallery, Henry Hathaway, Alfred Green, Henry Victor, R. D. Knickerbocker, and an unidentified man carry Barbara's casket. In the group following the casket, Rose (*center*) is steadied by William (*on her left*) and persons strongly resembling Henry (*on her right*) and appearing to be June (in white) moments before her collapse. Billy and an unknown woman follow behind.

in 1998). Unobstructed by prying crowds, the party proceeded with funeral guests to the Corridor Mausoleum. Final rites were uttered peacefully. Amid tears, Barbara's casket was lifted into a temporary receiving vault.[13]

Before her passing, Barbara had spoken to her parents of her desire to be cremated, the least expensive disposition. William had made arrangements for it at the cemetery. Paul implored him to reconsider; "She's too beautiful," he reasoned.[14] William cancelled the cremation and the receiving vault was purchased.

Loftier provisions were made March 24. A crypt was purchased in the cemetery's Cathedral Mausoleum, an elegant, commanding structure in the back section of the grounds. Patterned after ancient Greek and Roman temple architecture, the mausoleum features a Palladian portico and regal foyer lined on either side by statues of the twelve apostles. Branching off in both directions from the foyer, above-ground crypts fill marble corridors, gently lit through stained glass ceilings and windows. The cost of Barbara's crypt, $1,000 (around $13,400 today), was paid for with money provided by Paul. (Paul also paid for Barbara's funeral.)[15] The evening of March 24, Barbara's casket was quietly moved from its temporary vault to the Cathedral Mausoleum, down Corridor A, and placed in crypt 1308, its permanent resting place. Upon the crypt's marble facing, a solid bronze plaque bears the inscription "With God in the Joy and Beauty of Youth" beneath her name. The cemetery, also home to the remains of other illustrious notables who made early Hollywood and history—including silent film legends Rudolph Valentino, Douglas Fairbanks Sr., Cecil B. DeMille, Jesse Lasky, and William Desmond Taylor—has become known as the Cemetery of the Immortals.

Mourning for Barbara continued for some time. In the April 1926 issue of *Photoplay*, writer Margaret E. Sangster tendered words of comfort through a poem written in Barbara's honor:

> Somewhere, back of the sunset,
> Where loveliness never dies—
> She dwells in a land of glory,
> With dreams in her lifted eyes.
>
> And laughter lives all about her,
> And music sways on the air;
> She is far from all thought of sadness,
> Of passion, and doubt, and care!
>
> The flowers of vanished April,
> The lost gold of summer's mirth,
> Are wrapped, like a cloak, about her,
> Who hurried, too soon, from earth.
>
> And we who have known her splendor—
> A beauty that brought swift tears;
> Will cherish her vision, always,
> To brighten the drifting years!

As she entered her final year, Barbara evidently contemplated what she considered the greatest thing in life. "*Happiness.* Real happiness," she con-

BARBARA LA MARR
WITH GOD IN THE JOY AND BEAUTY OF YOUTH
1896   1926

Barbara's crypt, number 1308, in Hollywood Forever's Cathedral Mausoleum.

cluded, according to the *Movie Weekly* telling of her life story. "Not vying for sensational standards or for false pedestals, but the happiness that wells up from within and that cannot be taken away by external happenings." Often, she conceded that, in many respects, she had had an appalling life, but insisted she wouldn't change one bit of it. "Not one day of hunger," her *Movie Weekly* article continues. "Not one night of fear. Not one experience. Not one wish that I had a gown or one depressing moment when I knew the hat didn't match or the phone didn't ring." Money is nothing more than a means to an end and all things are relative, she is said to have declared. "Happiness . . . that's all."[16]

A year earlier, she was asked by an interviewer to provide a prescription for happiness for women. Barbara laughed. "I don't know exactly how many million women there are in the world, but however many million women there are, it takes that many million prescriptions," she replied. She stated that what is meat to some is poison to others; "experiences out of which one woman builds up a strong character that will stand on its own two feet and look the world in the eye and wring joy out of life, will wreck another woman." She added, "Some can't take their thrills from life without shipwreck. That's why they get them from the theater and the movies and reading." Artists, she said, must be strong enough to surmount the shipwrecks and use them to fuel their artistry.[17]

A few years after Barbara's death, Ben Lyon, in ruminating on his relationship with her during the summer of 1924, underscored a prevailing element of her nature. "I found in Barbara a generosity of heart that was a real and lasting lesson to me," he said. "Her heart was greater than her caution or her common sense. She gave until it hurt and that not being enough, she gave until she died. Barbara is best expressed in one word—generosity."[18]

Barbara gave of all she had and all she was. She gave herself fully to life itself, diving headlong into its every aspect, tasting it in its fullness. "Life is so *fluid*," she avowedly remarked. "People, times, fortunes, all change. So do opinions. So do hearts. One cannot draw definite conclusions, for the conclusion of today may well be the mistake or regret of tomorrow."[19] Even during times when the hope of death held greater appeal, she kept giving herself to life, somehow finding tragedy's lighter side. "The situation may be Tolstoian, but I can always see the Shaw view in places," she reputedly quipped.[20] Regardless of the scars wrought by her life experiences, she drew from the pain, giving vent to her self-admitted passion of expression that relentlessly drove her, giving the best she could to her art and the world. She gave because, in her giving, she came closest to experiencing a form of happiness that could not be taken from her.

In early 1925 Barbara recalled a discussion she had had with her longtime friend, actor Nat Goodwin. The topic, centering on a "futile, hopeless, persistent search" for an indescribable "something," was a recurring one between them. She identified with the tears he had wept as he chased illusion after illusion, seeking in vain for that which "so few of us ever find."[21]

Perhaps, in her placid Altadena bungalow, as she faced her greatest trial, Barbara's long, sorrowful search finally ended. Possibly, the peace that came over her in her last days brought a lasting happiness in which she realized more than ever the value of all she had. Her parents' devotion had sustained her through her illness, endured throughout her chaotic life, and given her, she indicated, a greater understanding of love. Her son, quick to smile at the mention of her, adored her regardless of her bank balance. Her friends, some of whom had long since seen through the pretenses she erected around herself, had continued loving her. Paul Bern (who, interestingly, possessed the qualities of friendship she had purportedly specified in her self-described ideal man), had many times seen her at her worst, and had not turned away when she was most in need. Even many of her fans and certain critics were still loyal, still believed in her despite her feelings of failure. And possibly, in considering her life afresh, Barbara saw through the devastating adversity she had known to the part of herself that had always endeavored to keep going, the part that had not been crushed.

Thirty-Three

When Barbara regained consciousness after her final collapse on the set of *The Girl from Montmartre* in October 1925, she believed her film career to be over. She also felt deep pride for her work and newfound faith in herself. She told those who were present, "I want to be remembered by my last picture."[1]

As far as Arthur Sawyer, Herbert Lubin, and First National executives were concerned, Barbara's death on January 30, 1926, made her wish impractical. Spooked by the public's inclination to shun deceased stars' films, the men elected to swallow a $250,000 loss (approximately $3.35 million today). Days after the general release of *The Girl from Montmartre* on January 31, they removed it from the market.

A week later, another idea occurred to them. Deciding to circulate the film as originally planned, they struck Barbara's name from all billing; Lewis Stone, her costar, was promoted instead. Bookings came in from exhibitors.

An unprecedented thing happened. Barbara's fans, undeterred by her death, flocked to view the film. From theaters countrywide came reports of record-breaking box office figures. Theaters not playing the film received countless phone calls from patrons, begging that it be shown.

Sawyer, Lubin, and First National shifted gears. Barbara's name was reinstated in the film's title and headlined all promotional materials. The film was hawked as a final chance to view her on the screen.

The Girl from Montmartre had its detractors. The preponderance of them knocked the concept of a former dancer winning her aristocratic lover after resuming her dancing to prove her unsuitability. Some were equally unimpressed with Barbara's performance. "She plainly shows the grip her illness had on her," *Film Daily* stated.[2]

Other reviewers saw something vastly different. Among them were those who found merit in the story, who credited the film's forceful dramatic scenes and delightful comedic interludes. Journalist Helen Klumph lauded director Alfred Green for making so worthy a film under nearly impossible conditions.

Thirty-Three

The majority who saluted the picture were most moved by Barbara. The *Los Angeles Times* asserted, "[she] is her old flaming self—vital and compelling, despite her evident illness." Patent differences were also noted in her. The Louisiana *Times-Picayune* commented, "The beauty and talent of the late Barbara La Marr seem to have flowered"; the reviewer assured Barbara she had nothing to regret. She succeeded in reinventing herself with her performance; she received tribute for her comedic skills and for breaking free of her stereotype. "Gone is the abundance of sex appeal that made her a screen vamp," observed the *New York Daily Mirror,* adding that she suffused the film with a "lovely, ethereal quality . . . that stirs sadness and awe in one's heart." The *Mirror* concluded, "She is exquisite." That she allowed her essence to shine forth was the decree of the *New York Graphic*: "This picture shows Barbara La Marr in her real nature—a generous, impulsive, whole-souled and loving girl." The *Brooklyn Daily Eagle* considered Barbara's performance to be "a last graceful gesture of adieu to a million filmgoers."[3]

In theaters worldwide, as *The Girl from Montmartre* was screened and upon its conclusion, audiences bade Barbara good-bye with hearty shouts of approval.

British musical duo Flanagan and Allen referenced Barbara's passing in their wildly popular 1932 song "Underneath the Arches," during a break in the singing when Chesney Allen reads 1926 newspaper headlines. Indeed, Barbara's death was one of the year's defining events. (Rudolph Valentino's that August was another.)

Explanations of exactly what killed Barbara were wide-ranging. Some were poetic. Adela Rogers St. Johns suggested she died simply "because the tale was told."[4] Writer Frances Marion likened Barbara to "a glorious sapling ultimately destroyed by barren roots."[5] Bert Ennis, referring to Barbara's "orchid-like beauty" and "orchid-like frailty," proposed that she was "killed by the thing which had sent her sky-rocketing into a world of headlines and Rolls Royces, only to plunge her into debt, sickness, and the obituary column."[6]

Other explanations were more straightforward, though differing. Following the declaration of Barbara's doctor that tuberculosis, nephritis, and her decision to cease medical treatment had caused her death, others presented theories. In certain circles, shattered nerves were blamed; it was inferred that her extreme vitality had nevertheless been no match for fame's brutal pace. Some considered the culprits to be her reckless lifestyle in New York and her insistence upon continuing her work. *Photoplay* contended that her dieting methods sealed her fate.

Five months after Barbara's death, *Photoplay* determined to end the diet frenzy that had seized American women. Catherine Brody wrote a series of articles exposing the unrealistic weight standards imposed upon film stars and the potentially lethal methods certain actresses had employed to slenderize. Specifically warning against thyroid pills, Brody maintained that they induced Barbara's tuberculosis and subsequent demise. Later *Photoplay* articles persisted in citing Barbara's tuberculosis as an example of a dieting regimen turned deadly.[7]

It has periodically been written that Barbara was a drug addict and died of a drug overdose. Writer and filmmaker Kenneth Anger, in his 1975 work *Hollywood Babylon*, a book based mainly on gossip and speculation, suggests she had a fondness for high-grade opium, kept cocaine in a golden casket atop her piano, and experimented with every form of dope until dying of a suicidal overdose.

Another book, established around rumor and (as stated in its preface) outright lies, is *The MGM Girls: Behind the Velvet Curtain*, written by Peter Harry Brown and Pamela Brown in 1983. The authors claim that Barbara received a morphine injection from a studio physician in 1923 after spraining her ankle during a *Souls for Sale* dance sequence. From there, they allege, she formed a morphine addiction. It should be noted that while the trades—which reported extensively on studio happenings—mention that Barbara and others suffered severe eye irritation from klieg lights while filming *Souls for Sale*, nothing is said of an ankle injury. Additionally, Barbara does not appear in a dance sequence in the film, though such a scene might have been cut. Possibly the rumor arose around the knee injury Barbara suffered while dancing in *The White Moth* (1924).

A few authors have stated that Barbara was arrested for possessing forty cubes of morphine but died before standing trial for the incident. In reality, however, it was black-haired, thirty-three-year-old actress Alma Rubens who, on January 5, 1931, was arrested for carrying forty cubes of morphine; Rubens died of pneumonia January 21, before her trial date. Period magazines and newspapers reported openly on Rubens's addiction, as they did in the cases of Wallace Reid and actress Juanita Hansen in the 1920s. These publications do not mention Barbara in connection with drugs. Reid's death certificate furthermore lists morphine addiction as contributing to his death. Barbara's death certificate does not allude to drug usage.

Those who knew Barbara well throughout various times in her life never alluded to it either. ZaSu Pitts certainly didn't. In his fifties, Barbara's son, questioning stories he had read about Barbara, confidentially asked Adela Rogers St. Johns if Barbara dabbled with narcotics. St. Johns, whose association with Barbara began when Barbara was sixteen and endured to her death, and who candidly wrote of Barbara's excessive drinking and Wallace Reid's drug usage, replied that she was unaware of it. To writer Jimmy Bangley in the 1980s, actress Alice Terry, Barbara's *Prisoner of Zenda* (1922) costar and friend, likewise admitted Barbara's partiality to "a good party and a good highball" but dismissed drug abuse claims.[8] "I don't believe all these things they printed about her," Terry said.[9]

Two men intimately connected with Barbara near the end of her life said the same. Ben Lyon acknowledged her alcoholism to Bangley in 1976 but said nothing of drugs.[10] Ben Finney resolutely defended her. "It is inconceivable that during our close friendship I would not have known if she were a junkie," he wrote in his memoir. "She did well enough with booze."[11]

Virginia Carville, besides enjoying an eleven-year friendship with Barbara, lived with her while she made her starring pictures in New York, and the women kept in contact throughout Barbara's final months. Virginia, like Robert Carville, spoke privately with Virginia Dodd (Virginia Carville's great-niece and Robert's granddaughter) of Barbara's drinking, but there she drew the line. She told Dodd Barbara "absolutely did not" use drugs. Dodd recalled, "She thought it was horrible what people said."[12]

It is unclear how tales of Barbara's supposed drug use originated. Finney proposed that her drinking might have spawned them. Unquestionably, her late-night lifestyle, dieting, illness, and nux vomica overdose (whether accidental or intentional) inflamed such conclusions.

Austrian-born dramatist and novelist Arnolt Bronnen is another source of some of the misperceptions beleaguering Barbara's memory. Known primarily for his plays, Bronnen tended toward violence, perverse eroticism, and opportunism in his work. In 1928, he authored *Film und Leben: Barbara La Marr* (The Life and Films of Barbara La Marr), a novel written in German and published in Berlin. He spared little of his fondness for amoral themes in the writing. At one point, for example, he has Barbara awakening in the middle of the night in 1918, running from a New

York hotel room she shared with Ben Deely to the room of a cocaine and white slave dealer across the hall, ripping off her clothing, writhing before him on the bed, and raving, "I'm a pig... I like doing things that are senseless, vulgar, and dirty. Everything that is good and fine is ridiculous to me ... there lies heavily within my soul a taste for the ugly, which seeks the vulgar, the filth, the awful things of life."[13] Although the book is fictional, flimsily woven around basic biographic details of Barbara's life and brimming with inaccuracies, it has been mistaken for a factual account.

During her life, Barbara had grown accustomed to being misunderstood. She believed that, in playing vamps, she had in some ways misrepresented her true character. Shortly before her passing, she asked her friend, writer Jim Tully, "Some day, Jim, will you write about me—and tell them that I wasn't everything I played on the screen?"[14]

To her most faithful friends, Barbara was someone other than her film image, was more than the scandals, headlines, and rumors she generated. These friends, including ZaSu Pitts and makeup artist Perc Westmore, lamented that she could be so misunderstood.

"She played [vamps] well because she was a superb actress," said Alice Terry. "The truth was, she was far from a vamp ... She was a wonderful person and my friend."[15]

Even Barbara's demons didn't shroud the truth of the woman her friends perceived her to be. "Barbara's weaknesses were all of the flesh," writer Willis Goldbeck purportedly stated. "Her virtues were of the mind and spirit. We shan't see her like again."[16] Adela Rogers St. Johns admonished the world, "Judge her as you will, admit her faults and weaknesses, as I do, none of you could have known her and not loved her."[17]

Barbara's public image and talent were as adored by her fans as her true self was by those who knew her. Throughout 1956 and 1957, committees that included Hollywood heavyweights Samuel Goldwyn, Cecil B. DeMille, Mack Sennett, Hal Roach, and Jesse Lasky convened to determine whom to honor with a star on the newly proposed Hollywood Walk of Fame. Barbara was among the 1,558 motion picture, television, radio, and audio recording artists selected. Her induction occurred at the groundbreaking ceremony February 8, 1960. Her star may be seen at 1621 Vine Street, a lasting testament to the twenty-six films in which she is known to have appeared, the respect accorded her by her peers, and the artistic excellence that inspired so many.

Thirty-Three

Barbara's star at 1621 Vine Street, Hollywood.

Barbara's star continued shining in filmdom's heavens long after her films exhausted their run and talking pictures extinguished an era. Many studios, unable to profit any longer from the silent films they had produced, destroyed them. Those films that escaped junk heaps were rolled into their canisters and left to die unpreventable deaths in studio vaults. Filmed on unstable cellulose nitrate film stock, they decayed, many of them crumbling to dust as decades passed. Others' stars eventually eclipsed Barbara's. She quietly faded from public memory.

Today, due to renewed interest in silent film history and the assiduous work of film preservationists and restorationists, Barbara's star is rising again. Approximately thirty thousand surviving prints of silent films are currently housed in archives worldwide, according to Peter Kobel, author of *Silent Movies: The Birth of Film and the Triumph of Movie Culture*. Kobel points out that until these films are catalogued, it's impossible to determine how many copies exist within collections. The silent film survival rate is presently estimated to be a mere 25 percent. Twelve of the twenty-six films Barbara is known to have acted in are included in this estimate. Modern audiences may readily enjoy her feisty turn in Douglas Fairbanks's *The Nut* (1921) and her acclaimed performance in Fairbanks's epic *The Three Musketeers* (1921). Barbara's celebrated work in Rex Ingram's *The Prisoner of Zenda* (1922), which convinced Ingram to star her in his prized thriller, *Trifling Women* (1922), may also be viewed. Likewise available to silent film aficionados is the star-studded *Souls for Sale* (1923), featuring Barbara's portrayal of a vamp with a heart of gold.

The remaining eight of Barbara's films confirmed to be extant are presently held in archives. *Harriet and the Piper* (1920), *The Eternal Struggle* (1923), *The White Moth* (1924), *The Heart of a Siren* (1925), and *The White Monkey* (1925), all of which showcase Barbara's vampy side, are among them, as are her personally cherished, sympathetic enactment in *Thy Name Is Woman* (1924), and her racy, gritty characterization in *The Shooting of Dan McGrew* (1924). Most recently, her hauntingly poignant final film appearance has been preserved in a fully restored version of *The Girl from Montmartre* (1926). In the past, some of these films have been seen by the public via theater screenings and private viewings at hosting archives. It is anticipated that they will continue to be shown in various theaters, screened at film festivals, and aired on Turner Classic Movies in the future.

Regrettably, as of this writing, fourteen of the films in which Barbara acted are unaccounted for. Equally lamentable is the apparent vanishing of the fruits of Barbara's career as a Fox Film Corporation story writer. The chances of those six films surfacing grew slimmer on July 9, 1937. Fire broke out in Fox's storage vault and, stoked by the flammability of the nitrate film stock, consumed most of the studio's pre-1935 original film negatives.

Perhaps, as more of the world's surviving silent film heritage is recovered and restored, Barbara's lost works will return to the public. Perhaps, through these films and those already known to have survived, today's film fans might be transported—as young Reatha Watson, a self-acknowledged incurable dreamer stargazing from her windowsill, was also transported—to the realm of the silent screen's legendary sirens, the realm of the most iconic figures of the 1920s, the realm of the "too beautiful" Barbara La Marr.

"May your Star of Destiny never grow dim—Barbara La Marr." Courtesy of Allison Francis.

Epilogue

Robert Carville's memories of his romance with Barbara stayed with him long after their dance partnership ended with a final turn across Harlow's Café in 1917, the day he enlisted in the war effort. In the years following her death, he considered penning a memoir of their relationship. Only one thing prevented it.

Paul Bern's love for Barbara persisted. Until his death in 1932, Paul saw to it that the vase affixed to her crypt never lacked for roses. When he purchased a Bavarian-style chateau in Benedict Canyon in the early 1930s, after rejoining Metro-Goldwyn-Mayer as a producer, he created a tribute to her. Overlooking the pool are four faces, each carved into a wooden beam protruding from the house into the patio. Paul explained to visitors that the carvings, created by studio artisans and representing the four winds, depict four people who had been closest to him: actor Douglas Fairbanks Jr., writer and producer Carey Wilson, an undisclosed woman (presumably Paul's institutionalized, common-law wife, Dorothy Millette), and Barbara.

So distraught was Paul by Barbara's passing that it was insinuated at the time that he attempted suicide. Later, in the aftermath of Paul's death (an alleged suicide), actor John Gilbert told the press he rescued Paul from "possible suicide" after Paul "brooded for days" over Barbara's death. Gilbert refused to provide details, stating, "The circumstances are too delicate and too close to my heart for me to disclose."[1] Gilbert's account took on a ridiculous, unsubstantiated life of its own. One rumor held that Paul attempted to drown himself by submerging his head in a toilet, and that his supposed suicide attempt occurred when Barbara wed Jack Daugherty (when in fact Paul facilitated the ceremony and acted as best man). Paul denied that Barbara's death caused him to attempt suicide.[2]

Robert told Paul of his intent to write about his own love affair with Barbara. A pitiable sadness clouded Paul's eyes. He asked Robert not to publish the story while he, Paul, was alive. "I could not resist his plea," recalled Robert. "To know Paul Bern was to love him. To meet him was to

Barbara's countenance as carved on a beam at Paul Bern's home. Courtesy of Valerie Franich.

know why he had succeeded . . . What compassion was reflected from those mellow eyes of his, love and compassion for his fellow man. He did not seem to care for gold nor fame, but only to make this world a happier place for you and me to live in."[3] Robert promised Paul he would keep his memories to himself.

Paul's unexpected death in 1932 absolved Robert of his vow. He narrated his account of the years he spent as Barbara's dance partner and lover to his third and final wife, Nancy Landis (half-sister of screen actors Cullen and Margaret), who typed as he spoke.

Robert opens his memoir with words he attributes to Barbara (perhaps overheard by himself or his sister, Virginia), apparently spoken a few weeks before Barbara's passing, when the end seemed imminent and close friends were summoned to say good-bye. She spoke of hating to leave Paul. "He's too fine and too noble and too sensitive for this cruel world," she said. "Life has treated us both very cruelly. I wish he were going with me, for I like Paul Bern." Robert next quotes her as saying, "There's only one man I ever really loved."[4]

Robert wrote of experiencing two haunting visions, one occurring at the beginning of his relationship with Barbara, the other at the end. The first took place in Barbara's San Francisco apartment as he reclined upon a divan in the living room, drinking wine, counting down the remaining hours of 1914, and becoming better acquainted with her. She knelt at his feet atop a pillow, garbed in a purple silken robe and pearl headdress. He recounted taking in her exotic beauty, inhaling the incense perfuming the room, and "drifting, floating away into space." The room transformed into a temple along the Nile River, he continued. Slaves appeared to be kneeling around him . . . More slaves, carrying golden cups of wine, materialized . . . In a corner of the temple, a chanting priest came into view . . . At the center of it all, still seated before him on the floor, was Barbara. Suddenly, she spoke, continuing a conversation they had been having in the living room, dissolving his reverie.

Robert's vision recurred in April 1917, the day the United States declared war on Germany and he joined the army. He and Barbara, both fearful about the future, had returned to their apartment after closing their Harlow's engagement. Barbara's hysterics and conviction that Robert would be killed in Europe intensified his own trepidation. He credited what transpired next to his "highly nervous state." Before his eyes, he recalled, Barbara's countenance shifted, her clothing giving way to a jew-

Epilogue

eled robe and headdress. She appeared to him to be seated upon a throne with slaves kneeling beside her. "I stepped back in fear and surprise," wrote Robert. "Shaking my head, I said, 'My God, where am I?'" The sound of Barbara's voice again drew him back to the apartment. "You were with me, Antony," he quotes her as saying, "back in Egypt in another existence. You've always been mine, but now I'm losing you."

For unknown reasons, Robert never published his manuscript. Written in 1935 and one of many manuscripts he composed, it was passed to his descendants when his painful battle with cancer ended with his suicide in 1967. Entitled "Two Lives, Two Loves," the story provokes a significant question: As Barbara's death loomed and—according to Robert—she spoke of loving only one man, was she referring to Robert Carville or Paul Bern? On one hand, Robert seems to imply he was the one love of Barbara's life. The farewell note she was said by Robert to have given him before his departure for training camp in 1917 appears to confirm this: "You are the only man I have ever loved, or ever will." The title of Robert's story, together with the mystical visions he describes, could theoretically reference a relationship with her in two separate lifetimes (though if this were the case, he would more likely have titled his memoir "Two Lives, *One Love*"). Hence, it could be surmised, based on what he wrote, that Barbara loved Robert and merely liked Paul. This might explain why Paul resisted the idea of Robert writing his memoir.

It doesn't necessarily explain, however, why Robert alluded to Paul in his story at all. Paul is mentioned only on the first page, primarily in the aforesaid exchange between him and Robert, Robert's remarks concerning Paul's character, and Barbara's purported comments near the end of her life. Conceivably, Robert's inclusion of him is more logical if Barbara indeed loved Paul. Robert concludes his story with his entrainment for camp and the ending of his affair with Barbara: "Two lives that were as one had been parted," he writes, "—two hearts that beat in unison were torn asunder." Consequently, might the title "Two Lives, Two Loves" denote Barbara's love for both Robert and Paul? (Since Robert doesn't mention his wives in the memoir—he briefly mentions Marjorie, his first wife, as his dance partner only—it's highly doubtful that they factor into his title.) Barbara's admission about a year before her death that she had yet to experience real love suggests she may have discovered it with Paul during her final months. Given this scenario, could Paul's reluctance to have the public learn of the love he and Barbara shared stem from his common-law marriage to Dorothy Millette (a union that for years he intended to resume should Millette recover her sanity)?

The meaning behind the phrase "I like Paul Bern. There's only one man I ever really loved" changes considerably depending upon the word emphasized when spoken. "*There's* only one man I ever really loved" refers to Paul being that man, whereas "There's only one man I ever really *loved*" denotes someone other than Paul. Not knowing which word Barbara stressed when she uttered the phrase makes interpreting her meaning doubly difficult.

The depth of Barbara's fondness for Paul Bern is certain. The nature of that fondness, whether Barbara believed herself to have known real love in her lifetime, and, if she did, whom it was with will perhaps remain riddles.

William and Rose spent the days after Barbara's funeral secluded in the Altadena bungalow where she died. As the court-appointed administrator of Barbara's estate, William was contacted by the press that same week. How much, asked reporters, did Barbara's heirs (as documented in her probate record), Jack Daugherty (their divorce suit was pending when she died), William, Rose, Sonny, and Billy, expect to receive of the incredible sums she had made in films? To one reporter, William commended his daughter's big heart, pointing out the thousands of dollars she donated each month to orphanages, hospitals, and others in need. To another, he commented, "She did not know the value of a dollar."[5] Barbara's remaining assets, consisting of her Whitley Heights home, its furnishings, and her clothing, were valued at under $10,000. (Jack had already waived his rights to her assets.)

Barbara had not left a will; she had, however, left unpaid debts. One by one, William received the claims against her estate. The first was a relatively minor bill for $100 due Rolls Royce of America for maintenance services. Two others were considerable. Although Barbara had been making regular payments (with money borrowed against her salary) to a creditor for jewels purchased in 1923, $13,133 (approximately $177,100 today) remained to be paid. Because Barbara's home had been attached over the matter, the property was seized and sold, the proceeds covering but half of the debt. The debtor submitted a claim for the outstanding amount, but the monies were never paid; apparently there was nothing left of Barbara's estate. Next was a $71,402 (about $962,700 today) claim from Arthur Sawyer and Herbert Lubin for salary advances and various payments made on Barbara's behalf. The men followed their claim with a proposal to forgo litigation via a compromise. Barbara had taken out a $150,000 life insurance policy, naming Sawyer and Lubin's company as beneficiaries and claiming a one-half interest for her estate. Sawyer and Lubin offered to withdraw their claim against Barbara if William withdrew his claim to half of the insurance payout. William accepted the offer, and the issue was closed. (Barbara's claims against Sawyer and Lubin for unpaid wages followed her to her grave.)[6]

The grief William and Rose felt over Barbara's death abided long after they left Altadena and settled throughout the Los Angeles area. Sustained by their love for each other, William's gentle sense of humor, and faith in God, they reconstructed their lives. William found solace behind his typewriter. Barbara remarked in 1924 that, since he left the irrigation and newspaper businesses in the early 1920s, he was forever writing a novel and hoping it would sell. William kept plugging away. His works, while never receiving the recognition he might have wished for, evidently earned a modest income before his passing in 1941. Rose died earlier, in 1936.

After William's cremation at Hollywood Cemetery (then called Hollywood Memorial Cemetery and now called Hollywood Forever), Barbara's brother Billy approached the cemetery's manager, Julian "Jules" Roth, with Rose's cremains and a request.

Roth had met Barbara in the summer of 1924, amid the boisterous roar of a New York City nightclub. He was "Jack" Roth then, vice president of oil promoter C. C. Julian's Julian Petroleum Corporation and the brains behind the outfit's advertising. Charged by California authorities with manipulating and illegally selling company stock, Julian and Roth had taken their operation east. Barbara, obviously charmed by the attractive, cultured adman, indulged him with a fling. Then Roth dropped by her apartment to pick her up for a date one evening and set eyes on Virginia Carville. Barbara yielded her beau to her best friend seemingly without hard feelings; Barbara had already trained her sights upon Ben Finney. When Roth finagled a release from San Quentin in 1937 after serving five years for grand theft in connection with his Los Angeles stock brokerage, he married Virginia, gained a foothold in Hollywood Memorial Cemetery (allegedly as a financial consultant), and took the place over, his scandalous past buried. A fragment of his past nonetheless remained. Roth was said to place flowers at Barbara's crypt.

Roth honored Billy's request to inter Rose and William with Barbara. It was stipulated, either by Billy or, more likely, Roth, that only the plaque inscribed with Barbara's name appear on the crypt.

Eight decades after Barbara's death in 1926, with a wistful tone in his voice, her son admitted to having no memories of her.

Yet a single, ephemeral image dwelt deep within his mind. He is three and a half. His mother's funeral has just concluded. He's in the backseat of a large automobile. Several weeping women, whom he believes to be pallbearers or pallbearers' wives, are with him. Suddenly, one of them turns to him. "Who do you think he will go to live with now?" the woman sobs to the other women.[7]

ZaSu Pitts, Tom Gallery, and their daughter, Ann, had already decided the matter amongst themselves. In the three months Sonny had lived in their home, he had lived in their hearts. Days before Barbara's funeral, Gallery announced his plan to adopt the little boy. Reporters considered it done; the press ran photographs of Sonny with his purported new family.

The news was premature. William and Rose wanted their grandson back. William refuted Gallery's announcement, telling reporters that the right to raise Sonny belonged to Barbara's relatives. ZaSu, declaring that Barbara had given Sonny to her, refused to hand him over. William petitioned the court to be made Sonny's legal guardian and reportedly prepared for a lawsuit.[8]

Two others were also in the running to parent Sonny. Billy was willing to rear him. A caption on the back of an International Newsreel photo stated that Paul Bern was "anxious to adopt" him.[9]

The battle dragged on for months. Sonny remained in the Gallerys' care. The Gallerys were unable to begin adoption proceedings without William's clearance. The Watsons grappled with the facts. William and Rose, in their late sixties, were living on a limited income. Although Billy had adopted a boy, Jimmy, a month after Barbara staged Sonny's sham adoption in 1923, he may have been divorced by 1926 (he would marry actress Deletta Williams, his final wife, by 1930), and the frequent traveling required by his profession made parenting difficult. Paul, despite the existence of his mentally ill, common-law wife, was, to all appearances, a bachelor.

By contrast, ZaSu Pitts and Tom Gallery seemed an ideal choice. ZaSu's acting career and salary had thrived since her starring turn in Erich

Epilogue

The Gallerys (*left to right*) Ann, Tom, ZaSu, and Donald. Courtesy of Donald Gallery.

Von Stroheim's *Greed* (1924). An actor no longer, Gallery made a decent living as head of the Hollywood Legion Stadium and would soon become a boxing promoter. Sonny had become attached to the Gallerys in the year he had lived with them.

William and Rose gave up the fight. That November, ZaSu and Gallery left a Los Angeles courtroom with a new son. They christened him Donald Michael Gallery.

ZaSu proved to be a wonderful mother, through good times and bad. Her marriage to Tom Gallery wasn't always the storybook romance the magazines purported it to be. About a week after finalizing Donald's adoption, the pair separated. Charging desertion, ZaSu filed for divorce in 1932. She was awarded custody of Donald and Ann. Gallery remained in the children's lives, visiting regularly. ZaSu married tennis champion turned broker John "Eddie" Woodall in 1933.

ZaSu made her children a priority, putting aside her aspirations of playing dramatic roles and sticking primarily to comedic parts that earned steady paychecks. Her efforts to keep her children unspoiled—among

Donald at sixteen. Courtesy of Donald Gallery.

them, celebrating their birthdays on the same day and giving them a single gift to share—moderated the splendor in which Donald lived. The Georgian-style mansion he called home was nestled in the star-studded Los Angeles suburb of Brentwood and afforded the best in boyhood amusement. Shirley Temple and Judy Garland were among his playmates. Clark Gable, Greta Garbo, Joan Crawford, Gloria Swanson, Barbara Stanwyck, and Elizabeth Taylor were neighbors at differing times and regular guests in his home. (An eye-popping glimpse of Garbo sunbathing nude by her swimming pool next door could often be had; Donald later admitted to charging his school pals a quarter each to catch their own peep.) Warmly recalling his atypical childhood and youthful innocence, ninety-year-old Donald chuckled, "I thought all kids grew up as I did!"[10]

As Barbara had hoped, her son became the man she dreamed he would. He received the fine education she had planned to provide, excelling as an honor student at Brentwood Town and Country School and later

Epilogue

the prestigious, character-building Webb Boarding Preparatory School for boys. His winning disposition—one part Barbara's magnetism, one part even-temperedness, and a dash of shyness—gained him friends wherever he went. ZaSu considered him a godsend. "Don Mike is an angel," she told a reporter in 1932.[11]

As he neared manhood, Donald learned that being a gentleman—and the epitome of the handsome, all-American "boy next door"—had advantages. Shirley Temple's safety was paramount to her parents and film studio. Her home next door was protected by an eight-foot-high enclosure, an armed watchman, and security sensors on doors and windows. Unwilling to trust their daughter to just any young man, the Temples selected Donald to escort the petite superstar (by now a teenager) to film premieres and other social gatherings. Donald later insisted they were merely friends, though Shirley apparently had other ideas. After Donald left for Stanford University, she often wrapped herself in his varsity sweater, even daring to wear it at her high school where, to avoid being caught in violation of a stringently enforced uniform policy, she pressed her books against her chest.

After a new family moved into Shirley's house, the family's anxious mother recruited Donald for a special assignment. Her preteen daughter had fallen hard for twenty-year-old actor Peter Lawford, an older man the mother considered an unacceptable companion. The mother instructed Donald, though himself nine years older than the girl, to occupy her time and, ideally, cause her to forget Lawford. Donald succeeded in his mission. He kept the relationship platonic, as her mother requested, though it tested his resolve. The girl had developed a crush on him and happened to be Elizabeth Taylor, the most beautiful creature he had ever seen.

His respectfulness and dependability aside, Donald broke the occasional heart. In September 1942, ZaSu's was the first. With the Second World War raging, he had left Stanford and enlisted in the U.S. Army Air Corps. Perhaps he also broke Shirley Temple's heart. ZaSu and Shirley's mother had hoped the couple would marry. But with an unknown future looming, Donald was unable to get serious with Shirley. In his absence, she accepted another man's marriage proposal.

As Donald completed fighter pilot training, ZaSu—still terrified by his decision to go off to battle—drew upon her connections behind his back, contacting a general she knew who was stationed abroad. The man was willing to help but, in exchange, asked ZaSu to get his daughter into films.

ZaSu agreed; the man's daughter came to Hollywood, appeared in films, and eventually married a wealthy studio mogul. Donald was transferred out of the Air Corps, given an assignment as a "spy catcher" in the Counter Intelligence Corps, or CIC (the precursor to the CIA), and assigned to Liverpool, England. The decision to employ Donald in this capacity was not made lightly; CIC agents were meticulously chosen for their solid reputation as upstanding men. Donald excelled at his duties, earned the coveted title of Special Agent, and remained with the CIC after the war's end, rounding up war criminals in Switzerland. He later served as a guard at the Nuremberg war crimes trials.

Donald returned to Los Angeles in 1946, resumed his education, and found a job investigating claims for an insurance company. He also found a bride. In 1947, he married Warner Bros. starlet Joyce Reynolds. The marriage ended after four years, however. "We were young," Donald later explained.[12]

Three decades later, as a newcomer to Catalina Island, Donald met the love of his life: a lovely local named Patricia. She became his wife in 1985. They remained on the island for years, Donald with a pizza parlor and ice cream store he purchased, Patricia with her jewel shop.

Sharing Barbara's zest for life, desire to perform and write, and philanthropic tendencies, Donald likewise lived to the fullest. He played bit parts in films and television, nurtured others' talents as president of a writer's group after retiring to Puerto Vallarta, Mexico, in 1993, and rescued stray animals with Patricia. Most important to him, though, was enjoying twenty-nine years with, as he was fond of saying, "the greatest wife in the world."[13]

At the contented age of ninety, Donald professed to have no regrets over the way his life turned out.

He had, however, harbored a persistent longing. "I wish I could have known Barbara," he admitted.[14] ZaSu told him as a boy what a lovely person Barbara was, and that he and Barbara had loved each other very much. Throughout the years, as Donald gazed at Barbara's image in yellowing clippings from 1920s film magazines and collected her photographs from memorabilia shops, his mind spun with unanswered questions. As an adult he sought to answer them, to know and understand Barbara. He spent hours beside her crypt, thinking of all he wished to say to her.

ZaSu had never spoken to him of William, Rose, and his Uncle Billy, and they had never, to his knowledge, attempted to see or contact him. By the time Donald began searching for the missing pieces of his life, William

Epilogue

and Rose had died; Billy died in 1952. Donald was unaware of Barbara's half-siblings, Donald's Aunt June and Uncle Henry, who were both still alive at that point. June, possessing a marital record surpassing Barbara's—she wed at least six men—lived as June Marston until her death in 1954. Henry, charged in 1928 with two counts of incest against his daughters, aged eighteen and fourteen, and (since the younger daughter was underage) one count of rape, pleaded guilty to one count of incest and spent twenty-five years in San Quentin before dying in 1966.[15]

The question Donald most yearned to put to Barbara continued haunting him over the years: he wondered who his father was. He had his own idea.

From as far back as he remembered, Paul Bern came to ZaSu's home each Sunday to see him, bringing gifts of toys and often taking him on outings. ZaSu told Donald that Paul was his godfather. Many in the film industry didn't accept that explanation. Leatrice Gilbert Fountain, Donald's lifelong friend, stated that her mother, actress Leatrice Joy, a close friend of Paul's, "always believed Don was the son of Paul Bern"; Fountain added, "that seems to have been the general opinion."[16] Young Donald, taken with Paul's kindness toward him, began believing it himself. Ten years old when Paul died in 1932, he would remember his days with Paul as some of the happiest he had known.

The older Donald became, the more he wanted to know the truth of his identity. Ben Lyon, among other men to whom Barbara had been romantically linked, was also rumored to be Donald's father. Donald spoke privately with Lyon as an adult. Lyon denied the rumor was true, adding that Barbara hadn't revealed his father's identity to him.

Donald would never learn what Jack Daugherty might have known. Debt-laden, Jack ended his life in 1938, living on in boys and men who idolized his red-blooded heroism long after rudimentary microphones and soundstages eradicated silent cinema, temporarily replaced rollicking action heroes, and ended his starring career in 1929.

Donald believed ZaSu and Tom Gallery knew who his father was. He asked them about it multiple times. Neither gave him an answer.

He implored Virginia Carville to tell him all she knew about the subject. She, too, kept whatever information she had to herself, answering, Donald said, "in such a way as to protect Barbara's reputation." Donald suspected that ZaSu, Gallery, and Virginia were protecting *him*. "People just didn't talk about those things in those days," he explained.[17]

One person was willing to talk.

A portal to Donald's lost years appeared unexpectedly in 1963. ZaSu Pitts, following an accomplished career encompassing film, theater, radio, and television, had just died of cancer. Donald was in his early forties. While rummaging through ZaSu's house, boxing up her belongings and moving them out, a letter, addressed to ZaSu and hidden away, stopped him cold.

It had been sent by Irene Almond. In it, Almond introduced herself as Barbara's former maid and "Sonny's" nurse. Her identity, she wrote, could be verified by Lew Cody or Ben Lyon. Almond stated that she had been Donald's nurse from the day Barbara gave birth to him until Ada Slater was hired, and was Barbara's maid until Barbara's death. She explained she was therefore acquainted with many instances in Donald's early life—including, Donald realized as his eyes dissected Almond's words, the knowledge he most desperately wanted. "On communication from you," Almond had typed in closing, "I should be very glad to give you some valuable information concerning the boy and his parentage."[18]

Donald looked again at the date on the letter. Almond had mailed it to ZaSu from New York in 1933, thirty years earlier. Donald had no way of knowing whether ZaSu ever contacted her. Nor could he locate a current address for Almond. He was unable to determine if Almond, who would have been in her late seventies when he discovered the letter, was still alive. (Almond appears to have died childless, nullifying the possibility that information could be gathered from direct descendants.) Donald's chance to find out what Almond knew was gone.

Donald's life went on. Barbara continued existing in his heart—a nebulous, ever-evolving amalgamation of others' memories, rumors, (often inaccurate) accounts he read about her, and his treasured hopes. Also in his heart was Paul Bern—an imagined father.

On the East Coast of the United States in 2014, Laura Riebman reflected upon her own familial ties. Over eighty years after his sensationalized death, Laura wondered about her great-uncle, Paul Bern. The discovery of Paul's body with an apparently self-inflicted gunshot wound came as a tremendous shock to his family in 1932. Paul's younger brother Henry (Laura's grandfather), following an immediate trip from New York to Los Angeles to conduct his own investigation, told the

Epilogue

press that he and his family were unconvinced of any specific suicide motive. Neither Henry nor the rest of the family spoke of Paul's violent demise after this; the pain was too great. Baseless rumors that arose about Paul after his death hurt just as much. Saddened by the misinformation enveloping her great-uncle's legacy, Laura set out to learn more. She researched and read about him. She considered rumors that he had fathered a son.[19]

A search led her to Donald Gallery that April. Introducing herself as his possible relative, she expressed her wish to know him and make her family whole. Laura was overjoyed when Donald agreed to undergo genetic testing to confirm whether he was Paul's son.

The fundamental test for verifying paternal ancestry, the Y-DNA test, compares the Y-DNA chromosome between two males. Found only in males, Y-DNA passes unadulterated from fathers to sons, generation after generation, until broken by a female offspring. Although the test cannot confirm specific male relationships, it unequivocally determines whether two males descended from the same paternal line. Assuming Donald was Paul's son, that line traced back to Paul and Henry's father, down through Henry to his only son, Raymond, and through Raymond's son, Paul Henry. Excited by the possibility of reuniting with his father's cousin, Paul Henry agreed to be tested with Donald.

Donald was thrilled by the prospect of proving himself to be Paul's son and connecting with blood relatives. The alternative seemingly worried him. "I've lived all my life believing myself to be a certain person," he said in reference to his parentage months before the subject of DNA testing came up.[20]

In comparing Donald's Y-DNA sample against Paul Henry's, the laboratory was looking for an identical match. The samples contained many differences. That Donald was Paul's son is impossible.[21]

Concern arose for how Donald would take the news. He was already distressed by symptoms of stroke-induced dementia, which he had been experiencing with increased regularity. He was also mourning a close friend's recent passing. To avoid hurting him further, it was decided not to tell him about the test results unless he asked. He never did.

Did Paul believe himself to be Donald's father? Might Barbara have believed it? The answers to these questions, as well as the identity of Donald's biological father, will likely never be known.

Donald and Patricia. Courtesy of Donald Gallery.

Donald Gallery passed away quietly in Puerto Vallarta at age ninety-two during his usual afternoon nap on October 11, 2014. His wife, Patricia, was beside him, watching television. His cheerful spirit, even to the end, was an inspiration. "He had the most peaceful, beautiful look on his face," Patricia said.[22]

Appendix

Musings of a Muse

Barbara's lifelong compulsion to express herself through the written word often took the form of poetry, pouring from her, she said, whenever she "was so full-up with emotion" she "just had to have an outlet." Free verse, a poetic form bereft of set structures, was her preferred medium of literary expression. To her it was "the freest of the free." She considered her poetry, as she considered all art, a substitute for life—albeit a relatively inferior one. "I suppose that if we could all live to the utmost, we wouldn't create very much, because art really isn't an effective substitute," she said.[1]

In 1922, as Barbara entered her mid-twenties atop a crest of breakout film roles, she often secluded herself on the sidelines of sets when not before the camera, transcribing her feelings into poetry. The following poems (and those on pages 307–10) represent what Barbara believed to be her finest work as a poet.[2]

Because
When I met PEDRO, I was thankful that my
hair was like pale sunshine through a golden
mist at dawn, BECAUSE—His was black and soft
as a moonless summer night!

When I met DAVID, I was thankful that my eyes
were dark and deep, and veiled, BECAUSE—His
were clear and grey, and searching!

When I met BILLY, for the first time in my life,
I was thankful that my nose was retroussé, BECAUSE—
Well, Billy had a sense of humor!

Appendix

When I met NAIFE, I was thankful that my
mouth was tender, with a wistful childish expression,
BECAUSE—His was red—too red—and just a bit cruel!

BUT—when I met YOU: I was thankful, oh, so
thankful, that my skin was soft, and white, BECAUSE—
WELL, JUST BECAUSE!

Love and Hate
I LOVE you—
Your lips, your hair, your eyes,
Your willful, reckless, tender lies,
I hate you!

I hate you—!
Your smile, your curls, your glance,
You pagan worshipper of Chance,
I love you!

Are You—?
Why should I—who worship Thought—
Unthinkingly bare my Soul unsought,
Dreams that memory cannot dim—
Why should I speak to you of HIM?

Why should I tell you all these things—
Of hours when Passion's wearied wings
Folded beneath the mauve-grey sky
Of dawn—that ever means "Goodbye"?

Of strange, mysterious, wonderful nights
When I have tasted the gods' delights;
Of lips I have kissed, and kissing burned—
Of loves I have left and loves returned.

When dreaming and close at my side
I felt the urge of Passion's tide.

Musings of a Muse

I closed my eyes and infinitely sad
Dreamed of that which—I have never had.

But why should I—who worship Thought—
Bare my Soul to you unsought—
Telling of dreams Time cannot dim,
Unless—perhaps—that you are him!

Reincarnated
Why do I dream at twilight
When the evening sun is low,
Of palm trees that quiver and
Golden waters that glow?

Perhaps I have found in some strange
Land a pair of eyes
That haunt me, thrill me, from beneath
Distant southern skies.

Perhaps, Adored, that Centuries ago
I knew things that I now not know,
Perhaps on primitive, desert shores
I found you, loved you, was wholly yours—
With love that all eternity survives;
And am still yours thru all these lives.
So in the Centuries to come I shall be
Wholly yours—tho' you may never
Know me.

Acknowledgments

It is said that life's plans for us are often greater than those we dream ourselves, and that many journeys, despite their fleeting frustrations and unexpected detours, bring as much joy as their destinations. These maxims have rarely proven truer for me since Barbara La Marr entered my life. I'm eternally grateful to those individuals—several of whom have become treasured friends—who illumined this journey and enabled me to complete this biography.

I thank film historian Karie Bible for introducing me to Barbara, for just happening to have my head-shot business card on her desk when she received the call from Brad Macneil, coproducer of *Channeling Hollywood*, inquiring if she knew an actress who could write Barbara's life story in monologue form and portray her in it. I thank Brad Macneil, director Richard Hilton, and Brad Price for casting me as Barbara, as well as the Pasadena Playhouse and Pasadena Museum of History for producing *Channeling Hollywood*.

I express profound gratitude to Donald and Patricia Gallery. From the moment Don returned home after seeing me perform in *Channeling Hollywood*, exclaiming, Patricia told me, "I finally met the person who is supposed to write this book!," the unwavering faith he placed in me and the friendship, love, and encouragement he and Patricia have given me have been invaluable. Although primarily focused on acting when I met Don and never intending to use my writing skills to author a book, I couldn't resist his entreaty that I write Barbara's biography any more than I could resist Barbara's compelling story. While I am saddened that Don passed on before this book's publication, I have often felt his supportive presence and am honored to have fulfilled his dream that Barbara's complete story be told. I hope I have made him proud.

I express appreciation to Virginia Jauregui and Virginia Dodd (Robert Carville's great-granddaughter and granddaughter) for serendipitously gracing my life in 2010 by contacting Don, days after I wished for greater insight into Barbara and Robert's relationship. "Something brought you to

Acknowledgments

us," Virginia Jauregui said after unearthing Robert's memoir deep within the family's storage shed.

Others likewise graciously donated their time, alternately relating family stories, supplying genealogical information, and clarifying facts. Laura Riebman, Paul Bern's great-niece, has additionally shared her journey to honor Paul's memory and been a welcome source of encouragement. Joan Barry Liebmann, granddaughter of Antonia Miether Melvill, shared, along with her grandmother's painting, the memories of her mother, Viola Barry, Barbara's friend. Thanks also to Shari Ainsworth Kroner, great-niece of Philip Ainsworth; Daphne Allen, great-niece of Pearl Allen; Paul H. Bern, great-nephew of Paul Bern; Dr. Connie A. Hailey of the Southeast National Tuberculosis Center; Leatrice Gilbert Fountain, daughter of John Gilbert and Leatrice Joy; Ruthie Primiano, great-granddaughter of George Ake; Robert Brown, great-grandson of George Watson (brother of William Watson); Sarah Cantor of the Holy Names Heritage Center; Darren Borgias, biographer of C. B. Watson; film historian Hugh Munro Neely; and Deborah Brugliera.

I offer gratitude to those who, like Donald Gallery, Virginia Jauregui, and Laura Riebman, kindly provided photographs: Allison Francis who further blessed me with her generosity; Valerie Franich; and Robert S. Birchard. I acknowledge Bryson Harris for beautifully restoring two of this book's photographs. Realtor Tim Swan was a source of pictures of the interior of Barbara's Whitley Heights home.

Librarians and archivists frequently assisted me with accessing articles and documents. I'm indebted to Julia Butler of the Heritage Park Library for combing the country to fulfill my interminable microfilm orders. Profuse thanks to William Chase of the Cleveland Public Library for sacrificing personal time to photograph Barbara's diary for me. I also sincerely thank Sandra Joy Aguilar and Jonathon Auxier of the University of Southern California's Warner Bros. Archives; Ned Comstock of USC Special Collections; Coralynn Petrie and Patty Scruggs at St. Mary's Academy; Sister Bernice Hollenhorst of the Sisters of the Holy Cross Archives; Theodore Hovey of Hollywood Forever; Chris Her at Fresno Public Library; Tamara Vidos Glencross of the University of Oregon's Knight Library; Mike Pepin of the American Film Institute; Mary Sholler of the Madera County Library; Katherine Krzys of Arizona State University Library's Special Collections; Josie Walters-Johnston at the Moving Image Section of the Library of Congress; Isa Lang of Chapman University's Rinker Law

Acknowledgments

Library; Fred LeBaron of the Loyola University Chicago School of Law Library; Donna Silvas of the Porterville Library; Barbara Scheibel of Onondaga County Public Library; Carolyn Seaman of Saddleback College Library; and Jan Becking of the University of California, Santa Cruz McHenry Library. Additional thanks to the accommodating staff at the Margaret Herrick, Multnomah County, and Katie Wheeler Libraries; Diocese of Fresno Archives; Mandeville Special Collections Library, University of California, San Diego; Altadena, Dallas, La Mesa, and Summit Historical Societies; San Diego History Center; the University of California, Los Angeles; and the Los Angeles, Tacoma, Spokane, Seattle, Medford, and Tehama Public Libraries.

I extend gratitude to my family and friends for seeing the best in me, to my mother for listening to innumerable readings of my manuscript, and to my parents for teaching me that nothing is impossible when one's entire heart is in it.

The infinite love and patience of my husband, Erik, sustained me throughout this undertaking, indulging me whenever I asked "just one more question" about my manuscript and enduring, to quote Barbara's husband Jack Daugherty, having yet not having a wife while this work consumed me.

Thanks also to Frank and Suzanne Cooper and Hollywood Forever for enabling me to continue presenting over many years the one-woman performance piece I wrote about Barbara.

I am grateful to author Christina Rice, my guiding light, for her advice and recommendation that I submit my manuscript to the University Press of Kentucky. I sincerely thank Anne Dean Dotson, Patrick O'Dowd, Cameron Ludwick, Mack McCormick, Jacqueline Wilson, Amy Harris, Ila McEntire, and the rest of the University Press of Kentucky team for their enthusiasm for this project and for being wonderful to work with. Moreover, I thank Donna Bouvier, author Mary Mallory, and the University Press of Kentucky's anonymous panel of readers; their highly valued, expert suggestions enhanced this manuscript.

I wish to remember those whose lives interconnected with Barbara's, who enliven these pages. I'm privileged to have written about them.

My final thanks go to Barbara. In giving your whole soul to your life, you have given me some of the greatest gifts of mine.

Filmography

The survival status noted for the films listed below was compiled from the following sources: the American Silent Feature Film Database, from the report "The Survival of American Silent Feature Films: 1912–1929," Library of Congress, http://memory.loc.gov/diglib/ihas/html/silentfilms/silentfilms-home.html (accessed March 2017); "Treasures from the Film Archives," http://fiaf.chadwyck.com (accessed November 2016); www.silentera.com (accessed November 2016). It should be noted that listings documenting the survival status of silent films, compiled by film institutes, are in constant flux as more films are recovered. The status of films below said to be lost is therefore subject to change.

Writer

The Mother of His Children (Fox Film Corporation, 1920). Director: Edward J. Le Saint. Writers: Barbara La Marr Deely (story) and Charles Wilson (scenario). Cast: Gladys Brockwell, William Scott, Frank Leigh, Nigel De Brulier, Golda Madden, Nancy Caswell, and Jean Eaton. No surviving prints of this film are known to exist.

The Rose of Nome (Fox Film Corporation, 1920). Director: Edward J. Le Saint. Writers: Barbara La Marr Deely (story) and Paul Schofield (scenario). Cast: Gladys Brockwell, William Scott, Herbert Prior, Gertrude Ryan, Edward Peil, Stanton Heck, Frank Thorne, Lule Warrenton, and Georgie Woodthorpe. No surviving prints of this film are known to exist.

The Little Grey Mouse (Fox Film Corporation, 1920). Director: James P. Hogan. Writers: Barbara La Marr Deely (story) and James P. Hogan (scenario). Cast: Louise Lovely, Sam De Grasse, Rosemary Theby, Philo McCullough, Wilson Hummel, Miss Gerard Alexander, Willis Marks, and Thomas Jefferson. No surviving prints of this film are known to exist.

Filmography

Flame of Youth (Fox Film Corporation, 1920). Director: Howard M. Mitchell. Writers: Ouida (Maria Louise Ramé) (story based on her 1874 novel *Two Little Wooden Shoes*), Barbara La Marr Deely (adaptation), and Frank Howard Clark (scenario). Cast: Shirley Mason, Raymond McKee, Philo McCullough, Cecil Van Auker, Adelbert Knott, Betty Schade, Karl Formes, and Barbara La Marr Deely (uncredited). No surviving prints of this film are known to exist.

The Land of Jazz (Fox Film Corporation, 1920). Director: Jules Furthman. Writers: Jules Furthman (story and scenario), and Barbara La Marr Deely (story). Cast: Eileen Percy, Ruth Stonehouse, Herbert Heyes, George Fisher, Franklyn Farnum, Hayward Mack, Rose Dione, Carry Ward, Blanche Payson, Wilson Hummel, Harry Dunkinson, Dick La Reno. No surviving prints of this film are known to exist.

My Husband's Wives (Fox Film Corporation, 1924). Director: Maurice Elvey. Writers: Barbara La Marr (story) and Dorothy Yost (scenario). Cast: Shirley Mason, Bryant Washburn, Evelyn Brent, and Paulette Duval. No surviving prints of this film are known to exist.

Actress

Harriet and the Piper (Louis B. Mayer Productions and Anita Stewart Productions, 1920). Director: Bertram Bracken. Writers: Kathleen Norris (story) and Monte M. Katterjohn (scenario). Cast: Anita Stewart, Ward Crane, Charles Richman, Myrtle Stedman, Margaret Landis, Byron Munson, Loyola O'Connor, Irving Cummings, Barbara La Marr Deely. A print of this film is filed at the Archives Françaises Du Film-CNC (Bois-d'Arcy, France).

The Nut (Douglas Fairbanks Pictures, 1921). Director: Theodore Reed. Writers: Kenneth Davenport (story) and William Parker (scenario). Cast: Douglas Fairbanks, Marguerite De La Motte, William Lowery, Gerald Pring, Morris Hughes, and Barbara La Marr. This film is currently distributed on DVD by Kino Lorber (USA) and available for viewing at www.archive.org/details/The_Nut.

Desperate Trails (Universal Film Manufacturing Company, 1921). Director:

Filmography

Jack Ford. Writers: Courtney Ryley Cooper (story based on his "Christmas Eve at Pilot Butte" published in *Redbook,* 1921) and Elliott J. Clawson (scenario). Cast: Harry Carey, Irene Rich, Georgie Stone, Helen Field, Edward Coxen, Barbara La Marr, George Siegmann, and Charles E. Insley [*sic*]. No surviving prints of this film are known to exist.

The Three Musketeers (Douglas Fairbanks Pictures, 1921). Director: Fred Niblo. Writers: Alexandre Dumas (story based on his 1844 novel *Les Trois Mousquetaires*) and Edward Knoblock (scenario). Cast: Douglas Fairbanks, Leon Barry, George Siegmann, Eugene Pallette, Boyd Irwin, Thomas Holding, Sydney Franklin, Charles Stevens, Nigel De Brulier, Willis Robards, Lon Poff, Mary MacLaren, Marguerite De La Motte, Barbara La Marr, Walt Whitman, Adolphe Menjou, and Charles Belcher. This film is currently distributed on DVD by Kino Lorber (USA) and available for viewing at www.archive.org/details/The_Three_Musketeers.

Cinderella of the Hills (Fox Film Corporation, 1921). Director: Howard M. Mitchell. Writers: John Breckenridge Ellis (story based on his 1913 novel *Little Fiddler of the Ozarks*) and Dorothy Yost (scenario). Cast: Barbara Bedford, Carl Miller, Cecil Van Auker, Tom McGuire, Wilson Hummel, and Barbara La Marr Deely. No surviving prints of this film are known to exist.

Arabian Love (Fox Film Corporation, 1922). Director: Jerome Storm. Writer: Jules Furthman (scenario and story). Cast: John Gilbert, Barbara Bedford, Barbara La Marr, Herschel Mayall, Robert Kortman, and William H. Orlamond. No surviving prints of this film are known to exist.

Domestic Relations (Preferred Pictures, 1922). Director: Chester (Chet) Withey. Writer: Violet Clark (scenario and story). Cast: Katherine MacDonald, William P. Carleton, Frank Leigh, Barbara La Marr, Gordon Mullen, George Fisher, and Lloyd Whitlock. No surviving prints of this film are known to exist.

The Prisoner of Zenda (Metro Pictures Corporation, 1922). Director: Rex Ingram. Writers: Anthony Hope (story based on his 1894 novel *The Prisoner of Zenda*), Edward Rose (based on his 1896 play *The Prisoner of Zenda: A Romantic Play and a Prologue in Four Acts,* from the novel), and

Filmography

Mary O'Hara (scenario). Cast: Lewis Stone, Alice Terry, Robert Edeson, Stuart Holmes, Ramon Novarro (billed as Ramon Samaniegos [sic]), Barbara La Marr, Malcolm McGregor, Edward Connelly, and Lois Lee. This film is distributed on DVD by Grapevine Video (USA), Warner Home Video (USA), and Lobster Films (France). Surviving prints may be viewed on site by appointment at the Academy Film Archive in Beverly Hills, California, and the Film and Television Archive, University of California, Los Angeles. Surviving prints are also filed at Gosfilmofond (Moscow, Russia) and George Eastman House (Rochester, New York).

Trifling Women (Metro Pictures Corporation, 1922). Director: Rex Ingram. Writer: Rex Ingram. Cast: Barbara La Marr, Ramon Novarro, Pomeroy Cannon, Edward Connelly, Lewis Stone, Hughie Mack, Eugene Pouyet, John George, Jess Weldon, B. Hyman, and Joe Martin (the orangutan). No surviving prints of this film are known to exist.

Quincy Adams Sawyer (Sawyer-Lubin Productions, 1922). Director: Clarence Badger. Writers: Charles Felton Pidgin (story from his 1900 novel *Quincy Adams Sawyer*), Bernard McConville (adaptation and scenario), and Winifred Dunn (titles). Cast: John Bowers, Blanche Sweet, Lon Chaney, Barbara La Marr, Elmo Lincoln, Louise Fazenda, Joseph Dowling, Claire McDowell, Edward Connelly, June Elvidge, Victor Potel, Gale Henry, Hank Mann, Kate Lester, Billy Franey, Taylor Graves, Harry Depp, Andrew Arbuckle, and Ray Thompson. No surviving prints of this film are known to exist.

The Hero (Preferred Pictures, 1923). Director: Louis J. Gasnier. Writers: Gilbert Emery (story from his 1921 play *The Hero: a Play in Three Acts*) and Eve Unsell (scenario). (Although uncredited, Barbara La Marr was likely at least partially responsible for writing the scenario.) Cast: Gaston Glass, Barbara La Marr, John Sainpolis, Martha Mattox, Frankie Lee, David Butler, Doris Pawn, and Ethel Shannon. No surviving prints of this film are known to exist.

Poor Men's Wives (Preferred Pictures, 1923). Director: Louis J. Gasnier. Writers: Agnes Christine Johnston (story and scenario), Frank Dazey (story and scenario), and Eve Unsell (titles). Cast: Barbara La Marr, David Butler, Betty Francisco, Richard Tucker, ZaSu Pitts, Muriel McCormac,

Filmography

and Mickey McBan. No surviving prints of this film are known to exist. Four of the film's seven reels, however, are on file at Gosfilmofond (Moscow, Russia).

Souls for Sale (Goldwyn Pictures, 1923). Produced, directed, and written by Rupert Hughes. Cast: Eleanor Boardman, Richard Dix, Frank Mayo, Barbara La Marr, Lew Cody, Mae Busch, Arthur Hoyt, David Imboden, Roy Atwell, William Orlamond, Forrest Robinson, Edith Yorke, Dale Fuller, Snitz Edwards, Jack Richardson, Aileen Pringle, Eve Southern, May Milloy, Sylvia Ashton, Margaret Bourne, Fred Kelsey, Jed Prouty, Yale Boss, William Haines, George Morgan, Auld Thomas, Leo Willis, Walter Perry, Sam Damen, R. H. Johnson, Rush Hughes, L. J. O'Connor, and Charles Murphy. Celebrity appearances by Hugo Ballin, Mabel Ballin, T. Roy Barnes, Barbara Bedford, Hobart Bosworth, Charles Chaplin, Chester Conklin, William H. Crane, Elliott Dexter, Robert Edeson, Claude Gillingwater, Dagmar Godowsky, Raymond Griffith, Elaine Hammerstein, Jean Haskell, K. C. B. (a.k.a. Kenneth C. Beaton), Alice Lake, Bessie Love, June Mathis, Patsy Ruth Miller, Marshall Neilan, Fred Niblo, Anna Q. Nilsson, ZaSu Pitts, John Sainpolis, Milton Sills, Anita Stewart, Erich von Stroheim, Blanche Sweet, Florence Vidor, King Vidor, Johnny Walker, George Walsh, Kathlyn Williams, and Claire Windsor. This film is distributed on DVD by the Warner Archive. A surviving print is also on file at the Museum of Modern Art (New York City) and may be viewed on-site by appointment.

Mary of the Movies (Columbia Productions with Robertson-Cole Pictures Corporation, 1923). Director: John McDermott. Writers: Louis Lewyn (story and scenario) and Joseph W. Farnham (titles). Cast: Marion Mack, Florence Lee, Mary Kane, Harry Cornelli, John Geough, Raymond Cannon, Rosemary Cooper, Creighton Hale, Francis McDonald, Henry Burrows, John McDermott, Jack Perrin, and Ray Harford. Celebrity appearances by David Butler, Marjorie Daw, Elliott Dexter, Louise Fazenda, Alec Francis, Wanda Hawley, Rex Ingram, J. Warren Kerrigan, Barbara La Marr, Edward J. Le Saint, Bessie Love, Douglas MacLean, Tom Moore, Carmel Myers, Eva Novak, ZaSu Pitts, Herbert Rawlinson, Anita Stewart, Estelle Taylor, Rosemary Theby, Maurice Tourneur, Richard Travers, Johnnie Walker, and Bryant Washburn. A partial print of this film is filed at the Film and Television Archive, University of California,

Filmography

Los Angeles. It is anticipated that the print will one day be available for onsite viewing.

The Brass Bottle (Maurice Tourneur Productions, 1923). Director: Maurice Tourneur. Writers: F. Anstey (story from his 1900 novel *The Brass Bottle*) and Fred Myton (scenario). Cast: Harry Myers, Ernest Torrence, Tully Marshall, Clarissa Selwyn, Ford Sterling, Aggie Herring, Charlotte Merriam, Edward Jobson, Sam De Grasse, Barbara La Marr, Otis Harlan, Hazel Keener, and Julanne Johnston. No surviving prints of this film are known to exist.

St. Elmo (Fox Film Corporation, 1923). Director: Jerome Storm. Writers: Augusta Jane Evans (story based on her 1866 novel *St. Elmo*) and Jules Furthman (scenario). Cast: John Gilbert, Barbara La Marr, Bessie Love, Warner Baxter, Nigel De Brulier, and Lydia Knott. No surviving prints of this film are known to exist.

Strangers of the Night (Louis B. Mayer Productions, 1923). Produced and directed by Fred Niblo. Writers: Walter Hackett (story based on his 1921 play *Captain Applejack: An Arabian Nights Adventure in Three Acts*), C. Gardner Sullivan (adaptation), Bess Meredyth (scenario), and Renaud (titles). Cast: Matt Moore, Enid Bennett, Barbara La Marr, Robert McKim, Mathilde Brundage, Emily Fitzroy, Otto Hoffman, and Thomas Ricketts. No surviving prints of this film are known to exist.

The Eternal Struggle (Louis B. Mayer Productions, 1923). Director: Reginald Barker. Writers: G. B. Lancaster (a.k.a. Edith Joan Lyttleton) (story based on her 1913 novel *The Law Bringers*), J. G. Hawks (adaptation), and Monte M. Katterjohn (scenario). Cast: Renee Adorée, Earle Williams, Barbara La Marr, Pat O'Malley, Wallace Beery, Josef Swickard, Pat Harmon, Anders Randolf, Edward J. Brady, Robert Anderson, and George Kuwa. Surviving prints of this film are filed at the Library of Congress (Washington, D.C.), the Warner Archive (Burbank, California), and Gosfilmofond (Moscow, Russia). The copy owned by the Library of Congress may be viewed at its Moving Image Research Center by appointment. (Because this print was gifted to the Library of Congress by Russia in 2010, it includes Russian intertitles. The library plans someday to translate them.)

Filmography

The Eternal City (Madison Productions, 1923). Presented by Samuel Goldwyn. Director: George Fitzmaurice. Writers: Hall Caine (story from his 1901 novel *The Eternal City*), Ouida Bergere (scenario), John Emerson (titles), and Anita Loos (titles). Cast: Barbara La Marr, Bert Lytell, Lionel Barrymore, Richard Bennett, and Montagu Love. Special appearances by Benito Mussolini and Victor Emmanuel III, King of Italy. No surviving prints of this film are known to exist. Two of the film's eight reels have been preserved, however, and may be viewed on-site by appointment at the Museum of Modern Art (New York City).

Thy Name Is Woman (Louis B. Mayer Productions, 1924). Director: Fred Niblo. Writers: Karl Schoenherr (story from his 1914 play *Der Weibsteufel* [*The She Devil*]), Benjamin Floyd Glazer (from his 1920 play *Thy Name Is Woman,* a translation of Schoenherr's work), and Bess Meredyth (adaptation and scenario). Cast: Ramon Novarro, Barbara La Marr, William V. Mong, Wallace MacDonald, Robert Edeson, Edith Roberts, and Claire McDowell. Surviving prints of this film are filed at George Eastman House (Rochester, New York) and Warner Archive (Burbank, California).

The Shooting of Dan McGrew (Sawyer-Lubin Productions, 1924). Director: Clarence Badger. Writers: Robert William Service (story from his 1907 book *The Spell of the Yukon and Other Verses*), Winifred Dunn (scenario), and Barbara La Marr (scenario, uncredited). Cast: Barbara La Marr, Lew Cody, Mae Busch, Percy Marmont, Max Ascher, Fred Warren, George Siegmann, Nelson McDowell, Bert Sprotte, Ina Anson, Philippe De Lacy, Harry Lorraine, Eagle Eye, Milla Davenport, and William Eugene. A surviving print of this film is filed at Gosfilmofond (Moscow, Russia).

The White Moth (Maurice Tourneur Productions, 1924). Director: Maurice Tourneur. Writers: Izola Forrester (story based on her work "The White Moth," originally featured in *Ainslee's Magazine*) and Albert Shelby LeVino (adaptation). Cast: Barbara La Marr, Conway Tearle, Charles De Roche, Ben Lyon, Edna Murphy, Josie Sedgwick, Kathleen Kirkham, and William Orlamond. Surviving prints of this film are available for on-site viewing by appointment at the Library of Congress Moving Image Research Center (Washington, D.C.) and the Museum of Modern Art (New York City). A surviving print is also filed at Gosfilmofond (Moscow, Russia).

Filmography

Sandra (Associated Pictures, 1924). Director: Arthur Sawyer. Writer: Pearl Doles Bell (story based on her 1924 novel *Sandra*) and Barbara La Marr (adaptation, uncredited). Cast: Barbara La Marr, Bert Lytell, Leila Hyams, Augustin Sweeney, Maude Hill, Edgar Nelson, Leon Gordon, Leslie Austin, Lillian Ten Eyck, Morgan Wallace, Arthur Edmund Carewe, Helen Gardner, and Alice Weaver. No surviving prints of this film are known to exist.

The Heart of a Siren (Associated Pictures, 1925). Director: Phil Rosen. Writers: William Hurlbut (story based on his 1923 play *Hail and Farewell*), Frederic and Fannie Hatton (scenario), and Arthur Hoerl (continuity). Cast: Barbara La Marr, Conway Tearle, Harry Morey, Paul Doucet, Ben Finney, Florence Auer, Ida Darling, William Ricciardi, Clifton Webb, Florence Billings, Mike Rayle, Katherine Sullivan, Arnold Daly, and Paul Ricciardi. Surviving prints of this film are available for on-site viewing by appointment at the Film and Television Archive, University of California, Los Angeles, and the Art Museum and Pacific Film Archive, University of California, Berkeley. A surviving print is also filed at George Eastman House (Rochester, New York).

The White Monkey (Associated Pictures, 1925). Director: Phil Rosen. Writers: John Galsworthy (story based on his 1924 novel *The White Monkey*), Arthur Hoerl (adaptation), and Louis Sherwin (titles). Cast: Barbara La Marr, Thomas Holding, Henry Victor, George F. Marion, Colin Campbell, Charles Mack, Flora Le Breton, and Tammany Young. Six of the film's seven reels are available for on-site viewing by appointment at the Library of Congress Moving Image Research Center (Washington, D.C.) and Wisconsin Center for Film and Theater Research (Madison).

The Girl from Montmartre (Associated Holding Corporation, 1926). Director: Alfred E. Green. Writers: Anthony Pryde (story based on his 1925 novel *Spanish Sunlight*), June Mathis (editorial director), Eve Unsell (continuity), and George Marion, Jr. (titles). (Although uncredited, Paul Bern was likely responsible for adapting the scenario.) Cast: Barbara La Marr, Lewis Stone, Robert Ellis, William Eugene, E. H. Calvert, Mario Carillo, Mathilde Comont, Edward Piel, Nicholas De Ruiz, Bobby Mack, and Lolita Lee (Barbara's double, uncredited). As of this writing, Warner Bros. has recently restored a surviving print of this film. It will undoubtedly be screened at festivals and archives worldwide. A partial print of this film, featuring a Spanish dance sequence (likely performed by Lolita Lee), is filed at the Film and Television Archive, University of California, Los Angeles. It is anticipated that the print will one day be available for on-site viewing.

Notes

Preface

1. Barbara La Marr, "The True Story of My Life," *Movie Weekly,* January 10, 1925, 15.

Prologue

1. "Beautiful Girl Disappears; 'Kidnapped,' Says Her Father," *Los Angeles Examiner,* January 3, 1913.
2. Adela Rogers St. Johns, "The Girl Who Was Too Beautiful," *Photoplay,* June 1922, 20.
3. "Beauty Too Dangerous, Girl Ordered from City," *Oakland Tribune,* January 25, 1914.
4. Jim Tully, "Jim Tully's Gallery of Women," *New Movie Magazine,* October 1932, 31.
5. Haines quoted in Marquis Busby, "The Wisecracker Reveals," *Photoplay,* October 1929, 128.
6. "Cartoonist to Address C.C. Banquet: Capp Opinionated, Amoozin'," *Abilene Reporter-News,* February 16, 1966.
7. Ed Wheelan, *Minute Movies: A Complete Compilation, 1927–1928* (Westport, CT: Hyperion Press, 1977), viii.
8. Bert Ennis, "Meteor Called La Marr," *Motion Picture,* February 1929, 40.

One

The Part I epigraph is from Barbara La Marr, "The True Story of My Life," *Movie Weekly,* December 13, 1924, 5.

1. Barbara La Marr, "The True Story of My Life," *Movie Weekly,* December 13, 1924, 4.
2. Ibid.
3. Warren H. Orr, "Nine Generations of Orrs in America," 87–88, manuscript given to author by C. B. Watson biographer Darren Borgias.
4. For William Watson's family and childhood, see ibid., 93; Darren Borgias, "The Early Years for Chandler Bruer Watson," Klamath County Museums, Klamath Falls, Oregon; Adela Rogers St. Johns, "The Life Story of Barbara La Marr," *Liberty Magazine,* December 1, 1928, 9. Although St. Johns tended to fictionalize portions of her articles, the probable accuracy of the relatively small amount of

Notes to Pages 8–11

information on the Watsons' history collected from this article (which was obtained by St. Johns after interviewing William and Rose Watson) has been supported via cross-checking.

5. Period journalists often refer to Chandler as "Judge" and "the Honorable"; Darren Borgias, his biographer, cites Chandler's tenure as collector of customs for the Southern District of Oregon as the reason for these honorifics.

6. Fred Lockley, "Impressions and Observations of the Journal Man," *Oregon Journal*, June 29, 1923.

7. W. W. Watson, "W. W. Watson Tells What He Sees after 35 Years' Absence," *Ashland Tidings*, February 15, 1915.

8. For information on Rosa (Rose) Contner's parents, childhood, marriages to Liles and Barber, and children (before her marriage to William Watson), see U.S. Census, 1850, James Contner, Utica, Licking, Ohio, https://familysearch.org/ark:/61903/1:1:MXQK-9YT (accessed November 2012); U.S. Census, 1860, James Contner, Benton, Oregon, https://familysearch.org/ark:/61903/1:1:MDQV-D7H (accessed November 2012); Adela Rogers St. Johns, "The Life Story of Barbara La Marr," *Liberty Magazine*, December 1, 1928, 9–10; Col. John Kelsay and Cornelia Contner wedding certificate, State of Oregon, County of Benton, January 4, 1864; entry for William Liles and Rose Contner in *Clark County, Washington, Marriages*, vol. 1, 23; "Marriages," *The People's Cause*, May 20, 1876, for Rose and Caleb's marriage (because the newspaper issue containing Caleb's obituary is missing from the microfilm reel and death certificates predating 1889 were not retained by the county recorder, Caleb's cause of death could not be determined); Violet June Marr passport application, March 27, 1920, images 673–74, https://familysearch.org/ark:/61903/1:1:QV5B-DV61 (accessed April 2011) (Redding as place of residence); *The People of the State of California vs. Henry Clay Barber*, case no. 671, Superior Court of the State of California, County of Madera, 1928, Madera (transcript cites Redding as place of residence and Henry mentions having two brothers); Certificate of Death, June Marston, date of death, February 1, 1954, State of California, County Clerk of Los Angeles, file 2166, Los Angeles; California Death Index, Henry C. Barber, 1966, https://familysearch.org/ark:/61903/1:1:VPCZ-P2N (accessed March 2013); U.S. Census, 1900, Rose Watson in household of William W. Watson, Multnomah, Oregon, https://familysearch.org/ark:/61903/1:1:MSDK-NXN (accessed January 2013) (number of Rose's children living). Curiously, Violet lists her father as Richard F. Barber on at least two of her marriage certificates; so far as could be deduced, however, Rose was wed to Caleb Barber at the time of Violet's birth.

9. Wm. W. Watson and Rosa M. Barber wedding certificate, State of Oregon, County of Washington, Hillsboro.

10. "W. W. Watson Tells What He Sees after 35 Years' Absence." For information on birth of William Jr., see U.S. Census, 1900, William W. Watson Jr. in household of William W. Watson, Multnomah, Oregon, United States, https://familysearch

.org/ark:/61903/1:1:MSDK-NXJ (accessed January 2012); Billy Wright DeVore, Certificate of Death, County of Los Angeles, April 4, 1952; 1885 U.S. Federal Census, Pierce County, Territory of Washington, http://www.digitalarchives.wa.gov (accessed April 2013); "Personal," *Daily Morning Astorian,* January 5, 1887. William Watson Jr.'s native state and year of birth are further confirmed by other early census records; he would, however, give differing years of birth and his birthplace as Kentucky in later records. The 1885 Pierce County census and the *Daily Morning Astorian* article place the Watsons in Tacoma from at least mid-spring 1885 through January 5, 1887.

11. Untitled article, *Oregonian,* November 19, 1893, 4.

12. "Away Below Zero: That Is Where the Police Dropped the 'Sunday Mercury,'" *Oregonian,* November 19, 1893; untitled article, *Capital Journal,* November 11, 1893, 2.

13. "Some Portland News," *Eugene Capital Journal,* December 8, 1891.

14. "Away Below Zero: That Is Where the Police Dropped the 'Sunday Mercury.'"

15. "Note and Comment," *Yakima Herald,* September 21, 1893.

Two

1. Mark Sullivan, *Our Times: America at the Birth of the Twentieth Century* (New York: Scribner, 1996), 36.

2. Ibid., 114.

3. *New York Herald* quoted in Peter Kobel, *Silent Movies: The Birth of Film and the Triumph of Movie Culture* (New York: Little, Brown and Co., 2007), 11.

4. Ibid.

5. John Higham, *Writing American History: Essays on Modern Scholarship* (Bloomington: Indiana University Press, 1972), 79, 82.

6. Barbara La Marr, "The True Story of My Life," *Movie Weekly,* December 20, 1924, 29.

7. Ibid., December 13, 1924, 5.

8. St. Mary's Academy Student Records for Reatha Watson (1903), St. Mary's Academy, Portland, Oregon; St. Mary's Academy Education Training Development handbook, Holy Names Heritage Center, Lake Oswego, Oregon; author's e-mail correspondence with Sarah Cantor of the Holy Names Heritage Center, February 4, 2011.

9. La Marr, "The True Story of My Life," December 13, 1924, 4; December 20, 1924, 29.

Three

1. Caroline Bell, "The Rebellion of Barbara," *Picture Play,* March 1926, 56.

2. Barbara La Marr, "The True Story of My Life," *Movie Weekly,* December 13, 1924, 4.

3. "Printer and Newsie Are Chief Funsters," *Oakland Tribune*, February 6, 1923.

4. Bell, "The Rebellion of Barbara," 56.

5. Ibid.

6. La Marr, "The True Story of My Life," December 13, 1924, 4.

7. Ibid.

8. Ibid., 5.

9. JoAnn Chartier and Chris Enns, *Gilded Girls: Women Entertainers of the Old West* (Guilford, CT: Globe Pequot, 2003), 31–32, 35–36, 38–40.

10. La Marr, "The True Story of My Life," December 13, 1924, 5.

11. Caroline Bell, "Writing, Dancing, and . . . That Is Just the Beginning of the Accomplishments of Barbara La Marr," *Picture Play*, August 1922, 56.

12. All quotes pertaining to Barbara's *Movie Weekly* article in this section are from La Marr, "The True Story of My Life," December 13, 1924, 5–6.

13. "New Bill at the 'Odeon' Next Week," *Tacoma Daily News*, February 25, 1905.

14. "Nobody's Child" by Phila Henrietta Case, from Flora N. Kightlinger, *The Star Speaker: A Complete and Choice Collection of the Best Productions by the Best Authors, with an Exhaustive Treatise on the Subject of Vocal and Physical Culture and Gesturing* (Jersey City, NJ: Star Publishing Co., 1892), 168–69.

15. William Watson quoted in Charles Carter, "The Death of Barbara La Marr," *Picture Play*, May 1926, 46.

16. La Marr, "The True Story of My Life," December 13, 1924, 6.

17. "Theatrical; 'Two Orphans' at Star," *Tacoma Daily News*, July 11, 1905.

18. "Amusements: 'A Texas Ranger' at the Star," *Tacoma Daily Ledger*, July 19, 1905; "Amusements: 'Camille' at the Star Theater," *Tacoma Daily Ledger*, August 10, 1905.

19. "Theatrical," *Tacoma Daily News*, July 17, 1905.

20. Mrs. Henry Wood, *East Lynne: A Drama, in Four Acts* (London: Richard Bentley, 1862), 12.

21. "Amusements: 'East Lynne' at Star" and "'East Lynne' at the Star," *Tacoma Daily News*, November 23 and 21, 1905.

22. "At the Theaters: Star Theater," *Tacoma Daily News*, July 17, 1906.

23. "Amusements: 'Zora' at the Star," *Tacoma Daily Ledger*, August 28, 1906.

24. La Marr, "The True Story of My Life," December 13, 1924, 6.

25. "Spokane Theaters Big after Turn of Century," *Spokane Daily Chronicle*, October 25, 1967.

26. "Jessie Shirley Called by Death," *Spokane Daily Chronicle*, May 30, 1918.

27. "Idaho, County Marriages, 1864–1950," George W. Ake and Neoma V. Ross (for unknown reasons, Violet used an alias), April 14, 1907, Latah, Idaho, https://familysearch.org (accessed March 2014).

28. Ruthie Primiano, telephone interview with author, June 24, 2014.

29. "'Uncle Tom's Cabin' Again," *Spokesman Review,* February 17, 1907.

30. "At the Auditorium," *Spokane Daily Chronicle,* February 21 and 22, 1907.

31. "Auditorium Glory Days Recalled," *Spokesman-Review* July 28, 1957.

32. "The World's Largest Stage," newspaper clipping, Auditorium Theater File, Spokane Public Library, Spokane, Washington.

33. Bell, "The Rebellion of Barbara," 56.

34. La Marr, "The True Story of My Life," December 13, 1924, 4; December 20, 1924, 15.

35. Ibid., December 13, 1924, 27.

Four

1. Barbara La Marr, "The True Story of My Life," *Movie Weekly,* February 7, 1925, 18.

2. Ibid., January 3, 1925, 11.

3. For St. Augustine's Academy information: Sister Bernice Marie Hollenhorst of the Sisters of the Holy Cross Archives, e-mail correspondence with author, September 23, 2011; *Tidings,* vol. 2, Fresno 1902–1909, 218, clipping contained within the Diocese of Fresno archives, Fresno, California; "St. Joseph's School Students Close Term Work," *Fresno Evening Democrat,* June 6, 1905 (St. Joseph's was renamed St. John's in 1907; it was the primary school companion to St. Augustine's Academy); "higher aims and loftier ideals" quoted in "Sixteen are Graduated," June 5, 1906, clipping from an unidentified Fresno newspaper, Sisters of the Holy Cross Archives, Notre Dame, Indiana. Unfortunately, student records from this period were not retained by the school. St. Augustine's (as well as its neighboring co-ed primary school component, St. John's School) was, however, the only convent school in Fresno during the time the Watsons resided there.

4. "Barbara La Marr and the Pace That Killed," *Oakland Tribune,* April 4, 1926.

5. "What Is Christian Science?" http://christianscience.com (accessed October 2011).

6. La Marr, "The True Story of My Life," December 20, 1924, 29.

7. Ibid., December 13, 1924, 27.

8. Delight Evans, "The True Life Story of Barbara La Marr," *Screenland,* March 1924, 94.

9. "Kidnapers of Pretty Girl Sought by Police," *San Francisco Call,* January 3, 1913.

10. La Marr, "The True Story of My Life," December 20, 1924, 29.

11. Ibid., 15.

12. Peter Kobel, *Silent Movies: The Birth of Film and the Triumph of Movie Culture* (New York: Little, Brown and Co., 2007), 40.

13. Samuel Goldwyn, *Behind the Screen* (Whitefish, MT: Kessinger Publishing, 2003 [first published 1923]), 16.

14. Geoffrey Macnab, "100 Years of Movie Stars," http://www.independent.co.uk./arts-entertainment/films/features/100-years-of-movie-stars-19101929-1876290.html (accessed November 2011).

15. Ibid.

16. Adela Rogers St. Johns, "The Life Story of Barbara La Marr," *Liberty Magazine*, December 1, 1928, 11. (St. Johns wrote the article following an interview with Rose and William Watson.)

17. Ibid.

18. Jimmy Bangley, "The Legendary Barbara La Marr," *Classic Images*, May 1996, 14.

Five

1. "Beautiful Girl Disappears; 'Kidnapped,' Says Her Father," *Los Angeles Examiner*, January 3, 1913.

2. "Kidnapers of Pretty Girl Sought by Police," *San Francisco Call*, January 3, 1913.

3. "Serious Charge against Couple," *Los Angeles Times*, January 5, 1913.

4. "Photos Aid Girl Hunt: Police Searching State," *Los Angeles Evening Herald*, January 3, 1913.

5. "Beautiful Girl Disappears; 'Kidnapped,' Says Her Father."

6. Ibid.

7. "Watson Girl Not Found; Coast Police Continue Hunt for Los Angeles Beauty," *San Francisco Call*, January 4, 1913.

8. "Beautiful Girl Disappears; 'Kidnapped,' Says Her Father."

9. "Efforts to Find Reatha Watson Unavailing," *Los Angeles Examiner*, January 4, 1913.

10. "Kidnapers of Pretty Girl Sought by Police."

11. "Efforts to Find Reatha Watson Unavailing."

12. Ibid.

13. "Star of First Comedies," *Charleston Gazette*, April 12, 1931.

14. "Efforts to Find Reatha Watson Unavailing."

15. "Girl Missing: Warrants Out," *Los Angeles Times*, January 3, 1913.

16. "Photos Aid Girl Hunt: Police Searching State," *Los Angeles Evening Herald*, January 3, 1913.

17. "Beautiful Girl Disappears; 'Kidnapped,' Says Her Father."

18. Ibid.

19. Ibid.

20. "Serious Charge against Couple."

21. "Efforts to Find Reatha Watson Unavailing."

22. "Serious Charge against Couple."

23. "Thrilling Escape Told by Kidnaped Girl," *Los Angeles Evening Herald,* January 4, 1913.

24. "Reatha Watson Is Home; Tells of a Wild Trip," *Los Angeles Examiner,* January 5, 1913.

25. "Thrilling Escape Told by Kidnaped Girl."

26. "Reatha Watson Is Home; Tells of a Wild Trip."

27. "Thrilling Escape Told by Kidnaped Girl."

28. "Reatha Watson Is Home; Tells of a Wild Trip."

29. "Serious Charge against Couple."

30. "Reatha Watson Is Home; Tells of a Wild Trip."

31. "Thrilling Escape Told by Kidnaped Girl."

32. Ibid.

33. "Alleged Child Stealers Surrender Themselves," *Los Angeles Times,* January 7, 1913.

34. All of Violet's quotes in this and the following paragraphs are from "Reatha Begged to Go, Declares Violet Ake," *Los Angeles Evening Herald,* January 8, 1913.

35. "Miss Watson Fights Eye Duel with Mrs. Ake at Arraignment," *Los Angeles Evening Herald,* January 18, 1913.

36. Ibid.

37. For this and all subsequent quotes in the following paragraphs, see "Miss Watson Hailed as California's Venus," *Los Angeles Evening Herald,* January 21, 1913.

38. Ibid.

39. "Watson Girl Tells Her Story in Court," *Los Angeles Examiner,* January 23, 1913.

40. "Complications on the Tapis," *Los Angeles Times,* January 23, 1913.

41. "California's Venus Faints as She Tells [of] Kidnaping," *Los Angeles Evening Herald,* January 29, 1913.

42. Ibid.

43. Ibid.

44. "Watson Girl Falls in a Faint on Stand," *Los Angeles Examiner,* January 30, 1913.

45. Ibid.

46. "'Reatha Watson Kidnapped? No'; Case Is Dismissed by Judge," *Los Angeles Examiner,* February 12, 1913.

47. Ibid.

48. "Watson Girl Father Appeals to Judge," *Los Angeles Evening Herald,* February 28, 1913.

Six

1. Matthew F. Bokovoy, "Inventing Agriculture in Southern California," *Journal of San Diego History* 45, no. 3 (Summer 1999), www.sandiegohistory.org/journal/99spring/agriculture.htm (accessed April 2013).

2. Robert Carville (Robert Dyer Hobday), "Two Lives, Two Loves," unpublished memoir, 1935, 10 and 3. Courtesy of Virginia Jauregui; all quotes from this document used with permission.

3. Barbara La Marr, diary, May 30, 1916 entry, Special Collections, Cleveland Public Library, Cleveland, Ohio. The studio where Reatha worked and met Reid is difficult to pinpoint. Robert Carville dates her fling with Reid after her return to Los Angeles. Since Reatha and Reid were both employed by the Nestor studio at varying times the previous year, it's possible their relationship occurred before Reatha left Los Angeles, although this is doubtful; Reid was noted to have been dating Davenport exclusively during his time at Nestor. Typically for bit players, Reatha does not appear in Paul C. Spehr's extensive directory, *American Film Personnel and Company Credits, 1908–1920* (Jefferson, NC: McFarland & Co., 1996) under any of the aliases she used at this time; nor, evidently, are her names listed in the major trade publications in conjunction with work at a specific studio. Reid worked at three different studios the summer of 1913: Bison, Powers, and Rex.

4. "Stolen Twice, Is Now Widow," *Duluth News-Tribune*, November 17, 1913.

5. See ibid. for this and subsequent quotes regarding Reatha's account of her marriage to Jack Lytelle.

6. Ibid.

7. Carville, "Two Lives, Two Loves," 10.

8. William Inglis, "Is Modern Dancing Indecent?" *Harper's Weekly*, May 17, 1913, 11; "Cabarets," *Variety*, February 13, 1914, 20.

9. Ethel Watts Mumford, "Where Is Your Daughter This Afternoon?" *Harper's Weekly*, January 17, 1914, 28.

10. "Two Pastors Find Text in 'The Sun': 'The Revolt of Decency' Editorial Read from St. Francis Xavier's Pulpit," *New York Sun*, April 7, 1913.

11. Mumford, "Where Is Your Daughter This Afternoon?" 28; and Inglis, "Is Modern Dancing Indecent?" 12.

12. Untitled article in *Variety*, February 20, 1914, 22.

13. "Barbara La Marr and the Pace That Killed," *Oakland Tribune*, April 4, 1926.

14. William Foster Elliot, "Not Like the Fan Stories," *Los Angeles Times*, September 17, 1922.

15. "Swart Wraith Lost to View," *Los Angeles Times*, March 4, 1914.

16. Adela Rogers, "C. V. Riccardi in His Own Story Denies He Is 'Love Pirate,'" *Los Angeles Evening Herald*, August 17, 1914.

17. Mumford, "Where Is Your Daughter This Afternoon?" 28.

18. Lewis A. Erenberg, *Steppin' Out: New York Nightlife and the Transformation of American Culture, 1890–1930* (Chicago: University of Chicago Press, 1981), 130, 132 (*Variety* quoted here).

19. "Mashers Galore: John Danger Becomes an Adept," *Los Angeles Record*, July 11, 1914.

Notes to Pages 61–69

20. "Too Beautiful for City, Girl Sent to Country for Safety," *Los Angeles Evening Herald,* January 22, 1914.

Seven

1. "Snares Beset Beauty's Path; Beware! Warns Reatha Watson," *Los Angeles Examiner,* June 15, 1914; "Bigamy Bride Returns to Parents," *Los Angeles Examiner,* June 6, 1914.
2. "Bigamy Bride Returns to Parents."
3. "Too-Beautiful Girl to Make L.A. Home," *Los Angeles Evening Herald,* March 16, 1914.
4. "'Too Beautiful Girl' Declares Beauty Is Curse of Her Life," *Los Angeles Evening Herald,* March 17, 1914.
5. "Warrant for Converse in Love Theft Manhunt," *Los Angeles Evening Herald,* June 4, 1914.
6. "Snares Beset Beauty's Path; Beware! Warns Reatha Watson."
7. "Bigamy Bride Returns to Parents."
8. Ibid.
9. "Snares Beset Beauty's Path; Beware! Warns Reatha Watson."
10. Max Lawrence and Beth Lytelle marriage license, 1914, California County Marriages, https://familysearch.org (accessed June 2012).
11. "Bigamy Bride Returns to Parents."
12. Ibid.
13. "Wife Charges He's a Bigamist," *Los Angeles Times,* June 4, 1914.
14. "Rope Tied about Neck by Mexicans," *El Paso Herald,* November 2, 1912.
15. For Lawrence's involvement with Mexican rebellion, see ibid.; "Americans Brutally Treated By Mexicans," *Trenton Sunday Times-Advertiser,* April 23, 1911; "Parents See Converse in Prison," *El Paso Herald,* February 27, 1911; "Both Had Arms When Arrested," *El Paso Herald,* February 23, 1911; "Converse Is Dead; Operation Failure; Fracture of Skull," *El Paso Herald,* July 1, 1914; and "Brown Claim Disallowed by U.S.; Gets the Same Consideration as Converse-Blatt Claim for Imprisonment," *El Paso Herald,* January 6, 1913.
16. "Parents See Converse in Prison."
17. Ibid.
18. "Americans Brutally Treated by Mexicans."
19. "Husband of El Paso Girl Faces Bigamy Charge," *El Paso Herald,* June 4, 1914.
20. "Converse in Jail; Baby the Cause," *El Paso Herald,* July 15, 1913.
21. "Converse Is Dead; Operation Failure; Fracture of Skull."
22. "Warrant for Converse in Love Theft Manhunt."
23. Ibid.
24. "'Bigamy Bride' Is in Hiding," *Los Angeles Examiner,* June 5, 1914.

25. *Los Angeles Examiner,* June 4, 1914; *Oakland Tribune,* June 4, 1914.
26. "'Bigamy Bride' Is in Hiding."
27. Ibid.
28. "Reatha Watson Bride Again," *Los Angeles Examiner,* June 4, 1914.
29. "'Bigamy Bride' Is in Hiding."
30. "Warrant for Converse in Love Theft Manhunt."
31. Ibid.
32. "Bigamy Bride Returns to Parents."

Eight

1. "Surplus Bride Returns Home," *Los Angeles Times,* June 6, 1914.
2. "Bigamy Bride Returns to Parents," *Los Angeles Examiner,* June 6, 1914.
3. Ibid.
4. "'Bigamy Bride' Helps Converse," *El Paso Herald,* June 20, 1914.
5. "Bigamy Bride Returns to Parents."
6. "Reatha Watson Did Not Know I Was Married," *Los Angeles Examiner,* June 7, 1914.
7. "Conquests of Heart Breaker Will Be Ended," *El Paso Herald,* June 10, 1914.
8. "Forsakes Gaiety for Simple Life," *Los Angeles Times,* June 7, 1914.
9. All courtroom quotes here and in subsequent paragraphs from "Legal Tangle Delays Trial of Converse; 'Too Beautiful' Girl Has Disappeared," *Los Angeles Examiner,* June 10, 1914.
10. "Snares Beset Beauty's Path; Beware! Warns Reatha Watson," *Los Angeles Examiner,* June 15, 1914.
11. "'Bigamy Bride' Helps Converse."
12. "Girl's Beauty Brings Down Hand of Law upon Man Who Married Her," *The Daily Book,* June 26, 1914, noon edition.
13. For this article and the quotations in the subsequent paragraphs, see "Snares Beset Beauty's Path; Beware! Warns Reatha Watson."
14. "Wife Charges He's a Bigamist," *Los Angeles Times,* June 4, 1914; "'Bigamy Bride' Helps Converse"; "'Matrimonial Aphasia,' Plea of Converse for Bigamy," *Los Angeles Examiner,* June 23, 1914.
15. "Gives Life to Prove Innocence," *Los Angeles Examiner,* June 28, 1914.
16. "'Matrimonial Aphasia,' Plea of Converse for Bigamy."
17. Ibid.
18. "Gives Life to Prove Innocence."
19. "'Matrimonial Aphasia,' Plea of Converse for Bigamy."
20. For this and subsequent quotes relating to Lawrence's surgery, see "Gives Life to Prove Innocence."
21. "Managers Place Ban on Beautiful Actress," *Oakland Tribune,* July 5, 1914.
22. Ibid.

23. "Local and Personal," *Ashland Tidings,* January 25, 1915.

24. "Mary Pickford Actress, Niece of Judge Watson," *Ashland Tidings,* May 18, 1914.

25. "Miss Watson Not Mary Pickford," *Ashland Tidings,* February 1, 1915.

Nine

The Part III epigraph is from Robert Carville (Robert Dyer Hobday), "Two Lives, Two Loves," unpublished memoir, 1935, 10. Courtesy of Virginia Jauregui; quoted with permission.

1. Lewis A. Erenberg, *Steppin' Out: New York Nightlife and the Transformation of American Culture, 1890–1930* (Chicago: University of Chicago Press, 1981), 170.

2. "The Dance Craze—If Dying—Is a Remarkable Invalid," *Vanity Fair,* February 1915, 34; for dancers' salaries, see Julie Malnig, *Dancing Till Dawn: A Century of Exhibition Ballroom Dance* (New York: New York University Press, 1992), 41.

3. Information in this and subsequent paragraphs involving Robert and Reatha in Nat Goodwin's café is from Robert Carville (Robert Dyer Hobday), "Two Lives, Two Loves," unpublished memoir, 1935, 2–3. Courtesy of Virginia Jauregui; quoted with permission.

4. Gale's identity could not be established via period trade publications and other records. During the summer of 1914, director Albert W. Hale—noted in the 1916 *Motion Picture Studio Directory and Trade Annual,* October 21, 1916, 111, as being five feet one-half inches tall and weighing 210 pounds—worked at the Majestic Studio with Wallace Reid before moving to the Kalem Studio in Santa Monica. Moreover, Hale is cited in "Doings at Los Angeles," *Moving Picture World,* November 7, 1914, 774, as being closely connected to Nat Goodwin (Hale lived in Goodwin's beach house while Goodwin was away on show business). Whether "Al" Hale is the overweight "Hal Gale" referenced by Robert is speculation on the author's part.

5. Carville, "Two Lives, Two Loves," 3.

6. Ibid.

7. William Lipsky, *San Francisco's Panama-Pacific International Exposition* (Mount Pleasant, SC: Arcadia Publishing, 2005), 7–8.

8. Regarding Robert's account that he christened Reatha as Barbara La Marr, it should be noted that, according to available sources, Robert's Kentuckian (maternal) grandmother was named Rebecca M. Hobday. (His paternal grandmother was named Eliza Hobday and resided in England.) It's unclear if his maternal grandfather was married more than once, if Robert's great-grandmother was named Barbara, or if Rebecca used the name Barbara as a nickname (other females in the family had adopted nicknames). See U.S. Federal Census, 1880, "Rebecca Hobday in household of Robert D. Hobday, Augusta, Bracken, Kentucky,"

Notes to Pages 89–97

https://familysearch.org/ark:/61903/1:1:MCC3-311 (accessed May 2013); Minnesota State Census, 1895, "Rebecka [sic] M. Hobday in household of William A. Hobday, Duluth City, St. Louis, Minnesota," https://familysearch.org/ark:/61903/1:1:MQDN-667 (accessed May 2013). Additional information was obtained from Virginia Jauregui, Robert's great-granddaughter, electronic message correspondence with author, May 24 and July 12, 2014. To avoid confusion here, it should also be mentioned that Robert's maternal and paternal grandparents indeed shared the surname Hobday, although they bore no blood relation.

9. All quotes involving Barbara and Robert in the Pavo Real café are from Carville, "Two Lives, Two Loves," 5–6.

10. All quotes involving Barbara and Robert in Barbara's apartment are from ibid., 8–11.

11. Ibid., 11.

12. Ibid., 12.

13. "Terpsichore Never Appeared in Stockings! Fair Dancer Prefers to Trip It Barefoot," *San Francisco Examiner*, July 15, 1915.

14. "Fair Dancer Will Appear," *Chicago Examiner*, August 27, 1915.

15. Carville, "Two Lives, Two Loves," 15.

16. Isadora Duncan, *My Life* (New York: Liveright, 1995 [first published 1927]), 60; Susan Cerny, "The Temple of Wings," http://berkeleyheritage.com/berkeley_landmarks/temple_of_wings.html (accessed April 2012).

17. Carville, "Two Lives, Two Loves," 12.

18. Ibid., 13.

19. Ibid., 14.

20. Ibid.

21. Ibid., 15.

22. Ibid.

23. "Miss La Marr Creates Many Dances," *San Francisco Examiner*, July 18, 1915.

24. "Terpsichore Never Appeared in Stockings! Fair Dancer Prefers to Trip It Barefoot."

25. "Barbara La Marr and the Pace That Killed," *Oakland Tribune*, April 11, 1926.

Ten

1. Robert Carville (Robert Dyer Hobday), "Two Lives, Two Loves," unpublished memoir, 1935, 21. Courtesy of Virginia Jauregui; quoted with permission. To protect Barbara from scandal after she became a film star, it was stated (in "The True Story of My Life," *Movie Weekly*, December 20, 1924) that she and Robert were indeed married during the time they performed together and that he was her first husband. Both statements are untrue.

2. "We Have with Us from California," *Chicago Examiner*, August 27, 1915.

3. Carville, "Two Lives, Two Loves," 17.

4. Ibid., 18.

5. Ibid.

6. Ashton Stevens, "Conway and LeMaire Hit; Plot Is Quickly Lost," *Chicago Examiner*, October 11, 1915.

7. "La Salle Show Is Improved," *Chicago Examiner*, October 24, 1915.

8. Carville, "Two Lives, Two Loves," 23.

9. Ibid.

10. Ibid., 24.

11. Ibid., 25.

12. Ibid., 26.

13. Barbara La Marr, diary, January 19, 1916 entry, Special Collections, Cleveland Public Library, Cleveland, Ohio.

14. Carville, "Two Lives, Two Loves," 28.

15. "Barbara La Marr and the Pace That Killed," *Oakland Tribune*, April 11, 1926.

16. Barbara La Marr, "The True Story of My Life," *Movie Weekly*, December 27, 1924, 12.

17. Carville, "Two Lives, Two Loves," 31.

Eleven

1. Fair Oaks Sanitarium brochure, from the J. Bryan Grimes Papers, Collection no. 54, East Carolina Manuscript Collection, J. Y. Joyner Library, East Carolina University, Greenville, North Carolina.

2. Robert Carville (Robert Dyer Hobday), "Two Lives, Two Loves," unpublished memoir, 1935, 31. Courtesy of Virginia Jauregui; quoted with permission.

3. Ibid.

4. Barbara La Marr, "The True Story of My Life," *Movie Weekly*, January 10, 1925, 14.

5. Carville, "Two Lives, Two Loves," 30.

6. Barbara La Marr, diary, June 4, 1916 entry, Special Collections, Cleveland Public Library, Cleveland, Ohio.

7. Carville, "Two Lives, Two Loves," 30.

8. "Blows for Kisses," *Los Angeles Times*, July 21, 1914.

9. Whether or not Barbara's decision to assume the name La Marr was inspired by her sister's surname rather than by Robert is open to conjecture. Although Barbara wouldn't meet Arthur Marr until July 10, 1916 (as recorded in her diary), it's possible June was already married to him when Barbara began using the name a year and a half earlier.

10. Barbara La Marr, diary, September 5, 1916 entry.

Twelve

1. "Her Hubby Back in Prison," *Oakland Tribune,* May 14, 1926.
2. Robert Carville (Robert Dyer Hobday), "Two Lives, Two Loves," unpublished memoir, 1935, 35. Courtesy of Virginia Jauregui; quoted with permission.
3. Phil Ainsworth and Barbara La Marn [sic] Watson, 13 Oct. 1916, Alameda, CA, Indexes to Marriage Licenses and Certificates, ancestry.com (accessed October 22, 2013).
4. Barbara La Marr, diary, October 13, 1916 entry, Special Collections, Cleveland Public Library, Cleveland, Ohio.
5. "Husband Sues for Divorce in Reatha Watson Love Tangle," *Los Angeles Evening Herald,* December 30, 1916.
6. "Dancer, Scantily Clad, Forced to Run for Her Life," *San Francisco Chronicle,* December 8, 1916.
7. "Cabarets," *Variety,* December 22, 1916, 15.
8. Carville, "Two Lives, Two Loves," 35.
9. Ibid.
10. "Threatens to Kill Hubby by Taking Breath from Lips with Her Own, Charge Made," *Evening Tribune,* December 10, 1916; "Husband Sues for Divorce in Reatha Watson Love Tangle."
11. "Husband Sues for Divorce in Reatha Watson Love Tangle."
12. For details of the automobile controversy, see "Auto Sale Involved," *Los Angeles Times,* January 6, 1917; Barbara La Marr, diary, August 8 and 9 and September 5, 1916, entries; "Barbara La Marr and the Pace That Killed," *Oakland Tribune,* April 11, 1916.
13. For Barbara and Robert at the recruiting office (including the quotations), see Carville, "Two Lives, Two Loves," 36–37.
14. "Watson Girl Is Alive," *Oakland Tribune,* June 1, 1917.
15. Ibid.
16. "Too Beautiful Wife Divorced by Ainsworth," *Oakland Tribune,* August 12, 1917.

Thirteen

1. Advertisement, "Jones and Deeley [sic]," *Variety,* May 27, 1911 (on second to last page).
2. "Multnomah Hotel Patrons," *Oregonian,* July 24, 1927; draft registration card for Robert Dyer Hobday, U.S. World War I Draft Registration Cards, 1917–1918, Los Angeles no. 6, California, familysearch.org (accessed December 2014).
3. Barbara La Marr, diary, entry written on pages inscribed September 13, 14, and 15, 1916. (Barbara crossed out the dates printed on each page and wrote by hand "Wed. Aug. 1917.")
4. Advertisement for "The New Bell Boy," *Variety,* December 20, 1912, 105.

5. "Fine Magic Is Seen," *Oregonian,* May 5, 1917; "The Theaters," *Grand Rapids Press,* September 19, 1916.

6. "Tulane Presents 'The Beauty Shop' and Orpheum Has Extra Bill for This Week's Offerings," *Times-Picayune,* November 11, 1917.

7. "Amusements," *Denver Post,* September 19, 1917.

8. "The Day among the Local Theaters," *Times-Picayune,* February 5, 1919.

9. Barbara La Marr, "The True Story of My Life," *Movie Weekly,* January 10, 1925, 29.

10. "Wouldn't Sell Bonds," *Variety,* May 3, 1918, 5.

11. *People vs. Philip Ainsworth,* case no. 18283, Superior Court of the State of California, County of Los Angeles, April 30, 1923, Los Angeles.

12. "Miss La Marr Jails Lawyer," *Los Angeles Times,* November 16, 1923.

13. Draft registration card for Nicholas Bernard Deely, U.S. World War I Draft Registration Cards, 1917–1918, New York City no. 158, New York, New York, familysearch.org (accessed May 2014).

14. Nicholas Bernard Deely and Barbara La Marr Watson wedding certificate, State of New Jersey, Borough of Fort Lee, Fort Lee, given to author by Donald Gallery, from his personal papers.

15. "In and Out," *Variety,* October 4, 1918, 19.

16. La Marr, "The True Story of My Life," January 17, 1925, 11.

17. "Barbara La Marr and the Pace That Killed," *Oakland Tribune,* April 11, 1926.

18. Adela Rogers St. Johns, "The Life Story of Barbara La Marr," *Liberty Magazine,* December 15, 1928, 64.

Fourteen

The Part IV epigraph is from Barbara La Marr, "The True Story of My Life," *Movie Weekly,* January 17, 1925, 12.

1. Quoted in Helen Lee, "The Gift for Glory," *Screenland,* December 1923, 25.

2. Barbara La Marr, "The True Story of My Life," *Movie Weekly,* January 17, 1925, 12.

3. Quoted in Lee, "The Gift for Glory."

4. John Emerson and Anita Loos, "Movies—The Eighth Art," *Vanity Fair,* March 1920, 104.

5. La Marr, "The True Story of My Life," January 17, 1925, 30.

6. Ibid.

7. "Earned Million, Left but $10,000," *Post Standard,* March 21, 1926.

8. "Fox Studio Doings," *Motion Picture News,* January 7, 1920, 889.

9. U.S. Census, 1920, Bernard N. Deely, Los Angeles, California, https://familysearch.org/ark:/61903/1:1:MH79–66Y (accessed December 2015).

10. Jack Jungmeyer, "Daily Movie Service: Barbara a Siren Only for the Movies," *Niagara Falls Gazette,* April 10, 1923.

11. La Marr, "The True Story of My Life," January 17, 1925, 12.
12. "The Mother of His Children," *The Moving Picture World*, April 17, 1920, 458; "Gladys Brockwell Scores New Success," *Charlotte Observer*, May 25, 1920.
13. "The Mother of His Children," *Wid's Daily*, April 11, 1920, 16; "A Tabloid Review," *Photoplay*, June 1920, 97.
14. "Gladys Brockwell in Rose of Nome," *Exhibitors Herald*, September 11, 1920, 88.
15. "Rose of Nome," *Motion Picture News*, August 7, 1920, 1239.
16. "Barbara La Marr and the Pace That Killed," *Oakland Tribune*, April 11, 1926.
17. Ibid.
18. "'Too Beautiful Girl' in Row over Auto," *Los Angeles Evening Herald*, June 7, 1920; "Deely Divorce Suit Is Dropped, Report," *Los Angeles Evening Herald*, January 31, 1921.
19. "Little Gray [sic] Mouse," *Variety*, December 24, 1920, 28.

Fifteen

1. "Do You Want to Break into the Movies?" *Movie Weekly*, March 12, 1921, 17.
2. Ibid.
3. Barbara La Marr, "The True Story of My Life," *Movie Weekly*, January 17, 1925, 30.
4. Ibid., January 24, 1925, 19.
5. "Harriet and the Piper," *Variety*, January 28, 1921, 40.
6. La Marr, "The True Story of My Life," January 24, 1925, 20.
7. "A Happy Picture That Will Please Both Young and Old," *Wid's Daily*, December 12, 1920, 10.
8. Ibid.; "The Flame of Youth," *Motion Picture News*, December 18, 1920, 4681.
9. "Title Promises Something Good but You Don't Get It," *Wid's Daily*, January 16, 1921, 15.
10. "Doug Fairbanks Makes Hit; Also Miss Renstrom," *Charlotte Observer*, November 18, 1922.
11. Donald Gallery's recollections of his conversations with Adela Rogers St. Johns to author via telephone, October 4, 2010.
12. Adela Rogers St. Johns, *Love, Laughter, and Tears* (New York: Doubleday, 1978), 150.
13. "What Makes Them Stars? 'Lure!' Says Fred Niblo," *Photoplay*, November 1923, 116.
14. Ibid.
15. Fairbanks quoted in La Marr, "The True Story of My Life," January 24, 1925, 20.
16. Ibid., 31.

Sixteen

The Part V epigraph is from Richard Griffith, *The Movie Stars* (New York: Doubleday, 1970), 25.

1. "Star Avers Women Prefer Acting for Career," *Oregonian*, July 30, 1922.
2. "Desperate Trails," *Moving Picture World*, July 2, 1921, 115.
3. *New York Tribune* quoted in "'Three Musketeers' Has Greatest Reception Ever Accorded a Film," *Moving Picture World*, September 10, 1921, 190.
4. *Los Angeles Express* quoted in "Praise 'Three Musketeers,'" *Motion Picture News*, September 17, 1921, 1514.
5. "'Three Musketeers' a Great Hit in Frisco," *Motion Picture News*, September 17, 1921, 1486.
6. "In the Words of D'Artagnan—Marvelous!!" *Wid's Daily*, September 4, 1921, 2.
7. "Girl of 'Too Much Beauty' Wins Fame," *Salt Lake Telegram*, October 23, 1921; "The Three Musketeers," *Movie Weekly*, September 24, 1921, 21; "The Celluloid Critic," *Motion Picture Classic*, November 1921, 50; untitled photo caption, *Picture Play*, March 1922, 42.
8. *N. Bernard Deely vs. Barbara Watson Deely*, case no. D-24555, Superior Court of the State of California, County of Los Angeles, 1923, Los Angeles.
9. *Salt Lake Telegram*, October 23, 1921; *Fort Worth Star-Telegram*, October 31, 1921.
10. "Cinderella of the Hills," *Motion Picture News*, November 5, 1921, 2481.
11. Fred Niblo, "What Makes Them Stars? 'Lure!' Says Fred Niblo," *Photoplay*, November 1923, 116.
12. Ouida Bergere, "Why Are We Afraid of Sex?" *Movie Weekly*, September 23, 1922, 10.
13. Ramon Romeo, "New Vamps for Old," *Moving Picture Stories*, June 15, 1926, 14, 15.
14. "Says Eighteen of Twenty 'Clean' Pictures Lost Money," *Variety*, March 11, 1921, 38. (Despite the title, the article reports that, of the twenty pictures, only eighteen had been released and, of those eighteen, sixteen were financial failures.)
15. Quoted in Mark Sullivan, *Our Times: America at the Birth of the Twentieth Century* (New York: Scribner, 1996), 381.
16. Delight Evans, "The True Life Story of Barbara La Marr," *Screenland*, March 1924, 94.
17. Barbara La Marr, "Why I Adopted a Baby," *Photoplay*, May 1923, 31.
18. "Gossip—East and West," *Photoplay*, November 1923, 99.
19. Liam O'Leary, *Rex Ingram: Master of the Silent Cinema* (Dublin: Academy Press, 1980), 42.
20. Whytock quoted in Michael Powell, *A Life in Movies* (London: Heinemann, 1986), 126.

21. Barbara La Marr, "The True Story of My Life," *Movie Weekly*, January 24, 1925, 31.

22. Ibid.

23. Metro Pictures Corporation Weekly Pay Roll July 2, 1921–December 30, 1922, Metro-Goldwyn-Mayer Accounting Department record, Margaret Herrick Library, Academy of Motion Picture Arts and Sciences, Beverly Hills, California.

24. O'Leary, *Rex Ingram*, 141.

25. Novarro quoted in DeWitt Bodeen, "Ramon Novarro," *Films in Review*, November 1967, 538.

26. Adela Rogers St. Johns, "The Life Story of Barbara La Marr," *Liberty Magazine*, December 15, 1926, 66.

27. Ramon Novarro, "Ramon Novarro Tells of His Screen Loves," *Movie Weekly*, April 25, 1925, 5.

28. Terry quoted in Jimmy Bangley, "The Legendary Barbara La Marr," *Classic Images*, May 1996, 17.

29. Goldbeck quoted in St. Johns, "The Life Story of Barbara La Marr," 66–67.

Seventeen

1. Adela Rogers St. Johns, "The Haunted Studio," *Photoplay*, December 1927, 96.

2. William Foster Elliot, "Not Like the Fan Stories," *Los Angeles Times*, September 17, 1922.

3. Barbara La Marr, "Why I Adopted a Baby," *Photoplay*, May 1923, 31.

4. Bob Moak, "The Girl Who Loved Laughter," *Silver Screen*, May 1931, 19; Jimmy Bangley, "The Legendary Barbara La Marr," *Classic Images*, May 1996, 20.

5. Leatrice Gilbert Fountain e-mail correspondence with author, July 24, 2009.

6. Leatrice Gilbert Fountain, *Dark Star* (New York: St. Martin's Press, 1985), 79.

7. Ibid., 80.

8. James A. Daniels, "The Trail of Tragedy That Haunted Paul Bern," *New Movie Magazine*, December 1932, 95.

9. "Samaritan of Hollywood," *Los Angeles Record*, September 6, 1932.

10. "Bern Riddle Increases," *Los Angeles Times*, September 10, 1932.

11. "Jurors Were Told Bern Was Slain," *New York Times*, November 10, 1934.

12. Hendry quoted in Samuel Marx and Joyce Vanderveen, *Deadly Illusions: Jean Harlow and the Murder of Paul Bern* (New York: Dell Publishing, 1990), 298.

13. Faith Service, "The Man Jean Harlow Has Married—Paul Bern," *Motion Picture*, October 1932, 51; Harrison Carroll, "Ex-Follies Beauty Deserts Stardom for Gilbert's Sake," *Los Angeles Evening Herald Express*, September 12, 1932.

14. "Bern's Kin Arrives," *Los Angeles Times*, September 8, 1932.

15. "Mystery Red-Haired Woman in Bern's Past," *Los Angeles Examiner*, September 8, 1932.

16. "Bern Riddle Increases," *Los Angeles Times,* September 10, 1932.

17. Marx and Vanderveen, *Deadly Illusions,* 251.

18. Ibid., 284.

19. "Hollywood's Headline Romances," *Modern Screen,* September 1932, 36.

20. Harrison Carroll, "Film Colony Is Stunned by Suicide," *Los Angeles Evening Herald and Express,* September 6, 1932.

21. Adela Rogers St. Johns, "Jean Harlow Tells the Inside Story," *Liberty Magazine,* November 26, 1932, 9.

22. Charles Higham, *Merchant of Dreams: Louis B. Mayer, M.G.M., and the Secret Hollywood* (New York: Donald I. Fine, 1993), 60–61.

23. Author's e-mail correspondence with Paul H. Bern, Paul Bern's great-nephew, July 7 and 10, 2014. Paul Bern gifted the shaker to his brother Henry Bern in 1930; Henry handed it down to his son, Raymond Bern, in 1954; and Raymond gave it to his son, Paul H. Bern, in 2004. In each instance, the shaker was inscribed with a date and the names of the giver and recipient. Confoundingly, Barbara's inscription is dated 1928, two years after her death. It's possible that her inscription may have been incorrectly backdated by either Paul Bern or Henry Bern when they passed the shaker on, although Paul H. Bern, Raymond Bern, and Laura Riebman, Paul Bern's great-niece, are unable to explain the discrepancy.

24. "Arabian Love," *Variety,* May 19, 1922, 41.

25. "Domestic Relations," *Moving Picture World,* June 17, 1922, 655.

26. Adela Rogers St. Johns, "The Life Story of Barbara La Marr," *Liberty Magazine,* December 15, 1928, 67.

27. "World-Wide Condemnation of Pictures as Aftermath of Arbuckle Affair," *Variety,* September 23, 1921, 46.

28. Murray Schumach, *The Face on the Cutting Room Floor: The Story of Movie and Television Censorship* (New York: William Morrow & Co., 1964), 19.

29. "'Screen Integrity to Be Protected'—Hays," *Variety,* March 3, 1922, 44.

30. "Exhibitors Warn Stars," *Variety,* February 17, 1922, 47.

31. Harry Carr, "The Hollywood Boulevardier Chats," *Motion Picture Classic,* September 1922, 63.

32. Gloria Swanson, *Swanson on Swanson: An Autobiography* (New York: Pocket Books, 1980), 242.

33. Adela Rogers St. Johns, "The Life Story of Barbara La Marr."

34. Adela Rogers St. Johns, "The Girl Who Was Too Beautiful," *Photoplay,* June 1922, 20–21, 106–7.

Eighteen

1. Metro Pictures Corporation Weekly Pay Roll July 2, 1921–December 30, 1922, Metro-Goldwyn-Mayer Accounting Department record, Margaret Herrick Library, Academy of Motion Picture Arts and Sciences, Beverly Hills, California.

2. Jack Jungmeyer, "Daily Movie Service: Barbara a Siren Only for the Movies," *Niagara Falls Gazette,* April 10, 1923.

3. Alma M. Talley, "Rex Ingram's New Find Triumphs in 'Trifling Women,'" *Movie Weekly,* October 28, 1922, 13.

4. James Ursini, "John F. Seitz Interview Transcript," 138; © 1972 American Film Institute, Louis B. Mayer Library, Los Angeles, California; used with permission.

5. Metro Pictures Corporation Weekly Pay Roll July 2, 1921–December 30, 1922.

6. DeWitt Bodeen, "Ramon Novarro," *Films in Review,* November 1967, 536.

7. "The History of Childbirth," excerpted from *The Way of the Peaceful Birther* by Amy Cox Jones (2010), http://www.birthologie.com/pregnancy/the-history-of-childbirth/ (accessed June 2013).

8. Jim Tully, "Funny Face," *New Movie Magazine,* February 1933, 106.

9. Barbara La Marr, "Why I Adopted a Baby," *Photoplay,* May 1923, 112.

10. "Her Real Life Tragedies More Startling than the Parts She Played in the Movies," *American Weekly,* February 7, 1926.

11. Letter from Irene Almond Harris to ZaSu Pitts, dated January 24, 1933 (given to author by Donald Gallery, from his personal papers).

12. "'Prisoner of Zenda' Gets High Praise from Critics," *Moving Picture World,* August 26, 1922, 674.

13. "The Prisoner of Zenda," *Moving Picture World,* May 6, 1922, 87; "A Confidential Guide to Current Releases," *Picture Play,* August 1922, 83.

14. Metro Pictures Corporation Weekly Pay Roll July 2, 1921–December 30, 1922.

15. Joan Drummond, "Beautiful Barbara," *Pictures and the Picturegoer,* April 1924, 44.

16. "A Brunette Vampire Speaks," *Movie Weekly,* August 26, 1922, 22.

17. Adebe Whitely Fletcher, "Across the Silversheet," *Motion Picture,* January 1923, 118.

18. C. S. Sewell, "Trifling Women," *Moving Picture World,* October 14, 1922, 597.

19. "'Trifling Women' Runs Second Week," *Moving Picture World,* April 7, 1923, 671; "Garrick Books 'Trifling Women' Starts Saturday," *Duluth-News Tribune,* December 28, 1922.

20. "Trifling Women," *Philadelphia Inquirer,* December 26, 1922.

21. "Sawyer and Lubin Build First Studio at San Diego," *Exhibitors Herald,* January 6, 1923, 36.

22. "Bert Ennis," *Exhibitors Herald,* March 4, 1922, 44.

Nineteen

1. Helen Klumph, "When Is Barbara Sincere?" *Picture Play,* September 1923, 63.

2. "Cartoonist to Address C.C. Banquet: Capp Opinionated, Amoozin'," *Abilene Reporter-News,* February 16, 1966.

3. Willis Goldbeck, "The Black Orchid," *Motion Picture Magazine,* November 1922, 64.

4. William Foster Elliot, "Not Like the Fan Stories," *Los Angeles Times,* September 17, 1922.

5. Joan Drummond, "Beautiful Barbara," *Pictures and the Picturegoer,* April 1924, 43.

6. Helen Klumph, "Pre-Views and First Impressions," *Picture Play,* March 1923, 18.

7. Malcolm H. Oettinger, "The Studio Lorelei," *Picture Play,* March 1924, 74.

8. "National Guide to Motion Pictures," *Photoplay,* March 1923, 66.

9. Ibid.

10. "Barbara La Marr Charms at Queen," *Dallas Morning News,* February 12, 1923.

11. Irene Kahn Atkins, *David Butler* (Lanham, MD: Scarecrow Press, 1993), 26.

12. "Poor Men's Wives," *Picture Play,* May 1923, 70; Roger Ferri, "Poor Men's Wives," *Moving Picture World,* February 10, 1923, 576; "Barbara La Marr Scores Once More," *Dallas Morning News,* February 19, 1923.

13. Barbara La Marr, "What I Would Do If I Were Poor Man's Wife," *Montgomery Advertiser,* June 24, 1923.

14. Jim Tully, "Funny Face," *New Movie Magazine,* February 1933, 106.

15. "'Souls for Sale' Shows Life behind the Scenes," *Lethbridge Daily Herald,* November 27, 1923.

16. Drummond, "Beautiful Barbara," 44.

17. James O. Kemm, *Rupert Hughes: A Hollywood Legend* (Beverly Hills, CA: Pomegranate Press, 1997), 127.

18. Gayle D. Haffner, *Hands with a Heart: The Personal Biography of Actress ZaSu Pitts* (Denver: Outskirts Press, 2011), 81–83. (Haffner's information was obtained via her interview with Madge Meredith, a close friend of ZaSu Pitts.)

19. Malcolm H. Oettinger, "Homespun," *Picture Play,* January 1924, 33.

20. Haffner, *Hands with a Heart,* 83.

Twenty

1. For information pertaining to Philip Ainsworth's interactions with Constantino Riccardi in this section, see *People vs. Philip Ainsworth,* case no. 18283, Superior Court of the State of California, County of Los Angeles, April 30, 1923, Los Angeles.

2. Ibid.

3. Donald Gallery's recollections of his conversations with Virginia Carville to author via telephone, February 20, 2010; Bert Ennis, "The Truth about Barbara's

Baby," *Pictures,* June 1926, 97; "Barbara La Marr to Be Feature of Automobile Show: Thousands Greet Star on Arrival," *Dallas Morning News,* February 12, 1923.

4. "Barbara La Marr to Be Feature of Automobile Show."

5. Ibid.

6. "Barbara La Marr Invites World to Auto Exposition," *Dallas Morning News,* February 12, 1923. An exhaustive search in hopes of turning up a recording of Barbara's voice has led me to the conclusion that no recordings exist of her WFAA broadcasts. Radio recording was done on a largely experimental basis in 1923; few recordings were made, and hardly any survived.

7. Letter dated January 15, 1926, from Emma Wylie Ballard to Barbara La Marr, Donald Gallery's personal papers shared with author.

8. Letter from Ballard to *Photoplay,* dated July 31, 1928, Donald Gallery's personal papers shared with author.

9. Details pertaining to Barbara's visit to Hope Cottage are from Donald Gallery's recollections of his conversations with Virginia Carville to author via telephone, September 18, 2007, and October 1, 2008; see also Ennis, "The Truth about Barbara's Baby."

10. Peter Kobel, *Silent Movies: The Birth of Film and the Triumph of Movie Culture* (New York: Little, Brown and Co., 2007), 111.

11. William A. Johnston, "Creatures of Celluloid," *Motion Picture News,* September 24, 1921, 1611.

12. Sonny's Hope Cottage file documents referenced here are from Donald Gallery's personal papers shared with author.

13. "Part of Dallas to Be Taken Along by Fair Movie Queen," *Dallas Morning News,* February 17, 1923.

14. "Auto Show Closes Most Successful Season in History," *Dallas Morning News,* February 19, 1923.

Twenty-One

1. Edwin Schallert, "What's This about Beauty?" *Picture Play,* October 1923, 98.

2. "Poor Men's Wives," *Movie Weekly,* March 3, 1923, 15; "Poor Men's Wives," *Photoplay,* April 1923, 72.

3. Letter dated March 14, 1923, from Arthur Sawyer to Louis B. Mayer, from Donald Gallery's scrapbook shared with author.

4. Grace Kingsley, "The Home Life of the Hollywood Screen Stars," *Movie Weekly,* April 5, 1924, 29.

5. "The Eternal Struggle," *Film Daily,* September 16, 1923, 5.

6. "The Eternal Struggle," *Movie Weekly,* November 10, 1923, 30.

7. Kingsley, "The Home Life of the Hollywood Screen Stars," 14.

8. Letter dated January 16, 1933, from Ada Slater (Sonny's nanny) to ZaSu Pitts, Donald Gallery's personal papers shared with author.

Notes to Pages 219–227

9. Grace Kingsley, "World's Wickedest Vamp Adopts a Baby," *Movie Weekly,* April 14, 1923, 11; Grace Kingsley, "Honeymooning in Venice," *Movie Weekly,* November 24, 1923, 10.

10. Kingsley, "The Home Life of the Hollywood Screen Stars," 15.

11. Kingsley, "World's Wickedest Vamp Adopts a Baby."

12. For the quotations here and in the following paragraphs, see Barbara La Marr, "Why I Adopted a Baby," *Photoplay,* May 1923, 31, 112.

13. "Barbara a Mother," *Chicago Herald Examiner,* February 17, 1923; "Hollywood," *Salt Lake Telegram,* September 6, 1925; Norman Zierold, *Sex Goddesses of the Silent Screen* (Chicago: Henry Regnery, 1973), caption on photo between 68 and 69.

14. Malcolm H. Oettinger, "The Studio Lorelei," *Picture Play,* March 1924, 73–74.

15. Helen Klumph, "When Is Barbara Sincere?" *Picture Play,* September 1923, 90.

16. Whitley quoted in Gaelyn Whitley Keith, *The Father of Hollywood* (El Dorado Hills, CA: BookSurge, 2009), 243.

17. Letter dated January 29, 1923, from Louis B. Mayer Studios to Arthur Sawyer, from Donald Gallery's scrapbook shared with author.

18. "Strangers of the Night," *Moving Picture World,* September 15, 1923, 264.

19. "Fantastic Story in 'Brass Bottle,'" *Dallas Morning News,* August 5, 1923.

20. "St. Elmo," *Photoplay,* October 1923, 76.

21. "In Movieland," *Winnipeg Free Press,* July 18, 1928.

22. Helen Ferguson, "Unquenchable Ardor, Pitying, Wise—," *Motion Picture Classic,* May 1924, 35.

Twenty-Two

1. Paul Bern quoted in Samuel Marx, *Mayer and Thalberg: The Make-Believe Saints* (New York: Random House, 1975), 47.

2. "Barbara La Marr to Wed," *Corsicana Daily Sun,* March 5, 1923.

3. Marquis Busby, "The Wisecracker Reveals," *Photoplay,* September 1929, 124; October 1929, 56.

4. Busby, "The Wisecracker Reveals," October 1929, 128.

5. Busby, "The Wisecracker Reveals," September 1929, 123.

6. Graber quoted in William J. Mann, *Wisecracker: The Life and Times of William Haines, Hollywood's First Openly Gay Star* (New York: Penguin Group, 1998), 65, 320.

7. Busby, "The Wisecracker Reveals," October 1929, 128.

8. Barbara La Marr, "The True Story of My Life," *Movie Weekly,* December 20, 1924, 15.

9. Graber quoted in Mann, *Wisecracker,* 65.

10. Busby, "The Wisecracker Reveals," October 1929, 128.
11. "Film Newlyweds Must Be at Studios Today," *Los Angeles Times,* May 7, 1923.
12. "Film Newlyweds Must Be at Studios Today"; Frances Hamilton, "The Dark Side of Fame," *Motion Picture Magazine,* February 1926, 63.
13. Hamilton, "The Dark Side of Fame."
14. Jack Daugherty, "His Greatest Thrill," *Film Daily,* June 3, 1923, 34.
15. "'I'm All Through with Husbands,' Said Barbara La Marr," *Syracuse Herald,* September 16, 1923.
16. "Film Newlyweds Must Be at Studios Today"; Samuel Marx and Joyce Vanderveen, *Deadly Illusions: Jean Harlow and the Murder of Paul Bern* (New York: Dell Publishing, 1990), 45.
17. "Film Newlyweds Must Be at Studios Today."
18. "Barbara La Marr Weds," *Los Angeles Times,* May 6, 1923.
19. "'I'm All Through with Husbands,' Said Barbara La Marr."
20. "Roth Hounded Her, Declares Picture Star," *San Francisco Chronicle,* November 18, 1923.
21. "Her Real Life Tragedies More Startling than the Parts She Played in the Movies," *American Weekly,* February 7, 1926.
22. "Film Beauty Free Again," *Los Angeles Times,* May 1, 1923.
23. Harry Carr, "On the Camera Coast," *Motion Picture Magazine,* October 1925, 61.
24. "Spouse Was Eclipsed by Studio Star," *Los Angeles Times,* September 14, 1923.
25. "Screen Beauty Troubled Again," *Los Angeles Times,* May 9, 1923.

Twenty-Three

1. Joan Drummond, "Beautiful Barbara," *Pictures and the Picturegoer,* April 1924, 42.
2. Alma M. Talley, "'I Never Knew What Love Was Before,' Says Barbara La Marr," *Movie Weekly,* June 23, 1923, 11.
3. Ibid.
4. Jack Dougherty [sic], "Why I Quit Being Mr. Barbara La Marr," *Photoplay,* October 1924, 28–29, 115.
5. "'I Never Knew What Love Was Before,' Says Barbara La Marr."
6. Fred J. Balshofer and Arthur C. Miller, *One Reel a Week* (Berkeley: University of California Press, 1967), 165–66.
7. "Whispers from the Studios," *Movie Weekly,* November 24, 1923, 21.
8. Grace Kingsley, "Honeymooning in Venice With Barbara La Marr," *Movie Weekly,* November 24, 1923, 10, 25.
9. Dougherty, "Why I Quit Being Mr. Barbara La Marr," 29.

10. Balshofer and Miller, *One Reel a Week,* 167.
11. *St. Louis Star* quoted in "The Eternal City," *Film Daily,* January 13, 1924, 10.
12. "She Was a Phantom Delight," *Motion Picture Classic,* March 1924, 42.
13. "The Eternal City," *Variety,* January 24, 1924, 26–27.
14. County of Los Angeles, California, probate case files, estate no. 79638, Barbara La Marr (1926), Schedule B, "Barbara La Marr Account," Los Angeles Superior Court, Los Angeles. See also "La Marr's Manager on Stand in Trial," *Los Angeles Evening Herald,* February 14, 1924; "Confirms Signing of La Marr as First National Star," *Exhibitors Herald,* December 1, 1923.

Twenty-Four

1. Gladys M. Connaughton, "How Many Kinds of Screen Personalities Are There?" *Movie Weekly,* December 22, 1923, 30.
2. Adela Rogers St. Johns, "The Hollywood Story," *Los Angeles Examiner,* September 2, 1951; Robert Carville (Robert Dyer Hobday), "Two Lives, Two Loves," unpublished memoir, 1935, 31 (courtesy of Virginia Jauregui; used with permission); Aline Mosby, "Buster Keaton Sneers at Today's Big Bosoms," *El Paso Herald-Post,* June 23, 1956.
3. Eleanore Griffin, "Hollywood's Haunted Hill," *The New Movie Magazine,* January 1934, 53.
4. Fred Niblo, "What Makes Them Stars? 'Lure!' Says Fred Niblo," *Photoplay,* November 1923, 116.
5. Helen Ferguson, "Unquenchable Ardor, Pitying, Wise—," *Motion Picture Classic,* May 1924, 76.
6. R.C., "Turning on the Tears," *Pictures and the Picturegoer,* October 1925, 11.
7. Willis Goldbeck, "The Black Orchid," *Motion Picture,* November 1922, 93.
8. Ferguson, "Unquenchable Ardor, Pitying, Wise—," 35.
9. Ibid., 73.
10. Malcolm H. Oettinger, "The Studio Lorelei," *Picture Play,* March 1924, 74.
11. Frances Hamilton, "The Dark Side of Fame," *Motion Picture Magazine,* February 1926, 108.
12. Regina Cannon, "'My Private Life's My Own Affair,' Declares Barbara La Marr," *Movie Weekly,* May 31, 1924, 3.
13. Oettinger, "The Studio Lorelei," 106.
14. "Barbara Says Temperament Is All Bunk," *Los Angeles Times,* September 22, 1923.
15. "'I'm All Through with Husbands,' Said Barbara La Marr," *Syracuse Herald,* September 16, 1923.
16. Oettinger, "The Studio Lorelei," 106.
17. Grace Kingsley, "The Home Life of the Hollywood Screen Stars," *Movie Weekly,* April 5, 1924, 15.

18. Barbara La Marr, "The True Story of My Life," *Movie Weekly*, January 3, 1925, 12; January 10, 1925, 14.

19. "Barbara La Marr Gave Lavishly to Charity, Father Reveals," *Post Standard*, March 21, 1926.

20. Grace Kingsley, "'Vamp' Plays with Kiddies," *Los Angeles Times*, March 31, 1923.

21. *The People of the State of California vs. R. D. Hobday*, case no. 21602, Superior Court of the State of California, County of Los Angeles, 1924, Los Angeles; *The People of the State of California vs. R. D. Hobday*, Lloyd R. Pugh Affidavit in Support of a Motion for New Trial, Superior Court of the State of California, County of Los Angeles, March 24, 1924, Los Angeles.

22. Virginia Dodd telephone interview with author, October 24, 2010.

23. Barbara La Marr, 1916 diary, June 26, 1916 entry, Special Collections, Cleveland Public Library, Cleveland, Ohio.

24. Hamilton, "The Dark Side of Fame."

25. Cannon, "'My Private Life's My Own Affair,' Declares Barbara La Marr," 29.

26. Helen Klumph, "When Is Barbara Sincere?" *Picture Play*, September 1923, 62.

27. La Marr, "The True Story of My Life," January 31, 1925, 18.

28. Joan Drummond, "Beautiful Barbara," *Pictures and the Picturegoer*, April 1924, 42.

29. Elaine St. Johns quoted in Jimmy Bangley, "Barbara La Marr: A Memorial Tribute," *Classic Images*, February 1999, 29.

30. Klumph, "When Is Barbara Sincere?"

31. Helen Lee, "The Gift for Glory," *Screenland*, December 1923, 104.

32. Harry Reichenbach, *Phantom Fame* (New York: Simon and Schuster, 1931), 226.

33. Drummond, "Beautiful Barbara," 43.

34. La Marr, "The True Story of My Life," January 31, 1925, 18.

35. Cannon, "'My Private Life's My Own Affair,' Declares Barbara La Marr," 29.

36. Ferguson, "Unquenchable Ardor, Pitying, Wise—," 76.

37. La Marr, "The True Story of My Life," February 7, 1925, 17–18.

Twenty-Five

1. "Trial of Roth Is Begun," *Los Angeles Times*, February 8, 1924.

2. "Movie Vampire's Tears Halt Trial of Lawyer Accused as Blackmailer," *Syracuse Herald*, February 14, 1924.

3. "Her Real Life Tragedies More Startling than the Parts She Played in the Movies," *American Weekly*, February 7, 1926.

4. "Miss La Marr Halts Trial," *Los Angeles Times*, February 14, 1924.

5. "Tells of Bills Taken off Roth," *Los Angeles Times*, February 9, 1924.

6. Helen Ferguson, "Unquenchable Ardor, Pitying, Wise—," *Motion Picture Classic,* May 1924, 35.

7. Kevin Thomas, "'New Chinese Cinema' Focuses on Revolution," *Los Angeles Times,* February 14, 1994.

8. Harry Reichenbach, *Phantom Fame* (New York: Simon and Schuster, 1931), 225–26.

9. "Thy Name Is Woman," *Motion Picture Magazine,* June 1924, 55.

10. *San Francisco Chronicle* quoted in "Thy Name Is Woman," *Film Daily,* March 9, 1924, 16; Tamar Lane, "That's Out; Is Barbara La Marr Another Clothes Rack?" *Motion Picture Magazine,* November 1924, 113.

11. "Ramon Will Try Talkies," *Los Angeles Times,* August 5, 1928.

12. Novarro quoted in Adela Rogers St. Johns, "The Life Story of Barbara La Marr," *Liberty Magazine,* December 15, 1928, 66.

13. Ramon Novarro, "Ramon Novarro Tells of His Screen Loves," *Movie Weekly,* April 25, 1925, 32.

14. Perc Westmore, "Secrets of the Makeup Room," *Modern Screen,* May 1934, 118.

15. Barbara La Marr, "The True Story of My Life," *Movie Weekly,* January 3, 1925, 11.

16. Ferguson, "Unquenchable Ardor, Pitying, Wise—."

17. Joan Drummond, "Beautiful Barbara," *Pictures and the Picturegoer,* April 1924, 42. (Although the interview ran in 1924, it was conducted in the spring of 1923.)

18. Westmore, "Secrets of the Makeup Room."

Twenty-Six

1. "Gossip—East and West," *Photoplay,* April 1924, 94.

2. "Plays and Players," *San Antonio Express,* July 6, 1924.

3. Myrtle Gebhart, "Film Is Frank Appeal to Eye," *Los Angeles Times,* February 10, 1924.

4. "Whispers of the Film Flapper," *Movie Weekly,* February 23, 1924, 33.

5. *New York World* and *New York Post* quoted in "Newspaper Opinions," *Film Daily,* June 12, 1924, 5; "Shooting of Dan McGrew," *Variety,* June 11, 1924, 28; "The Shooting of Dan McGrew," *Film Daily,* March 30, 1924, 9.

6. Barbara La Marr, "The True Story of My Life," *Movie Weekly,* January 31, 1925, 19.

7. *The People of the State of California vs. Herman L. Roth,* case no. 21253, Superior Court of the State of California, County of Los Angeles, February 25 and 29, 1924, Los Angeles.

8. "Miss La Marr Halts Trial," *Los Angeles Times,* February 14, 1924.

9. Ibid.

10. "Roth Trial to Be Given to Jury," *Los Angeles Evening Herald*, February 20, 1924.

11. "Will Beg for Clemency for Her Persecutor," *Gettysburg Times*, February 25, 1924.

12. *The People of the State of California vs. Herman L. Roth*, case no. 21253, February 29, 1924.

13. "News From the Dailies: Pacific Coast," *Variety*, September 2, 1925, 10; "'Round the Square," *Variety*, August 19, 1925, 12.

14. *N. Bernard Deely vs. Barbara Watson Deely and Jack Dougherty* [sic], case no. D-24555, Superior Court of the State of California, County of Los Angeles, November 26, 1923, and March 21, 1924, Los Angeles.

15. "Miss La Marr to Testify in Roth Case," *Los Angeles Evening Herald*, February 9, 1924.

16. "The Husbands of Barbara," *Moving Picture Stories*, August 19, 1924, 2.

17. Bert Ennis, "Meteor Called La Marr," *Motion Picture*, February 1929, 94.

18. County of Los Angeles, California, probate case files, estate no. 79638, Barbara La Marr (1926), Schedule A, "Amount Due Associated Pictures Corporation: March 22, 1924," and Schedule 3, "Paid for A/C Barbara La Marr," Los Angeles Superior Court, Los Angeles.

19. "Barbara La Marr Escapes Arrest as Court Gets Facts," *Los Angeles Evening Herald*, February 19, 1924 (the article incorrectly lists Barbara as a witness in a suit involving her husband, Jack); "Barbara La Marr Sued on Jewelry," *Los Angeles Times*, February 21, 1924; Dorothy Donnell, "From Hollywood to You," *Moving Picture Stories*, April 1, 1924, 13; County of Los Angeles, California, probate case files, estate no. 79638, Barbara La Marr (1926), "Installment Note to William Koeberle."

20. *E. Burton vs. Barbara La Marr*, case no. 150556, Superior Court of the State of California, County of Los Angeles, January 8, 1925, Los Angeles; "News From the Dailies: Los Angeles," *Variety*, January 27, 1926, 12.

21. Letter from Arthur H. Sawyer to Mr. R. A. Rowland, Associated First National, Inc., January 25, 1924, "Barbara La Marr Correspondence," Folder no. 16079A, Box no. WB1, Warner Bros. Archives, School of Cinematic Arts, University of Southern California, Los Angeles.

22. "The White Moth," *Variety*, June 18, 1924, 23.

23. Bebe Daniels and Ben Lyon, *Life with the Lyons: The Autobiography of Bebe Daniels and Ben Lyon* (London: Odhams Press, 1953), 130.

24. Ibid.

25. Ben Lyon, "Vampires I Have Known," *Photoplay*, February 1925, 28, 113.

26. "La Marr Idol of Film Colony," *Davenport Democrat and Leader*, March 30, 1924; "Studio News and Gossip: East and West," *Photoplay*, June 1924, 50; untitled, undated International Newsreel caption, from Donald Gallery scrapbook shared

with author; "Jinx Finds Home on Tourneur Lot," *Los Angeles Times,* March 16, 1924.

27. Perc Westmore, "Secrets of the Makeup Room," *Modern Screen,* May 1934, 118.

28. "The White Moth," *Photoplay,* August 1924, 50; "The Screen in Review," *Picture Play,* September 1924, 57; Oliver Owl, "Sexy Stuff Ruins Grosses," *Variety,* October 22, 1924, 19; *San Francisco Examiner* quoted in "'The White Moth'—1st Nat'l," *Film Daily,* June 10, 1924, 5.

29. Alma Whitaker, "Commerce and the Angels," *Los Angeles Times,* April 10, 1924.

Twenty-Seven

The Part VI epigraph is from Barbara La Marr, "The True Story of My Life," *Movie Weekly,* February 7, 1925.

1. Bert Ennis, "Meteor Called La Marr," *Motion Picture,* February 1929, 94. Ennis recalled the incident as occurring in St. Charles, Louisiana; the *New Orleans States* reported it as happening in Lafayette.

2. Meigs O. Frost, "Must Be in Love to Act, Says Star," *New Orleans States,* April 9, 1924.

3. "Only Moral Vamps Get By," *New York Evening Post,* May 23, 1924; "Henle's Column," *Herald-Star,* April 18, 1924; "Barbara La Marr's 'Immorality' Story," *Variety,* April 16, 1924, 20.

4. "Barbara La Marr's 'Immorality' Story," 45.

5. "Barbara La Marr Is Put under Ban," *Oakland Tribune,* April 17, 1924.

6. Regina Cannon, "'My Private Life's My Own Affair,' Declares Barbara La Marr," *Movie Weekly,* May 31, 1924, 29.

7. March 4, 1924, letter to Mr. Wm. Darby from Ed Fletcher, Box 9, Folder 22; May 7, 1924, letter to Mr. C. C. Kompley, District Attorney, from Ed Fletcher, Box 64, Folder 14; May 9, 1924, letter to The Shareholders of S-L Studios from "the committee appointed to examine the books and business of the S-L Studios," Box 64, Folder 15; September 23, 1924, letter to Mr. Claude L. Chambers from Ed Fletcher, Box 4, Folder 30; December 23, 1924, letter to The Shareholders of S-L Studios from the Trustees of S-L Studios, Box 64, Folder 15. These documents, and all details in this section pertaining to S-L Studios, are from Ed Fletcher Papers, MSS81, Mandeville Special Collections Library, University of California, San Diego.

8. "Over the Teacups," *Picture Play,* November 1924, 27.

9. Ibid., October 1924, 31.

10. "Hollywood's Very Friendly Ex-Wives and Husbands," *Syracuse Herald,* June 28, 1925.

11. Barbara La Marr, "The True Story of My Life," *Movie Weekly,* January 31, 1925, 19.

12. Jack Dougherty [sic], "Why I Quit Being Mr. Barbara La Marr," *Photoplay,* October, 1924, 28.
13. Ibid., 29, 115.
14. Ibid., 115.
15. Ibid., 28.
16. Ibid., 29, 116.
17. Bebe Daniels and Ben Lyon, *Life with the Lyons: The Autobiography of Bebe Daniels and Ben Lyon* (London: Odhams, 1953), 130.
18. Ben Lyon, "Vampires I Have Known," *Photoplay,* February 1925, 113.
19. "New York paper" quoted in "Barbara La Marr's Last Fight for Life Revealed," *Los Angeles Record,* February 1, 1926.
20. La Marr, "The True Story of My Life," January 10, 1925, 15.
21. Cannon, "'My Private Life's My Own Affair,' Declares Barbara La Marr."
22. Frances Hamilton, "The Dark Side of Fame," *Motion Picture Magazine,* February 1926, 108.

Twenty-Eight

1. "Four 1st Nat'l Stars," *Film Daily,* January 10, 1924, 6.
2. "Over the Teacups," *Picture Play,* October 1924, 31; Donald Gallery telephone interview with author, September 18, 2007.
3. Michael G. Ankerich, *Broken Silence: Conversations with 23 Silent Film Stars* (Jefferson, NC: McFarland, 1993), 76.
4. Perc Westmore, "Secrets of the Makeup Room," *Modern Screen,* May 1934, 118.
5. "Barbara La Marr and the Pace That Killed," *Oakland Tribune,* April 4, 1926.
6. "And Romance, Too!" *Sandusky Register,* September 10, 1931.
7. Bert Ennis, "Meteor Called La Marr," *Motion Picture,* February 1929, 95.
8. Caroline S. Hoyt, "Let's Paint Hollywood Red," *Modern Screen,* July 1934, 83.
9. Norman Zierold, *Sex Goddesses of the Silent Screen* (Chicago: Henry Regnery, 1973), 69.
10. Ben Finney, *Feet First* (New York: Crown Publishers, 1971), 43, 53.
11. Ibid., 71.
12. Ibid., 72, 74.
13. Ibid., 53.
14. Ibid., 74, 76.
15. "Broadway Hears Finney to Wed Marilyn Miller," *Syracuse Journal,* January 6, 1926.
16. "Barbara Denies Suicide Story," *Syracuse Journal,* November 8, 1924.
17. "Poisoned?" *Syracuse Herald,* November 9, 1924; Edward J. Doherty, "Actress Gives Hubby Freedom; To Wed Again," *Danville Bee,* November 11, 1924.
18. "Barbara Denies Suicide Story."

Notes to Pages 294–302

19. "'Three Close Friends,' Says La Marr's Husband of Triangle," *Oakland Tribune,* November 16, 1924.

20. "Presenting the New Mr. La Marr," *Los Angeles Times,* November 14, 1924; "Barbara La Marr Reported Engaged to B. F. Finney, Jr.," *Richmond Times-Dispatch,* November 27, 1924.

21. "Sandra," *Film Daily,* January 4, 1925, 6.

22. Helen Ferguson, "Unquenchable Ardor, Pitying, Wise—," *Motion Picture Classic,* May 1924, 35.

23. *Boston Traveler* quoted in "'Sandra—1st Nat'l; Olympia, Boston," *Film Daily,* December 22, 1924, 4.

24. *St. Louis Globe-Democrat* quoted in "'Sandra—1st Nat'l; Grand Central, St. Louis," *Film Daily,* November 23, 1924, 16.

25. "Sandra," *Photoplay,* January 1925, 62.

26. Barbara La Marr, "The True Story of My Life," *Movie Weekly,* February 7, 1925, 27.

27. Martin B. Dickstein, "The Cinema Circuit: 'Heart Trouble,'" *Brooklyn Daily Eagle,* April 8, 1925.

28. "Film Reviews: My Husband's Wives," *Variety,* December 31, 1924, 26A.

29. "Amusements: Endicott Strand," *Binghamton Press,* January 28, 1925; "Amusements: Temple Theater," *Cortland Standard,* December 16, 1924; "My Husband's Wives," *Moving Picture World,* November 22, 1924, 359.

Twenty-Nine

1. Catherine Brody, "Wholesale Murder and Suicide," *Photoplay,* August 1926, 124; Katherine Albert, "Diet—The Menace of Hollywood," *Photoplay,* January 1929, 33.

2. Bert Ennis, "Meteor Called La Marr," *Motion Picture,* February 1929, 95.

3. "Studio News & Gossip: East and West," Photoplay, April 1925, 88.

4. "How the Movie Queens Keep Thin," *San Antonio Light,* November 29, 1925.

5. Ennis, "Meteor Called La Marr"; Dorothy Manners, "The Flesh and Blood Racket," *Motion Picture Magazine,* April 1929, 118.

6. Brody, "Wholesale Murder and Suicide," 30.

7. Myrtle West, "The Price They Paid for Stardom," *Photoplay,* November 1926, 29.

8. Jimmy Bangley, "The Legendary Barbara La Marr," *Classic Images,* May 1996, 20.

9. "Heart of a Siren," *Film Daily,* March 15, 1925, 12; "Heart of a Siren," *Moving Picture World,* March 21, 1925, 271; "Heart of a Siren," *Variety,* April 8, 1925, 38.

10. Letter from Ada Slater to ZaSu Pitts, January 16, 1933, Donald Gallery's personal papers shared with author.

11. "White Monkey Youth Symbol in New Picture," *Los Angeles Times*, July 19, 1925.

12. Caroline Bell, "The Rebellion of Barbara," *Picture Play*, March 1926, 56.

13. Ibid.

14. "White Monkey," *Moving Picture World*, September 12, 1925, 151.

15. "'White Monkey' Unimposing," *Los Angeles Times*, July 20, 1925; *New York Sun* quoted in "The White Monkey—First Nat'l," *Film Daily*, June 14, 1925, 11.

16. *New York Telegram* quoted in "The White Monkey—First Nat'l"; "The Screen in Review: Bad Pictures from Good Books," *Picture Play*, September 1925, 58; "The White Monkey—First National," *Photoplay*, August 1925, 103.

17. Ben Finney, *Feet First* (New York: Crown Publishers, 1971), 80.

18. Ibid., 80, 85.

19. Ibid., 85.

20. Ennis, "Meteor Called La Marr," 94–95.

21. Barbara La Marr, "The True Story of My Life," *Movie Weekly*, January 10, 1925, 14–15.

22. Helen Ferguson, "Unquenchable Ardor, Pitying, Wise—," *Motion Picture Classic*, May 1924, 76.

23. Barbara La Marr, "My Screen Lovers," *Photoplay*, November 1923, 63.

24. Ferguson, "Unquenchable Ardor, Pitying, Wise—."

25. Barbara La Marr, "Why I Adopted a Baby," *Photoplay*, May 1923, 31.

26. Poetry quoted with permission of Donald Gallery.

27. Barbara Miller, "La Marr Faces 'Last Chance,'" *Los Angeles Times*, September 13, 1925.

28. Letters from Ada Slater to ZaSu Pitts, January 16, 1933, and January 30, 1940, Donald Gallery's personal papers shared with author.

29. "Enjoyable Parties," *Troy Times*, August 1, 1925.

30. Caroline Bell, "The Rebellion of Barbara," *Picture Play*, March 1926, 98.

Thirty

The Part VII epigraph is from John Montgomery, "Too Beautiful Again Spells T-r-o-u-b-l-e," *Los Angeles Herald Examiner*, January 14, 1962.

1. "Obituary: Barbara La Marr," *Variety*, February 3, 1926, 49.

2. "Six Theatres Now Planned by Roxy, Sawyer, and Lubin," *Exhibitors Trade Review*, August 1, 1925, 13. The Roxy chain subsequently envisioned by Sawyer and Lubin never materialized; the project rendered them insolvent. The Roxy Theatre was eventually purchased by Warner Theatres.

3. Certificate of death: Barbara La Marr (Reatha Dale Watson), date of death January 30, 1926, State of California, County of Los Angeles, file no. 253, Los Angeles; "Barbara La Marr and the Pace That Killed," *Oakland Tribune*, April 11, 1926.

4. "On the Set and Off," *Movie Weekly*, September 19, 1925, 29.

5. Perc Westmore, "Secrets of the Makeup Room," *Modern Screen,* May 1934, 118.

6. Russell J. Birdwell, "Hollywood!" *Ogden Standard-Examiner,* November 1, 1925.

7. "Studio News and Gossip: East and West," *Photoplay,* October 1925, 42.

8. For Barbara's allegations against Sawyer and Lubin, see letter from Milton Cohen to Fred Spring, First National Pictures, August 21, 1925, and letter from Milton Cohen to Associated Pictures Corporation, November 5, 1925, "Barbara La Marr Correspondence," Folder no. 16079A, Box WB1, Warner Bros. Archives, School of Cinematic Arts, University of Southern California, Los Angeles.

9. Caroline Bell, "The Rebellion of Barbara," *Picture Play,* March 1926, 56, 98.

10. Ibid., 98.

11. Samuel Marx, *Mayer and Thalberg: The Make-Believe Saints* (New York: Random House, 1975), 80.

12. Bell, "The Rebellion of Barbara," 98.

13. "Miss La Marr Resumes Work in Film Studio," *Oakland Tribune,* October 18, 1925.

14. Barbara La Marr, "The True Story of My Life," *Movie Weekly,* February 7, 1925, 27.

15. Westmore, "Secrets of the Makeup Room," *Modern Screen,* 119.

16. Margaret Reid, "Looking On with an Extra Girl," *Picture Play,* January 1926, 54.

17. "Liberty: 'The Girl from Montmartre,'" *Terra Haute Sunday Spectator,* February 6, 1926.

18. Ibid.

19. Bell, "The Rebellion of Barbara," 98.

20. Westmore, "Secrets of the Makeup Room," 119.

21. Ibid.

22. Ibid.

23. Ibid.

24. Ibid.

Thirty-One

1. Alma Whitaker, "Lolita Would Rather Act Than Eat—and She Has," *Los Angeles Times,* December 4, 1927; "Miss La Marr's Film to Be Shown; $25 If You Can Find Double in Picture," *Plain-Dealer,* March 7, 1926.

2. Letter from Milton Cohen to Associated Pictures Corporation, November 5, 1925, "Barbara La Marr Correspondence," Folder no. 16079A, Box no. WB1, Warner Bros. Archives, School of Cinematic Arts, University of Southern California, Los Angeles.

3. Letters from Milton Cohen to Fred Spring and from S. Spring to Milton Cohen, August 21, 1925 and September 15, 1925, respectively, ibid.

4. Virginia Dodd telephone interview with author, October 24, 2010.

5. Caroline Bell, "The Rebellion of Barbara," *Picture Play,* March 1926, 98.

6. Barbara La Marr, "The True Story of My Life," *Movie Weekly,* December 27, 1924, 29.

7. Ibid., November 29, 1924, 7.

8. "Siren Wooing Back Old Charm: Star Battles for Health," *Los Angeles Times,* November 10, 1925.

9. Joan Barry Liebmann, Viola's daughter, in-person interview with author, June 2, 2012.

10. "Hollywood's Headline Romances," *Modern Screen,* September 1932, 36.

11. "Barbara La Marr and the Pace That Killed," *Oakland Tribune,* April 11, 1926.

12. Ibid.

13. Russell J. Birdwell, "Hollywood!" *Salt Lake Telegram,* January 10, 1926.

14. "Barbara La Marr and the Pace That Killed."

15. Jack Carberry, "Barbara La Marr's Last Fight for Life Revealed," *Los Angeles Record,* February 1, 1926.

16. For information on Christian Science, see Deborah Abbott and Stephen Gottschalk (eds.), *The Christian Science Tradition: Religious Beliefs and Healthcare Decisions,* 10, www.che.org/members/ethics/docs/1276/Christian%20Science.pdf (accessed May 2015); "First Church of Christ Scientist: Questions and Answers," http://www.christianscienceinriverside.org/Questions.php (accessed May 2015).

17. Charles Carter, "The Death of Barbara La Marr," *Picture Play,* May 1926, 46.

18. Ibid.

19. Marjorie Driscoll, "Barbara La Marr Dies in Altadena: End Comes after Long Health Fight," *Los Angeles Examiner,* January 31, 1926, 3.

Thirty-Two

1. Certificate of death, Barbara La Marr (Reatha Dale Watson), date of death, January 30, 1926, State of California, County of Los Angeles, file no. 253, Los Angeles.

2. "Barbara La Marr's Last Fight for Life Revealed," *Los Angeles Record,* February 1, 1926.

3. Perc Westmore, "Secrets of the Makeup Room," *Modern Screen,* May 1934, 119.

4. "Milestones," *Time,* February 15, 1926, 36.

5. "Baby Rose Dwarfs Floral Bier," *Los Angeles Times,* February 3, 1926.

6. "Women Riot at Star's Funeral," *Los Angeles Times,* February 6, 1926; undated, untitled news clipping from unknown source, from Donald Gallery's scrapbook shared with author; Donald Gallery telephone interview with author, September 18, 2007.

7. "Women Riot at Star's Funeral"; news clipping from Donald Gallery's scrapbook.

8. "5,000 Defy Police and Mob La Marr Funeral Chapel," *Los Angeles Examiner,* February 6, 1926; "Barbara La Marr Is Laid to Rest," *Moving Picture World,* February 20, 1926, 3; "Police Guard La Marr Hearse as 5,000 Storm Funeral Party," *Los Angeles Evening Express,* February 5, 1926.

9. "5,000 Defy Police and Mob La Marr Funeral Chapel."

10. "Milestones"; "Final Rites for Barbara La Marr," *Hollywood Daily Citizen,* February 5, 1926; "Barbara La Marr Is Laid to Rest."

11. "Police Guard La Marr Hearse as 5,000 Storm Funeral Party."

12. "Milestones"; "5,000 Defy Police and Mob La Marr Funeral Chapel"; "Throng at La Marr Funeral Near Riot; Five Women Faint," *Los Angeles Evening Express,* February 6, 1926.

13. "Women Riot at Star's Funeral"; Theodore Hovey (Hollywood Forever), e-mail correspondence with author, October 8, 2013.

14. Donald Gallery telephone interview with author, September 18, 2007.

15. Cost of Barbara's crypt obtained from Theodore Hovey (Hollywood Forever), e-mail correspondence with author, October 8, 2013. For information on Paul Bern paying for Barbara's funeral and crypt, see Faith Service, "The Man Jean Harlow Has Married—Paul Bern," *Motion Picture,* October 1932, 76; Robert Carville (Robert Dyer Hobday), "Two Lives, Two Loves," unpublished memoir, 1935, 1 (courtesy of Virginia Jauregui; used with permission).

16. Barbara La Marr, "The True Story of My Life," *Movie Weekly,* February 7, 1925, 27.

17. Meigs O. Frost, "Must Be in Love to Act, Says Star," *New Orleans States,* April 9, 1924.

18. Madge Dressen, "Keeping Baby Single," *Motion Picture,* September 1928, 96.

19. La Marr, "The True Story of My Life," February 7, 1925, 18.

20. Ibid., December 20, 1924, 15.

21. Ibid., January 10, 1925, 14–15.

Thirty-Three

1. "Barbara La Marr Dies Suddenly," *Oakland Tribune,* January 31, 1926.

2. "The Girl from Montmartre," *Film Daily,* March 7, 1926, 9.

3. "Barbara La Marr Film Is Magnet," *Los Angeles Times,* April 20, 1926; "Schiro's Tudor: 'The Girl from Montmartre,'" *Times-Picayune,* May 7, 1926; *Daily Mirror* and *New York Graphic* quoted in "Newspaper Opinions," *Film Daily,* February 28, 1926, 197; "The Cinema Circuit: Adolphe Menjou and Vincent Lopez Co-featured at the Strand—'The Girl from Montmartre,'" *Brooklyn Daily Eagle,* February 22, 1926.

4. St. Johns quoted in Jimmy Bangley, "The Legendary Barbara La Marr," *Classic Images*, May 1996, 20.

5. Marion quoted in Jimmy Bangley, "Barbara La Marr: A Memorial Tribute," *Classic Images*, February 1999, 28.

6. Bert Ennis, "Meteor Called La Marr," *Motion Picture*, February 1929, 40, 95.

7. Catherine Brody, "Wholesale Murder and Suicide," *Photoplay*, July, August, and September 1926 (for information on Barbara, see July 1926, 30); Katherine Albert, "Diet—The Menace of Hollywood," *Photoplay*, January 1929, 30; Dr. H. B. K. Willis, "Diet for Health and Beauty," *Photoplay*, February 1929, 90.

8. Bangley, "The Legendary Barbara La Marr," 17. (The article was published years after Bangley's interview with Terry.)

9. Allan R. Ellenberger, "Alice Terry: The Girl from Vincennes," *Films of the Golden Age*, Summer 1997, 77.

10. Bangley, "The Legendary Barbara La Marr," 20.

11. Ben Finney, *Feet First* (New York: Crown Publishers, 1971), 79.

12. Virginia Dodd telephone interview with author, October 24, 2010.

13. Arnolt Bronnen, *Film und Leben: Barbara La Marr* (Berlin: Rowohlt Verlag, 1928). English translation by Audrey R. Langer; transcript from Donald Gallery's personal papers given to author.

14. Jim Tully, "Jim Tully's Gallery of Women," *New Movie Magazine*, October 1932, 104.

15. Jimmy Bangley, "The Legendary Barbara La Marr," *Classic Images*, May 1996, 17.

16. Goldbeck quoted in Adela Rogers St. Johns, "The Life Story of Barbara La Marr," *Liberty Magazine*, December 15, 1928, 67.

17. Ibid., December 22, 1928, 58.

Epilogue

1. "Jean Harlow, Grilled by Police, Collapses," *Washington Post*, September 7, 1932.

2. Samuel Marx, *Mayer and Thalberg: The Make-Believe Saints* (New York: Random House, 1975), 80.

3. Robert Carville (Robert Dyer Hobday), "Two Lives, Two Loves," unpublished memoir, 1935, 1. Courtesy of Virginia Jauregui; quoted with permission.

4. All quotes pertaining to Robert Carville's memoir in this section are from ibid., 1, 10, 36–37.

5. "Barbara La Marr Leaves $10,000 of Million She Made," *Oakland Tribune*, February 28, 1926.

6. For information on the settlement of Barbara's estate, see County of Los Angeles, California, probate case files, estate no. 79638, Barbara La Marr (1926), "Amended Petition for Letters of Administration"; "Return and Account of Sale by

Trustee"; "Creditor's Claim" (Organizers Holding Corporation); "Petition to Compromise Claim"; "Order to Compromise," Los Angeles Superior Court, Los Angeles.

7. Donald Gallery e-mail correspondence with author, May 21, 2013.

8. "Studio News and Gossip: East and West," *Photoplay,* June 1926, 102; "El Hijo Adoptivo de Barbara La Marr Causa de un Litigio," *Heraldo de Mexico,* February 11, 1926.

9. International Newsreel caption dated February 26, 1926, from the back of a photo of Paul Bern found on eBay.

10. Donald Gallery telephone conversation with author, October 17, 2012.

11. "ZaSu Pitts Returns to Hope Cottage, First Home of Her Son, John [sic] Mike," partially dated *Dallas Dispatch* article, January 1932, Donald Gallery's personal papers shared with author.

12. Donald Gallery telephone conversation with author, February 20, 2010.

13. Ibid., July 2, 2010.

14. Ibid., September 18, 2007.

15. "Information" and "Proceedings on Sentence: Reporter's Transcript," *The People of the State of California vs. Henry Clay Barber,* case no. 671, Superior Court of the State of California, County of Madera, July 11, 1928 and August 3, 1928; "Determining Term of Confinement," Henry Clay Barber, case no. 671, Superior Court of the State of California, Board of Prison Terms and Paroles, California State Prison at San Quentin, February 13, 1941. These documents are from the Superior Court of the State of California, County of Madera, Madera.

16. Leatrice Gilbert Fountain e-mail correspondence with author, July 24, 2009.

17. Donald Gallery telephone conversation with author, March 4, 2009.

18. Letter from Irene Almond Harris to ZaSu Pitts, January 24, 1933, Donald Gallery's personal papers shared with author.

19. Laura Riebman e-mail correspondence with author, May 7, July 3, and October 14, 2014.

20. Donald Gallery e-mail correspondence with author, September 25, 2013.

21. Author's arrangement for Donald's testing, including conveying lab results to both families.

22. Patricia Gallery telephone conversation with author, October 14, 2014.

Appendix

1. William Foster Elliot, "Not Like the Fan Stories," *Los Angeles Times,* September 17, 1922.

2. Barbara's poetry used with permission of Donald Gallery.

Selected Bibliography

Ankerich, Michael G. *Broken Silence: Conversations with 23 Silent Film Stars.* Jefferson, NC: McFarland, 1993.
Atkins, Irene Kahn. *David Butler.* Lanham, MD: Scarecrow Press, 1993.
Balshofer, Fred J., and Arthur C. Miller. *One Reel a Week.* Berkeley: University of California Press, 1967.
Borgias, Darren. "The Early Years for Chandler Bruer Watson." Klamath County Museums, Klamath Falls, OR.
Bronnen, Arnolt. *Film und Leben: Barbara La Marr.* Berlin: Rowohlt Verlag, 1928.
Chartier, JoAnn, and Chris Enns. *Gilded Girls: Women Entertainers of the Old West.* Guilford, CT: Globe Pequot, 2003.
Daniels, Bebe, and Ben Lyon. *Life with the Lyons: The Autobiography of Bebe Daniels and Ben Lyon.* London: Odhams, 1953.
Duncan, Isadora. *My Life.* New York: Liveright, 1995 (first published 1927).
Erenberg, Lewis A. *Steppin' Out: New York Nightlife and the Transformation of American Culture, 1890–1930.* Chicago: University of Chicago Press, 1981.
Finney, Ben. *Feet First.* New York: Crown Publishers, 1971.
Fountain, Leatrice Gilbert. *Dark Star.* New York: St. Martin's Press, 1985.
Goldwyn, Samuel. *Behind the Screen.* Whitefish, MT: Kessinger Publishing, 2003 (first published 1923).
Griffith, Richard. *The Movie Stars.* New York: Doubleday, 1970.
Haffner, Gayle D. *Hands with a Heart: The Personal Biography of Actress ZaSu Pitts.* Denver: Outskirts Press, 2011.
Higham, Charles. *Merchant of Dreams: Louis B. Mayer, M.G.M., and the Secret Hollywood.* New York: Donald I. Fine, 1993.
Higham, John. *Writing American History: Essays on Modern Scholarship.* Bloomington: Indiana University Press, 1972.
Keith, Gaelyn Whitley. *The Father of Hollywood.* El Dorado Hills, CA: BookSurge, 2009.
Kemm, James, O. *Rupert Hughes: A Hollywood Legend.* Beverly Hills, CA: Pomegranate Press, 1997.
Kightlinger, Flora N. *The Star Speaker: A Complete and Choice Collection of the Best Productions by the Best Authors, with an Exhaustive Treatise on the Subject of Vocal and Physical Culture and Gesturing.* Jersey City, NJ: Star Publishing Co., 1892.

Selected Bibliography

Kobel, Peter. *Silent Movies: The Birth of Film and the Triumph of Movie Culture.* New York: Little, Brown and Co., 2007.

Lipsky, William. *San Francisco's Panama-Pacific International Exposition.* Mount Pleasant, SC: Arcadia Publishing, 2005.

Malnig, Julie. *Dancing Till Dawn: A Century of Exhibition Ballroom Dance.* New York: New York University Press, 1992.

Mann, William J. *Wisecracker: The Life and Times of William Haines, Hollywood's First Openly Gay Star.* New York: Penguin Group, 1998.

Marx, Samuel. *Mayer and Thalberg: The Make-Believe Saints.* New York: Random House, 1975.

Marx, Samuel, and Joyce Vanderveen. *Deadly Illusions: Jean Harlow and the Murder of Paul Bern.* New York: Dell Publishing, 1990.

O'Leary, Liam. *Rex Ingram: Master of the Silent Cinema.* Dublin: Academy Press, 1980.

Orr, Warren H. *Nine Generations of Orrs in America.* Chicago: [n.p.,] 1954.

Powell, Michael. *A Life in Movies.* London: Heinemann, 1986.

Reichenbach, Harry. *Phantom Fame.* New York: Simon and Schuster, 1931.

Schumach, Murray. *The Face on the Cutting Room Floor: The Story of Movie and Television Censorship.* New York: William Morrow & Co., 1964.

Sullivan, Mark. *Our Times: America at the Birth of the Twentieth Century.* New York: Scribner, 1996.

St. Johns, Adela Rogers. *Love, Laughter and Tears.* New York: Doubleday, 1978.

Swanson, Gloria. *Swanson on Swanson: An Autobiography.* New York: Pocket Books, 1980.

Wheelan, Ed. *Minute Movies: A Complete Compilation, 1927–1928.* Westport, CT: Hyperion Press, 1977.

Wood, Mrs. Henry. *East Lynne: A Drama, in Four Acts.* London: Richard Bentley, 1862.

Zierold, Norman. *Sex Goddesses of the Silent Screen.* Chicago: Henry Regnery, 1973.

Index

Page numbers in italics refer to photographs.

Adorée, Renée, 213, 214
Ainsworth, Barbara La Marr. *See* La Marr, Barbara
Ainsworth, Philip, 120, *121,* 123, 206, 231–32; Barbara and, 120; Barbara's divorce suit against, 133–34, 205; beating of Barbara and, 122–23, 126; divorce suit of against Barbara, 123, 124, 125–26, 133, 205; illegitimacy of Barbara's marriage to Ben Deely and, 133–34, 205–6, 207, 231, 254, 268; marriage to Barbara and, 121–24, 133, 205–6, 232
Ake, George, 25, 27, 28, 39
Ake, Violet. *See* Barber, Violet June (half-sister)
Alabama, 68, 135
Alderman, Edwin Anderson, 291
Alexander the Great, 29
Alexandria Hotel, 58, 65, 142
Allen, Chesney, 345
Allen, Pearl, 20–22, 23–24. *See also* Allen Stock Company
Allen Stock Company, 19, 20–22, 23, 24, 25, 28
Al Levy's, 58, 256, 267
Almond, Irene, 188, 200, 204, 208, 248, 275, 282, 305, 327, 364
Alone at Last (show), 106

Altadena, CA, 327, 328, 330, 335, 343, 356
Ambassador Hotel, 171, 315, 316
Anger, Kenneth, 346
Arabian Love (film), 176–77
Arbuckle, Roscoe, 177–78, 210, 250, 254
Aristotle, 29
Arizona, 56, 90, 145, 279
Ashland, OR, 10, 79–80, 81
Ashland Tidings, 79–80
Associated First National. *See* First National
Associated Holding Corporation, 315. *See also* Associated Pictures
Associated Pictures, 243, 257, 262, 269, 282, 304, 310, 315, 318, 328. *See also* Lubin, Herbert; Sawyer, Arthur; S-L Pictures
Astoria, OR, 12
Astor Theatre (New York, NY), 188
Auditorium Theater (Spokane, WA), 24–25, 26
Auditorium Theatre (Los Angeles, CA), 88
Auer, Florence, 301
Aurelius, Marcus, 29
Avery, Charles, 44
Avery, Russ, 266, 267

Badger, Clarence, 190, *191,* 263, *263*
Ball, Russell, *218, 231, 239, 246*
Ballard, Emma Wylie, 209–10

425

Index

ballroom dancers, 85
Band, Phil, 92–93
Bangley, Jimmy, *272, 300,* 347
Bara, Theda, 2, 8, 127, 164–65, 280
Barber, Caleb Austin, 11, 11n8
Barber, Henry (half-brother), 11, 16, 34, 337, 338, *339,* 363; death of, 363
Barber, Violet June (a.k.a. June Marr; June Marston; Violet Ake; Violet Ross) (half-sister), 11, 15–16, 19, 34, 39, 47–48, 89, 363; on Barbara, 47–48, 53; Barbara and, 25, 27, 28, 39–40, 115–16, 117, 337, 338, *339;* Barbara's kidnapping allegement and, 40–45, *46,* 47–49, 51–53, 89, 115; death of, 363; marriages of, 15, 25, 39, 115–16, 363
Bardot, Brigitte, 291
Barker, Reginald, 213
Barry, Viola Melvill, 330–31. *See also* Melvill, Viola
Barrymore, Lionel, 236, 237, *237,* 238, *240*
Baxter, Warner, 224, *224*
Beaux Arts, 259
Bedford, Barbara, 163–64, 176
Beery, Wallace, 213, 226
Bell, Caroline, 318–19
Bell, Pearl Doles, 295
Ben Deely & Co., 130–31, 135, 139. *See also* La Marr, Barbara: vaudeville career of
Bergere, Ouida, 165, 237, 238, 245
Bergquist, Rudolph, *191,* 325, 327
Bern, Friedericke, 173
Bern, Henry, 174, 364–65
Bern, Paul, 2–3, 172–74, *176,* 332, 352–53, 354, 364–65; Barbara and, 172, 175, *176,* 200, 226, 227, 230, 259, 275, 319, 343, 354, 355–56;

Barbara's fatal illnesses and death and, 319, 327, 331–32, 335, 337–38, 339–40, 352; Donald Gallery and, 331, 358, 363, 364–65; love for Barbara of, 175, 198, 332, 352, *353,* 355
Bern, Paul Henry, 365
Bern, Raymond, 365
Bernhardt, Sarah, 19, 24
B. F. Keith (vaudeville circuit), 130
Biograph Studios, 80–81, 286
Bitler, Don C., 55
Black Orchids (film), 166–67, 170, 175–76, 177, 180–81, *182–83,* 183–84, 188, 191; Barbara's pregnancy and, 184–85, *186–87,* 187; synopsis of, 181, 183. *See also Trifling Women* (film)
Blatt, Edward, 66, 67
Blood and Sand (film), 168
Bloomington, IL, 131
Boardman, Eleanor, 201, 216
Booking Guide, 274
Boston Street (Altadena), 327
Boston Traveler, 294
Bow, Clara, 2
Bowers, John, 190
Boxley, Clark, 39, 41–42, 43–45, 47, 48–49, 51–53, 89
Bracken, Bertram, 148–49
Brass Bottle, The (film), 222, 223, 224, 269
Brent, Evelyn, 296
Brentwood, CA, 360
Broadway (New York, NY), 96, 103–4, 105, 106, 109, 110. *See also* New York, NY; New York State
Brockwell, Gladys, 142, 143, 144, 145, 146, 338
Brody, Catherine, 346
Bronnen, Arnolt, 347

426

Bronson Avenue (Los Angeles), 317, 326
Brooklyn Daily Eagle, 345
Brown, Milton, *196*
Buddhism, 261
Buffalo, NY, 102–3
Burbank, CA, 45, 62, 64
Burns, Frankie, 118
Bushman, Francis X., 216
Butler, David, 198

Cad, the Tomboy (play), 24
Café Frontenac, 101, 102
Café Nat Goodwin, 86–87
Café Royale, 98
Caine, Hall, 237–38
Camille (play), 22
Campbell, Colin, *304*
Canada, 20, 68–69, 127, 145, 213, 310, 311
Canary Cottage, The (show), 120
Cannon, Pomeroy, 181
Capp, Al, 2, 193
Carey, Harry, 161
Carleton, William P., 177
Carmichael, John, 173
Carmichael, Winifred, 174
Carr, Harry, 283
Carroll, Harrison, 174, 255
Carville, Robert (a.k.a. Robert Hobday), 85–86, 88, 124, 129, 200, 249–50; Barbara and, 55, 86–87, 88–91, 92–93, 98–103, 106–7, 108–11, 113–14, 118, 123–24, 128, 249–50, 332, 347; as Barbara's dance partner, 88, 90, 91, 92, 93–99, *95,* 100–1, 102, 103–5, 106, 109–10, 118–19, 123, 124, 200; Barbara's name given by, 88–89, 89n8, 116n9; love affair with Barbara, 87, 91, 103, 112–13, 114–15, 116–17, 118, 119, 120–21, 124–25, 129, 352, 354–55; marriage to Philip Ainsworth and, 120–21, 122–24, 126
Carville, Virginia (a.k.a. Virginia Hobday), 200, 208, 211, 275, 293, 328–29, 332, 347, 354, 357, 363
Casino Company, 27
Castle, Irene, 85, 94, 99, 106
Castle, Vernon, 85, 94, 99, 106
Castles in the Air, 106, 107, 110
Caswell, Nancy, 144
censorship, film and, 79, 143, 178–79. *See also* La Marr, Barbara: censorship and films of
Chaney, Lon, 190
Chaplin, Charles, 94, 132, 150, 161, 164
Charles A. Taylor Company, 27–28
Chicago, IL, 97–99, 100, 101, 130, 131, 133, 134, 229, 293
Chicago Examiner, 97, *98,* 99
Christian Science, 31, 102, 103, 333, 337
Christie, Al, 42
Christie Hotel, 255
Cinderella of the Hills (film), 163–64
Clair, Ethlyne, 289
Claridge Hotel, 111
Clark, Frank Howard, 150
Clark County, WA, 11
Clarke, George, 297
Classic Images, 272, 300
Cleveland, OH, 133
Cocoanut Grove, 171
Cody, Lew, *176,* 201, 262, 265, 364
Coeur d'Alene, ID, 25
Cohen, Milton, 250, 268, 318, 328, 338
Columbia Productions, 203
Columbia River (WA), 28, 190
Columbia University, 107

Index

Compson, Betty, 290
Confucianism, 261
Connelly, Edward, 184, *186*
Contner, Charlotte Brown (maternal grandmother), 10
Contner, James (maternal grandfather), 10
Converse, Amelia, 65, 67–69, 70, 71, 74–75, 77, 78
Converse, Charles, 65, 66, 67
Converse, Flora, 65, 66, 69, 78
Converse, Lawrence (husband), 65–68, 70, 77–78; Barbara and, 62, 63–65, 68–75, 70, 76–77, 78–79, 89–90, 179; death of, 78–79. *See also* Lawrence, Max
Corvallis, OR, 10
Counter Intelligence Corps (CIC), 362
Count of Monte Cristo, The (play), 22
Coxen, Edward, 161
Crane, Ward, 148
Crawford, Joan, 2, 360
Cryer, George, 274
Curran, Lenore, 122, 126

Dallas, TX, 207–8, 209, 211, 212
Dallas Automotive Trades Association, 207
Dallas Morning News, 198, 208, 212, 222
dance craze, 58–59, 60, 85
Danse de Follies, 109
Darling, Ida, 301
Darwin, Charles, 29
Daugherty, Jack (husband), 228–29, 230, 293, 363; on Barbara, 229, 236, 241, 284, 285, 293–94; as corespondent in Ben Deely divorce suit against Barbara, 254, 257, 266, 268, 282, 292; divorce suit of against Barbara, 293–94, 356;

marriage to Barbara, 229–31, *231*, 235, 236, 240–41, 252–53, 263, 281, 283–84, 293, 352, 356; separations from Barbara and, 268, 282, 283–84, 292, 293
Daugherty, Virgil Ashley. *See* Daugherty, Jack
Davenport, Dorothy, 56, 56n3, 178
Davis, Clifton, 173
Davis, Jefferson, 10
Davis, Samuel, 10
Deane-Tanner, William Cunningham. *See* Taylor, William Desmond
De Brulier, Nigel, 144, 155, *224*
Deely, Barbara (La Marr). *See* La Marr, Barbara
Deely, Ben (husband), 127–29, *128*, 130–31, 134, 139, 141, 143, 292, 296; alleged illegitimacy of marriage to Barbara and, 133–34, 205, 230, 254, 257, 268, 292; Barbara and, 127, 128–29, 130–31, 132, 133–35, 139, 292, 296, 348; Barbara's divorce suit against, 146, 155; death of, 292; divorce suits of against Barbara, 146, 155, 254–55, 257, 268, 269, 292; Herman Roth's blackmailing of Barbara and, 254–56, 266, 267; marriage to Barbara, 133–34, 136, 139, 141, 142, 143, 145–46, 155, 157, 162, 175, 205
Deely, Nicholas Bernard ("Ben"). *See* Deely, Ben
Deer's Head Inn, 310
De Grasse, Sam, 147, 223
De Lacy, Philippe, 265
De La Motte, Marguerite, 150, 152
DeMille, Cecil B., 36, 172, 340, 348
Dempsey, Jack, 161–62
Denver, CO, 131, 207

428

Index

Denver Post, 131
De Roche, Charles, 269
Desperate Trails (film), 161
Detroit, MI, 100, 101
DeVore, Billy (a.k.a. William Watson Jr.) (brother), 132, 135, 358, 362–63; Barbara and, 130, 135, 230, 263, 335, 337, *339,* 356, 357–58; death of, 363; vaudeville career of, 34, 130, 132, 135, 263. *See also* Watson, William, Jr.
Díaz, Porfirio, 66, 67
Dietrich, Marlene, 2
Dix, Richard, 201
Dodd, Virginia, 347
Doherty, Edward, 255
Domestic Relations (film), 177
Douglas Fairbanks Pictures Corporation, 150
Douglas Fairbanks Studios, 232. *See also* Fairbanks Studios
Doyle, Gerald, 65, 68, 69, 74–75, 77, 125–26
Dramatic Life of Abraham Lincoln, The (film), 299
Dressler, Marie, 216
Drew, Frank, 205, 254, 256, 268
Drew, Mrs. Sidney (a.k.a. Lucille McVey), 140
Dumas, Alexandre, 22, 153
Duncan, Isadora, 92
Dunn, Winifred, 262
Duse, Eleonora, 244
Dymond, John, 256
Dyris, Jacqueline, 255

East Lynne (film), 127
East Lynne (play), 23
Eaton, Jean, 144
Eddy, Mary Baker, 31. *See also* Christian Science

Edison, Thomas, 14, 33, 87, 250
Edison Company, 165
Edison Trust, 33
El Centro, CA, 55, 56, 58, 60–61, 62
El Fey Club, 289, 290, 306
Elite Cafeteria, 88
Elliot, William Foster, 194
El Paso, TX, 66, 67–68
Elvey, Maurice, 295
Emery, Gilbert, 197
Emmanuel, Victor, III, 238
Ennis, Bert, 192, 213, 236, 270, 274, 275, 279, 280, 328; on Barbara, 3, 268, 289, 298, 307, 345; Barbara's adoption of son and, 208, 209, 210, 211, 220
Ernst, Eleanor, 34
Escoto, Miguel, 281
Eternal City, The (Caine), 237
Eternal City, The (film), 233–34, 236, 237–39, *239, 240,* 241–43, *242,* 245, 248, 251, 259
Eternal Struggle, The (film), 213–14, *215,* 226, 350
Evans, Augusta Jane, 224
Exceptional Photoplay Committee of the National Board of Review, 198
Exhibitors Herald, 192

Face in the Dark, The (film), 131
Fairbanks, Douglas, Jr., 352
Fairbanks, Douglas, Sr., 132, 150, 152–53, 155, *156,* 161, 162, 340, 350; Barbara and, 150, 152, 153, 154, 156, *156,* 244, 350
Fairbanks, John, 153
Fairbanks Studios, 152, 153, 154. *See also* Douglas Fairbanks Studios
Fair Oaks Sanitarium, 108–9
Famous Players Film Company, 109
Farnum, William, 145, 146

Index

Fay, Larry, 289. *See also* El Fey Club
Fazenda, Louise, *247*
Felton, Verna, 20, 21, 24
Ferguson, Helen, 225, 244
Fidler, Jimmie, 244
Film Daily, 177, 214, *264,* 265, 294, 302, 344
film industry, 2, 8, 14, 32–34, 148, 185, 210, 297–98; filmmaking, 33, 35, 143, 161, 183, 184, 197, 201–2; scandals and, 79, 177–79, 203; writing for the silent screen, 140–41, 143. *See also* censorship; vamps
Film und Leben: Barbara La Marr (Bronnen), 347–48
Finney, Ben, 290, 291, 299, *301,* 306; on Barbara, 291–92, 305–6, 347; Barbara and, 290–92, 293, 294, 299, *301,* 303, 305–6, 357
Finney, Benjamin Ficklin ("Ben"). *See* Finney, Ben
First National, 269, 271, 273, 282, 321, 338; Barbara's contract with, 243, 256, 280, 283, 286, 299, 301, 303, 306, 310, 319, 328, 344
First World War, 87, 124, 130, 132, 133, 135, 229
Fisher, George, 151
Fitts, Buron, 281
Fitzmaurice, George, 237–38, 241
Five Senses, The (painting), 35, *36*
Flagstaff, AZ, 145
Flame of Youth (film), 150–51, 295
Flames of the Flesh (film), 141
Flaming Youth (film), 271
Flanagan and Allen, 345
Fletcher, Ed, 192, 281–82
flickers, 32
Florrie Meets a Gentleman (film), 310
Flynn, Emmett, 142

Folly (a.k.a. Barbara La Marr), 58, 63, 86, 88, 205. *See also* La Marr, Barbara
Fool There Was, A (film), 164
Ford, Henry, 87
Ford, Jack, 161
Fort Lee, NJ, 133, 299, 304
Fountain, Leatrice Gilbert, 172, 363
Four Horsemen of the Apocalypse, The (film), 166
Fox, William, 141, 146, 151
Fox Film Corporation, 127, 141–42, 143, 164, 165, 295; Barbara and, 141–43, 145, 146–48, 149–51, 163, 176, 224, 295, 350
Francisco, Betty, 198
Frederickson (judge), 48, 52, 53
Fresno, CA, 29, 34, 39, 316
Friganza, Trixie, 120
Frost, Meigs O., 279–80, 281
Frothingham, J. L., 157, 163, 165
Furthman, Jules, 151

Gable, Clark, 360
Gale, Hal, 86–87, 86n4
Gallery, Ann (a.k.a. ZaSu Ann Gallery), 203–4, 327, 328, 358, 359, *359*
Gallery, Donald (son), 218, 310, 347, *360,* 361–66, *366;* adoption of by Barbara, 200, 204–5, 207–8, 209–13, 219–21, 302–3; on Barbara, 60, 284, 362; Barbara and, 199–200, 204–5, 214, *215,* 218, 221, *221, 231,* 235–36, *247,* 265, 302–3; Barbara's parenting of, 204, 219, 243, 252, 282, 302, 332; birth of and Barbara's pregnancy and, 180, 184–88, *186, 187, 191,* 302–3, 364; Barbara's illness and death and, 327–28, 331, 337–38, 356,

430

Index

358–59, 362–63; death of, 366; father of, 187–88, 363–64, 365; Paul Bern and, 331, 363, 364, 365; ZaSu Pitts and, 187, 327–28, 337, 358–62, *359,* 363–64
Gallery, Patricia, 362, 366, *366*
Gallery, Tom, 203, 328, 337, 338, *339,* 358–59, *359,* 363
Gallery, ZaSu Pitts. *See* Pitts, ZaSu
Galloway, Clinton E., 316, 317, 322, 324, 326, 330, 332, 333, 335
Galsworthy, John, 303, 304
Garbo, Greta, 2, 360
Garfield, James A., 9
Garland, Judy, 360
Gasnier, Louis J., 195–98
Gee, George, 53
Geissinger, James, 64, 65, 69, 72, 75
George (Barbara's driving instructor), 115
George Washington Carver Institute, 250
Georgia, 135
Gettysburg, PA, 292
Gilbert, Aletha, 74
Gilbert, John, 171–72, 176, 197, 224, *224,* 352
Girl from Montmartre, The (film), 319, 321–25, *322–23,* 326–27, 344–45, 350
Girl of Tomorrow, The (show), 99
Glass, Gaston, 197
Glendora, CA, 65, 67, 69
Goldbeck, Willis, 170, 172, 193, 348
Goldwyn, Samuel, 33, 159, 233, 235, 237–38, 241, 251, 348
Goldwyn Studios, 141, 172, 201, 226, 227
Goodwin, Nat, 86–87, 343
Goose Lake, CA, 11
Graber, Ted, 227

Graham, Ralph, 74–75, 76, 77
Grand Rapids, MI, 134
Grauman, Sid, 96
Great War, The. *See* World War I
Greed (film), 359
Green, Alfred ("Al"), 321, 324, 326, 338, *339,* 344
Green Teapot Hotel, 291, 306
Griffith, Corinne, 306
Griffith, D. W., 150, 222
Guatemala, 303
Guinan, Texas, 289, 290

Haines, William, 2, 226–28, *228*
Hale, Albert W., 86n4. *See also* Gale, Hal
Hanford, WA, 28, 29
Hanford Columbian, 28
Hansen, Juanita, 346
Harlow, Jean, 173, 174, 175
Harlow's, 123, 124
Harriet and the Piper (film), 148–49, 151, 250, 350
Hathaway, Henry, 338, *339*
Hays, Will, 178, 283
Hays Office. *See* Hays, Will
Hazel Kirke (play), 22
Healy's, 106, 128
Hearst, William Randolph, 95–96, 97
Heart of a Siren, The (film), 299, *300,* 301–2, *301,* 350
Hendry, Whitey, 173
Hero, The (film), 197, 198, 213, 260
Heyes, Herbert, 151
Hill, John, 266, 267
Hill Island Inn, 111
Hillsboro, OR, 10, 11
His Brother's Wife (film). See *Hero, The* (film)
Hobday, Ann, 91, 92
Hobday, Betty, 129, 250

Index

Hobday, Robert. *See* Carville, Robert
Hobday, Virginia (Robert [Carville] Hobday's daughter), 129
Hobday, Virginia (Robert [Carville] Hobday's sister). *See* Carville, Virginia
Hogan, James P., 147
Holding, Thomas, 155, 304, *304*
Hollywood, CA, 14, 214, 216, 338, 340; Barbara and, 2, 42, 62, 89, 90, 213, 249, *249*, 267, 280, *341, 349*; film industry and, 8, 154, 174, 177, 201, 203, 348. *See also* film industry
Hollywood Babylon (Anger), 346
Hollywood Cemetery. *See* Hollywood Forever
Hollywood Forever, 338, *341,* 357
Hollywood Memorial Park. *See* Hollywood Forever
Hollywood Orphans' Home, 249, *249*
Hollywood Walk of Fame, 348, *349*
Holmes, Stuart, 168
Honduras, 303
Hoover (art studio), *194, 195*
Hope Cottage, 209–10, 211, 219
Hotel Angelus, 51
Hotel Cadillac, 101
Hotel Knickerbocker, 106
Hotel Nassau, 111
Howard, Joe, 99
Hughes, Birdie, 62, 63, 64, 65, 71, 72, 74
Hughes, Howard, 201
Hughes, Rupert, 201, 202–3
Hume, W. T., 12

Ibsen, Henrik, 29
Illinois, 8, 33, 131, 134, 135; divorces in, 133–34, 205. *See also* Chicago, IL
Ince, Thomas, 192

Indiana, 131, 135, 207
Indianapolis, IN, 135
Ingram, Rex, 165–68, *169,* 170, 177, 179, 180, 181, 183, 184–85, 191, 350
In Pursuit of Polly (film), 134
Inslee, Charles, 116
Inter-Californian, 34, 39
Italy, 235, 237–38, 240, 241, 243. *See also Eternal City, The* (film)

Jamaica, 303
Jessie Shirley Company, 20, 24–25, 26, 27, 28
Johnston, William, 210
Jones, Edward, 173
Joy, Leatrice, 172, 175, 363
Juarez, Mexico, 66–67
Julian, C. C., 357

Kansas City, MO, 157
Kaufman, Albert, 109
Kazan (film), *128*
Keaton, Buster, 244
Kentucky, 11n10, 86, 88, 135
Keystone Studios, 192
Kiesler, Hedwig Eva Maria, 3
Kilbane, Johnny, 118
Kinemacolor Company of America, 190
Kingsley, Grace, 214, 216, 218, 219
Kipling, Rudyard, 164
Klieg eyes, 201–2
Klumph, Helen, *247,* 344
Knickerbocker, R. D., 255, 268, 338, *339*
Knoblock, Edward, 153
Kobel, Peter, 14, 210, 349
Koran, the, 261

Laemmle, Carl, 33, 80
Lafayette, LA, 279

Index

Lake County Examiner, 10
Lakeview, OR, 9, 10
La Marr, Barbara, *ii*, 1–3, 7, 37, *41, 73, 80, 163, 176, 189, 194–96, 218, 237, 266,* 277, 313, *351, 353;* acting of, 2, 155–56, 161, 168, 180, 213, 244–45, 257–58, 279–80, 301; adolescent behavior in Los Angeles nightclubs of, 58–60, 63, 153; adolescent rebellion of, 32, 39–40, 49, 55, 57, 60, 63, 71, 74, 153; adoption of son, (*see* Gallery, Donald: adoption of by Barbara); alcoholism and drinking of, 60, 101, 102, 107–8, 109, 120, 123, 259, 260, 263, 287, 289, 305–6, 347; Associated Pictures Corporation contract of, 243, 255, 268, 269, 297, 310, 318, 328 (*see also* Sawyer, Arthur); banned from working as actress, 79, 86; banning of films of, 280, 281; "too beautiful" for Los Angeles, 61, 62, 79–80, 153–54, 179; beauty of, 41, 49–51, *50,* 59, 61, 62–63, 75–76, 77, 79, 97, 162, 243, 244, 251, 318–19, 336; as Beth Lytelle, 57–58, 64, 76; as Beth (Watson), 31, 331; birth of, 8, 13–14, 47, 88; blackmailing of, 89–90, 93 (*see also* Roth, Herman); and books, 17, 19, 29; censorship and films of, 79, 156, 181, 183, 264, 265, 270, 280, 283, 286, 287, 305 (*see also* censorship); as Southern California chambers of commerce representative, 274–75, 279–80; as "California's Venus," 49–51, *50,* 52; character of, 3, 14–15, 18–19, 26, 31–32, 39, 156, 168–70, 171, 193–95, 227, 244–47, 294, 348; as child actress, 19–20, 21–26, 27–28, 29, *30;* childhood and girlhood of, 5, 8, 13–14, 15–20, *16,* 21–28, 29–32, *30,* 34–36, *35–36,* 47–48; as comic strip inspiration, 2; crypt of, 339–40, *341,* 358; Dallas trip of, (*see* Texas); dancing of, 58, 59, 91–92, 96, 325; dancing career of (partnered), 91, 122, 200 (*see also* Carville, Robert: as Barbara's dance partner); dancing career of (solo), 91–92, 94, 96, *98,* 110, 119, 125, 127, 135; death of, 334–40, *337, 339,* 344, 345–46, 347, 352, 354, 356–57, 358; delinquency application against, 54; diary kept by, 56n3, 103, 109–12, 113–15, 116–17, 119, 121–22, 123, 129, 250n23; dieting and weight of, 297–99, 305, 311, 346; domestic life of, 199, 248, 252 (*see also* Gallery, Donald: Barbara's parenting of); (alleged) drug use of, 346–47; education of, 16–17, 18, 22–23, 29–31, 32, 34; failed attempts of to work in films, 34–36, 42, 55, 56, 79, 86–87, 109; family background of, 8–13; fatal illnesses of, 260–61, 289, 299, 305, 315–16, 317, *320,* 322, 324–26, 327, 328, 330, 332–35; fictionalized background of, 7–8, 80–81, 88, 89–90, 91, 96, 97n1, 110, 179–80, 212, 220, 251–52; as film actress, 55, 62–63, 76, 148–49, 151, 152, 154, 155, 157, 163, 165, 166–68, 243, 348, *349* (*see also* Sawyer, Arthur: Barbara's contracts with); financial woes of, 98–101, 102, 103, 118, 139, 250, 269, 289, 307, 315, 318, 356–57; First National contract of, (*see* First National); as

Index

La Marr, Barbara *(cont.)*
Folly, (*see* Folly); Fox Film Corporation contract of, 142; funeral of, 335, 336–39, *339*, 340, 358; generosity of, 15, 201, 248–49, *249*, 250, 289, 342, 356; illnesses of, 31, 113, 117, 131–32, 134–36; insecurities of, 108–9, 114, 148, 149, 250–52, 287, 299, 307, 319; intelligence of, 29, 172, 271, 287; Italy trip of, (*see* Italy; Rome, Italy); kidnapping allegement of, 39, 40–47, *41, 46,* 48–49, 51–54, 89, 115, 179; lost films of, 349–51 (*see also Filmography on page 375*); on marriage, 76, 121, 137, 144, 162, 199, 204, 212, 230–31, 283–84; on men and love, 187, 188, 220, 229, 235, 280, 307, 329, 354–56; modeling of, 35, *36,* 49–51, 87, 88; money from men and, 92, 93, 102, 106, 110–11, 113–14, 115, 116, 117, 122, 123; on motherhood, 188, 199–200, 204, 212, 219–21, *221;* name changed to Barbara La Marr, 88–89, 89n8, 90, 116n9; nervous breakdowns of, 102, 107–9, 113, 136, 292–93, 299, 310–11; notoriety of, 53–54, 56, 79, 89–90, 126, 154, 162–63, 177, 179–80, 232–33, *266,* 274–75, 280–81; nun aspiration of, 17, 30–31, 103; poetry of, 17, 29, 143, 307–10, 367–69; pregnancy and childbirth of, (*see* Gallery, Donald: birth of and Barbara's pregnancy and); probate record of, 356–57; professionalism of, 155–56, 201, 245, 248, 271–73, 322–23, 324; radio broadcasts of, 208, 208n6; religion and spirituality of, 17, 30–31, 102–3, 261, 333; reviews of dancing of, 96, 99; reviews of films acted in, 149, 152, 161, 162, 164, 177, *183,* 188, 191–92, 198–99, 202–3, 213, 214, 222, 223, 224–25, 242–43, 258, 259–60, *264,* 265, 274, 294–95, 302, 304–5, 344–45; reviews of films written by, 144, 145, 147, 151, 296; reviews of theater acting of, 23–24, 26; reviews of vaudeville performances of, 131; sadness of, 244–45, *247,* 258, 260, 274, 285, 343; salary of (dancing), 94–95, 97–98, 99, 100, 103, 105; salary of (film acting), 3, 149, 168, 181, 188, 213, 222, 234, 243, 318 (*see also* Sawyer, Arthur: salary advances made to Barbara by); salary of (screenwriting), 142; salary of (vaudeville), 130; sanitarium stay of, 107–9; as screen idol, 2, 193, 225, 235, 236, 243, 244–49, *246–47,* 250–53, 284, 285; screenwriting career of, 141–45, 146–48, 149–52, 295–96, 350; sex appeal of, 2, 156, 193, 244, *246,* 262, 268, *270,* 274; son of, (*see* Gallery, Donald); sprained knee of, 271–73, 346; suicide attempts of, 136, 292–93, 299; uncredited screenwriting of, 197, 262, 283, 286, 287; vamp film roles of, 148–49, 152, 155–56, *156,* 161, 162, 163–64, 176–77, 181–83, *182–83, 186–87,* 190–92, *191,* 201, *202,* 213–14, 222–25, *223–24,* 262–65, *263–64,* 269–70, *270, 272, 273,* 274, 286–87, *287–88,* 294–95, 299–302, *300–1,* 303–5, *304,* 350; vamping style of, 190, 244, 251, 279–80; vamp typecasting of, 2,

163–65, 190, 191, 213, 219, 220, 251, 262–63, 270, *270,* 279–80, 318–19, 348; vamp typecasting of and deviation from, 2, 193–94, 198–99, *199,* 213, 244, 260, 318–19, 345, 348; vamp typecasting and motherhood of, 210–11, 219, 220–21, 222; vaudeville career of, 129, 130–31, 132–33, 134–36, 139; Whitley Heights home of, 214, 216–19, *217–18,* 221, *231,* 244, 269, 316–17, 356; writing of, 7, 139–40, 141–43, 144, 329
La Marr, G. V., 311
Lamarr, Hedy, 3
La Marr, Ivan. *See* Gallery, Donald
La Marr, Marvin Carville. *See* Gallery, Donald
La Mesa, CA, 192, 281
Landis, Cullen, 354
Landis, Margaret, 148, 354
Landis, Nancy, 354
Land of Jazz, The (film), 151–52
Larkin, Mark, 153
La Salle Opera House, 99
Lasky, Jesse, 321, 340, 348
Last of the Mohicans, The (film), 222
La Venta Inn, 325
Lawford, Peter, 361
Lawrence, Florence, 33
Lawrence, Max (a.k.a. Lawrence Converse), 63, 64, 65, 69, 76. *See also* Converse, Lawrence
Lee, Lolita, 326–27
Leigh, Frank, 144, 177
LeMaire, Charles, 299, *300*
Le Saint, Edward J., 143, 145
Levy, Paul. *See* Bern, Paul
Liberty Bonds, 132
Li'l Abner (comic strip), 2. *See also* Capp, Al

Liles, William, 11
Lincoln, NE, 131
Little Grey Mouse, The (film), 147
Little Princess, The (film), 203
Lord & Taylor, 111
Loren, Sophia, 291
Los Angeles, CA, 214; Barbara and, 41, 49, 54, 55, 81, 127, 139, 143, 150, 243, 274, 311, 327, 335; Barbara as "too beautiful" for, 61, 62, 79, 153–54, 179; Barbara as unaccompanied minor in, 55, 56–58, 59–61, 62, 63; Barbara's dancing career and, 123, 124; Barbara's film acting and, 34–35, 79; film industry and, 33. *See also* Hollywood, CA
Los Angeles Chamber of Commerce, 274–75, 280
Los Angeles Evening Herald, 42, *46,* 47, 49, *50,* 51, 62, 71, 153–54
Los Angeles Examiner, 37, 41, *41,* 42, 43, 53, 70, *70,* 71, 72, *73,* 77, 255
Los Angeles Express, 162
Los Angeles Herald Express, 255
Los Angeles Times, 42, 55, 62, 74, 194, 230, 255, 256, 262, 274, 304, 318, 330, 345
Louis B. Mayer Pictures, 148. *See also* Mayer, Louis B.
Louisiana, 131, 135, 274, 279
Louisiana Times-Picayune, 345
Love, Bessie, 224, 338
Love, Montagu, 237, *237*
Lovely, Louise, 146–47
Lowery, William, 152
Lubin, Barney, 315, 316, 317, 321, 327, 328
Lubin, Herbert, 190, 192, 243, 282, 315, 315n2; Barbara and, 243, 283, 297, 303, 315, 318, 319, 328, 344,

435

Index

Lubin, Herbert *(cont.)* 357. *See also* Associated Pictures Corporation; S-L Pictures; S-L Studios
Lyon, Ben, 269, 270, 271, 364; Barbara and, 271, *272,* 283, 284–85, 293, 342, 347, 363
Lyric Theater (New York, NY), 161
Lytell, Bert, 237, *237,* 238, 242, *242,* 286, *287,* 333, 338, *339*
Lytelle, Beth (a.k.a. Barbara La Marr), 57–58, 64, 76. *See also* La Marr, Barbara; Watson, Beth
Lytelle, Folly. *See* Folly
Lytelle, Jack (purported husband), 56–57, 90

MacDonald, Katherine, 177
Mack, Marion, 203
MacLaren, Mary, 155
Madden, Golda, 144
Madero, Francisco, 66, 67
Madison, Cleo, 166
Majestic, RMS, 306
Majestic Theatre, 132
Male and Female (film), 197
Man from Home, The (film), 241
Man from Texas, The (play), 24
Mann, William J., 227
Marden, Leo, 60–61, 62, 153–54
Marion, Frances, 203, 345
Marion, George F., 304, *304*
Mark of Zorro, The (film), 150, 153
Marmont, Percy, 262, 265
Marr, Arthur, 116, 116n9
Marr, June. *See* Barber, Violet June (half-sister)
Marshall, Thomas, 207
Marston, June. *See* Barber, Violet June (half-sister)
Martin, Joe, 183–84, *187*

Marvin, Zebina ("Zeke") E., 209, 210, 211
Marx, Samuel, 259
Maryatt, Mildred Gray, 232, 233
Maryatt, Oscar, 232–33
Mary of the Movies (film), 203
mashers, 60–61
Mason, Shirley, 145, 150, 295, 296
Mathis, June, 321
Matteawan (hospital), 109
Mayer, Louis B., 3, 148, 173, 213, 222, 226, 257, 259. *See also* Metro-Goldwyn-Mayer
Mayo, Frank, 201
McBan, Mickey, *199*
McCabe, John, 24
McCormac, Muriel, *199*
McCormick, John, 338
McCullough, Philo, 147, 151
McGuire, Tom, 164
McKee, Raymond, 151
McKim, Robert, 222
McVey, Lucille (a.k.a. Mrs. Sidney Drew), 140
Medford, OR, 113, 114, 115, 116, 117
Medford Mail Tribune, 114
Melvill, Antonia Miether, 35, *36*
Melvill, Viola, 35, *36. See also* Barry, Viola Melvill
Memphis, TN, 131
Menjou, Adolphe, 155
Metro-Goldwyn-Mayer (a.k.a. MGM), 3, 173, 319, 332, 346, 352
Metro Pictures, 166, 167, 168, 170, 180, 181, 184–85, 187, 188, 190, 260, 262
Mexico, 33, 56, 62, 63, 66, 67, 167, 362
Mexico City, Mexico, 67
Miami (film), 290
Miami, FL, 290, 303
Michael Strogoff (play), 22

436

Index

Michigan, 120, 134, 135. *See also* Detroit, MI
Midway Gardens, 97, 98
Miller, Arthur, 238, 241
Miller, Barbara, 318
Miller, Marilyn, 306
Millette, Dorothy, 174–75, 352, 356
Milligan, J. C., *215*
Milner, Marjorie, 86, 88, 355
Minneapolis, MN, 131
Minter, Mary Miles, 178
Minute Movies (comic strip), 2
Missouri, 135, 229
Mitchell, Howard M., 150, 163
Moebs, William, 101, 102
Mong, William V., 257
Moore, Colleen, 271, 306, 321, 338
Moore, Herbert, 131
Moore, Matt, 222, *223*
morality clauses in studio contracts, 179, 255
Mother of His Children, The (film), 139–40, 141, 142, 144–45
Motion Picture, 191
Motion Picture Classic, 243
Motion Picture Magazine, 193, 232, 259–60
Motion Picture News, 145, 151, 164, 210
Motion Picture Producers and Distributors of America, 178. *See also* Hays, Will
Movie Weekly, 148, 213, 214, 240, *242;* Barbara's life story in, 7–8, 105, 109, 343; Barbara's life story in (childhood and girlhood), 5, 7, 8, 15, 18–19, 20, 24, 26–28, 29, 32, 252; Barbara's life story in (husbands and men), 97n1, 283–84, 329; Barbara's life story in (Barbara's illnesses), 131–2, 135; Barbara's life story in (fictionalized family background), 7; Barbara's life story in (film acting career), 148, 149, 150, 167, 250–51, 252–53, 265, 295; Barbara's life story in ([additional] quotes credited to Barbara from), 137, 227, 248, 261, 277, 285, 307, 340, 342; Barbara's life story in (screenwriting career), 142, 144, 329
Moving Picture Stories, 165, 268
Moving Picture World, 177, 188, 191, 198, 222, 282, 302, 304
Mumford, Ethel Watts, 58
Murphy, Edna, 269
Mussolini, Benito, 237–38, 239, 241
Myers, Harry, 223
My Husband's Wives (film), 295–96
My Pardner (play), 22
Myrtle Vane Company, 27–28

Naldi, Nita, 165, 280
National Board of Review, 143, 198
Neale, Earle, 291
Negri, Pola, 338
Neilan, Marshall, 338
Nestor Studios, 42, 56n3
"New Bell Boy, The" (vaudeville act), 127, 130, 131, 134
New Haven, CT, 134
New Jersey, 33, 108, 132, 133. *See also* Fort Lee, NJ
New Mexico, 279
New Orleans, LA, 131, 274, 279
New Orleans States, 279. *See also* Frost, Meigs O.
New York, NY, 25, 161, 174, 188, 198, 242, 315; Barbara and, 109, 111, 113, 131, 133, 235, 259, 274, 289, 357; Barbara's dancing career and, 95, 96, 97, 102, 103, 110; the making of Barbara's films and, 241, 259, 282. *See also* New York State

Index

New York Daily Mirror, 345
New York Graphic, 345
New York Herald, 14
New York Post, 265
New York State, 33, 59, 165, 172, 190, 227, 290, 306, 332; Barbara and, 128, 136, 236, 243, 250, 280, 282–83, 292, 294, 297, 303, 310, 311, 346, 347; Barbara's dancing career and, (*see* Buffalo, NY; Broadway [New York, NY]); the making of Barbara's films and, 248, 282, 286, 318. *See also* Broadway (New York, NY); Buffalo, NY; New York, NY
New York Sun, 59, 304
New York Telegram, 305
New York Tribune, 9, 162
New York World, 265
Niblo, Fred, 150, 153, 155–56, 165, 167, 222, 244, 257
nickelodeons, 32
Nobody's Child (poem), 21
Nodler, Morris, 281
Normand, Mabel, 178, 317
North Carolina, 135, 290
Northwest News, 10
North Yakima, WA. *See* Yakima, WA
Novak, Jane, *128*
Novarro, Ramon, 167, 168–69, *169,* 180, 181, 185, 257; Barbara and, 2, 167, 168–69, *169,* 181, *182, 183,* 184, *187, 257, 259,* 260, 330, 337
Nut, The (film), 152, 350

Oakland, CA, 117, 118, 120, 122, 123, 124, 126, 200, 263
Oakland, Iowa, 65
Oakland Tribune, 221
O'Brien, Eugene, 216
Odeon Theater (Tacoma, WA), 20

Oettinger, Malcolm H., 245, *246*
Ohio, 8, 10, 133, 135
Old Faithful Inn, 94–95, 100
O'Leary, Liam, 166
Omaha, NE, 131
O'Malley, Pat, 213
One Reel a Week (Balshofer and Miller), 238
Oregon, 9, 10, 11, 12, 15, 93, 139. *See also* Ashland, OR; Medford, OR; Portland, OR
Oregonian, 9, 10, 12, 15
Oregon Journal, 9
Orozco, Pascual, 66
Orpheum (vaudeville circuit), 130
Orpheum Theater (Denver, CO), 131
Orpheum Theater (Tacoma WA), 19, 20
Orpheum Theater (Salt Lake City, UT), 130
Orpheum Theater (San Francisco, CA), 139
Orr, Warren, 8
Orting Oracle, 12
Ouida (a.k.a. Maria Louise Ramé), 150

Palace Hotel, 93
Palace Music Hall (Chicago, IL), 99, 134
Palace Theater (New Orleans, LA), 131
Paramount Pictures, 139, 178
Paris, SS, 236–37, *237*
Patchwork Girl of Oz, The (film), 127
Paterson, NJ, 132
Pathé Frères, 196
Patterson, T. W., 230
Patton, George, 132
Pavo Real, 88
Pendleton, C. W., 47, 48, 49, 51, 52
Pennsylvania, 10, 292, 310

Index

People of the State of California vs. Herman L. Roth, The, 265–68, *266.* See also Roth, Herman
Percy, Eileen, 151
Peter Stuyvesant, the, 105
Photoplay, 153, 177, 180, 191, 198, 213, 219, *240,* 262, 271, 274, 284, 294, 297, 298, 299, 305, 317, 332, 340, 346
Pickford, Jack, 306
Pickford, Mary, 80–81, 132, 150, 161, 164, 203, 306
Picture Play, 162, *183,* 188, 198, 213, *246–47,* 274, 305
Pictures, 210
Pictures and the Picturegoer, 197, *247*
Pike County, IL, 8
Pitts, ZaSu, 203–4, 358–59, *359,* 364; Barbara and, 187, 203–4, 327–28, 337, 338, 347, 348, 358; Donald Gallery and, (*see* Gallery, Donald: ZaSu Pitts and)
Plato, 29
Pomp (screenplay), 329
Poor Men's Wives (film), 198–99, *199,* 203, 213
Portland, OR, 9, 10, 12, 15, 17, 24
Portola-Louvre, 122
Portsmouth Times, 246
Prairie City, OR, 15
Prairie City Miner, 15
Preferred Pictures, 177, 197
President Jackson (ship), 306
Primiano, Ruthie, 25
Prior, Herbert, 145
Prisoner of Zenda, The (film), 166, 167, 168, 169, *169,* 170, 180, 181, 188, *189,* 260, 263, 350
Pryde, Anthony, 321
Puerto Vallarta, Mexico, 362, 366
Purviance, Edna, 94

Quebec, Canada, 310
Queen's Evidence (play), 24
Quincy Adams Sawyer (film), 188, 190–91, *191*

Ramé, Maria Louise (a.k.a. Ouida). *See* Ouida
Rappe, Virginia, 177
Ratcliffe, Morelle, 207
Rector, George, 104, 105
Rector's, 104–6
Redding, CA, 11
Reed, Theodore, 152
Reeder, Fern, 250
Reeve, Sidney, 76, 77
Reichenbach, Harry, 251, 259
Reichenbach, Lucinda, 251
Reid, Margaret, 322–24
Reid, Wallace, 55–56, 56n3, 86, 86n4, 178, 346–47
Reynolds, Joyce, 362
Riccardi, Constantino, 59–60, 205–7, 211, 231
Rich, Irene, 161
Richman, Charles, 149
Rich Men's Wives (film), 198
Richmond, VA, 109–10
Riebman, Laura, 364–65
Riverside, CA, 44, 49
Riverside Drive (NY), 105, 282, 292, 293
Roach, Hal, 348
Robert Brunton Studios, 154
Roberts, Cliff, 141
Rome, Italy, 234, 237–38, 241. See also *Eternal City, The* (film)
"Rosary, The" (song), 325
Rosen, Phil, 299, 301, 302, 304, 305
Rose of Nome, The (film), 145
Ross, Mona (a.k.a. Ross, Violet) (niece), 16, 39, 47, 48, 115, 116, 117

Index

Ross, Orval, 15, 25
Ross, Violet (a.k.a. Mona Ross) (niece), 16, 39
Ross, Violet (a.k.a. Violet June Barber). *See* Barber, Violet June (half-sister)
Roth, Herman, 254–57, 261, 265–68, 281, 319
Roth, Julian "Jules" (Jack), 357–58
Roxy Theatre, 315, 315n2
Rubens, Alma, 346

Sacramento, CA, 139, 174, 280–81
Sacramento Bee, 139
Saddle Rock, 118, 119, 120
Sainpolis, John, 197
Salt Lake City, UT, 125, 130
Salvain, Paul, 105
San Antonio, TX, 212
Sandberg, Alex, 106, 110–13, 114, 115, 116, 117, 122, 123
Sandra (film), 283, 286–89, *287–88*, 294–95, 297
Sandusky Star Journal, 266
Sandusky-Stockdale Company, 27
San Francisco, CA, 86, 87, 162, 174, 177, 206, 207, 231, 326; Barbara and, 42, 43, 45, 51, 52–53, 87, 93, 117, 139, 205, 262, 281, 354; Barbara's dancing career and, 88, 92, 93–94, 96, 122
San Francisco Call, 42
San Francisco Chronicle, 260
San Francisco Examiner, 96, 97, 274
San Francisco World's Fair (1915 Panama-Pacific International Exposition), 87, 93–94
Sangster, Margaret E., 340
Santa Barbara, CA, 45, 47, 89, 230
Santa Monica, CA, 67, 86
Santa Paula, CA, 44
Sawyer, Arthur, 190, 192, 254, *263*, 281–82, 315, 315n2; Barbara and, 188, 190, *263*, 283, 295, 297, 316, 328; Barbara's adoption of son and, 200, 208, 209–11; Barbara's alleged affair with, 254, 255, 266–67; Barbara's contracts with, 192, 243, 255, 268, 269, 297, 306, 310, 318, 328; Barbara's distrust of, 315, 318, 328, 357; exploitation of Barbara's sex appeal by, 262, 269, 270, 286–87, 294, 299, 305, 318–19; Herman Roth's blackmailing of Barbara and, 254–56, 266–67; management of Barbara's career by, 192, 210–11, 213, 214, 222, 225, 233, 243, 257, 262, 281–82, 299, 302, 303, 316, 318–19, 328, 344; salary advances made to Barbara by, 269, 315, 356–57
Sawyer, Incorporated, 190
Schofield, Paul, 145
Schubert, Lee, 106
Schubert Theatre, 106
Scott, William, 144, 145
Seattle, WA, 19, 27–28, 34, 39, 42, 306
Seitz, John F., *169*, 183–84, 185
Selective Service Act, 133
Seneca, 29
Sennett, Mack, 348
Service, Robert William, 262, 265
Sheehan, Winfield, 141–42
Ship Hotel and Café, 146
Shirley, Jessie, 20, 24–25, 26, 27
Shooting of Dan McGrew, The (film), 262–65, *263–64*, 350
Siccardi, Rosa, 240
Slater, Ada, 282, 302, 303, 310, 327
S-L Pictures (a.k.a. Sawyer-Lubin Pictures), 190, 192, 243, 262, 265. *See also* Associated Pictures; Lubin,

Index

Herbert; Sawyer, Arthur; S-L Studios
S-L Studios, 192, 281–82, 315. *See also* S-L Pictures
Socrates, 29
Souls for Sale (film), 201–3, *202,* 227, 329, 346, 350
South Bend, IN, 135
Southwestern Automobile Show (Southwestern Automobile Show and Food and Home Exposition), 207, 208. *See also* Texas
Spanish influenza, 134, 135
Spanish Sunlight (Pryde), 321. See also *Girl from Montmartre, The* (film)
Spencer, Amelia (a.k.a. Amelia Converse). *See* Converse, Amelia
Spokane, WA, 24–26, 27
Spokane Daily Chronicle, 25, 26
Spring, Fred J., 77
Spring-Rice, Cecil, 110
Spurr, Melbourne, *246*
Squaw Man, The (play), 28
Stanwyck, Barbara, 360
Star Theater (Tacoma, WA), 20, 21, 22, 23, 24
State Line Herald, 9, 10
St. Augustine's Academy, 29–31, 32
Staulcup, M. P., 299
St. Clair, P. V., 43, 48–49
St. Elmo (film), 224, *224*
Stewart, Anita, 148
St. Francis Hotel, 177
St. Johns, Adela Rogers, 10, 153–54, 168, 170, 180, 251; on Barbara, 1, 10, 15, 153–54, 171, 175, 179–80, 244, 245, 283, 345, 347, 348; Barbara and, 153–54, 347
St. Johns, Elaine, 251
St. Louis Globe-Democrat, 294
St. Louis Star, 242

St. Mary's Academy, 16–17
stock theater, 21–22, 29. *See also* La Marr, Barbara: as child actress
Stone, Lewis, 168, 181, *186,* 321, *322,* 344
Stonehouse, Ruth, 151
Storm, Jerome, 176, 224
Strand Theatre (New York, NY), 242
Strand Theatre (San Francisco, CA), 162
Strangers of the Night (film), 222, *223*
Strathmore, the, 282
Strickling, Howard, 173, 180
Summit, NJ, 108
Sunday Mercury, 12, 15
Sunday Welcome, 15
Swanson, Gloria, 165, 179, 197, 225, 280, 285, 338, 360
Sweet, Blanche, 190, *191,* 216, 338

Tacoma, WA, 11, 12, 18, 19, 20, 24
Tacoma Daily Ledger, 22, 23
Tacoma Daily News, 18, 20, 22, 23, 24, 25, 27
Tacoma New Age, 18
Tagore, Rabindranath, 261
Taylor, Charles A., 27–28
Taylor, Elizabeth, 360, 361
Taylor, Estelle, 174
Taylor, Laurette, 27
Taylor, William Desmond, 177–78, 340
Tearle, Conway, 269–70, 299, 301
Techau Tavern, 92, 93, 94, 95
Temple, Shirley, 360, 361
Tennessee, 135, 290
Terry, Alice, 36, 167, 168, 169, 347, 348
Texas, 66, 67, 68; Barbara and, 207–8, 211, 212, 279
Texas Ranger, A (play), 22
Thalberg, Irving, 259

Index

Thomas, Kevin, 258
Thomas A. Edison Foundation, 250
Three Musketeers, The (film), 153, 154–57, *156*, 162, 163, 222, 350–51
Thy Name is Woman (film), 257–60, *258–59*, 265, 350
Times-Picayune, 345
Toland, Gregg, *246*
Torrence, Ernest, 223
Tourneur, Maurice, 222–23, 269, 270, 271
Trifling Women (film), 191, 193, 197, 260, 263, 301. See also *Black Orchids* (film)
True to His Flag (play), 22
Tucker, Richard, 198
Tuller Hotel, 100
Tully, Jim, 2, 187, 200, 348
Turlock, CA, 29, 34
Turner Classic Movies, 350
Two Little Wooden Shoes (Ouida), 150
Two Lives, Two Loves (unpublished memoir), 355. See also Carville, Robert
Two Orphans, The (play), 22

Uncle Tom's Cabin (play), 25–26, 27
Underhill, Harriette, 290
United Artists, 150
United Studios, 222, 271, 319, *323*, 326
Universal, 161, 165, 166, 228, 233, 299, 303
Unsell, Eve, 197
Utah, 125, 127, 130, 131

Valentino, Rudolph, 106, 166, 168, 216, 225, 248, 321, 340, 345
"Vampire, The" (poem), 164
vamps, 164–65, 190, 244. See also *under* La Marr, Barbara
Van Auker, Cecil, 164

Van Cleve, J. W., 65
Vane, Myrtle, 27, 28
Variety, 59, 60, 132, 133, 134, 135, 139, 147, 149, 177, 178, 243, 265, 270, 296, 302
vaudeville, 130, 131, 134. See also La Marr, Barbara: vaudeville career of
Veitch, Arthur, 44, 48–49, 51, 52, 53
Ventura, CA, 230
Vernon Country Club, 58
Victor, Henry, 304, *304*, 338, *339*
Victory (film), 139
Virginia, 88, 109–10, 135, 252, 290, 291, 306
Vitagraph, 165, 192
Von Stroheim, Erich, 358–59
Vorkapich, Slavko, 173

Wagner, Rob, 49–51
Walter C. Blue Company, 335, 336
Walters, Barbara, 210
Warfield, David, 265
Warner Bros. Studios, 273
Washburn, Bryant, 296
Washington, D.C., 110, 250
Washington State, 8, 25, 28, 39, 190. See also specific cities
Watson, Benjamin (uncle), 9, 10, 12
Watson, Beth (a.k.a. Barbara La Marr), 31, 331. See also La Marr, Barbara; Lytelle, Beth
Watson, Chandler Bruer (a.k.a. C. B. Watson) (uncle), 9, 9n5, 12, 79, 80
Watson, Jane Mitchell (paternal grandmother), 8
Watson, Reatha (a.k.a. Barbara La Marr). See La Marr, Barbara
Watson, Rose (a.k.a. Rosa May Contner Watson) (mother), 17, 114, 139, 143, 357; background of, 10–11; on Barbara, 26, 39–40, 42,

Index

49; Barbara and, 8, 87, 113, 114, 116–17, 125, 139, 146, 205, 230, 317, 343; as Barbara's biological mother, 8, 13; Barbara's childhood and girlhood and, 8, 13, 15, 20, 25, 27, 28, 29, 31, 32, 34–35, *35*, 47, 55, 58, 59, 62, 63; Barbara's death and, 334, 337, 338, *339*, 356; Barbara's fatal illnesses and, 311, 316, 317, 327, 329–30, 332, 334; Barbara's kidnapping allegement and, 39–40, 42, 44, 47, 48, 49, 51, 52, 53, 54–55, 115; Barbara's marriage to Lawrence Converse and, 64, 70, 71, 72, 74; death of, 357, 358; Donald Gallery and, 214, 358, 359, 362–63; protectiveness of Barbara and, 15, 32, 39–40, 42, 54, 74, 114

Watson, William (father), 12, 13, 39, 79, 139, 357; background of, 8–10, 11–13; on Barbara, 21, 26, 40, 42–43, 72–73, 80, 248, 333, 356; Barbara and, 8, 113, 114, 116, 139–40, 146, 205, 248, 343; as Barbara's biological father, 8; Barbara's childhood and girlhood and, 8, 15, 17, 18, 20, 21, 25, 27, 28, 29, 31, 32, 34, 39, 47, 55, 58, 59, 60, 62, 63; Barbara's death and, 334–35, 336, 337, 338, 339, *339*, 356–57; Barbara's fatal illnesses and, 311, 316, 317, 322, *323,* 324, 326, 327, 329–30, 332, 333–34; Barbara's kidnapping allegement and, 40–43, 44, 47, 48, 54–55, 115; Barbara's marriage to Lawrence Converse and, 64, 70–71, 72–73, *73*, 74, 79; Barbara's writing and, 17, 139–40, 141, 143; death of, 357, 358; disapproval of Barbara's acting ambition by, 34, 42; Donald Gallery and, 358, 359, 362–63; newspaper career of, 9–10, 11–13, 15, 18, 25, 27, 28–29, 34, 39, 55, 62, 79, 114, 139, 357; protectiveness of Barbara and, 32, 39, 54, 60, 114, 322

Watson, William, Jr. (a.k.a. Billy DeVore) (brother), 11, 11n10, 15, 18, 19, 28, 29, 34. *See also* DeVore, Billy

Watson, William T. (paternal grandfather), 8

Wayne, Marie, 129, 296

Webb, Clifton, 301

Webb, Frank, 174

West, Claire, 286

West, Myrtle, 299

Westmore, Perc, 273–74, 316, 317, 322, 324, 325, 326, 335–36, 348

Wheelan, Edgar S. ("Ed"), 2

Whitaker, Alma, 274–75

Whitehead, Joseph, 173

White Monkey, The (film), 303–5, *304*, 350

White Monkey, The (Galsworthy), 303, 304

White Moth, The (film), 269–70, *270*, 271–73, *272–73*, 274, 283, 299, 346, 350

Whitley, Hobart, Mrs., 221

Whitley, Hobart Johnstone, 214, 221

Whitley Heights, 214, 216–17, *217. See also* La Marr, Barbara: Whitley Heights home of

Whytock, Grant, 166

Wid's Daily, 151

Wiedemann theater company, 19

Williams, Deletta, 358

Williams, Earle, 213

Wilson, Carey, 352

443

Wilson, Charles, 143
Wilson, Woodrow, 110, 124, 133
Windsor, Claire, 333, 338
Winter Gardens, 106
Withey, Chet, 177
Witzel, *247*
Wood, C. E. S., 12
Wood, Ellen, 23
Woodall, John ("Eddie"), 359
Woodbury, James A., *163*
Wooten, Myrtle, 129
World War I, 87, 124, 130, 132, 133, 135, 229
Would You Forgive? (film), 143
Wright, Clara, 52–53
Wright, Orville, 14
Wright, Wilbur, 14

writing for the silent screen, 140–41, 143

Yakima, WA, 8, 12, 13, 28, 34, 88
Yakima Daily Times, 12
Yakima Herald, 8, 12
Yakima Republic, 27, 28
Yancey Mills, VA, 291
Yost, Dorothy, 295
Yuma, AZ, 56

Zaza (play), 23
Ziegfeld, Florenz, 109
Ziegfeld Midnight Frolic (Broadway show), 109
Ziegfeld's Follies (Broadway show), 305
Zora (play), 24

Screen Classics

Screen Classics is a series of critical biographies, film histories, and analytical studies focusing on neglected filmmakers and important screen artists and subjects, from the era of silent cinema to the golden age of Hollywood to the international generation of today. Books in the Screen Classics series are intended for scholars and general readers alike. The contributing authors are established figures in their respective fields. This series also serves the purpose of advancing scholarship on film personalities and themes with ties to Kentucky.

Series Editor
Patrick McGilligan

Books in the Series

Mae Murray: The Girl with the Bee-Stung Lips
 Michael G. Ankerich
Hedy Lamarr: The Most Beautiful Woman in Film
 Ruth Barton
Rex Ingram: Visionary Director of the Silent Screen
 Ruth Barton
Conversations with Classic Film Stars: Interviews from Hollywood's Golden Era
 James Bawden and Ron Miller
You Ain't Heard Nothin' Yet: Interviews with Stars from Hollywood's Golden Era
 James Bawden and Ron Miller
Von Sternberg
 John Baxter
Hitchcock's Partner in Suspense: The Life of Screenwriter Charles Bennett
 Charles Bennett, edited by John Charles Bennett
My Life in Focus: A Photographer's Journey with Elizabeth Taylor and the Hollywood Jet Set
 Gianni Bozzacchi with Joey Tayler
Hollywood Divided: The 1950 Screen Directors Guild Meeting and the Impact of the Blacklist
 Kevin Brianton
He's Got Rhythm: The Life and Career of Gene Kelly
 Cynthia Brideson and Sara Brideson
Ziegfeld and His Follies: A Biography of Broadway's Greatest Producer
 Cynthia Brideson and Sara Brideson
The Marxist and the Movies: A Biography of Paul Jarrico
 Larry Ceplair
Dalton Trumbo: Blacklisted Hollywood Radical
 Larry Ceplair and Christopher Trumbo
Warren Oates: A Wild Life
 Susan Compo

Improvising Out Loud: My Life Teaching Hollywood How to Act
    Jeff Corey with Emily Corey
Crane: Sex, Celebrity, and My Father's Unsolved Murder
    Robert Crane and Christopher Fryer
Jack Nicholson: The Early Years
    Robert Crane and Christopher Fryer
Anne Bancroft: A Life
    Douglass K. Daniel
Being Hal Ashby: Life of a Hollywood Rebel
    Nick Dawson
Bruce Dern: A Memoir
    Bruce Dern with Christopher Fryer and Robert Crane
Intrepid Laughter: Preston Sturges and the Movies
    Andrew Dickos
Miriam Hopkins: Life and Films of a Hollywood Rebel
    Allan R. Ellenberger
John Gilbert: The Last of the Silent Film Stars
    Eve Golden
Stuntwomen: The Untold Hollywood Story
    Mollie Gregory
Saul Bass: Anatomy of Film Design
    Jan-Christopher Horak
Hitchcock Lost and Found: The Forgotten Films
    Alain Kerzoncuf and Charles Barr
Pola Negri: Hollywood's First Femme Fatale
    Mariusz Kotowski
Sidney J. Furie: Life and Films
    Daniel Kremer
Albert Capellani: Pioneer of the Silent Screen
    Christine Leteux
Mamoulian: Life on Stage and Screen
    David Luhrssen
Maureen O'Hara: The Biography
    Aubrey Malone
My Life as a Mankiewicz: An Insider's Journey through Hollywood
    Tom Mankiewicz and Robert Crane
Hawks on Hawks
    Joseph McBride
Showman of the Screen: Joseph E. Levine and His Revolutions in Film Promotion
    A. T. McKenna
William Wyler: The Life and Films of Hollywood's Most Celebrated Director
    Gabriel Miller
Raoul Walsh: The True Adventures of Hollywood's Legendary Director
    Marilyn Ann Moss

Veit Harlan: The Life and Work of a Nazi Filmmaker
    Frank Noack
Harry Langdon: King of Silent Comedy
    Gabriella Oldham and Mabel Langdon
Charles Walters: The Director Who Made Hollywood Dance
    Brent Phillips
Some Like It Wilder: The Life and Controversial Films of Billy Wilder
    Gene D. Phillips
Ann Dvorak: Hollywood's Forgotten Rebel
    Christina Rice
Michael Curtiz: A Life in Film
    Alan K. Rode
Arthur Penn: American Director
    Nat Segaloff
Claude Rains: An Actor's Voice
    David J. Skal with Jessica Rains
Barbara La Marr: The Girl Who Was Too Beautiful for Hollywood
    Sherri Snyder
Buzz: The Life and Art of Busby Berkeley
    Jeffrey Spivak
Victor Fleming: An American Movie Master
    Michael Sragow
Hollywood Presents Jules Verne: The Father of Science Fiction on Screen
    Brian Taves
Thomas Ince: Hollywood's Independent Pioneer
    Brian Taves
Carl Theodor Dreyer and Ordet: *My Summer with the Danish Filmmaker*
    Jan Wahl